Sovereignties

Also by Raia Prokhovnik

RATIONAL WOMAN
RHETORIC AND PHILOSOPHY IN HOBBES'S 'LEVIATHAN'
SPINOZA AND REPUBLICANISM

Sovereignties

Contemporary Theory and Practice

Raia Prokhovnik
Reader in Politics
Open University, UK

palgrave
macmillan

First published 2007 by
PALGRAVE MACMILLAN
Houndmills, Basingstoke, Hampshire RG21 6XS and
175 Fifth Avenue, New York, N.Y. 10010
Companies and representatives throughout the world

PALGRAVE MACMILLAN is the global academic imprint of the Palgrave
Macmillan division of St. Martin's Press, LLC and of Palgrave Macmillan Ltd.
Macmillan® is a registered trademark in the United States, United Kingdom
and other countries. Palgrave is a registered trademark in the European
Union and other countries.

ISBN 13: 978–1–4039–1323–4   hardback

This book is printed on paper suitable for recycling and made from fully
managed and sustained forest sources. Logging, pulping and manufacturing
processes are expected to conform to the environmental regulations of the
country of origin.

A catalogue record for this book is available from the British Library.

A catalogue record for this book is available from the Library of Congress.

10   9   8   7   6   5   4   3   2   1
16   15   14   13   12   11   10   09   08   07

Transferred to Digital Printing in 2009

For Madeline, Kaz and Mia

Contents

Preface

This book owes much to the inspiration of discussions with Rob Walker, Laura Brace and others at the ECPR panel on sovereignty in Budapest, October 2005, and to discussions at the 'Politics of Protection' workshop in London in July 2003 organised by Jef Huysmans with Neil Walker, Rob Walker and others. As always, Quentin Skinner and Conal Condren are intellectual touchstones for my thinking. I would like to thank colleagues at the Open University for debates, discussions and friendships over the past seven years – Jef Huysmans, Mike Saward, Andy Dobson, Grahame Thompson, Kath Woodward, Stephanie Taylor, Rachel Thomson, Jane Ribbens-McCarthy, Wendy Hollway, Gillian Rose, and Elizabeth Silva. I would also like to thank Gary, Eleanor, Conal, Anna, Madeline, Kaz, Mia, Nick, Alan, Hilary, Stuart, Jen, and Scott and Susan, Angela, Lorraine, Caroline, and Jane for their sustaining love and warm friendship.

Introduction
The Meaning of Sovereignty:
The Politics and Ownership of the
Concept

This book puts forward an argument that sovereignty has a plurality of conceptions and is currently open to positive reconceptualisation. It also tackles a range of problems and conundrums that stand in the way of recognising this viewpoint. These problems and conundrums include the narrow scope allowed for the concept by the conventional distinction between legal and political sovereignty, the ultimately conceptually unworkable but politically driven internal/external distinction that operates to maintain exclusion in international relations, the conceptually unwarranted exclusive equation of sovereignty with modern state sovereignty, the depoliticisation of sovereignty in the mainstream political theory discourse, and confusion due to the intangibility of sovereignty as a political concept.

One way into the concerns of this book is through the critique of the conventional distinction between political and legal sovereignty. The starting-point for studying sovereignty in political theory is through the division between legal sovereignty as the supreme jurisdictional authority (in a hierarchy of law-making bodies and practices) and political sovereignty as the highest authority to rule or govern (and so to make rules and policy sanctioned in legislation). Claims to sovereignty of this kind are thought to sustain the polity *as* polity. Political sovereignty has a very limited meaning here, concerned only with ruler sovereignty – covering issues of ultimate authority, the relation between rulers and ruled, and the question of popular sovereignty. Seen from the perspective developed in this book, the way in which legal and political sovereignty are twin concepts, both focusing on the question of *ultimate* authority, indicates firstly the common ground between them and only secondarily a distinction between them. The narrowness of the orthodox definition is partly due to the development of the hugely important dominant *Rechtstaat* tradition of modern western sovereignty. In the conventional definition, political sovereignty is only political in the narrow sense that it is about government, governance, and rule. Moreover, this conventional definition of political sovereignty is radically depoliticised – both because the scope of the political is so narrow (limited to government) and because of the reification of the authority concept (political sovereignty is about the authority relationship rather than about power). This makes it ripe for Foucault's telling criticism of the way authority can mask coercive and oppressive power relationships.

The key work that authority is meant to provide in the modern predominantly liberal political theory tradition (the senses in which it is a 'liberal' tradition is explored in Chapter 2) is to distinguish polities supposedly based on claims to authority and on law from despotisms on the one hand and those on the other like the model of the complexly hierarchical medieval polity whose ultimate legitimation came from divine law and power. The authority relationship in the modern sovereign state recommends itself in its founding myth of ruler-ordered power reconciled through a claim to authority which is based on voluntary contract. The authority relationship supposedly allows for distance from the supposed brute and arbitrary power exercised by despotic rulers on the one hand and the elaborately mediated medieval arrangements that constrained rulers of different degrees and ruled alike in a potentially emasculating but binding web of obligation and allegiance on the other. In crucially distancing political (temporal ruling) from religious authority, and in setting itself against the 'other' of primitive and modern despotisms, modern secular sovereignty promises a streamlined myth of individualised and contractual, autonomous and rational, intentionally willed and sanctioned, justified and legally warranted, self-validatingly legitimate, permitted and domesticated relations of authority.

Because of its emphasis on ruler sovereignty, the conventional modern conception of political sovereignty regards as secondary or neglects to take seriously the other functions that we ask it to perform for us, to do with political identity, the manner in which political stability is underpinned, and the meaning and boundaries of political practices. In Chapter 4 I develop another notion of 'political sovereignty', in contrast with this conventional definition of ruler sovereignty, analysing there the important and undervalued work the concept of sovereignty also does for us, in any particular polity, in conditionally settling the meaning of the content of politics, the limits of politics, and the boundary between the political and the unpolitical. In this sense politics is not simply an autonomous realm of activity (for instance in Arendt's terms). Its volatile and dynamic quality render it not completely self-validating, and it gains its broader parameters not just from the rules and prescriptions expressed in law but also and more fundamentally from political sovereignty in the sense developed here.

The argument offered in Chapter 4 is both a contribution to the understanding of sovereignty as a concept – a 'meta-take' on sovereignty – and a new conception of sovereignty. It focuses on the way political sovereignty acts as the umbrella or overarching framework under which the scope of politics is conditionally settled, political identity is given form, political stability is enabled, *and* the 'highest authority' of ruler sovereignty is specified. What count as legitimate and illegitimate political practices and rules and what can be done through politics varies from polity to polity according to the political mentality of the specific polity – its vocabulary and discourses, traditions, history, culture, geo-political situation, specific understanding of the relation to law, its social values, and ideological points of reference. This sense of political sovereignty broadens out the notion of politics to explain what makes an issue or event contentious, politically controversial. This analysis is also based in a more concrete idea of politics, recognising the role of the particular political mentality and political identity of a specific polity (for instance in the meaning given to street protest in France, the iconic status of the constitution in the US, the role of the 'basic law' in Germany), in contrast with the conventional notion of politics found in the ruler sovereignty definition, which is very abstract, universalised, and so naturalised.

Neil Walker usefully draws attention to the idea of the 'irreducible core, the non-negotiable given of any sovereign order' (N. Walker 2003b, 28). He defines sovereignty as 'the discursive form in which a claim concerning the existence and character of a supreme ordering power for a particular polity is expressed'. He notes that this 'supreme ordering power purports to establish and sustain the identity and status of the particular polity *qua* polity and to provide a continuing source and vehicle of ultimate authority for the juridical order of that polity' (N. Walker 2003b, 6). In the terms developed here it is within this 'irreducible core' that legal (rule authority) and political (ruler authority) sovereignty, *and* political sovereignty as described in Chapter 4 (the content and boundaries of the political, as a key aspect of political identity) operate. It is on this basis that, as Walker confirms, a 'sovereign order must assume its own continuing or self-amending sovereignty within its sphere of authority (rules of recognition and change) and must retain interpretive autonomy (rules of adjudication), deciding the boundaries of that sphere of authority' (N. Walker 2003b, 28). Conventional legal and political sovereignty by themselves cannot account for the activity of politics.

Chapter 5 takes this idea a step further and argues that in the context of the European Union this notion of political sovereignty can provide all the 'glue' that is necessary for the political community to cohere. While the question of 'ultimate political authority' remains firmly with the member states, political sovereignty in my sense can supply the minimal political identity and stability that is sufficient to maintain the EU level. Political sovereignty in my sense provides a solid but 'light touch' 'glue'. This proposal has distinct advantages over the main four lines of argument that are currently on the table for envisioning the EU as a polity, namely the advocacy of 'constitutionalisation', demands to construct a European demos to rectify the 'democratic deficit', functionalist hopes of coherence through political 'spillover', and allowing the lawyers to continue to run the integrationist show. The logic of the first three of these, if not all four, would lead to integration to the point of forming a European state on the model of the modern state, a cumbersome super-state Leviathan that swallows up the autonomy and valuable diversity of the current poly-centric arrangement, unworkable because its constitution would be full of empty rhetoric, undemocratic because on this scale political control is even more captured by political elites, unstable because functionalism on its own cannot generate a coherent political identity, and legally ambiguous because a sound legal system needs strong political underpinning. The proposal put forward in Chapter 5 identifies a plausible and viable polity that is not modelled on the state form and so does not suffer from any of these problems.

I became interested in the concept of sovereignty because its meaning seemed so opaque and unclear. Received definitions of sovereignty did not get at the heart of the matter, which seemed shrouded. The outcome of the investigations of this research is an advocacy to recognise and reassert the overwhelming primacy of sovereignty as a *political* concept. The argument holds that the obscurity around the meaning of the concept is due to a whole range of intersecting historical and conceptual factors. The identification of sovereignty with one conception, the state form, and the difficulty of thinking beyond it, is a familiar complaint, as is the influence of the realist international relations (IR) paradigm in making the mainstream definition – the division into internal and external dimensions, what they each contained, and how they mirrored and complemented each other – seem given and natural. Less familiar was the realisation of the enormously influential role played by law in the sovereignty story – the way the modern western legal definition of sovereignty bound up with the state and realist form, powerfully fused in the idea of the *Rechtstaat* (a polity based upon law as a moral concept), overshadowed the broader political meanings and functions of the concept. By this I mean that sovereignty as a political concept is not first and foremost about making rules (as is, necessarily, the impetus of legal thinking) but about negotiating a space for politics. Other factors helping to obscure the meaning of sovereignty were the way, in political theory, discussion of sovereignty languished in a deeply depoliticised discourse, the confusion of conception with concept, the approach to the modern state conception as homogeneous and the reluctance to think of sovereignty in terms of multiple conceptions, and confusion around the way sovereignty is a concept and a 'discursive form' and so is not 'real', even though it has very real effects.

The final factor was the claim by some globalisation 'theorists' that the concept of sovereignty no longer contained explanatory power or value, thereby confusing the grip of realist thinking over the state conception with the concept. Sovereignty is sometimes regarded as a concept with a fixed meaning, as something that can only be kept or lost, and which at the present time is under threat from globalisation, the erosion of the nation state, cosmopolitanism, forms of theocratic politics, and European integration, and on this basis the jettisoning of sovereignty as an important idea has been widely advocated. Neil Walker describes well the seeming crisis facing sovereignty due to the idea of its redundancy and irrelevance in contemporary international politics. This is the argument that we now live 'in a world in which many circuits of power operate beyond the direct control of the sovereign state, a trend which is clearly exacerbated by processes of globalisation or trans-nationalisation of productive forces, informative exchange, political capacities, social identities etc.'. In such a world, 'sovereignty figures lower and lower in the register of explanatory variables which may be invoked to make sense of that world' (N. Walker 2003b, 6). Other scholars have echoed this view. Walker and Mendlovitz asserted that 'state sovereignty offers only a misleading map of where we are' (Walker and Mendlovitz 1990, 2). Similarly, Camilleri and Falk referred to 'the ambiguities which at every level now surround the principle of sovereignty' (Camilleri and Falk 1992, 39). James argued that formal academic definitions, based on unsubstantiated claims of sovereignty, are not helpful in discussing and making sense of what happens in international relations between states; he also saw the ambiguity of the term as a reason to discard it in political discourse (James 1986, 85). And Habermas, arguing for an implausible and dangerous 'world citizenship', contended that the 'obsolescence of the state of nature between bellicose states has begun, implying that states have lost some sovereignty' (Habermas 1995, 279).

Many early pronouncements on globalisation held that sovereign states no longer had a central role to play in regulating economic markets, and some liberal internationalists bypass sovereignty to advocate forms of cosmopolitan global governance (even if they fall short of amounting to a global government) based on a human rights culture. As an example of the latter, Bohman and Lutz-Bachmann announce about their book that '[a]ll the philosophers in this volume reject the unqualified principle of internal sovereignty, especially as it is incorporated in the international law of the existing nation-state system'. Most of the contributors to that book 'seek something stronger than Kant's "federation of free states" but weaker than a single world republic' (Bohman and Lutz-Bachmann 1997, 13). The re-emergence in international politics of the importance of world religions both brings together in unlikely common cause members of the Muslim Umma across different states and reinforces the universalism and unilateralism of George W. Bush's advocacy of American values and perspectives.

The key question about globalisation for this book is whether it is transformative of the space and whole geography of Westphalian sovereignty in terms of a set of individual polities. The view of this book is that there are not convincing arguments for that thesis. We are still dealing with an international political space in which states understood as polities (as well as other bodies) matter most. What we do encounter is neo-liberal capitalist economics triumphant and intensifying, especially in economic interconnection between the trilateral regionalisms of the US, Europe and Asia. In the main, third world countries do not gain from the 'benefits' of globalisation, but are instead in thrall to rich and powerful economies in a system supported by the World Bank and other powerful agents, with the market prompting migration to sweat shops in new slum cities and the depletion of rural workforces. The continuities with the past, and in particular with the pattern of imperial economic gain in the wake of colonisation, is very strong. Such patterns have much greater political salience than much-heralded changes such as new developments and innovations in deterritorialised internet protest movements, the spread of television in the poorest countries, and the growth in international NGOs and other political actors. The approach to sovereignty undertaken here sees strong continuities between nineteenth, twentieth and twenty-first century patterns of international politics.

This book seeks to make a case for the importance of retaining sovereignty as a key concept in our political vocabulary in thinking about both domestic and international politics. In repudiating sovereignty, too narrow a version of it has been employed. Sovereignty has been spurned too hastily and in favour of potentially dangerous interest groups. This book seeks to draw upon the richness of the legacy of thinking about sovereignty that has been substantially overlooked, and to indicate how some of the resources of that legacy can help to re-imagine domestic political society and international politics. A re-invigorated sovereignty can also potentially provide a bulwark against the dangers of 'global governance' and secular and religious fundamentalisms, as well as against the encroachment, through the legitimating label of 'globalisation', of neo-liberal economic ideas to dominate the domain of politics. This book develops a strong argument for sovereignty as a robust concept with many conceptualisations in the past and capable of further fruitful reconceptualisation in the future.

The argument here also rejects the idea that the only solution to issues like the regulation of economic globalisation, environmental problems, and inequalities that are currently left off or not high enough up the current political agenda by the status quo structure of nation-states in the international order, is a cosmopolitan one driven by a rights culture. More imaginative conceptualisations of sovereignty can help to break down the barriers of internal and external sovereignty without abandoning a political unit like the state as the locus of national political allegiance and democratic politics. The problems associated with a global rights culture – its liberal origins and western bias, its trumping of cultural differences, and its moralisation of politics – are all well-rehearsed. In going against the grain of these recent trends in international politics the argument here is not a conservative one seeking to preserve an outdated system of privilege or stand in the way of progressive and emancipatory politics. This book argues that domestic and international politics can be transformed, and privileged positions and inequalities in contemporary politics overcome by drawing much more fully on the historical and philosophical resources that are available for thinking about sovereignty. In this way it is possible to avoid the unimaginative mapping of the domestic polity onto the European or global realms, and to think beyond the dichotomy between internal and external politics and the perception of politics as necessarily hierarchical. Neither a coercive and systematic international law nor a hegemonic rights-driven global democratic political institution – with all the dangers for oppression and lack of political accountability that such moves contain – need form an apex of international politics.

The book will engage with the literatures on sovereignty from political theory, international political theory, international relations, legal theory, and European integration theory. It seeks to offer a clear analysis of interlinked debates within these literatures, to indicate the politics between them, and to show how these debates pertain to current political developments. The aim of this book is to demonstrate the continuing salience of sovereignty as a political concept. The argument is that the conceptual analysis of sovereignty and the practical relevance of establishing a reconceptualised sovereignty in the debate over Europe are interdependent.

The subheading of the book signals this distinctive feature of it. The two elements of the subheading, *Contemporary Theory and Practice*, point to the two parts of the book. The first part explores contemporary reconceptualisation of the idea of sovereignty, and the second part engages with a contemporary political issue with crucial practical and institutional implications. The subheading also, however, registers that theory (including its historical dimension) and practice are involved in both parts. The argument is also built upon the understanding that each conception of sovereignty (say from Bodin to Foucault) has a history and is contextually-grounded, and is a theory contributing to Europe's intellectual history and potentially having a direct effect upon the structures of practice in organising the political community and relations with other polities. The book makes a case for keeping in view a plurality of conceptions of sovereignty. Historically the resources of our tradition of political thought – during the early-modern and modern period often regarded as characterised by a single hegemonic conception of state sovereignty – offer a vivid range of conceptualisations that are only with great loss reduced to a single meaning. While theory (along with its historical dimension) and practice are understood as deeply implicated in each other's constitution there is nevertheless an important element of contingency in their construction, which prevents us trying in any simple fashion to use theory and its history for instance to tell us how to comprehend practice. Equally the conditions of sovereignty help us to appraise its forms but that appraisal is not reducible to nor derived from those conditions. Conceptually, this book endorses Connolly's and Gallie's arguments about essential contestability.

In order to forward this project, this chapter has three aims, helping to set the framework for the contemporary discussion of the term. After considering the discourses in which sovereignty occurs, to identify the meaning of sovereignty in the range of its usages, there is a discussion of the general features of sovereignty and the political nature of the concept. These general features of sovereignty are a thread running through the book that is discussed in different forms in the different chapters. Then, the examination of the value of the ways in which epistemology precedes ontology for sovereignty, leads on to an examination of sovereignty as a political concept. In order not to pre-empt the discussion in Chapter 4 and because there is plenty to analyse about the dominant conception of sovereignty, this chapter concentrates on political sovereignty primarily in terms of its mainstream 'ruler sovereignty' form, focussing upon the agency of the sovereign body acting as an individual.

The meaning of sovereignty: how the concept is used

The issue in this section of the chapter is how to get at the meaning of sovereignty in its usages. The focus here is not to understand sovereignty through analysis and definition of the concept but rather through the variety of discourses and the types of argument in which sovereignty is already employed.

What does sovereignty mean? How can we establish what it means? This book takes the view that one useful way of getting at the meaning of sovereignty is to see that its meaning depends in part on how it is *used*, and in part on the resources from conceptual analysis and from the past and connections in the present. 'How it is used' means three things here – usage in contemporary discourses, conceptual analysis, and historical usages. Tully is getting at a combination of these three things when he characterises the modern history of the concept of sovereignty in terms of 'diverse solutions...offered to this remarkably constant problematisation of legitimacy and obedience' (Tully 1999, 126). However, also crucially involved in the study of both historical usages and contemporary discourses is the sense that the politics of sovereignty is very much part of what is being studied. Claims about the meaning of sovereignty are integral to the politics of sovereignty. While it is possible to do no more than identify a set of historical conceptions of sovereignty and define at a very abstract level the general features of the sovereignty concept, this would fall short of setting out the 'meaning' of sovereignty. In addition, as well as examining what sovereignty means and how we can establish its meaning, this book is concerned with the related question of what sovereignty *can* mean. Its future reconceptualisations are not determined by present usages and past meanings, but they are a good place to start.

What is at stake here is the politics and ownership of the sovereignty concept. It takes seriously Connolly's argument that the 'language of politics is not a neutral medium that conveys ideas independently formed'. Rather, the language of politics 'is an institutionalised structure of meanings that channels political thought and action in certain directions' (Connolly 1993, 1). One important way of getting at the meaning of sovereignty is to look at how it is constructed differently in the major sub-disciplines around Politics in which it is debated – primarily in political theory, international relations theory, security studies, and international law. Each of these discourses focuses on different general features of the concept, or different clusters of features, and employs a different mode of argument – different mixtures of explanatory, descriptive, conceptual, normative, functional argument, critique and deconstruction. This section of the chapter seeks to map these sometimes competing positions and perspectives on sovereignty, to combine insights from the different discourses, and to highlight through comparison their distinctiveness and limits. The approach taken in this chapter has advantages over approaches that proceed by contesting, asserting or stipulating a meaning of sovereignty, because it seeks to attend to how sovereignty is perceived in these different discourses, and pulls together the insights into the concept gained from this range of sub-disciplines. The following chapters in Part I contribute a historical dimension to the debate by pointing to the richness and pertinence of some of the (often overlooked) resources for discussing contemporary sovereignty in the canon of the history of political thought.

Another way of making this point is that the meaning of sovereignty in current debates is raised within three problematics. In the 1990s, in the light of claims about globalisation, ideas gained ground about the supposed effects of economic and political globalisation and the redundancy of the nation-state as the dominant political unit, and ideas for strengthening or working towards cosmopolitan or global political institutions. As a consequence, sovereignty was regarded as eroded, as no longer carrying explanatory force. Second, in areas of international relations theory and international law critical of the realist approach, the spectre of state sovereignty is invoked as an ethical issue. Thirdly, in political theory deeply indebted to Marxist or post-Marxist forms of antipathy to the state and state power, sovereignty is the expression of political power understood as broadly aligned with economic interests, and by Foucault sovereignty is dismissed as a sham. It is important, the argument developed here contends, to take all these debates seriously and not to reduce or dismiss them.

These three problematics are cross cut by some other issues, including questions of formal and informal, *de facto* and *de jure* sovereignty; the way sovereignty underpins the constitutionalism and so legitimacy of a modern state; the significance of the differences between how sovereignty is studied in political theory and IR; and the idea of sovereignty as political, about state power, contrasted with the idea of sovereignty as unpolitical, a purely descriptive designation about a universal relation of ruling. The argument of this book holds that a broad perspective can help to work out what sovereignty means given all these debates in the western tradition. It would also be instructive, though beyond the scope of this book, to examine other, non-western traditions of political theory and practice about the issues and ideas sovereignty deals with.

There are at least six contemporary discourses on sovereignty. The first three are deeply problematic, tending to essentialise and depoliticise sovereignty in different ways. The second three contain great potential for revitalising the notion of sovereignty.

The mainstream international relations discourse sees sovereignty as paradigmatically ordaining hierarchy at home and anarchy abroad, with inter-state relations taking place on the basis of national interest and power. This discourse relies heavily on an analogy between the modern liberal rational, calculating, autonomous individual agent and the sovereign state. This supposedly neutral and descriptive discourse has an important, often unacknowledged, normative dimension.

The tradition of political theory that deals with political concepts has emphasised the authority relationship by which sovereignty is seen to establish the domestic legitimacy and stability of government, a liberal constitutionalism, and the political obligation of the governed. While the authority relationship is crucial to the understanding of sovereignty, the mainstream political theory discourse on sovereignty tends to be a tamed and depoliticised, abstract, analytical and ahistorical discourse of conceptual analysis in which sovereignty is linked narrowly to the concepts of authority and legitimacy, on the whole celebrating the liberal principles of autonomy and negative freedom, and illustrated by a canon of past thinkers. This discourse has been mainly concerned, without fully explicating its scope, let alone analysing it, with domestic or internal sovereignty, and has worked with an explanatory and normative conception of sovereignty.

The discipline of international and constitutional law utilises a descriptive argument that also has a normative dimension, to point to the role of sovereignty in establishing the rule of law and constitutional government, and sometimes makes a normative argument for extending such legal institutions. The international law discourse takes for granted that sovereignty focuses on the highest law-making body, and so tends to conflate the legal and the political. Part of this discourse is allied to a cosmopolitanism driven by a rights culture promoting ahistorical rights-bearing agents. We have already noted that there are strong grounds for taking the view that neither a coercive and systematic international law nor a hegemonic rights-driven global 'democratic' political institution – with all the dangers for oppression that such moves contain, and based on a mistaken 'domestic analogy' – need form an apex of international politics.

The critical international relations theory discourse, of which Rob Walker is so important and thoughtful a proponent, presents a powerful critique of the realist tradition of IR theory and practice, in particular of functionalist assumptions about interest-based calculation of power politics. It also provides a powerful critique of political theory and of the spectre of state sovereignty, using writers such as Foucault, Schmitt, Agamben, and Derrida. It focuses primarily on external sovereignty through the features of a bounded territory and state association. The strengths of this discourse, from the perspective of this book, are that it reveals how political sovereignty, in the sense developed here, challenges the realist reification of state sovereignty. Outstanding issues with this discourse, from this book's point of view, are that the meaning of sovereignty that it employs is tied to the narrow and self-serving realist definition of state sovereignty, and that by metaphorical shift it draws its force from a generalised attack on forms of 'sovereign judgment' and 'sovereign meaning'. Sovereignty is constructed in this discourse as the master concept of modernity, fundamental to the set of dichotomies (the logic of exclusion of internal/external mapping onto culture/nature, man/woman, object/subject, etc.) that have characterised theory and practice, and that have defined truth and knowledge in the modern period. While this perspective contains great insight, these two orientations taken together mean that it is difficult, only on this basis, to develop a broader and relational conception of sovereignty.

Critical security studies highlights the territorial, state, and monopoly of violence general features of the concept. This discourse deconstructs the security pronouncements and practices of powerful states and their implications for internal and external sovereignty. Its aim is to disclose the governmentalising implications of the state being seen as the exclusive security referent. Its strength is that it re-politicises naturalised security techniques and reinstates mechanisms of securitisation as a field of politics. The problem with this discourse, from the perspective of this book, is that the normative dimension of its critique of securitising speech remains implicit, both in terms of the source of its normative thrust and its positive proposals. The discourse would be strengthened both by making its political perspective explicit, and by being able to differentiate more clearly between the securitising practices of different kinds of political regimes.

Finally, the critical political theory discourse finds Foucault's critique of sovereignty both devastating and limited. This discourse on sovereignty is committed to drawing out what is political about the sovereignty concept and accepts Foucault's criticism of the role a naturalised juridical discourse has played, but argues with Connolly that authority is not reducible to power, that the political is not reducible to the social, that sovereignty is not the same as social relations of power, and that the sham of juridical sovereignty does not tell the whole story. Foucault broaches a key distinction between (social) sovereign power and sovereign statehood, but there is also scope for a wider conception of the relation of ruling and of sovereignty's political functions. Part of the meaning of the 'politics of sovereignty' is the attempt of a concept inspired by Foucault, Schmitt, and Agamben to territorialise the field of debate about sovereignty. This book seeks to resist that take over. Foucault's approach is valuable especially in showing the operation of sovereign power in *social* interaction, but there are also other things to say about sovereignty.

This book locates itself primarily in the framework of the last three of these six discourses. It takes its bearings from the inadequacy of the idea that sovereignty is a concept with a fixed and homogeneous meaning, necessarily associated with the state, and as something that can only be kept or lost. Specifically, the features of sovereignty such as territoriality, state, monopoly of violence, authority relationship, and stability, have been taken to have unchanging significations. However, conceptually and historically it is the case that the way any one of these dimensions is understood can change, develop and evolve, without the meaning of sovereignty itself being in jeopardy. For instance, while it has been overstated, the meaning of the state may well have become more fluid under the impact of greater connectedness between states and between states and other political actors. Thus the wider context of this book is the viewpoint that there is a strong argument for sovereignty as a robust concept with many conceptualisations in the past and capable of further fruitful reconceptualisation in the future. One of the ways that this book seeks to contribute to the politics of the sovereignty concept is to reinforce the view that the meaning of sovereignty is rich and enduring, and that a focus on the resources from the discipline of Politics and on the political conflict over its meaning, result in it having a strong future. Structuring this viewpoint is the argument that sovereignty can be part of a progressive politics, by drawing much more fully on the historical and philosophical resources that are available for thinking about sovereignty. The wider resources of sovereignty can play a part in transforming domestic and international politics and overcoming privileged positions and inequalities in contemporary politics.

This section of the chapter ends by drawing attention to some of the ways that sovereignty is political. The focus here on the 'politics and ownership of the sovereignty concept' leads to a recognition of what a *political* perspective can offer, the view that sees politics (in the sense of operating with power relations and interests, bargaining, making side deals, distributing resources, negotiating intractable differences, managing contestation, holding accountable) as central, to highlight and reinstate the *political* nature of current sovereignty relations. This is separate from the way in which the history of political thought canon and the political theory discourse has been largely apolitical (seen itself as politically neutral) in recent years. In the discourse of external politics, sovereignty is seen as much more political.

'Sovereignty' is a technical concept for political theory, international relations and law, though its meaning varies across each of these fields according to which general features of the term are being highlighted. But alongside those technical meanings, 'sovereignty' as a political, rhetorical term is used with a political purpose to support interests. Sovereignty is political in that it is a counter to be traded. Sovereignty is also political because it is not just an intangible 'concept', a way of conceptualising political order and the relations between ruled and ruler. Sovereignty is also, as Zizek puts it, a 'concrete network of the material conditions of existence of an ideological edifice'. It is 'that which ideology itself has to misrecognise in its "normal" functioning' (Zizek 1999, 76). The given 'theoretical meaning' and the institutional expression of sovereignty can both be contested, and in this way both are political. Another way in which sovereignty is political is that particular constructions and conceptions of sovereignty have very much influenced the meaning of politics.

Sovereignty is political also in the sense that it is seen in the political theory tradition as associated with 'good' concepts like democracy, self-government and constitutionalism, and in the Foucauldian tradition with 'bad' concepts like domination, regulation, and oppression. Both are political. The meaning of sovereignty is affected by the conceptual company it keeps.

Sovereignty is also political in that it relates to how politics is enacted. For instance in my book *Spinoza and Republicanism* I tried to show how politics was done in the United Provinces in the seventeenth century. The meaning of sovereignty and Spinoza's conception of it were closely associated with how politics was done and normative ideas about how it should be done. The theories of sovereignty of Bodin and Kant, among others, were designed to make an impact on how politics was done – Bodin in connection primarily to ruler sovereignty and Kant with reference to the further articulation of the *Rechtstaat* and to relations between states. In the discourse of domestic politics, sovereignty most normatively establishes (or for Schmitt problematises) the overarching constitutional settlement. Standardly, the constitution is seen as non-political, establishing the frame *within* which messy politics is played out and conflict is constrained. Sovereignty is seen as a key element of the constitution, setting out the locus of supreme legal power, and the authority of governments to make law, go to war, and punish offenders through a criminal justice system. But we can also ask about the political nature of sovereignty and problematise the way sovereignty and the constitution have been seen as above politics.

Modern state sovereignty is conceived as a neutral – politically-neutral – concept, but this account masks a very political construction. Paul Keal draws out an example from the end of the nineteenth century of the 'political' dimension of sovereignty, where a condition was laid down that was not neutral politically, and which has significant repercussions for conceptualising claims to indigenous sovereignty, which is worth considering in some detail. The example highlights an instance of the move from a formulation which is clearly culturally specific to one which dresses its cultural specificity in universalised language. Keal relates how the great powers of Europe 'proclaimed "the standard of civilisation" as the criteria for membership of international society'. In order to be 'counted as members of international society, and consequently as subjects of international law, political entities had first to attain this standard, which stipulated a level of political and social organisation recognised by Europeans'. In this way, he demonstrates, the 'standard of civilisation was thus a crucial instrument for drawing the boundaries between the "civilised" and "uncivilised" worlds, and for determining who did or did not belong to international society' (Keal 2003, 29). Keal identifies that, conceived in this way, 'international society is necessarily limited to states with similar domestic arrangements based on a shared political culture'. In other words, the notion of international society was not based simply on mutual recognition as a marker of the sovereignty system. It precisely did not imply 'a pluralistic international society in which, so long as there are rules to guide mutual relations, the internal relations should not matter' (Keal 2003, 30).

The 'political' character of sovereignty in this sense also extends to the notion of legitimacy. Keal quotes Martin Wight, for whom legitimacy entailed 'the collective judgment of international society about rightful membership of the family of nations, how sovereignty may be transferred, and how state secession is to be regulated, when large states break up into smaller, or several states combine into one' (Keal 2003, 31). Such judgement is not neutral. Moreover, in contemporary world politics the *domestic* arrangements of states are, Keal notes, 'increasingly important in determining which states are regarded as legitimate'. The status and moral authority of states depends, perhaps more than ever before, Keal underlines, on 'factors such as their human rights record, their treatment of indigenous populations, whether they are governed by democratic institutions, and the degree of social justice that obtains in them'. This recalls an earlier time when legitimacy was not necessarily extended to non-Christian rulers (Keal 2003, 31).

The meaning of sovereignty: general features

Each theory of sovereignty focuses upon a different cluster of general features, attributes, marks, properties, and conditions to define and indicate the location and meaning of sovereignty, and no theory includes them all. The identity of sovereignty varies across the different conceptions of it that have been developed. For Hobbes it is a hypothetical single, meaningful, performance. For Locke it is a technical requirement, and for Rousseau it is an ongoing activity rather than a 'thing'. For Schmitt sovereignty is again a performance, invoked in the decision to acknowledge an exception, while for Foucault it is a dead letter and a false alibi.

The general features of sovereignty cover a range of subjects within and related to politics, including government, law, state theory, international relations, ethics, diplomacy, defence, security studies and policing. The sub-disciplinary discourses emphasise different clusters of general features but these also overlap. The general features highlighted in the mainstream political theory discourse include the authority relationship between rulers and ruled; sovereignty as a recognition concept, relying upon the recognition of others in order to be established; sovereignty as a regulative ideal establishing political stability; sovereignty as a way of designating the 'whole' realm of a political unit; sovereignty as functional rather than territorial; and modern sovereignty establishing a modern constitutional state but also possibly overridden by the constitution. The legal and constitutional discourse focuses upon the idea of sovereignty as self-government; the capacity to make law but take commands from none; as specifying the highest legal authority and establishing the rule of law; the idea of jurisdiction; the competence to initiate constitutional change; unequalled power; sovereignty's perpetual character over time across different office-holders; independent power; self-management; full authority; strong leadership; independence; supreme rule; self-reliance; autonomy; and control over one's own affairs. In the international relations discourse sovereignty is used to designate the idea of a fixed and bounded territory; territory as marking the border between internal and external sovereignty; security for and the boundaries of property and wealth; a monopoly on the use of violence within that territory and in the name of the state in external intervention; the power to declare war and make peace; to posit formal juridicial equality between states; state infrastructure (in particular for state theorists); the spectre and sanctioning of dominance (for state and critical IR theorists); and relations between states as setting the framework for the ideas of international relations, global politics, international politics, relations between state and non-state actors, foreign policy, international power relations, 'international society' (defined by Keal (2003, 30) as 'a community of mutual recognition' of each others' legitimate right to sovereign independence), and international community.

There is also a tradition of utilising a cluster of Latin terms to define and discuss sovereignty (Bartelson 1995, Coleman 2005, Armitage 1998). Concepts such as *imperium* (command), *jurisdictio* (administration of justice), *dominion* (rule), *potestas* (power), and *officium* (office-holding) can all shed light on the meaning of sovereignty. Franklin (1992), for instance, renders sovereignty as *maiestas* or majesty, and other authors select different combinations of these terms and give them varying weights.

Having set out a range of general features of sovereignty, one can ask how these features are related. Do they mutually reinforce each other? Are they interdependent, or intersect, or interlinked? Do they together form an edifice? Does one or more underpin the others? Is there a core to sovereignty, given that no one general feature is a requirement for all conceptions? How are the features related conceptually, and politically (for example, there is a strong connection between the rule of law and the monopoly of violence by the state)? Or are these features disjunctive, features that simply arose historically without fitting logically together but with particular histories and meanings in different places, with no universal logical theory? Moreover, what would answers to these questions mean for how the relation between the features can be reconceived? The book seeks to provide a clearer picture of some of these questions.

The concept of sovereignty is characterised not only by a range of general features but also by a series of distinctions. The distinction between legal and political sovereignty was discussed at the beginning of this chapter and comes up again throughout the book. Another distinction is between *de jure* and *de facto* sovereignty and this distinction is again problematic – here because its reference is slippery. It can be seen as aligned to the way sovereignty as the authority to make rules and to govern, subject to no higher law, is differentiated from the idea of autonomy, the actual capacity to act independently, free of international and transnational constraints. Here the *de jure/de facto* distinction maps onto that between legal and political sovereignty. Loughlin, for instance, maintains that the difference between legal and political sovereignty is that the former is about competence (power to enact law, and jurisdiction in the sense both of having a viable system of rule and being an entity in international politics) and capacity, concerns the 'expression of official power' and focuses on 'the institutional and public', while the latter is 'the product of a political relationship' between rulers and ruled and is about authority and power (Loughlin 2003, 69). While this is helpful as far as it goes, this formulation of the distinction does not clarify whether the key meaning of legal sovereignty refers to a) the highest legal body, that is, superiority, b) the capacity to make law (legislative bodies), or c) legitimacy (legal sanction). It also leaves open the question of whether the relationship depicted between the law and politics is neutral or political, and raises the question of the uneasy relationship between sovereignty and a constitution. We will return to this question in Chapter 4.

Dicey's authoritative distinction between legal and political sovereignty again aligns with the *de jure/de facto* separation. Legal sovereignty here rests on the belief that ultimate and final authority resides in the laws of the state. This also describes *de jure* sovereignty; the idea that supreme power is exercised on the basis of legal authority; the right to require somebody to comply, as defined by law. Political sovereignty was *de facto* sovereignty;

the actual distribution of power, the ability to command obedience, based on a monopoly of coercive force. Legal and political, *de jure* and *de facto* sovereignty are, however, closely related in practice, and there are reasons to argue that neither alone constitutes a viable form of sovereignty. Part of the slipperiness of this distinction comes from the difficulty of disentangling the concept of sovereignty from the liberal conception which, for instance, sees it as axiomatic that there is a distinction to be made between legal and political sovereignty, that sovereignty is associated with a modern emancipatory constitution, some sort of separation of powers, and the rule of law in the context of a *Rechtstaat*.

The *de jure/de facto* distinction can also be taken to represent the importance of accommodating sociological evidence about states with the principled basis of sovereignty. The assumption is that, strictly speaking sovereignty is by definition *de jure* and to say so is tautological, but that the idea of *de facto* sovereignty is used to show a willingness to negotiate and be flexible in the light of the contingencies of the real world of messy politics. However, the *de facto/de jure* distinction is often used in practice as a means of denying to some states (for instance so called 'failed' states and 'rogue' states) the full status of *de jure* sovereignty. Like the civilised/ uncivilised distinction it operates as a coded means of referring to a normative classification of states. Another reference for the *de jure/de facto* distinction aligns with the idea of sovereignty as a *formal* designation, counterposed to the informal messy reality of international politics. The implications of this meaning of the distinction are taken up in the next section of the chapter.

The meaning of sovereignty: epistemology constructs ontology

Rob Walker and others have demonstrated conclusively how modern state sovereignty, absolutist in a very real sense, has been used by dominant political actors to further their powerful interests. Such writers have detailed the patterns of marginalisation and exclusion that have been the clear outcome of a realist theory of sovereignty that prioritises epistemology over ontology and ignores 'empirical tendencies'. However, there are several ways in which insights can also be gained into the meaning of sovereignty and the politics of sovereignty by elucidating how, with the sovereignty concept, epistemology (theories of knowledge) constructs ontology (theories of being and reality), and what is taken to be knowledge constructs what is taken as reality.

Strictly speaking epistemology and ontology are inter-constitutive. Knowledge and reality (theory and practice) help to construct each other and there is unavoidably a two-way process of meaning-formulation at work. The idea that (political) concepts *describe* the world (theory deriving from reality) is necessarily interdependent with the ideas of using concepts to critically *reflect upon* the world, using concepts to critically *evaluate* the world (in both cases theory preceding reality), using concepts to make *normative* ('should') judgements about the world, using concepts to make political action more *effective*, and realising for instance the transformative *effects* on groups of people that emancipatory concepts can have (MacKenzie 2005, 6). In making a case for the primacy of epistemology over ontology I am not suggesting that sovereignty is a mere epiphenomenon or abstraction. Rob Walker is right to argue that sovereignty is a principle, an institution and a practice 'that always works both as abstraction and as a material social form' (Walker 2004, 245).

In addition there is an epistemology-ontology hermeneutic circle at work in this book. My interest in sovereignty is shaped by the history of the concept and its conceptions. But the interpretation of that history put forward here is also shaped by my current questions about it. The two interlock. 'What does sovereignty mean?' includes all the answers that have been given, and this means that the appropriate response is a historical endeavour. This is where two of the sides of the 'meaning' question posed in this chapter are connected. However, having registered the inter-dependence of knowledge and reality it is useful to highlight the ways in which epistemology does precede ontology for the meaning of sovereignty, to counteract the common view that the meaning of sovereignty derives simply from political 'facts' about the world. Rob Walker's target is the political effects of sovereign power, while the target here is the positivist and empiricist grip on commonsense understanding and social science explanation that denies the constructedness of meaning and reality.

Five ways in which it is important for understanding sovereignty to recognise that epistemology precedes ontology will be discussed here. They are the manner in which ideas mediate our understanding of the world; the way what counts as knowledge is organised through concepts; the gap between the abstract, conceptual nature of sovereignty and the 'real' world of political action; insights arising from Cooper's observations about rule-governed, conventional behaviour; and what sovereignty shares with and how it differs from other political concepts.

In the first place, ideas always mediate action, behaviour, and meaning. The way we are predisposed to see things shapes the way we understand them. Epistemic privilege is a feature of cognition. What we think and accept sovereignty to mean, structures the real world of political and legal practices within which we work. Ontology is not independent of epistemology. This applies not just to sovereignty but to all political concepts that help structure our understanding of the field of politics. Moreover, the big question posed here, 'what does sovereignty mean?', is an epistemological question. The reality and the ontology are shaped by the epistemology. Kant endorses this view when he sums up his idealist and metaphysical position in the Appendix to the *Metaphysics of Morals*. It is the idealist side of the argument that is relevant here. He says '[e]very actual deed (fact) is an object in *appearance* (to the senses). On the other hand, what can be represented only by pure reason and must be counted among *ideas*, to which no object given in experience can be adequate – and a perfectly *rightful constitution* among human beings is of this sort – is the thing in itself' (Kant 1999, 505).

Furthermore, the idea that epistemology logically precedes ontology through ideas mediating our understanding of the world implies a strongly constructionist methodology. Connolly, for instance, points to an important aspect of the priority of epistemology over ontology when he identifies 'the theory-embedded character of political concepts, the contestability of key political concepts, the normative implications of conceptual decisions in empirical inquiry, and the primacy of interpretation over law-like explanation' (Connolly 1993, vii). Connolly argues persuasively for the 'constructed, contestable, contingent, and relational character of established identities' (Connolly 1993, xi), and this applies to sovereignty as much as other forms of political identity. Sovereignty as an 'essentially contested concept' refers both to the way one concept has a variety of historical and contextual meanings, and to the way differences in contemporary interpretations of the same concept are a source of disagreement. It also remains the case that social constructions can have powerful effects. Just because something is socially constructed doesn't mean it is easy to shift.

Arguments concerning the priority of epistemology over ontology that are relevant here include the contingently situated essential contestability of concepts; the primacy of interpretation; the concept/conception distinction; the interplay between theory and practice in the construction and disputing of meaning; and how the conceptual organisation of knowledge changes over time and in different political circumstances and cultures.

In this respect we can recognise that the political nature of the sovereignty concept arises from three sources – the inevitable indeterminacy between theory and its application to practice, the contested quality of political concepts, and the mistaking of a conception for the concept. The gap between theory and practice discussed below, which is a characteristic of the relation of all concepts to the 'real' world, is expressed in features such as the intangibility of political concepts; the 'as if' or 'conventional effect' logic that enables political concepts to work; our understanding of rule-governed behaviour and 'secondary rules', and the articulations of political concepts in overlapping clusters. The contested quality of political concepts refers to the performativity of political concepts; the urge to depoliticise in conceptual analysis; sovereignty as a state (in the sense of polity) concept; sovereignty as a recognition concept and so dependent on acknowledgment; and sovereignty as related to representation and constitutionalism but not to accountability. Sovereignty, like other political concepts is unavoidably performative in the sense that it is known necessarily through its effects, its practices, through the acts done in its name. Here the 'as if' is cashed in. The political nature of sovereignty emerging from the eliding of conception and concept, discussed further below, is found in the dominance of the liberal legacy of political concepts.

Frazer spells out with the example of feminist interpretation the way in which epistemology operates to shape ontology in this first sense of ideas mediating action and understanding. She notes that '[f]acts about sexual difference frequently reveal that sexual difference is *a priori*: a set of presumptions, in the light of which particular characteristics are discerned and labelled sexual. It is not just sexual difference that is *a priori*, but, rather sexual hierarchy'. The general point here, Frazer underlines, is that '[c]oncepts are prior to observation and are an ingredient in interpretation – this seems to be the best way to understand how "prejudice" and "bias" work' (Frazer 1997, 217). Moreover, she urges, conceptual analysis can itself be thought of as a form of interpretation, whether it be conceptual analysis within established boundaries by philosophers, by Wittgenstinian language users, or by political theorists that seek to thoroughly destabilise concepts such as 'woman'. Frazer also draws the conclusion here that 'conceptual analysis is intimately bound up with textual analysis' (Frazer 1997, 218).

The second aspect of the idea that epistemology precedes ontology is that a theory about what counts as knowledge organises its argument in terms of concepts and conceptual relations. For instance, different theories of sovereignty over time (putting forward what counts as knowledge about sovereignty) have employed different conceptions of what the concept of sovereignty means. Bartelson explores a kind of concept/conception relation, arguing that 'the concept of sovereignty is filled with a historically variable content. As such, sovereignty does not stand in a predetermined and internal relation to knowledge, nor in an undetermined and external relation to it. Rather, the relation between sovereignty and knowledge is undetermined *and* internal, and is therefore also a historically open and productive circuit' (Bartelson 1995, 7). The upshot is that epistemology preceding ontology means that different historical theories of sovereignty cannot be related or constructed into a teleological story of progress, but must be recognised as incommensurably different (responding in particular ways to different problems, questions, norms and vocabularies, as well as in some cases reacting to previous theorisations) and that sovereignty has irreducibly multiple interpretations. The unique and specific political and intellectual context in which each conception of sovereignty was formed deserves to be listened to if we are really to discover the resources this legacy offers. Prokhovnik (2008 forthcoming) demonstrates this point.

What is being distinguished here is a thin abstract concept and multiple thick conceptions. A circularity in the argument is avoided (the thin set of attributes derived from the thick set of conceptions identified as examples of the thin concept) because of the openness in the range of ideas, conceptions, questions and perspectives available. One of the benefits of approaching sovereignty here in terms of a concept/conception distinction is that sovereignty doesn't begin with a fixed meaning, in terms of which each thinker is judged and measured. But one of the problems attached to using the distinction, which is hopefully avoided here, is that it can lead to a thin, dull, and perhaps essentialist definition of the concept, shorn of any real meaningfulness, together with a very diverse set of conceptions with no way of assessing and comparing their worth apart from their individual historical value.

Another example is the debate between the mainstream sovereignty canon and Foucault, which is a contestation over the relevant and appropriate concepts to use in the cluster with sovereignty. The mainstream legacy regards sovereignty as closely intertwined with authority and legitimacy, and with law. Foucault rejects this and seeks to undercut it by linking sovereignty with social relations of power. The view taken here about this struggle for conceptual pre-eminence, this form of the politics of sovereignty, is that both are valuable but that the two both coexist and are incommensurable.

Different conceptions of sovereignty shape political reality very differently, then. Sovereignty has a massive effect on the way we conceive politics. An example is found in the way the development of the concept of globalisation, particularly in its earlier stages, has been characterised by the attempt to squeeze the concept of sovereignty out of the picture as a major player in defining political reality. But the relationship between political concepts and political reality is two-way and both are moulded by the interplay between agency and structural constraints, and the concept of sovereignty still has life in it.

However, what counts as knowledge is not only organised through concepts, but the organisation of political knowledge is organised through concepts which are profoundly political. Conceptually, the book endorses Connolly's argument about essential contestability, which is an argument about the political character of concepts like sovereignty. By 'essential' he means 'central rather than trivial or peripheral', but not 'in principle irresolvable' (Connolly 1993, 120). He holds that 'a particular network of concepts [such as power, authority, persuasion, coercion] is contestable' because the 'standards and criteria of judgment it expresses are open to contestation', and that 'such a network is *essentially* contestable' because 'the universal criteria of reason…do not *suffice* to settle these contests definitively'. Ball offers a qualification to the idea of essential contestability that does not affect the value of Connolly's insights, positing 'contingent contestability' to take into account the political as well as philosophical basis of the contestability of concepts, giving the example of 'once-heated arguments about "republic" [that] have cooled considerably since the late eighteenth century' (Ball 1997, 36). Underpinning Connolly's view here is a convincing challenge to those who seek to neutralise or, in his words, 'transcend the politics of discourse' and who 'practice an academic politics of depoliticisation through reification of the terms of political discourse' (Connolly 1993, 225). It follows from this view of concepts that, in doing conceptual analysis, there is a need to attend to the discourses in which concepts are used and gain meaning. What we are looking at are historically located conceptual and political meanings of sovereignty.

Connolly argues that it is a positive quality of politics in general, that it deals characteristically with essentially contested or disputed concepts, concepts whose very definition depends upon actual people making practical decisions about their meaning. He also notes that Gallie, who coined the phrase 'essentially contested concepts', 'argues that mutual awareness among adversaries that some of their shared concepts are subject to essential disputes contributes to the intellectual development of all protagonists' (Connolly 1993, 11). However, it needs to be borne in mind that Gallie's formulation, while extremely useful, is also not itself politically neutral, and expressed the classic essential pluralism of political positions espoused by liberal thinkers from Locke to Mill to Berlin. In doing so, it rules out of court other perspectives.

The priority of epistemology over ontology (as well as referring to the way ideas mediate our understanding of the world, and that what counts as knowledge is organised through concepts, giving rise to the changing meanings over time and in different political circumstances and cultures) also gives the concept of sovereignty a flexibility in use that is exploited by political actors and in the different discourses about it. But it also causes a range of problems, for instance in seeming to leave a gap between 'facts' and the 'real world of politics' and conceptual intangibility. As a result there is a sense of sovereignty being an illusion, a sleight of hand, merely symbolic, a delusion, not 'real' in the way the territorial materiality of states is real. This has also fuelled the idea of sovereignty as a myth – a fiction, a falsehood, an imaginary thing, an untruth. But trusting in the territorial materiality of states is itself a construction, based on a natural science positivism and empiricism, and on modern map-making that figures space as territory. Stankiewicz (1969, 4) recognises that sovereignty is 'a set of logically related ideas – and not a simple, empirically verifiable condition'. The way in which sovereignty is a recognition concept, dependent upon recognition by others, also heightens the gap between meaning and reality. The 'as if' and fictive aspects of sovereignty, the way in which sovereignty is a 'necessary hypothesis', a 'regulatory fiction', contribute to both the flexibility and problems associated with the concept. Relatedly, part of sovereignty being a recognition concept is that sovereignty is a status. Status is again an intangible thing, something that is clearer in its effects in the world than in any essential meaning, and mediated by our understanding of the status ladder.

Thus another part of the 'meaning' of sovereignty in this sense refers to the intangibility that goes with political concepts. Hegel addresses this intangibility well, that sovereignty is an idea rather than a thing, and an attribute of the whole, not reducible to any of the parts. With sovereignty as with other political concepts, this intangibility is due to epistemology constructing ontology. Neil Walker's formulation runs parallel with this view. This intangibility is also closely related to MacIntyre's point, that ideas necessarily mediate our observation and understanding of the world, relating back to the discussion above. Part of what it means to do conceptual work is to conceptualise – here sovereignty as political order, etc. So in part the abstract, 'not real' aspect of sovereignty is a direct result of the level of attention being employed, in using ideas.

One attempt to overcome the gap between the abstract, conceptual nature of sovereignty and the 'real' world of political action comes from the 'as if' argument. We operate as if the model of politics and the paradigm of political action represents a truth. This is a benign form of the way in which we naturalise our conceptions. The relation is taken on trust; it involves the use of a hypothetical but not conditional argument. The 'as if' argument is characteristically 'modern', western, abstract, and universal, and is also similar to Hobbes's use of the hypothetical which, while ambiguous, has been often misunderstood (Prokhovnik 2005). The enhanced use and value given to maps for politics and warfare from the seventeenth century onwards also contributed to the potency of the 'as if' mentality we have, in prioritising the schematic map as the preferred representation of the terrain, in turn affecting how the terrain was developed. While the 'as if' argument is used or at least presupposed in the discourse of political theory, the mainstream IR discourse takes as literal what the 'as if' posits.

The modern logic has been that 'as if' (sovereignty as if it was absolute, etc.) provides the ontological terms of reference, from which we can proceed with political action and engagement and understanding. In this way also the epistemological precedes the ontological. The 'as if' logic ignores the historical – the tradition that covers different kinds of thinking about sovereignty, and the way our thought and action are shaped by what has gone on before. The 'as if' logic leaves us suspended in space, divorced from the real world. This helps to account for the shock and clamour when it seemed that the state had been eroded, and the subsequent invention of 'globalisation'.

Another aspect of epistemology preceding ontology in this third sense is that part of the flexibility of political concepts is that their force does not depend upon their descriptive precision. John Dunn argues that despite the fact that no actual nation-state conforms to the bald, stipulative definition, it is not this that undermines the validity of the concept of the nation-state. He says 'Nations consist of those who belong together by birth...States consist of those who are fully subject to their own sovereign legal authority'. A true nation state, he surmises, 'would consist only of those who belonged to it by birth and of those who were fully subject to its sovereign legal authority'. By this criterion, Dunn notes, 'it is unlikely that there is a single nation state in the world at present, and moderately unlikely that any such state has ever existed'. However, he points out, 'as with most political ideas, the force of the idea of the nation state has never come principally from its descriptive precision' (Dunn 1994, 3).

Similarly with the notion of sovereignty itself, the fact that no political community since the late sixteenth century has in practice had the uncontested power and authority promised by the definition of sovereignty, has not in itself been enough to undermine as a myth the existence of sovereignty. No state has ever had the complete internal capacity to pursue policies without regard for the expressed views of its subjects or citizens, whether or not the government is democratically-arrived at. And no state has ever had complete external independence, in the international arena to make policy unconstrained by consideration of the power and authority of other states.

Hinsley also draws attention to the way sovereignty is intangible and depends upon recognition. For instance, Hinsley notes that 'men do not wield or submit to sovereignty. They wield or submit to authority or power. Authority and power are facts...[but] sovereignty is not a fact. It is a concept which men in certain circumstances have applied...to political power' (Hinsley 1986, 16). He continues, arguing for the political character of sovereignty, 'in a word, the origin and history of the concept of sovereignty are closely linked with the nature, the origin and the history of the state'. Hinsley's statement that sovereignty is not a fact, points to an important aspect of its character. Just as political obligation is intangible, an idea about a relationship rather than an empirical fact, so sovereignty is a concept whose plausibility and validity depend entirely on actual people recognising it, acknowledging it, and using it. It does not exist unless there is a shared recognition between both parties of the relationship that it does define and constitute the relationship between them.

A fourth sense in which epistemology constructs ontology is brought out by David Cooper. He makes an interesting point about sovereignty that is relevant here, bringing together Austin's notion of performative utterances and Hart's account of sovereignty. Cooper distinguishes between 'the tree in my garden [that] is logically independent of any person's having gone through some rule-governed, conventional (including verbal) behaviour. The existence of the vast majority of things is independent in this way'. However, things like a promise (for instance by A) depend upon A's having gone through some rule-governed procedure, some performative utterance, like saying 'I promise' or nodding. As Cooper notes, 'Austin points out that for certain performances to "come off", such as promising, "there must exist an accepted conventional procedure having a certain conventional effect"' (Cooper 1971, 161, quoting Austin). Cooper argues that sovereignty is in the same class as promises, guarantees, contracts, gifts, marriages, and legal rights. Sovereignty, for Hart, notes Cooper, 'only belongs to a person or body in virtue of certain "secondary rules" – rules, that is, which "confer powers, public or private...which lead...to the creation of...duties or obligations". At some point, in other words, rules must be stated or implicitly govern behaviour, if someone is to be counted as the sovereign' (Cooper 1971, 161, quoting Hart).

The value of Cooper's insight is threefold. He points to the sense in which there is a 'conventional effect' (and this relates to the 'as if' argument) that enables the idea of sovereignty to work. It is not a 'thing' like a tree, but is understood as an effect that bestows powers. He also points to the way in which sovereignty is both the product of a relationship and conceptualises that relationship. The 'secondary rules' that define how sovereignty functions (possibly in a constitution, or understood in terms of divine or natural right) mediate between ruler and ruled, and between the ruled. The source of this is not just legal but also cognitive, part of our capacity to have ideas, mediate our experience of the world through ideas, and understand the salience of rule-governed behaviour and 'secondary rules'. The use of the concept of sovereignty trades on all this, but implicitly. And it is this understanding, of the cognitive as well as legal structure of sovereignty that Foucault misinterprets. He thinks sovereignty as a juridical relationship is a sham, and so dismisses sovereignty out of court, without recognising the cognitive work that goes on in forming and discussing political concepts. In reducing the political to the social, sovereignty to social power relations, Foucault overlooks the crucial role of the cognitive in the political. Prokhovnik (2008 forthcoming) develops this view.

The sense in which sovereignty is not just legal but also depends on cognitive connections, is different from the idea of sovereignty being an 'abstraction'. The tradition of liberal thinking is rightly criticised for its positing of abstract individualism, removing all the 'accidents' of gender and ethnicity and other forms of embodiment, in the misguided attempt to distil a common core of human rationality that can operate as the model of the pre-political individual, the fundamental element of the liberal political landscape. The loss involved in the liberal form of abstraction involves a reductiveness and a curtailment of personal and political identity to disembeddedness and disembodiment, by disuniting and disengaging what are lived and felt as multiple and intersubjective identities. The abstractness of the cognitive recognition of 'secondary rules' does not involve this kind of loss.

The third part of the value of Cooper's insight lies in the distinction between sovereignty and legal rights as both things that depend upon performative utterances. Cooper argues that '[w]hether or not a person has the right to do *x* is logically dependent upon some rule or convention by reference to which such a right may be ascribed'. It may be a written statute, a judicial decision, or take another form (Cooper 1971, 162). This is different from sovereignty as forming a relationship (ruler-ruled, or between the ruled) and as forming a whole (state). Moreover, what Cooper is pointing to is not a distinction between legal and political sovereignty, because political sovereignty can be defined in terms of popular sovereignty, that is, as Berki puts it, the 'political sense...that the "people" can and should form a united community without the instrumentality of an individual sovereign ruler, that they can control their destiny through conscious direction of the constitution, and that the people should be concerned with deliberation and decision-making' (Berki 1971, 208).

The fifth and final aspect of epistemology preceding ontology for sovereignty concerns what it shares with other political concepts. We have already noted the intangibility and fugitive quality about sovereignty, and some of this quality comes from it being a political concept and from the way in which all political concepts necessarily prioritise epistemology over ontology. So one way of getting at the meaning of sovereignty in this sense would be to attempt to specify what sovereignty shares with other political concepts, how sovereignty is connected to other specific concepts, and how sovereignty differs as a political concept from others.

A problem with the discourse of political concepts tends to be (with notable examples such as Connolly) its abstractness, whereby the discourse is conducted at a very high level of generality and often adrift from any systematic historical understanding. These properties point again to the way in which the discourse is not normatively neutral. In setting out a group of historical conceptualisations of sovereignty to balance what can be delivered by conceptual analysis, this book seeks to provide a more grounded understanding of the concept of sovereignty.

So what can be said about political concepts in general? Political concepts set out a framework for political debate and academic discussion of politics, and a shared vocabulary for doing so. However, as Connolly rightly observes, central to politics 'is the ambiguous and relatively open-ended interaction of persons and groups who share a range of concepts, but share them imperfectly and incompletely' (Connolly 1993, 6). We have already noted that political concepts are 'essentially contestable'. In addition, all political concepts are persistently unstable, malleable, constructed, and concern dispute and cooperation, because an important meaning of 'the political' is 'that which is highly-charged'. A further feature of political concepts in general is that, as Condren notes, ideas, concepts, and theories are 'not like battles and earthquakes. Significant degrees of interpretation' are required to understand the meaning they have in a context (Condren 1997, 52). Frazer enriches the meaning of the idea of 'essentially-contested concepts' when she confirms that '[m]eaning is indeterminate [because it is conventional and changes over time] and interpretation is unavoidable' (Frazer 1997, 224). Indeed, we have already noted that all political concepts describe, explain, normatively intervene, and evaluate the world. Another important feature of political concepts we have noted is the concept/conception distinction. At stake here are not contradictions or ambiguities but distinctively different conceptions, between which, however, there is a family resemblance.

A further feature of political concepts in general is that the meaning of political concepts comes in part from their positions in overlapping clusters, whereby a concept 'involves the elaboration of the broader conceptual system within which it is implicated' (Connolly 1993, 14). In a grammar of concepts of this kind 'political obligation', for instance, relies on agency, obedience, the limits of obedience, authority. Another feature held in common by political concepts is that they are parts of the answer to the question, 'how do we live together?' (and 'can we live together?' and 'should we live together?'). We assume that part of the answer to this will be 'with fairness' rather than, for instance, 'with slaves and concubines'. Political concepts are also involved in answers to the questions 'who gets what?' and 'says who?', that is, in the distribution of goods and power. Furthermore, all these concepts in the modern understanding are secular, taken to be and seeking to be fair, reasonable, and capable of being rationally justified, not having recourse to warrant from divine or other non-secular sanction. In addition, all political concepts are conventional, operate with a political society lived in by conventions, routines, everyday givens, all of which become naturalised if not re-politicised and highly charged, questioned and re-justified.

A problem that all political concepts share, and which the study of political concepts faces, is the urge to depoliticise. Political concepts are (relatively) settled meanings, and in studying political concepts there is an urge to set out a neutral (impartial, shared) language of political discourse, even or especially when dealing as politics does with contestability and deeply-held differences. In addition there is a tendency to think that the study of political concepts has greater legitimacy and so trumps uses of political concepts by engaged practitioners. Sovereignty confronts this problem particularly acutely. Whereas the concepts of democracy, representation, and power, for example, contain within them a degree of volatility and dynamism, sovereignty seeks to establish or define order. In defining the whole, the unit, of the polity, conceptions of sovereignty take the question about the nature, scope and limits of that whole, that unit, out of the realm of political debate. Like constitutionalism it seeks to be above the fray. Moreover, in seeking to establish stability in the link between rulers and ruled, and between the ruled, definitions of sovereignty resist attempts to destabilise those links.

All political concepts require some minimal acknowledgment or consent to operate. But concepts in the sovereignty/authority/legitimacy/obligation cluster also require additional recognition, and that recognition is a political act in the sense that it is part of citizenship. This is closely related to the 'as if' point. In addition, all political concepts imply rules, consent, consent to rules, and rule-bound behaviour. We are familiar with the idea of games and rule-following. For instance, any definition of social justice can issue in rules that are set out in tax and distribution policies that affect people and which they must abide by. But sovereignty, legitimacy, etc. as authority concepts, entail acknowledgment as well as rules. However, it would be mistaken simply to conceive of authority is an umbrella concept under which sovereignty is found, because sovereignty is related to claims to power, especially in the effects of power, as much as to claims to authority.

Nevertheless the notion of authority is important to the meaning of sovereignty in several ways. The concept of authority combines unquestioning recognition (and so there are links with naturalisation and the givenness of the commonsensical and commonplace), with the idea of power without coercion, and a logical relationship (as in Hobbes's theory of authorisation and representation). Arendt observes that the hallmark of authority is unquestioning recognition, a political model involving 'a relationship in which the compelling element lies in the relationship itself and is prior to the actual issuance of commands' (Arendt 1977, 109). The same reasoning applies to sovereignty, and operates through the way that, as Gadamer puts it, the authority of persons is 'ultimately based not on the subjection and abdication of reason but on an act of acknowledgement and knowledge'. Gadamer also illuminates the manner in which 'authority cannot actually be bestowed, but is earned, and must be earned if someone is to lay claim to it'. Authority, Gadamer emphasises, 'rests on acknowledgment and hence on an act of reason itself which, aware of its own limitations, trusts to the better insight of others'. Authority thus is not about 'obedience to commands'. Indeed, as Gadamer shows, 'authority has to do not with obedience but rather with knowledge' (Gadamer 1975, 279).

Connolly identifies an important paradox about sovereignty that links with the gap between concepts and the 'real' political world discussed earlier, at the root of which is the role of authority in sovereignty. He observes that sovereignty 'always occurs after the moment it claims to occupy'. The 'paradox of politics/sovereignty resides in this temporal gap between act and the consent that enables it'. Connolly also articulates the insight that, 'the temporal gap contains an element of arbitrariness that cannot be eliminated from political life' (Connolly 1995, 139).

The importance of authority for the concept of sovereignty is attested to in a wide range of theorising, including in Krasner's description of authority as crucial to three of the four kinds of sovereignty he outlines. He argues that domestic sovereignty embraces both authority and control, inter-dependence sovereignty (command of transborder flows) involves only control, and that Westphalian sovereignty (no higher or external authority) and international legal sovereignty (mutual recognition) depend upon authority alone. Krasner identifies authority as 'based on the mutual recognition that an actor has the right to engage in a specific activity, including the right to command others. Authority might, or might not, result in effective control. Control can also be achieved through the use of force' (Krasner 2001, 7).

We have already begun to consider how sovereignty is related to other specific concepts. We have discussed how sovereignty depends upon acknowledgment (that I recognise you as having authority, that I recognise myself as having an obligation), and that sovereignty, along with authority, legitimacy and political obligation, is more intangible than some other concepts. The political concept of power, in contrast, has a more visible presence, and coercion depends less on acknowledgment. The 'spectre' of sovereignty arises in part from this intangibility and in part from the power effects of sovereignty. Another point is that both sovereignty and to some extent authority need to be expressed in public office whereas, for example, legitimacy and political obligation can be outcomes. A further point is that political obligation is about agency, obedience, limits of obedience, and authority, whereas sovereignty has a more distant and buffered relation between the individual and the polity, in the sense that sovereignty is concerned with the link established between rulers and ruled, and between the ruled.

Sovereignty is a slippery concept, not just because epistemology logically precedes ontology. It is a slippery, open-ended and extended concept, in the same way that the concept of 'politics' is. Sovereignty is also slippery because it is an indirect term. 'Security' is a much more direct, immediately meaningful, straightforward notion. The meaning of sovereignty is mediated by other considerations. Sovereignty, like obligation, needs a context to interpret its significance for political theory. It is also slippery because there is no foundational reality, no ontological base to appeal to for sovereignty. Thus it is constructed in another sense as well.

Sovereignty is allied with the concept of citizenship in that sovereignty expresses the whole, the unit that citizens share in, belong to, compose, and have in common. Modern western notions of sovereignty are associated with the concept of constitutionalism in that sovereignty occurs within a *Rechtstaat*, a polity governed by the rule of law. Sovereignty is allied with the concept of nationalism in establishing or asserting the identity of the whole or unit. Obligation is one of the political concepts focusing on individuals that are closely related to sovereignty. As Dunn argues, 'states which are in fact effective in promoting the security of their subjects undoubtedly win (and deserve) a higher degree of loyalty than those that fail lamentably to furnish anything of the kind' (Dunn 1994, 5).

Having considered some of the things that all political concepts share and how sovereignty is related to other concepts, it remains to discuss how sovereignty differs from other political concepts. Brown *et al* confidently make four claims about the relation of sovereignty to law, authority and power, all of which can be challenged. They argue that sovereign 'or supreme authority is often confused with unlimited authority'. But, they hold, 'there is, in fact, no such thing: because the authority to govern is always conferred by laws, it is necessarily limited by law'. However, this chapter has already made a strong case for the priority of politics over law in respect of sovereignty. Second, they assert that, 'just as authority (which is the right to govern) is often confused with power (the ability to govern effectively), sovereignty is easily confused with unlimited power'. But, they maintain, 'there is no such thing as unlimited power, either: because its effective use always depends on circumstances, power can never be total. "Totalitarian" regimes may seek unlimited power, but they cannot achieve it'. However, we have already seen that the appeal to empirical evidence cannot be decisive with regard to political concepts like sovereignty. Third, they claim that defining sovereignty 'as a kind of power suggests, moreover, that a government's right to rule is dependent on its power'. But, they reason, 'just as the authority of a law is independent of a government's ability to enforce it effectively, so a government's ability to enforce its laws, though one of the conditions of its existence, is not the criterion of its authority'. However, there are strong grounds for recognising the role played by power and politics in the exercise of sovereignty. Finally they take the view that it 'took several centuries for theorists to unravel the tangle of confusions spun by careless use of the word "sovereignty"' (Brown *et al* 2002, 249–50). However, to argue in this way is to fall into the teleological trap and to subscribe to the exclusive equation of sovereignty with the modern state conception of it.

Some other political concepts are granted a measure of ambiguity or indeterminacy. For instance, democracy, where the outcome is contingent, and there is an ambiguity about 'authority', which can mean 'this or that authority to be followed', or 'works by authority rather than power' is of this kind. Justice, liberty and equality all also have grey areas. But sovereignty is not allowed to be ambiguous. What is the highest law-making body, who are included within the scope of the ruled, what links rulers and ruled, and what links the ruled to each other, must all be clear. What government the ruled give allegiance to, who represents the country abroad, and the absence of independent countries within it, must all be clear, despite anomalies in practice such as disputed territory, dual nationality, stateless persons, and dissident groups.

Writers like Rob Walker and Mark Neocleous rightly highlight the dangers of an important facet of sovereignty, its lack of affinity with the concept of accountability. The notion of accountability is not found in the sovereignty cluster of concepts. Sovereignty is located where accountability stops; it is absolute in the sense of being accountable to no further authority or power. Given the importance in our tradition of political concepts of the cluster of democracy, representation, rights, liberty, and accountability, this aspect of sovereignty is difficult to justify when the effects of sovereignty can be to exclude and discriminate against certain classes of people such as refugees. The inherent contestability of politics and political concepts is particularly difficult to square with a concept like sovereignty, with its move towards a depoliticised and untouchable position above the fray of politics.

We have briefly specified some features of sovereignty as a political concept, and have noted a variety of ways in which sovereignty, sovereignty claims, and discourses about sovereignty are political. For instance we saw that different conceptions of sovereignty shape political reality very differently, and that sovereignty has a massive effect on the way we conceive politics. Chapter 4 goes on to identify an important characteristic of the concept of sovereignty, and thereby state a key mystery about sovereignty. Sovereignty is outside of politics and yet it is also politically negotiable.

The first part of the book, analysing contemporary reconceptualisations of sovereignty, will critically engage with broad mainstream notions of sovereignty as a relation of ruling establishing a political order; as an instrument of political power; as a key feature sustaining the stability of a polity and its equality with other self-governing political communities; as having linked internal and external dimensions; as a status dependent upon recognition; and as important in discussing both the state and other political forms, and individual subjectivity. Part I includes chapters on the internal/external dualism characteristic of the modern paradigm of sovereignty; the impact of liberal ideas on the development of state sovereignty; and an argument for the role of the metaphor and metaphorical patterning in understanding sovereignty beyond its polity form. Part I ends with the argument about political sovereignty in Chapter 4 that is both the culmination of contemporary reconceptualisation – a new conception – and a 'meta-take' on the meaning of the concept. These chapters use important new developments in international political theory and feminist theory as well as in political theory, to extend challenges that have been made over the past ten years to the mainstream and dominant modern Western notion of sovereignty. This part examines and further advances those critiques, and develops positive ideas about the future theorisation of the concept of sovereignty on relational terms.

The second part of the book brings to bear recent theoretical moves in the light of a diversity of historical conceptions in order to consider a case-study of great relevance to contemporary political practice in the European Union (EU). '"Less is More": Sovereignty in Europe', will contribute to the analysis which proposes that what is needed in the public political form or polity of the EU is not the centralising logic of a unified and fully-fledged 'European sovereignty' but a looser relational conception focusing on political identity which fits the polycentric character of Europe. This chapter will engage with the theoretical literatures on European integration and law as well as political theory.

Part I
Contemporary Theory

1
From Internal/External to Post-States and Other Actors: Political Theory, International Relations, and International Relations Theory

This chapter is the first of four addressing contemporary debates about the meaning and utility of the concept of sovereignty, and building up a conception of sovereignty in relational terms. The aim in these chapters is to draw upon some of the continuities and discontinuities with the plurality of previous ideas and discourses about sovereignty (see Prokhovnik 2008 forthcoming), and to demonstrate that sovereignty remains a salient concept in politics and political theory. These chapters, but this one in particular does not attempt to represent the literature exhaustively but to use some contemporary arguments in the literature to advance the case developed here.

This chapter picks up on the contemporary set of discourses about sovereignty described in the Introduction. It clarifies the disjunction between how the concept of sovereignty has been studied by political theorists, how it is used in mainstream international relations, and how it has been conceptualised in international relations theory, and investigates an alternative to the dominant internal/external dichotomy that each of those discourses not only subscribes to but also reflects in their own practice. Chapter 2 outlines the liberal character of orthodox state sovereignty and the intractable problems associated with it, and builds on the reconceptualisation of sovereignty begun in Chapter 1. The theorisation of 'post-states' advanced in Chapter 1 approaches sovereignty from the external side, while the rethinking in Chapter 2 comes at liberal state sovereignty from the internal side. The initial sections of these two chapters are especially designed with readers with a political theory background in mind. They rehearse some material which is already familiar to those with an IR background. Chapter 3 examines an important but under-explored aspect of sovereignty, namely the explanatory power of metaphorical shifts associated the idea of sovereignty, and again furthers the case for a relational conception of sovereignty. Chapters 1–3 seek to break down the 'natural, neutral and normal' character of the modern state sovereignty form. On this basis Chapter 4 advances the rethinking of the concept of sovereignty by bringing together insights into the political character of sovereignty and examining the 'mystery' of sovereignty. The final chapter of the book examines the empirical case of sovereignty in the European Union and proposes a rethinking in the light of the historical and contemporary reflections on sovereignty that have been discussed.

This chapter, then, explores the significance of the disjunction between three of the major contemporary discourses about sovereignty. It highlights the profound indebtedness of the study of international relations to the realist tradition and pinpoints how all three discourses are in thrall to the modern, realist, state sovereignty model. Moreover the political theory, international relations and international relations theory discourses do not represent three equally-weighted alternative perspectives on sovereignty. The mainstream international relations discourse of states in anarchy is the dominant discourse. The historical political theory discourse has largely succumbed to seeing itself as the 'internal' arm of an internal/external division of labour, while the attempts of the various kinds of international relations theory to challenge the dominant discourse are hampered by their starting point of accepting much of the mainstream settlement.

The understanding that underpins the argument of the chapter is that the internal/external state sovereignty settlement, of self-determination and immunity from intervention, was formed by what became known as the realist tradition of international relations practice, supported by and articulated in the modern European realist, liberal ideology counterposing 'civilised' and other states. Recognition of the historical and cultural specificity of both the modern state paradigm and the discourses about it opens the way to puncturing the universalist claims of this model and to rethinking sovereignty beyond the modern state form. We have inherited a realist usage in which states, the internal/external division, and international anarchy are all 'given' structures of practice and of thinking. Historical evidence and the analysis of discourses both help to denaturalise those structures. On the one hand the presuppositions of that practice and ideology formed the basis of the academic study of International Relations and so the International Relations discourse. While political theory has a long and self-conscious pedigree the sub-discipline of International Relations, significantly, was only constituted after the First World War to understand and reform international politics. On the other hand the internal/external settlement is unchallenged by the mainstream contemporary political theory discourse, rendering it a deeply conservative discourse. International relations theory has not substantially moved out of the shadows of the settlement. Focusing on discourses in this chapter, rather than attempting to assert an ontological truth, gives this argument leverage to unseat the centrality of the internal/external lens through which to reconceive contemporary sovereignty and international politics.

The argument of the chapter is developed in three sections. In the first section the character of sovereignty in the political theory and international relations discourses is analysed and the significance of the unstable meaning of 'international relations theory' is explored. Untangling the politics of these discourses sets the scene for opening up a challenge to the internal/external distinction upon which the division of labour between political theory and international relations theory is seemingly naturally based. This first section is concerned to show how disciplinary boundaries within the study of Politics and the naturalised internal/external distinction have actively mutually reinforced each other. Discussion of the meaning of 'international relations theory' leads on to an analysis of its context in 'international political space'. The second section discusses historical evidence that challenges the weight placed upon the 1648 Peace of Westphalia in the mainstream international relations narrative, and considers what this means for rethinking sovereignty. Subjecting the status of Westphalia in the modern state conception to historical evidence and argument is a case study for the larger argument about the unacknowledged specificity of the modern conception. The third section makes a case for a reconceptualisation of internal/external in the light of the conclusions of the previous sections.

What is under the spotlight in this chapter is political theory, international relations and international relations theory on the one hand and internal and external sovereignty on the other. An important and familiar factor at stake here is the realist tradition in IR and its alternatives, but other factors are at work as well. Interacting with the importance of the realist legacy is the high place accorded to the legalised discourse on sovereignty in the *Rechtstaat* and in international law and thus the dominance of modern legal discourse in modern debates over sovereignty. Also at stake are liberal political principles (discussed in detail in the following Chapter 2), and the moralised character of the normative discourses of the rights and international justice discourses that represent the major alternative to the realist position. This chapter seeks to highlight a set of intersecting problems – the depoliticisation of the political theory discourse on sovereignty and also its moralised tone, the profound indebtedness of the academic study of international relations to the realist assumption of the state as natural and given, and the struggle of international relations theory to claim a discourse of its own and escape the confines of mainstream international relations. The normative argument of the chapter is to propose a shift from the normalised internal/external settlement sanctioned by the realist tradition and a legalised view of sovereignty to an understanding of post-states and other actors operating in a political field.

The view taken here is that any discussion of internal and external sovereignty must take as its starting point Rob Walker's ground-breaking critique of the universal, naturalised and depoliticised claims of the barrier set up by the conception of modern state sovereignty. The view presented by the realist tradition of sovereignty and its portrayal of the international sphere in large measure constitutes those concepts. As Rob Walker cogently observed, the realist perspective 'can be understood as an expression of the claim to state sovereignty rather than as an attempt to explain the consequences of state sovereignty' (Walker 1995, 33). However, this chapter seeks to take the discussion a step further by questioning again *all* the terms at stake – internal, external, and the supposed relation between them in terms of the meaning of 'international politics'. The role played by the disciplinary discourses of political theory and international relations reinforces and further obscures the debate about how to understand international politics.

Political theory, international relations, and international relations theory

The emergence of the state system led to a specific categorisation of what is to count as internal and what as external, and to the barrier model of sovereignty, but the story is further complicated by the manner in which disciplinary discourses have functioned. The argument of this section begins by examining the depoliticisation of the political theory discourse on sovereignty and the meaning of sovereignty in international relations. The scope and aims of different strands of IR theory are then explored and the character of the 'international political space' in which they operate is studied. Then the question of in what sense IR is an autonomous field of politics is addressed. This first section of the chapter argues that 'internal' and 'external' sovereignty do not correspond to a neat division of labour between political theory and international relations (theory) but were only constructed in this form with the entrenchment of modern state sovereignty and the realist tradition of international relations. Moreover, the salient comparison is not between political theory and international relations theory but still between political theory and international relations. While it is important to acknowledge the diversity of political theory and IR discourses, it is the dominant ones, namely Anglo-American political theory and analytical political philosophy, and realist IR that are at stake here.

According to the problem Rob Walker highlighted, political theory supposedly dealt with internal sovereignty and international relations supposedly dealt with external sovereignty, with the internal and external aspects treated as two mutually exclusive sealed units unproblematically establishing order at home and balance in anarchy abroad. According to the internal/external settlement, the functions of sovereignty internally are to enact law as supreme (and if possible legitimate) authority and to govern competently. The functions of sovereignty externally in the early modern period were for autonomous and bounded polities as states in territorialised space to exchange ambassadors, regulate trade, make treaties and alliances, and to wage war in a paradigm of international relations as a struggle for power. To the extent that external sovereignty is about war – the conduct of war, the prevention of war, the justification for war, morality and war, strategic alliances for maximising one's position, and military hardware – then the territorial dimension of sovereignty becomes crucial.

The definition of the legitimate rules of engagement in the international sphere for the realist tradition is defined on the basis of a balance of power in post-Napoleonic Europe. This balance of power was conceived, as Teschke puts it, as 'rooted in exclusive territoriality as the fundamental building-block of inter-state relations' (Teschke 2003, 2). External sovereignty is now summarised in the idea of competing national interests in the absence of a central authority or common standard, and on the basis of self-help, regulated by the principles of non-intervention, diplomatic relations, the conventions of warfare, but also rules governing the normal relations between states, of cooperation and shared enterprises. Key aspects of the dominant view of states and the sphere of operation which they create is summed up by Krasner, Spruyt, Bull, and Wendt. Krasner defines neo-realism and neo-liberalism (both part of the broad realist tradition) as international relations theories for which 'sovereign states are the basic ontological given: the actors in international politics are unitary, territorial, autonomous entities; they are sovereign states' (Krasner 2001, 6). Spruyt notes that 'the agents that make up the state system thus create a particular structure of interunit behavior' (Spruyt 1994, 17). Bull also authoritatively defined the neorealists' subscription to the 'logic of anarchy' in terms of 'absence of rule' and not as 'disorder, confusion' (Bull 1966, 35). Wendt distinguishes classical realists from neo-realists on the basis that the former 'attributed egoism and power politics primarily to human nature', while the latter 'emphasize anarchy' and power politics as structures of the international system (Wendt 1992, 395).

The naturalised internal/external dichotomy and the assumption that all actors are states is also reproduced in legal thinking, international law corresponding to external relations between states and constitutional law corresponding to the internal relations within a state. The fiction that all actors are states is maintained despite the manner in which the heteronomy and anarchy of external sovereignty is qualified by and exists alongside factors which are deeply ingrained in the identity of states. Factors apart from independent statehood shaping international relations include patterns of alliances governed by regional position, economic resources, size of territory, geopolitical strategic position, relation to superpowers, ideological orientation, religion, ethnic mix and minority populations.

The distinction between domestic and international, let alone domestic and international sovereignty, does not accurately align with that between political theory and international relations. For it is from the perspective of IR that political theory is about the domestic; and it is for IR that the domestic/international dichotomy is cogent. However, increasingly as political theorists become interested in questions of international politics, they tend unwittingly to confirm that IR distinction. Moreover, while Wight's view that the state is 'an organisation for survival in international anarchy' (quoted in Atack 2005, 12) has been influential, the situation is more complex. The idea of international anarchy and the formation of the system of sovereign states have constituted and mutually reinforced each other.

Thus, on reflection the issue is quite different one from a neat mirroring of political theory articulating internal sovereignty and international relations articulating external sovereignty. Modern political theory has assumed and has generally been incurious about a horizon provided by the limits of the polity, limits which were deemed to be ethical and normative (often based on the notion of homogenous ethnic national populations), the extent of the reach of shared principles and values, rather than simply territorial. It was for international relations – the realist model and the idea of state sovereignty that accompanied it – that the question of internal and external arose.

This means that the disjunction between the two discourses on sovereignty is even greater than previously realised. They are not counterparts, nor mirror images of each other, and they are not using sovereignty in the same sense. Malcolm represents the view which regards as unproblematic that internal and external sovereignty, 'sovereignty at home and away', 'are two sides of the same coin' (Malcolm 1991, 15). For political theory sovereignty has been a depoliticised discourse about authority and obligation that simply assumes the legitimacy of authority as the overarching concept in this discussion. For international relations it is the internal sovereignty of states (primarily defined in legal terms) that sanctions and provides an alibi for the behaviour of international actors (states) in anarchy. According to this view, internal sovereignty as a realm of legality and order mirrors external sovereignty as a realm of non-legality and lack of order. For the realist tradition of international relations, internal and external are co-constitutive and reciprocal, together exhausting all possibilities for the way things can be. Or, rather, the modern realist view has constructed *both* the domestic and international realms by its claims.

For the realist paradigm, internal sovereignty (now significantly territorial and legal in character) is not important in itself, but acts as the facilitator of politics as a play of state interests on the world stage unregulated by any overarching legal, moral, or coercive framework, enabled by the system of diplomatic norms. The nineteenth-century European model of diplomacy that is still the (instrumental rather than normative, and deliberately so) basis of interaction between states posits a unified political actor for each state, a political leader who represents that state, and an internal/external dichotomy that sets out the boundary between the legal and the non-legal, ordered and disordered realms. The dichotomy was not a tension or disjunction but acted as a positive and fruitful framework in which international politics could operate. Various forms of exclusion that resulted from this system were largely accepted with equanimity.

The idea that sovereignty for political theory and international relations have somehow naturally mirrored a separation between internal and external sovereignty is not borne out by the historical record. The twentieth century split between political theory and IR represented a disciplinary separation that expresses the realist mentality rather than a natural division. The background to the contemporary disjunction between the discourses on sovereignty in political theory and international relations is that since at least the early modern period political theorists have discussed the character of sovereignty, most of them (including Grotius, Pufendorf, Hobbes, Kant, Hegel amongst others) recognising the importance of both the 'internal' and 'external' aspects of the topic.

Political theory

The political theory discourse, then, has used the term 'sovereignty' rather than adding the prefix of 'internal' or 'domestic' sovereignty. It has also been dominated by the abstract analysis of concepts, which depoliticises them. It has concentrated on concepts around governing and government rather than politics more broadly, which further depoliticises a concept like sovereignty.

Over the past three decades mainstream political theory has focused on the concept of social justice, finding a reinvigoration of the discipline in response to John Rawls's *Theory of Justice*, after political theory had been pronounced dead in the post-war period. During this time the concept of sovereignty has been an unfashionable one to explore within political theory. However, the 'long silence' of political theory about sovereignty can also be seen as due to the victory of the dominant realist conception. This state of affairs contrasts with the current explosion of interest in sovereignty in international politics. Underlying this contrast between the two discourses is the very different intellectual legacies of the conceptions of sovereignty presented in the last century by political theorists and in international politics, resulting in the situation that these two ways of conceiving sovereignty are not symmetrical.

One example of the depoliticisation of the political theory discourse is identified by Edgley. She notes that 'political theory is strangely resistant' to acknowledging the international character of the state. The state is predominantly viewed 'as a discrete phenomenon' focusing on 'the relationship of the state to its own population', whereas if 'we give equal attention to the international dimensions of a state's actions then distinctions between democratic and fascist states become blurred'. She questions the practice whereby a liberal democracy retains 'its progressive claims' when 'in the process of securing favourable international conditions, representatives not only pursue economically undemocratic ends but also employ profoundly undemocratic means' (Edgley 1995, 153–5).

In political theory and the history of political thought canon, sovereignty is studied in part in terms of the elucidation of the concept of authority. Recent examples of analytical political philosophy such as Swift (2001), Wolff (1996) and Simon (2002) reassert the restrictive view of political theory as a part of moral philosophy, whose aim is to clarify political concepts and develop normative arguments (that is, arguments framed in terms of 'should') about the future of political society (which rulers can then implement in public policy). For instance, Simon asserts that '[p]olitical and social philosophy is concerned with the moral evaluation of political and social institutions' (Simon 2002, 2). This discourse, while having some undoubted benefits, also has the effect of 'not getting its hands dirty'. Raphael, in his influential work, *Problems of Political Philosophy*, argues explicitly that the 'concept of sovereignty should be used only of the legal authority, and not of the coercive power, of a state' (Raphael 1990, 16). The narrowly conceptual and normative basis of this discourse tends to result in (often well-meaning but ineffective) lofty prescriptions at some distance from full engagement with the effects of either inequalities and power relations, or the non-universal character of encultured practices and socially-specific norms. This 'ideal' normative discourse has the effect of normalising and depoliticising serious unjustified power inequalities and discrimination. Furthermore, this discourse is primarily concerned with government, 'good government' and so with politics only in a narrow sense, and thus with what we can identify as 'ruler sovereignty' (which is different from Franklin's usage with respect to Bodin).

However, the dilemma that analytical political philosophy presents itself with, of finding a reasonable balance between autonomy and authority in the context of 'good government', is not the only political problem at stake in the meaning of sovereignty. Dicey, Austin, Hinsley, Jouvenal and Laski, amongst others, could be invoked here. Furthermore, some of the reflection on the state by political theorists including Habermas, Rawls (1993a, 1993b) and Connolly (1984), has reinforced a discourse which has concentrated almost exclusively on the internal dimension. In such work the 'political' and the 'social' are closely intertwined, such that politics is seen as concerned with social conflict and social justice in particular communities. Rawls (1993a, 1993b) offers an unsophisticated view of international relations and does not help to integrate the internal and external dimensions of sovereignty. Examples of political theorists prominent in shaping the contemporary political theory debate whose vision is firmly state-centric include Nozick (1974), Berlin (1991) and MacCallum (1991). In the final chapter of *Identity/Difference* (1991) however, Connolly does consider the merits of democracy across and against territorial sovereign state boundaries.

This book recognises that sovereignty *is* an authority concept as well as acknowledging the truth in Foucault's critique in which alienated and disenchanted citizens are kept in submission in social power relations that disempower them and which make a mockery of the idea of an authority relationship between rulers and ruled. The two things go on concurrently and that they do so is not a contradiction. At the same time sovereignty is not only an authority concept and in Chapter 4 an argument is developed for recognising the under-acknowledged political work that sovereignty does for us.

In the course of the modern tradition of thinking about sovereignty, theorists have provided very different answers to the question, where does sovereignty rest? Rousseau argued for the sovereignty of the people, Hobbes for the sovereignty of the ruler, Dicey for the sovereignty of parliament, Hegel for the sovereignty of the state, and for Austin sovereignty rests in the 'monarch in parliament'. Sovereignty can also be taken to reside in the constitution, in a supreme court that can determine whether acts of the legislature are constitutional, or in the body with the power to amend the constitution. For Schmitt sovereignty is about having the capacity to make the critical decision about political crisis, not the capacities to exercise coercive power, or to rule. According to Schmitt, the most fundamental example of the exercise of sovereignty concerns the capacity and authority to decide when a situation amounts to an exception.

International relations

The two significant features of the mainstream international relations discourse are that it has only existed as a separate sub-discipline for around a hundred years and that it is dependent on the dominant realist practice and its understanding and construction of the international sphere. The problem with this dependence is that, in purporting to describe reality rather than recognising its constructed character, it provides little critical scope for the international relations discourse, depoliticises the inequalities with respect to 'uncivilised', indigenous, colonised, and post-colonised peoples, and naturalises the 'given' definition of the international sphere. The key issue with the realist outlook is not so much issues concerning the assumptions of anarchy, interests and balance, but the assumption that it is describing a bedrock reality and so the lack of acknowledgment of the constructedness of realism. Wendt draws attention to this problem when he argues, as Williams notes, for 'the importance of reflective judgment and the transformative potential opened up by the relational nature of identity' (Williams 2004, 658).

The mainstream political theory tradition and the mainstream international relations tradition in a sense have opposite defects. The former has been largely and uncritically attuned only to the formal and moralised conceptual relations at work while the latter has been uncritically attuned to the realist practices of power politics, the exercise of national interests, and the realpolitik at work in relations between states. Bartelson describes well how the naturalisation of the state occurred in the realist perspective, how the component states were 'regarded as immutable thanks to the purported transhistorical character' of sovereignty (Bartelson 2001, 156). Moreover the two discourses are linked in that the modern realist way of splitting the world into international politics as external and domestic politics as internal, 'domesticates' politics inside the state and tames political theory even though it doesn't regard itself as tamed.

For the dominant realist tradition of international relations the definition of sovereignty revolves around territorial integrity (of the state), political independence (of the state), and domestic order (of the state, encompassing juridical order and a legal monopoly over coercion). The mainstream discourse of external sovereignty has also raised an empirical condition (the territoriality of states) to the status of primary epistemological significance, and the primary explanatory force of external sovereignty has derived from the idea of the recognition of an entitlement by states not to be invaded.

A further difference between political theory and international politics as sub-disciplines of Politics was that political theory was built on a tradition of normative theorising, whereas (in academic disciplinary terms) international relations in every real sense developed out of foreign policy and strategic studies and military history, all of which were closely derived from mainstream practice. As a result international relations has operated with a supposedly God's-eye view, which is at the same time western-centric and moulded by realist and liberal traditions of IR, with western practice and the study of IR in an unhealthy 'explanatory' symbiosis. While the political theory discourse has been more sophisticated, in operating with some reflective distance, it has also been less progressive, focused on and mired in formal matters of constitutionalism.

Krasner describes the different meanings of state sovereignty used within the realm of international politics, by sociologists, international lawyers, and political scientists. For sociologists, sovereignty refers to 'a script, a shared cognitive map that facilitates but does not determine outcomes', whereas for international lawyers 'individual states are the basic building blocks of the international system'. He notes that 'these states are sovereign in the sense that they are juridically independent and can enter into treaties that will promote their interests as they themselves define them'. Krasner contends that what is 'critical for international lawyers is not the substance of these agreements but rather that they not be coerced'. He also distinguishes between political scientists for whom sovereignty 'has sometimes been an analytic assumption, as in the case of neorealism and neoliberal institutional, where states are assumed to be rational, unitary, independent actors', and English School political scientists for whom sovereignty is 'a set of normative principles into which statesmen are socialized, the most important of which is non-intervention in the internal affairs of other states' (Krasner 2001, 1).

Krasner's point is to argue that there are four different 'ways of talking' about sovereignty, and so four ways in which sovereignty can be a problem. He makes the interesting claim that the different components are not necessarily present in all cases, and that countries can validly claim some kinds of sovereignty but lack others. Interdependence sovereignty refers to control over transborder movements, which for instance Palestine lacks and which is thought by some to be eroded by globalisation. Domestic sovereignty is defined by the internal authority structure and the state's effectiveness, which for example so-called 'failed states' do not possess. International legal sovereignty entails recognition by other states, a *de jure* independence that is lacking in the cases of Taiwan and Tibet. Recognition is important not just for legal status and formal equality but also because it facilitates the making of contracts, because alliances enhance security, because it enhances a ruler's domestic support, and because 'membership in the World Trade Organisation can increase access to markets' and 'membership in the World Bank can provide financial resources'. On the other hand recognition does not guarantee either interdependence sovereignty or domestic sovereignty (Krasner 2001, 9–10). Westphalian sovereignty means the absence of external authority over a state, a *de facto* autonomy which Hong Kong, Palestine, Bosnia, and former Soviet republics such as Uzbekistan and Tajikistan lack. He makes the case that the role of the principle of non-intervention as a *grundnorm* has been overstated, overlooking instances of voluntary arrangements that compromise the domestic authority of a state (Krasner 2001, 11–12).

For our purposes the value of Krasner's description is that it indicates the internal variation within the mainstream state sovereignty discourse of international politics, and that it may offer a way of envisioning sovereignty that can appeal to scholars of both political theory and international politics. His approach is also important in showing that the study of what happens with anomalies indicates not the failure of the sovereignty concept (understood as fixed rules) but its resilience and flexibility. He even notes that '[c]onquest and absorption is not a challenge to rules of sovereignty but merely a redrawing of boundaries' (Krasner 2001, 10). The innovative character of this aspect of Krasner's work is highlighted when contrasted with James's lament, in an outline of the orthodox view in which sovereignty is resolutely depoliticised, for the 'absence of legislative control over semantic practice'. For James such absence leads to the license with which the term sovereignty is 'freely introduced' and the 'profusion of concepts [that] is being paraded' (James 1999, 457). Krasner's approach here is also greatly preferable to the punitive language of 'quasi-states' and 'failed states' favoured by some international relations writers.

Krasner's view is also of great value in pointing to the political use to which the components of sovereignty can and have been put. For instance he notes that recognition, the key to international legal sovereignty, 'has been used as a political instrument; it has been withheld from some governments that met widely recognized criteria and extended to those with only tenuous or even no control over the territory they claimed to govern', citing India as 'a member of the League of Nations and signatory of the Versailles settlements even though it was a colony of Britain' and so did not have juridical independence (Krasner 2001, 9). However, the problems with Krasner's view are that it is a form of modelling based on a historical reading, lacking any strong conceptual underpinning, and tied to the modern state-centric understanding of sovereignty. He does not provide an argument for why these four 'ways of talking' about sovereignty constitute the whole enquiry or exhaust the field of explanation, and how conceptually they fit together, and confusingly speaks of these 'ways of talking' about sovereignty as also 'components' or 'aspects' of sovereignty.

The contemporary discourses on human rights and international justice, focusing on humanitarian issues and aid but spilling over at times into calls for military intervention, seek to present an alternative to the lack of a moral motivation and the resolutely state focus of the realist tradition. In these discourses the invocation of sovereignty is sometimes disparaged on the grounds that sovereignty is concerned with the 'merely' formal level of political discourse and activity. However these discourses are hampered not just by the overwhelming capacity of powerful states to ignore calls to act for moral motives but also by their western-centric and universalising viewpoint, and by their myopia that cosmopolitan solutions are the only alternative to the state-centric system of international space. Moreover, there is an intractable and irreducible gap between the moral imperatives of the human rights and international justice discourses and the benchmarks of the dominant realist view, which hold that there is no common ground on which to establish shared normative principles, and that the anarchic international field means that no overarching authoritative principles can be imposed. At best, according to the dominant view, there is formal juridical equivalence between states. As Atack observes, political realism 'ignores the hierarchy of states within the international system (with the US at its pinnacle) and how this must influence international relations' (Atack 2005, 20). This, together with the universalising and so naturalising of the state form, is an example of realism's depoliticisation.

In the realist tradition states are regarded as being essentially self-interested and intrinsically self-regarding. States by their nature seek power, security and/or wealth in their relations with others in the international system, the story goes. States are necessarily realist and operate in an anarchic, 'inherently self-help, Realist world' (Wendt 1999, 241). However, this view represents only a piece of circular realist logic. Before the time that states were identified in terms of definitive territories and populations, the interests of polities in Europe were defined in much more complex ways, through intersecting allegiances to God, Emperor, Pope, princes, lords and magistrates. Pieces of territory near (often disputed) borders and marginal segments of population were not the issue in relations with other, often overlapping and cooperating corporate or collective political agents. The realist view appertains to the modern conception of the state but is not the only one available for rethinking the internal-external connection. Moreover, even on its own terms, the orthodox realist position is flawed. In regarding the material aspect of territory and population as central, this discourse does not take account of the constituent parts of the state as social relations and social structures, and ignores the crucial mediation of 'material facts' and action by ideas and values, all developed within particular histories of meaning.

Philpott notes that the most prominent upholders of the dichotomy between domestic politics informed by notions of justice and international politics 'awed by power', along with Marxists, materialists and prophets of technology, 'has been the Realist school, which regards war, alliances, balances of power, and the rises and falls of states and empires as the germane international events, and which holds that the contest over the international distribution of military and economic power', that is, the material interests of states, 'is what propels these events' (Philpott 2001, 5).

Wendt makes a strong case for the social construction of the realist belief that international relations is structured by power politics and anarchy. He contends that 'self-help and power politics do not follow either logically or causally from anarchy and that if today we find ourselves in a self-help world, this is due to process', that is interaction and learning, 'not structure' (Wendt 1992, 394). He gives a good example of the intersubjective basis of state action in the differentiation in US attitudes to British and Russian missiles. Wendt shows how shared or 'collective meanings...constitute the structures which organise our actions', and how 'identities are inherently relational' (Wendt 1992, 397). He also underlines how identities and 'collective cognitions do not exist apart from each other; they are "mutually constitutive"' (Wendt 1992, 399). In addition, Wendt makes a case for sovereignty as relational and intersubjective when he refers to stable territoriality and sovereignty as 'internationally negotiated terms of individuality' (Wendt 1992, 402). Wendt argues that realists reify 'self-help in the sense of treating it as something separate from the practices by which it is produced and sustained' (Wendt 1992, 410).

Wendt's rearticulation of the constructedness inherent in the very idea of sovereignty is useful both for the critique of realism (which is what he uses it for) and for the reconceptualisation of sovereignty. He looks to the upside of the state sovereignty settlement (it introduces a substantial element of inter-subjectivity into an otherwise simple state of nature situation) rather than the downside that other critics of realism focus on (the sovereignty system covertly constructs and so sanctions a free play of power in an international sphere devoid of law or morality, which benefits the interests of the power-ful). In taking this approach Wendt is not only revealing the constructivist formation of naturalised patterns of behaviour, but is also advocating the value of intersubjective practices and cooperation in international affairs. He usefully takes a performative approach, using the phrase 'sovereignty prac-tices' to refer to the importance of the ongoing commitment of states to certain intersubjective actions for the persistence of the meaning of sov-ereignty. He argues that the principle of sovereignty transforms a situation of pure power politics in a state of nature. It introduces elements of social con-struction, first because it sets up a social basis of a pattern of required reci-procal recognition, and second because it necessarily assumes the existence of equal others. As an institution, Wendt holds, sovereignty 'exists only in virtue of certain intersubjective understandings and expectations'. By setting up a particular kind of state – a sovereign state – and a particular kind of community – one based on 'a mutual recognition of one another's right to exercise exclusive political authority within territorial limits' – these 'reci-procal permissions' constitute a 'spatially rather than functionally differ-entiated world', organised 'around "domestic" and "international" spaces rather than around the performance of particular activities' (Wendt 1992, 412). Sovereignty norms, says Wendt, 'are now so taken for granted, that it is easy to overlook the extent to which they are both presupposed by and an ongoing artefact of practice', and the 'sovereign state is an ongoing accom-plishment of practice, not a once-and-for-all creation of norms that some-how exist apart from practice' (Wendt 1992, 413). Wendt also notes that there are competing principles for the organisation of political space and identity in the contemporary international system, such as spheres of influ-ence and informal empires, which coexist with the practice of sovereignty, with the implication that the continuing efficacy of sovereignty depends upon continued subscription to its practices (Wendt 1992, 414).

Reus-Smit argues cogently that a 'symbiotic embrace' between internal and external sovereignty developed in the twentieth century, evident for instance in Wilsonian internationalism and the Versailles peace settlement. He documents 'the emerging idea of the state as the political manifestation of the nation, and state policies as the political expression of the national interest'. These developments, he contends, 'encouraged the assump-tion that when the principle of national self-determination is upheld', a 'symbiotic embrace' is achieved (Reus-Smit 2001a, 530).

International relations theory and the character of international political space

There is, significantly, no settled agreed meaning for 'international relations theory' (the umbrella term used here to describe all kinds of theorising about politics in the 'international' domain). The argument put forward here is that international relations theory is best understood not as injecting a normative dimension into realist IR (which keeps the realist and state sovereignty settlement largely in place), nor by offering the international sphere to political theorists (which results in a moralised but conservatively understood state sovereignty settlement), but by approaching international politics as a realm of politics. Cynthia Weber's review of how some strands of international relations theory have taken on trust the meaning of state sovereignty and thereby begun their enquiries at the point after all the important, fundamental questions have been asked is pertinent here. She accurately identifies and is critical of the way they treat 'state sovereignty as an already settled question' (Weber 1995, 2).

Bartelson's caution about the gap between discourses and the 'reality' they examine is also salutary in thinking about international relations theory. He notes that political discourse and political order 'rarely evolve in tandem, and their respective evolutionary paths are never unilinear or uniform' (Bartelson 2001, 187). He is pointing to the way that there is no exact correspondence or precise symmetry between the things studied here and the discourses in which they are studied, for those discourses take on lives of their own, have internal politics of their own and agendas of their own, not always dependent on the character of the thing studied.

The meanings of both political theory and international relations theory are affected by a set of broader perceptions and distinctions, usefully outlined by Brown *et al*. For instance, whether one takes, in Brown *et al*'s words, a universalist or particularist viewpoint, will impinge on how one understands political theory and international relations theory. Whether one gives primary allegiance to a general principle such as Christendom, Christian pacifism, Islam or some other cosmopolitan ideal, or to a local or national identity respectively, will have a powerful impact on one's view of the world. Brown *et al* also observe that in many cases allegiance may be complex, given to a primary identity (such as the polis or a nation) but then qualified by other identities, for instance fellow feeling with other Greeks around the world or between peoples of the book (such as other Jews or Christians), distinguished from groups designated as barbarians or unbelievers (Brown *et al* 2002, 9). In the same way, the meaning of the difference between political theory and international relations theory, and between internal and external, partly hinges on whether one subscribes to a distinction 'between a power-oriented, anarchic, international realm, and a normatively integrated, governed, domestic society' (Brown *et al* 2002, 11), or whether one thinks that the same moral stance (human rights, religious norms) should apply to both, or whether there are other possibilities, for instance that both the domestic and the international are to some extent characterised by conflict and the exercise of power as well as by rule-governed behaviour. Brown *et al* note that, according to realists, 'because each state must defend its own interests, there can be no moral limits on the competition of states for power. Reason of state, here, means that international relations is a realm in which the rules of civil society do not apply: rules guiding personal conduct or domestic politics are irrelevant to foreign policy' (Brown *et al* 2002, 245).

Brown *et al* also usefully throw light on the distinctiveness of international relations theory. They observe that whereas 'conventional political theory explores the development of community within a collective context which is taken for granted, international political theory focuses more self-consciously on the way in which one particular notion of collective identity comes to dominate others in the creation of separate communities, and the relationship between this process and the process of relating to external others'. Significantly, the question arises for international political theory in a way it doesn't necessarily for political theory of the extent to which the 'outside' constitutes the inside. The Greek word 'polis', they note, meant 'fortified place', indicating 'that families that came together to create cities did so as a means of collective self-defense', and this demonstrates that 'at the very beginning of Western experience of these matters, the presence of an external enemy, outsiders, is crucial to the constitution of insiders, fellow citizens'. Brown *et al* use this argument to make the radical claim that the scope of international political theory 'should not be restricted to writings on the external relations of collectivities; there is a place also for the study of the internal constitution of collectivities by these external relations' (Brown *et al* 2002, 8).

Brown *et al* also distinguish between attitudes towards 'an international system, held together, if at all, by a balance of forces, and an international society based on law' (Brown *et al* 2002, 11). This is a contrast between collectivities that see themselves as having 'responsibilities only towards their own members and that relations with other collectivities rest simply on the contingencies of power and interest', the realist position, where those relations 'may be regular and patterned, that is, they may form a system, but they are not normatively grounded', and collectivities which acknowledge 'each other's rights and duties', conceived in legal terms. This latter idea of international society, in which relations are norm-governed, is crucially seen as subject to international law (Brown *et al* 2002, 10), though there are conflicting views about whether this notion of international society should exist simply 'to allow coexistence or to promote positive goals' (Brown *et al* 2002, 11).

In another work Brown develops this distinction further and expresses the relatively popular view that ethical imperatives should have a role in analysing international politics and in defining international relations theory. He argues that the term 'international political theory' heralds a move away from the older view that '"international relations", the subject matter of the discipline IR, were *sui generic*, different from other kinds of social relationship by their very nature, and thus that they had to be studied in an equally distinctive way'. He contends (but while retaining a state-centric lense) that international political theory moves forward from the old disjunction between political theory and international politics, in part because normative questions are now being asked, especially challenging the assumption of the priority given to caring for 'us' over caring for 'them' (Brown 2002, 2–3).

We have already noted the problems associated with the development of ethical theorising of politics on the world stage. Nardin and Mapel (1992) provide a survey of two kinds of ethical approach to international political theory, both of which are impelled by the rejection of the lack of normative motivation in the realist tradition. For these two approaches ethical theorising represents a coming of age for international relations theory. One broad strand is based on notions of cosmopolitanist human rights, global social justice and economic redistribution, resulting in the advocacy of forms of in global politics. The other rests upon communitarian notions of ethical relations between states according to an upgraded but still limited international law, resulting in the recommendation of a politics of international society. Brown (1992) clearly elucidates the issues at stake in the cosmopolitan/communitarian distinction, although areas of overlap between the two have increasingly been accented in the discourse in the last few years.

The situation in IR theory is made more complex not only by the disjunction between advocates of IR statecraft that includes both realists and English School protagonists (who argue that the international is a neutral realm) and IR theorists of the kind who hold that normative ideas are not only appropriate but essential to acting upon issues in the international realm. In addition, advocates of a rights culture, some of whom have a background in law and some coming from a continental philosophy tradition, and international justice theorists, some of whom come from a political theory background, both tend to overlook the distinctive character of international political space and so misunderstand the international realm on a straightforward domestic analogy.

Hutchings makes a strong argument for 'doing normative international theory as *international political theory* rather than as either *international relations theory* (realism) or *applied ethics* (idealism)' (Hutchings 1999, 182). In other words, IR theory needs to forge a critical and reflective approach towards its own distinctive subject matter. Hutchings also makes an important point when she advocates using the term 'international' to specify a broader context than just inter-state relations (Hutchings 1999, xvi), recognising the importance of redefining international political space beyond the narrow realist definition. It is with this proviso in mind that the chapter continues to use the still inadequate term 'international', rather than a term like 'geopolitics' which does not satisfactorily differentiate the international from the domestic domain since national politics is not un-geographical.

Some international relations theorists take the view that IR theory consists in constructing a canon of historical theorists who have discussed the international. Grotius, Pufendorf, Vattel, Groswinckel and others are the writers with a place in that canon, with Hobbes the key player. However, while it is useful to recover the ideas of past thinkers in this way, IR theory needs to recognise that as a discourse self-consciously separate from the realist tradition it is only just beginning to establish an independent identity. The work of IR theory is not concluded simply by asserting a pedigree. It also follows from the way historical study proceeds, that IR theory also needs to engage with contestation and interpretation rather than presenting canonical thinkers as expressing a timeless 'truth'. IR theory must also recognise the importance of cultivating a reflective and critical approach, as Hutchings recognises. The work of writers like Rob Walker, Teschke, and Simpson is vital, for example, in challenging the fictions and ideological givens inherited from the realist tradition. For instance, work bringing real historical investigation and analysis to bear on the significance of 1648 for international politics, and on the double standard which operated for Great Powers and 'outlaw states', is valuable. International relations theory with a proper theoretical dimension remains in the shadow of the dominant mainstream tradition driven by the ahistorical stereotypes and models of the realist perspective mapped onto practice and, because of its ideologically-driven purpose, not interested in investigating or understanding more fully its own presuppositions. What is clear, however, is that international relations and its forms of theory is a distinctive realm, which cannot be subsumed under political theory.

In relation specifically to sovereignty, international relations theory starts from a deep asymmetry with political theorists. IR theorists draw upon a tradition of interest in sovereignty as the defining principle of the mainstream IR unit of measurement and function and operation, namely the state. Sovereignty represents, as a starting point, the key political principle, useful for examining how states interact, whether that be conceived in terms of an international 'system' or 'community'. Political theorists have historically seen sovereignty in terms of the depoliticised relation between rulers and ruled, rendered unproblematic until Foucault and especially Schmitt in their different ways questioned it. The asymmetry between the two discourses on sovereignty is not only due to IR having been a realist stronghold, and the distribution of different concerns about sovereignty in its supposed internal and external faces (which is, in any case, circular), but is also due in part to the differences between the two domains they study.

The constructedness of international space defined in the realist paradigm as 'states in anarchy', which buttresses the universalised state sovereignty model, is disclosed by showing the historicity of the idea of territory. The conception of state sovereignty developed in the seventeenth century when the idea of territorialised power was new. A useful factor in reconceptualising sovereignty is to use the geographers' distinction between territory and space. According to this distinction, territory and space are not the same, and territoriality is only one way that space is utilised. Other forms of political society such as hunter-gatherer tribes, nomadic peoples, and seaborne empires are all conceived as occupying some sort of space, not predicated on strict territorial boundaries. It was only in the second half of the seventeenth century that an abstract sense of spatial relationships in terms of 'territory' was developed, and it was expressed in the new technology of scientific map-making. Moreover, the modern state naturalised notion of territoriality, in which authority is locked into territorialised modes of power, is made more complex by consideration of what it hides, what it has licensed and other ideas of space it marginalises. The notion of mutually-recognised borders actually define jurisdiction rather than territory as such. Historically, the consolidation of state territories was spurred along by the development of mercantile economics and capitalism. Powerful states have always been able to undertake military action and exercise economic power elsewhere, beyond the confines of their own territory. In contrast with the constructedly territorial conception of modern states an alternative, network form of domination is now used to posit diffused power and exercises control over flows rather than over territory.

All these points work to deconstruct the modern state sovereignty fusion of space and territory. This understanding, together with the view developed in this book that the proposal for international relations theory which carries the most potential is one that focuses on international space as a sphere of politics rather than primarily of moral action or of political theory, leads to the view that the designation 'international political space' best describes the international domain conceptualised beyond the realist 'states in anarchy' and its internal/external dichotomy. It also follows from the idea of international space as a sphere of politics that the international domain is not an inherently violent one.

In sum then, political theory is not simply mirrored by international relations theory, and this is significant. In addition there are a range of protagonists of diverse meanings of the 'international' and its theorisation seeking to capture the discourse. The continuing power of the realist mode of international relations, figured not as a theory but as a set of pragmatic principles for statecraft and diplomacy, shapes the debate. There is also the indeterminacy arising from the relatively new academic discipline of IR and the new field of inquiry of international relations theory, and debates about the newly constructed canon of reflections and speculations on international politics. There is a strong push to define IR theory as the project to extend moral principles to the international sphere, and there is the valuable critical IR theory of writers like Ashley and Walker to deconstruct the discourses of state sovereignty. There is also work by Bartelson and others to reimagine politics wherever it occurs, and so to conceive of the international domain as 'international political space'. But this view is cautious of the inflated claims about the transformative potential of global politics, transnational political activism, and the international rights culture.

International political space as an autonomous field of politics?

The discussion of IR theory has shown that there is a connection between conceptions of IR theory and ways of conceiving the international realm. The idea of a critical and reflective IR theory that moves beyond the assumptions of the realist tradition and is instead associated with the notion of an international political space has already been proposed. Later in the chapter the content of that 'international political space' will be explored, but meanwhile a question that arises here concerns the autonomy of this space separate from the political space examined by political theory, and separate from economic, technological and cultural actions and interactions in international space. The international domain and what goes on within it has been depicted in IR theory in terms of, among other things, an 'international society of states', 'international society', 'system of states', 'international community', 'global community', 'international relations', 'international politics', 'global politics', a 'geopolitical system', and 'world politics'. Each designation conceives of the space, units and their relations differently.

Wight's work highlights particularly clearly some of the issues at stake in whether IR is an autonomous field of politics. He asked 40 years ago 'Why is There No International Theory?', no parallel theoretical tradition about relations between states, the society of states, the family of nations, or the international community to that concerning the good life within a polity. Wight observed that there was a legacy of work on international law, writings on statecraft, and the speculations of a few political philosophers, but no sustained and systematic set of reflections in international theory. He identified the 'intellectual prejudice imposed by the sovereign state' as one of the reasons for this lack. This prejudice, he thought, consists of the belief that the sovereign state is 'the consummation of political experience and activity which has marked Western political thought since the Renaissance', the identification of international politics with the pre-contractual state of nature, a belief that '[i]international anarchy is the one manifestation of the state of nature that is not intolerable', that the 'division of the world into sovereign states is necessary and natural', that no individuals can be members of international society except as representatives of states, and that since the sixteenth century 'every individual requires the protection of a state'. As a result, Wight announced, international politics has become 'the untidy fringe of domestic politics' (Wight 1966, 21, 23, 31).

However, Wight also identifies two further reasons for the absence of international theory, which centre on the character of the international realm. One is that 'international politics differ from domestic politics in being less susceptible of a progressivist interpretation', and is characterised by recurrence, repetition and political action rather than being based on a belief in progress (Wight 1966, 26). Wight argues that the lack of a canon of international theory is no accident, but has gone on alongside a thriving practice from Elizabeth I to Bismarck of a system based on the balance of power and the concept of the national interest. International politics has been a flourishing realm, studied under the name of foreign affairs, problems in foreign policy, diplomacy, and international law. According to Wight, history shows that 'the highest form of statecraft...is the regulation of the balance of power'.

The second reason Wight gives for the want of international theory is the 'recalcitrance of international politics to being theorised about', which is due to the inappropriateness of the given language of political theory for this purpose, according to Wight. The language of political theory is indeed appropriate for considering 'man's control of his social life', of action 'within the realm of normal relationships and calculable results', and in the 'theory of the good life'. But the domain of international politics, Wight contends, is about survival, the extreme case rather than the regular case, with 'the ultimate experience of life and death, national existence and national extinction', war, intervention, and security (Wight 1966, 33). As Krasner (1995/6, 117) puts it 'nothing', no policy option, 'is ever off the table'. The international system, he maintains, 'is a less stable and less institutionalised environment than established domestic polities. Authority structures' and the Westphalian model itself 'cannot dominate power asymmetries' and differences in normative frames of reference derived from domestic constituencies (Krasner 1995/6, 148).

While Wight's insights are useful in helping to think about the character of international political space his rejection of the 'intellectual prejudice imposed by the sovereign state' does not extend far enough. Huysmans accounts for the distinctiveness of the international realm within the mainstream tradition in a more thorough-going way than Wight, mapping Schmitt's notion of the exception onto the international realm. The split between domestic politics and international politics, Huysmans argues, 'is a particular solution to the question of where politics is within the framework of sovereignty'. This split 'externalises the question of the exception and the decision it requires. In other words, the split between inside and outside territorialises the key problem of the rule of law'. As a result, Huysmans notes, the 'normal and the legal are contained within a territorially defined state', the constitutional order. In this way, the 'exceptional and the extra-territorial legitimacy are moved to the space of international relations' (Huysmans 2003, 215). What Huysmans is valuably doing here is indicating that the view of the distinctiveness of international politics as defined by commentators like Wight is itself a construction, a choice to see things that way, a choice among several. As Huysmans puts it, the international 'is the game in which the exception in domestic politics becomes the normal condition of politics'. Huysmans also questions the view that globalisation is challenging sovereignty, and argues that interrogating the control and authority to command of the territorial state leads, rather, 'to the re-emergence of the question of the political: that is, where and what is politics?' (Huysmans 2003, 216).

Koskenniemi adds an interesting specific historical dimension to the view that international politics represents a distinct field of activity, of naked struggle and power, different from political theorising of the domestic realm. He makes the case that the 'distinction between a tranquil domestic normality and the struggle for survival in the international realm came about through a projection at the international level of a distinct sensibility that the German refugees' to the United States, who founded the international relations discipline, 'brought from Weimar about matters political, a sensibility which in Schmitt's case has been aptly described as an "aesthetics of horror" and which in Morgenthau appears in a thoroughly pessimistic outlook on human nature and society' (Koskenniemi 2001, 467).

There is a tendency to think that the alternative to the internal/external arrangement is to merge international and domestic politics into a single form of politics discussed within a single discourse. However, there is more than one option to the upholding of an exclusionary internal/external dichotomous barrier. The unitary politics and unitary discourse solution does not recognise the value of the concept of sovereignty in recognising the particular identities a range of polities and other actors have within international political space. Conceiving of the international realm as a distinctive domain does not make this view a realist one though, because a range of political and sectoral actors is acknowledged and the porousness, diversity and interdependence of polities is recognised. The proposal of this chapter would be to keep the notion of the international realm as distinctive, but as relational rather than fully autonomous, not just modelled on the criteria of the individual (let alone liberal individual) or the domestic realm (let alone liberal polity) writ large. But while rejecting the domestic analogy, the proposal sees the idea of politics as now on a continuum rather than the state border forming an irreducible separation between us and them. This proposal recognises and sees as political (that is, not just as a given) the play of power politics and other forms of politics without valorising them (as the realist tradition does with respect to the power politics of states). Domestic and international politics are no longer compartmentalised in the realist mode, but at the same time the pitfalls of both the rights regime and the international justice discourse are avoided, neither of which can recognise enough the Western bias they bring to the international sphere.

The meaning of 'international' (and so of 'domestic', 'internal', and 'external') changes over time

The link between conceptions of IR theory and ways of conceiving the international realm is clear, and it has already been hinted that a critical and reflective IR theory that moves beyond the assumptions of the realist tradition is associated with the notion of an international political space. What underpins this viewpoint is a broader awareness that the meaning of the 'international' varies enormously over time. Teschke, Spruyt, and Brown *et al* have illuminating contributions to make in this respect. These historical points are not just quaintly decorative additions to an argument. They show and shock us into realising the extent to which we have naturalised the realist set-up, fixing as real and longstanding the ideas of state and international.

For a start Teschke recognises that 'although the medieval, early modern, and modern geopolitical systems are all characterised by anarchy, they reflect fundamentally different principles of international relations'. Indeed, he notes, 'the indeterminacy of anarchy, variations in the character of international systems, the political regimes of their constitutive actors, and their forms of conflict and co-operation can be theorised on the basis of different social property relations' that 'form the constitutive core of different geopolitical orders'. As a result, Teschke shows, it is clear that 'personalised, decentralised, feudal political authority was replaced by personalised but more centralised absolutist rule, which was in turn replaced by depersonalised, centralised capitalist political order: modern sovereignty' (Teschke 2003, 217). What is new about the modern state is that '"the state" is no longer required to interfere directly into processes of production and extraction'. Instead, 'its central function is confined to the internal maintenance and external defence of a private property regime' (Teschke 2003, 256).

Broadening out from this point, Teschke makes a strong general case that 'the character of international systems expresses the nature of their constitutive units'. The case of the medieval geopolitical order shows that it 'lacked both the differentiation between the domestic and the international and the differentiation between the economic and the political'. Teschke argues that this 'double absence' can be accounted for best in terms of the 'specific relations of exploitation between lords and peasants institutionalised in lordship – the constitutive unit of feudal order – establishing political access to peasant produce'. Moreover, and very differently from the modern case, 'the nexus between individual noble appropriation and the right to resist, fixed in the noble right to bear arms, precluded a state monopoly of the means of violence'. It follows crucially that '[i]nterlordly relations were therefore by definition neither "international" and hence anarchic, nor domestic and hence hierarchic'. In consequence, sovereignty was 'parcellised among politically appropriating lords' (Teschke 2003, 73). Teschke goes on to outline how international relations under early-modern absolutist sovereignty and proprietary kingship, by contrast, were conducted on the basis of 'empire-building, political marriages, wars of succession, dynastic "international" law, bandwagoning, and an inter-dynastic compensating equilibrium that eliminated smaller polities'. Teschke makes a strong case that it was such institutions and practices that 'structured early modern modes of aggression, conflict resolution, and territoriality' (Teschke 2003, 218). It is only in the modern period that the consolidation of exclusive sovereignty occurred, with the 'internal monopolisation of the means of violence, translated into rulers' exclusive control of the instruments of foreign policy – the army, diplomacy, and treaty-making' (Teschke 2003, 2–3).

Spruyt reinforces this historicised understanding of the meanings of internal and external sovereignty and the relations between them, specifically with respect to 'a change in the character of the constitutive units of the international system' (Spruyt 1994, 156). Spruyt and others help to chip away at the lense of statism through which we view the world, and the statist intellectual predispositions we have inherited in trying to rethink political community. Spruyt makes the case plainly that prior to the development of the sovereign state, in 'none of the three modes of organisation under study can we define or distinguish domestic from international politics. Feudal lords, church, and empire operated in systems of crosscutting jurisdictions. Juridical competence depended on the specific issue at hand' (Spruyt 1994, 36).

Moreover, the designation of a unit as a state is political rather than automatic and natural. As Spruyt says, the 'very fact that some institutions are empowered as states, whereas others are denied that status, demonstrates how constraints have been placed on the subsequent choices of social actors' (Spruyt 1994, 17). The secular nature of the equality presupposed by the sovereign state system is also crucial. Spruyt makes the argument that 'rule that legitimates itself as religiously sanctioned cannot accept other political authorities as equals. Yet...territorial sovereignty implies exactly that states are equal' (Spruyt 1994, 197).

Spruyt also pours scorn on realist attempts to read back the internal/external conceptual distinction into pre-sovereign state times. In medieval Europe, complex 'networks of rival jurisdictions overlaid territorial space.

Church, lords, kings, emperor, and towns often exercised simultaneous claims to jurisdiction. Occupants of a particular territorial space were subject to a multiplicity of higher authorities'. Spruyt argues that given 'such a logic of organisation, it is impossible to distinguish the acts conducting "international" relations, operating under anarchy, from those conducting "domestic" politics, operating under some hierarchy. Bishops, kings, lords, and towns all signed treaties and waged war'. As a result, there 'was no one actor with a monopoly over the means of coercive force. The distinction between public and private actors was yet to be articulated'. Moreover, the answers as to whether lords were subject to kings, the king subject to the church, the church subject to the emperor 'were inevitably contextual and intersubjective' (Spruyt 1994, 12). Spruyt notes that the medieval system 'was quite different than that of the contemporary state system'. Jurisdiction in the earlier system 'was neither discrete – jurisdictions overlapped – nor exclusive – different authorities might claim final jurisdiction on the same matter' (Spruyt 1994, 13).

Spruyt also illuminatingly discusses how empires in the past did not have a sense of the external and the international in the way the state system has brought into being. He notes that the Ottoman Empire had a different logic or organisation, 'a universalist logic of authority' based on Islam (Spruyt 1994, 17). Spruyt identifies this asymmetry in the logic of organisation, rather than differences in society and culture, to account for the difficulty the Ottomans had in playing a role in the European state system, because they did not subscribe to the shared understanding of international 'rules of the game' of the European states. Spruyt notes that China and the Parthian Empire 'could exist in their respective spheres of influence without having to formally agree upon borders', and that the Roman Empire conceived its outer limits 'not as a boundary, but as a temporary stopping place where the potentially unlimited expansion of the Pax Romana had come to a halt' (Spruyt 1994, 16).

Brown *et al* also address the historicity of the notion of the international. They note that 'there have been many periods in the past when the idea of a clear-cut distinction between the "international" and "domestic" has not existed' (Brown *et al* 2002, 1). However the situation is more complex than Brown *et al* imply, for there have been differing conceptions of what the domestic, the foreign, and the relations between them have been over time. Brown *et al* seem to suggest that the distinction between international and domestic has existed at different periods with intervals in between when it was in abeyance. They also imply that the meaning of the distinction was constant. Furthermore they reject the idea that 'the "international" has no predetermined meaning...a notion that is negotiated afresh by every age' (Brown *et al* 2002, 5). All these assumptions present a picture that is misleading, for the distinction between relations within collectivities and between collectivities has been constructed in various ways over time as collectivities have been more or less permeable, their political identities more or less prominent and fixed, and the bases of their identities changed.

Brown *et al* are right to maintain that international relations can take place between 'cities in classical Greece and between papacy, emperor, corporation, and prince in the middle ages as well as between modern nation-states', but they make the questionable statement that international relations can refer to relations between any kind of collectivities, so long as it is a 'collectivity with an identity which distinguishes them from others'. They argue that there 'is a sense in which all politics is "international"', on the grounds that typically a collectivity is 'itself an ensemble of other collectivities' (Brown *et al* 2002, 7). This is to render the term 'international' almost devoid of meaning. Brown *et al* note that the 'unitary actor which plays such a large part in the assumptions of a great deal of international theory can only come into existence as the result of a successful negotiation of internal collective identities to create a new meta-identity' or, for instance in modern nation-states, through 'the suppression of such different collective identities by one dominant faction' (Brown *et al* 2002, 8).

However, Brown *et al* do recognise that 'the idea of the international as a separate sphere of social life is not one that medievals would accept' (Brown *et al* 2002, 5), and they usefully note that the term 'international' was coined by Jeremy Bentham in 1789 in the context of discussions about international law. Roman law had discussed a *ius gentium* but originally in relation to commercial transactions, and so was a private international law. The modern usage identified international law as 'governing legal relationships among politically autonomous units' and so became a public international law (Brown *et al* 2002, 6–7). Brown *et al* make the point that the term 'international law' did 'not come into general use until the nineteenth century. Even then the rules governing international relations were sometimes referred to as the "public law of Europe", highlighting the way the "international" is steeped in European tradition. But most writers clung to the antiquated and equivocal term "law of nations"…struggling to describe new modes of diplomacy using a conceptual vocabulary inherited from ancient Rome and medieval Christendom' (Brown *et al* 2002, 311).

The significance of the myth of 1648

This section is concerned to show how the enormous significance attached to the Peace of Westphalia in the mainstream IR tradition plays a key role in supporting the view of sovereignty as necessarily composed of and fully explained by mutually exclusive internal and external dimensions. More generally here, the status of Westphalia is questioned by the use of historical evidence and argument. In the dominant tradition of international relations Westphalia 'explains' not only the emergence of modern (state) sovereignty and the state system but also the concept itself, as well as being taken as the paradigm of the structure of an international treaty. Spruyt indicates the resilience and well-constructedness of the Westphalian narrative. The ideas of territorial demarcation and mutual recognition, plus the state system 'produced by mutual empowerment', led to a very strong and 'systematised pattern of interaction in international affairs' (Spruyt 1994, 192). The section then goes on to consider the impact of the historicity of Westphalia on the meaning of the state sovereignty paradigm.

Brown *et al* put forward the orthodox view that 'the Peace of Westphalia recognised the right of the princes, bishops, and cities of the empire to conduct their foreign affairs as independent states, thereby reinforcing the principle of sovereignty as the cornerstone of the international order'. By the seventeenth century, they continue, 'the idea that the world was divided among a number of independent states whose sovereigns held supreme authority within their own territories but no authority in the realms of other sovereigns was firmly entrenched in European political thought and practice' (Brown *et al* 2002, 250). Krasner places the role of the Westphalian aspect of modern state sovereignty in context when he distinguishes the Westphalian state definition of sovereignty from four other definitions, in terms of the organisation and effectiveness of domestic authority structures, the ability to control transborder movements of goods, people and ideas, the right to make international agreements, and formal international law ideas of sovereignty (Krasner 1995/6, 121).

The dominant narrative about Westphalia operates as a myth in four respects. It confidently selects from the overall historical context to tell a particular story, and is unconcerned about its perpetuation of historical inaccuracy. It is a triumphalist and teleological story about progress towards the modern nation-state. Focusing directly on the teleological quality of the Westphalian model, Keating argues that the 'Westphalian fallacy' arises from 'a teleological interpretation of what happened in the subsequent three hundred years and an assumption that the seeds must have lain in this event' in an unhelpful manner for considering what sovereignty means in the contemporary world (Keating 2003, 194). Thirdly, the Westphalian narrative is a normative story that is all about the rejection of an older, tangled and unsatisfactory way of doing things, in favour of a secular, neat, rational, territorial way. And lastly, it assumes an uncomplicated, given legal meaning for sovereignty. What is at issue here is not that 1648 is a myth *per se*, for myths are necessary ideological tools and exercise a potent force. The reason it matters to point out that it is a myth is to counter the dominant realist view that the Westphalian system is 'really' how political actors operate on the international stage, a given and naturalised set up. This section draws on the valuable work of Keating,

Philpott, Krasner, Teschke, Reus-Smit and others, bringing a variety of important historical insights to bear.

Mainstream international relations subscribes to a given and naturalised idea of state sovereignty derived from a version of Hobbes, of the relation between sovereign states as a billiard-ball antagonistic connection between states. This narrative not only misrepresents Hobbes, is not Hobbes's full position on the matter, and involves transposing from domestic to international sphere. This narrative also involves ignoring other theorists who were clearer that international relations not just a state of warfare or anarchy. For Pufendorf for instance, as Dufour notes, '[a]s well as *anthropological* and *social* considerations [in his notion of sociality], there is also *historical* evidence that societies in the state of nature are not perpetually engaged in warfare, but rather have ties of amity' (Dufour 1991, 572).

Keating briskly dismisses the role of the Peace of Westphalia ('referred to erroneously as the Treaty of Westphalia') as the historical source for the claims made for the Westphalian system of sovereign states in mainstream international relations. He notes that 'neither the Treaty of Munster or that of Osnabrück contains any reference to sovereignty or to anything like the sovereign state'. He adds that while Westphalia 'did provide for the "nationalisation" of religion as a way of coping with a problem that had threatened public order over the previous hundred years', this 'can scarcely be its main legacy since European countries have long abandoned the idea that religious uniformity is a defining task of the state'. He argues that Westphalia 'did not establish the present system of European states, and indeed the only state which still has its 1648 borders is Portugal'. Keating contends that its 'main achievement was the prolongation of the Holy Roman Empire for another 150 years' (Keating 2003, 194).

Historical examination indicates three crucial and interesting ways in which the Peace of Westphalia differs from its orthodox image in international relations. The aim of the Peace of Westphalia was to cede to princes sovereignty over religious practice, whereas the orthodox figure is secular in character. Secondly, one of the provisions of Westphalia was that states must be Christian. Philpott notes that, on this basis 'Russia and Poland, but not the Ottoman Empire, were admitted, and given full diplomatic privileges', and observes that this 'requirement was gradually dropped over the following couple of centuries'. Thirdly, the stipulation of non-intervention, 'the key prerogative of sovereign states, was not explicitly stated in the settlement, and would not be until the eighteenth century, when philosophers and lawyers openly espoused it' (Philpott 1999, 582). These points demonstrate the unacknowledged malleability of the significance of Westphalia in contrast with the fixed and stable settlement represented in the international relations orthodoxy. If a key provision was 'gradually dropped', we can ask about other changes that can be made to the meaning of sovereignty here while keeping the conception of sovereignty intact. Likewise, Philpott's case that the rules for membership 'evolved' from demanding Christianity to a 'secularised "standard of civilisation" for aspiring states' Philpott (1999, 583) does not explain very effectively, but only relies on a Darwinian metaphor without justifying its utility or relevance.

Krasner supports this view, arguing that the Peace of Westphalia of 1648 is a myth, both because its status as the founding document of the states system is 'mythological' and because its provisions enforcing religious toleration in Germany infringe its own declaration of individual princes' control over deciding the religious allegiance of its population (Krasner 1995/6, 141).

Teschke and Krasner highlight that the Westphalian narrative has been common ground beyond the realist tradition in international relations. Teschke makes a strong case that Westphalia is a myth, a 'conventional account, shared by Realists, members of the English school, and Constructivists alike', according to which 'the Westphalian treaties were a decisive turning point in the history of international relations' (Teschke 2003, 2). While Krasner's perspective is limited by taking as given the equation of sovereignty with modern state sovereignty, he usefully identifies how the Westphalian model is critical for 'actor-oriented approaches' to international relations such as neo-realism and neo-liberal institutionalism as well as for the international society view. For neo-realists, the 'ontological givens in the international system are Westphalian states, understood as unitary rational actors operating in an anarchic setting and striving to enhance their well-being and security', constrained only by 'the power of other states', while for and neo-liberal institutionalists the Westphalian state holds the solution to key problem of international relations, namely market failures. International society perspectives regard all players in the international sphere, such as public officials, diplomats, statesmen and political leaders, as having a 'shared intersubjective understanding' and for whom the role of sovereign Westphalian states is to permit 'some kinds of activities but not others' (Krasner 1995/6, 121–2). Actor-oriented approaches work on the assumption that actors (that is Westphalian states) 'create institutions to promote their interests' (Krasner 1995/6, 146).

Krasner also argues convincingly that neither neo-realist nor constructivist approaches have provided 'much guidance for understanding the pattern of weakness and persistence that has characterised how the Westphalian model has actually worked' (Krasner 1995/6, 145). He makes a strong case that 'the model has persisted because it does serve some of the interests of some actors', especially the weaker states but also some strong ones (Krasner 1995/6, 149). The Westphalian model 'has never been an accurate description of many of the entities that have been called states', Krasner maintains, because the 'assumption that states are independent rational actors' is 'misleading' when empirically not all rulers have been autonomous. He also holds that breaches of the Westphalian model do not constitute fatal blows to that system. He contends that there 'has never been some golden age of the Westphalian state', and that this model 'has never been more than a reference point or a convention'. Krasner portrays the Westphalian state as flexible, dynamic, and volatile and holds that it 'has never been some deeply confining structure' (Krasner 1995/6, 115).

Underlying Teschke's perceptive analysis is the sense that 'periodisation is no innocent exercise' (Teschke 2003, 2). Using close historical analysis, he argues that Westphalia did not inaugurate the modern state system and the distinctive understanding of international relations associated with it, 'the founding charter of a modern system of sovereign states' (Teschke 2003, 37), and did not mark the transition from medieval to modern political relations. The view that 'the Westphalian settlement organised the European order on the basis of sovereign states adhering to distinctly modern principles of conflict and co-operation', and 1648 as marking the 'origin of modern international relations', is incorrect (Teschke 2003, 2). In Teschke's interpretation, the 'standard IR account of Westphalia's modernity is radically rejected and revised' (Teschke 2003, 151).

Teschke's thesis is that Westphalia registered the transition from the feudal pattern of relations to a dynastic pattern dominated by absolutist states, and that 'further massive transformation' took place before the modern state-system was in place. The myth he is attacking is the assumption by the orthodox realist tradition, 'conflating the Westphalian with the modern states-system' and 'conflating absolutist with modern sovereignty' (Teschke 2003, 31). He argues persuasively that the 'logic of inter-dynastic relations structured the early modern geopolitical order [that is, the 'relations between public carriers of political power' (Teschke 2003, 12)] until the regionally highly uneven and protracted nineteenth-century transition to international modernity' (Teschke 2003, 217).

A strong plank in Teschke's argument is that, while an important part of the story about Westphalia handed down in the international relations tradition is that the Peace established a system of states as equal and like units, the historical evidence points rather to 'the temporal coexistence of heterogeneous international actors in a "mixed-case" scenario'. While 'France, Austria, Spain, Sweden, Russia, Denmark-Norway, Brandenburg-Prussia, and the Papal States were absolutist' states, the 'Holy Roman Empire remained a confederal elective monarchy until 1806', and the 'Dutch General Estates established an independent oligarchic merchant republic'. At the same time, 'Poland was a "crowned aristocratic republic" and Switzerland a free confederation of cantons', Italian 'merchant-republics struggled against being transformed into monarchies', and 'England became a parliamentary constitutional monarchy presiding over the world's first capitalist economy'. Nevertheless, with all this diversity, it was 'the numerically and power-politically preponderant dynastic states' that dominated the early modern international system (Teschke 2003, 218).

For Teschke, one of the reasons for the IR misinterpretation of Westphalia, which has proceeded by 'tacit acceptance...passed down unexamined' (Teschke 2003, 2), is that 'in its preoccupation with the external marks of sovereignty, international relations are usually theorised in abstraction from the internal constitution of the units of geopolitical systems', such that 'the historically diverse nature of political communities is generally undertheorised'. Other reasons are that the notion of the state tends to be understood only in 'institutional, static, comparative terms', and that Weber's definition of the modern state is 'mistakenly projected on to differently structured pasts'. The final reason for the misinterpretation is that absolutism is incorrectly identified with 'Weberian notions of state rationalisation and bureaucratic centralisation', whereas absolutist sovereignty is defined more satisfactorily in terms of proprietary kingship, the model for which is the 'nexus between a non-capitalist agrarian economy and a parasitic patrimonial state apparatus' in France, resulting in the conclusion that 'absolutist sovereignty was neither absolute nor modern' (Teschke 2003, 152).

Reus-Smit pays attention to an important aspect of the politics of the 'state sovereignty system' which breaks down its universal and abstract claims. While Ruggie holds the typically abstract view that sovereignty is a principle that specifies 'the basis on which the constituent units are separated from one another' (quoted in Reus-Smit 2001a, 527), Reus-Smit reminds us that up to the early 1960s 'the world was divided into a hierarchy of political forms, with the system of sovereign states at the pinnacle surrounded by a range of dependent colonies, protectorates, and mandates'. The hierarchy was based not just on economic and military power but on 'the European application of a standard of civilisation which distinguished between civilised, barbarian, and savage peoples' (Reus-Smit 2001a, 533).

Jackson shows that in practice state sovereignty was not neutral but normatively-loaded. Under the old game the European powers used a 'standard of civilisation' to determine and guard the membership of international society. Only those that demonstrated 'empirical sovereignty', that is 'the wherewithal to provide political goods for citizens' were granted sovereign status. Under the new game, with the wave of decolonisation after World War II, weak states were accorded 'juridical sovereignty', that is a right of constitutional autonomy, without exhibiting the trappings of empirical statehood (Jackson 1990, 29).

Krasner points to the historical malleability of the state conception of sovereignty that lies behind the use of Westphalia as rigid 'benchmark'. He argues that contemporary theses that sovereignty is at risk and being transformed are 'not well-founded', because 'violations of the principles of territoriality and autonomy', which he identifies as the key features of the system of political authority operating in the Westphalian model of the state, 'have been an enduring characteristic of the international system both before and after the Peace of Westphalia' (Krasner 1995/6, 123). He contends that it is 'historically myopic to take the Westphalian model as a benchmark that accurately describes some golden age when all states exercised exclusive authority within their own borders', and maintains that in the 'contemporary world, peace and stability would be better served by explicitly recognising that the Westphalian model has, in fact and in theory, always been contested' (Krasner 1995/6, 150). Krasner also makes the case that the 'rules of sovereignty', by which he means the rules of state sovereignty, 'are not absolutely constraining' and that new rules are possible and conventional ones ignored, so long as the actors involved 'can reach voluntary agreements' or, alternatively, if 'some powerful states are willing to engage in coercion' (Krasner 2001, viii).

Krasner also notes another disjunction between the abstract Westphalian ideal and the resilience of actual practice. He discusses how conventions such as human rights accords, and contracts such as international agreements (mechanisms used by stronger states), and coercion and imposition (to which weaker states are subject) 'have all been enduring patterns of behaviour in the international system'. Krasner underlines how every 'major peace treaty since 1648 – Westphalia, Utrecht, Vienna, Versailles, and Helsinki – has violated the Westphalian model in one way or another'. It follows, he argues, that compromising the Westphalian model, either by invading other states or setting up authority structures that cross-cut states, is 'always available as a policy option because there is no authority structure to prevent it'. As a result, Krasner underlines, the Westphalian model is neither an empirical regularity nor an analytic assumption about the capacity of rulers to act within international constraints, but is best understood as a convention or reference point without the power to predict the behaviour of policy-makers (Krasner 1995/6, 117).

Impact on the meaning of state sovereignty

Historical work by Simpson, Pagden, and Koskenniemi discloses the impact of the myth of Westphalia on the subsequent history of state sovereignty. Simpson's work is also useful in challenging the orthodox story which seeks to contrast a pre-Westphalian period, 'in which hierarchy and centralised authority were the dominant features', with the Westphalian era, 'where the state system is organised around a strong principle of sovereign equality' (Simpson 2004, 9). Simpson asks what work the notion of 'sovereign equality' performs in the international arena, and notes that it acts in three capacities whose content is not precise. Sovereign equality is a legal principle 'designed to regulate the inter-state system', and so 'operates to define the relationship between states and their standing in international organisations'. It also 'forms the backdrop to a series of rights' such as 'the right to self-defence, the right to regulate the behaviour of its national'. Thirdly, the legal principle provides the context for immunities such as 'the immunity from exercise of another state's jurisdiction in its territory' (Simpson 2004, 39).

Simpson also revises the standard meaning of sovereignty in the light of historical analysis, this time regarding the way international legal norms emerge. His work is particularly insightful in teasing out the parallel logic of normative values and judgements which exists alongside the assertion of state sovereignty as a neutral and universal set of principles by the realist tradition. His work is all the more powerful for concentrating on legal, formal sovereignty, sovereignty in the context of international law, and distinguishing between legal and political sovereignty, since the dual standards he identifies are not simply the result of messy (contingent, pragmatic, instrumental) politics but are at the heart of legal thinking and practice. His work is also valuable for underlining the more general political point that formal principles such as sovereignty are always understood and acted upon in the context of broader cultural values and practices. He identifies a 'mystery' about the international legal order, and argues for the contemporary resonance of the nineteenth-century twin-track mentality in international law that asserted and legitimised intervention on the basis of a distinction between civilised and uncivilised states alongside a recognition of formal equal sovereign status between states. Rather than accepting the orthodox explanation of an inevitable theory/practice tension between the formal rules of equal state sovereignty and political and contingent factors that lead to inequalities of power between states, he sees a continuity between the aggressive statements and actions of Great Powers (an elite group of western states) in the nineteenth century against 'uncivilised' or 'pariah' states (for instance about Turkey), the exclusion of the 'outlaw' Bolshevik Russia from the League of Nations, and the statements and actions of today's major powers against 'outlaw' or 'rogue' states (such as Iran, Iraq and recently, Serbia). Simpson is keen to take 'history seriously', to show 'how particular arguments (for example those concerning equality and hierarchy) recur in the international law of the modern period' (Simpson 2004, 11).

The principle of sovereign equality is not fiction, Simpson maintains (Simpson 2004, 8). But alongside the inclusionist, universalist and pluralist impulses of the UN Charter, he sees another, exclusionist, conception of legal order that retains its potency. He notes that '[i]mmunity was disposable in cases involving outlaws but tenaciously applied to the personnel of the Great Powers themselves'. His general point here is that the 'way international law worked...was dependent on the identity of the protagonists involved' (Simpson 2004, xiii). Therefore, he argues, the 'conventional image of international law as a system in which states are at least equal *in law*', that is, the sovereignty equality assumption 'is incomplete' (Simpson 2004, 6).

Simpson judges that for nearly two centuries the (western) Great Powers have used formal equality to justify their power and underwrite their ostracism of states deemed to be beyond the pale by virtue of their internal politics or moral considerations. He therefore highlights the disjunction between states judged according to their formal (universal) sovereign equality and those judged according to particular, 'anti-pluralist' considerations. The particular mixture of Great Power prerogatives, the designation of deviant states, and formal equality (which he terms 'juridical sovereignty') has, says Simpson, characterised the international legal order since 1815, and has established a 'legalised hegemony', the 'realisation through legal forms of Great Power prerogatives', in which 'the Great Powers see themselves as acting in the shadow of international law', but that 'the shadow they see is their own', for they 'make and remake (but rarely break) international law' (Simpson 2004, x).

Challenging 'the apparent innocence of an international legal order based on sovereign equality' (Simpson 2004, xiv), he contends that, in the light of this skewed equality, wars 'are fought not between adversaries but between the international community and international renegades or between the universal and the particular, e.g. "human rights" and "Islamic terrorism"'. The central figure is the 'outlaw state: a figure whose estrangement from the community of nations and demonisation by that community has long been required as part of the project of creating and enforcing international "society"' (Simpson 2004, xi). Simpson usefully identifies how international legal theory written under the banners of 'democratic governance, liberal internationalism, neo-Kantianism and republicanism' pose 'a challenge to the dominant pluralist tradition' (Simpson 2004, 21). He also points to the way scholars 'concerned to elaborate norms with universalisable potential', for instance in debate about the lawfulness of intervention in Afghanistan in 2002, start from the wrong basis of assuming 'a rough juridical parity among the various protagonists in that war' (Simpson 2004, 320), when what is needed is to recognise that sovereign equality is 'qualified by the existence of legalised hegemony and anti-pluralism' (Simpson 2004, 319). He describes as a 'puzzle' or 'enigma' the lack of attention given to the way this 'highly interventionist normative system' has interacted and continues to interact with the much-vaunted principle of sovereign equality (Simpson 2004, 353).

Simpson locates his approach to international law and politics as a modification of the English School position. He quotes Bull and Watson's definition of international society as a group of states that 'not merely form a system, in the sense that the behaviour of each is a necessary factor in the calculations of the others, but also have established by dialogue and common consent rules and institutions for the conduct of their relations and recognise their common interest in maintaining these arrangements' (quoted in Simpson 2004, 231). Like mainstream realists the English School concentrate upon states as the key actors on the international stage, but appeal to norms rather than to rules, take international law seriously, and see states acting in a social environment. In the context of the English School position Simpson, then, emphasises the non-consensual as well as consensual aspects of international society, and that the present international order 'can best be understood as struggle between these two conceptions of international society', the universalist and egalitarian pluralist conception with its norms of non-intervention, sovereign immunity and state equality, and the anti-pluralist conception based on the notion of two spheres of order – the core of liberal states committed to a deepening constitutionalism around common values, and outlaws and outsiders (Simpson 2004, 231).

Pagden's investigation into how the ideas of Locke 'and his fellow ideologues' were used to deny sovereignty to the Amerindians, supports the case that sovereignty has been used to oppress and dominate. It also shows how the meaning of sovereignty changes over time. The reason given, ignoring available ethnological evidence, for the view that the Amerindian rulers 'exercise very little Dominion, and have but a very moderate Sovereignty' (quoted by Pagden 1998, 44), was that they remained in a state of nature and had not yet 'surrendered their "natural power" to a political community and established a legal system and judiciary', but were still in a state of 'individual self government' (Pagden 1998, 44). Underlying this logic was the *res nullius* argument that America was 'in the same condition as all the world had been before the creation of human societies' (Pagden 1998, 43), and the argument set out by Grotius that in order 'to be *rights*, claims to both property and sovereignty (*dominium*) have to be exercised'. Pagden notes that the '"agriculturalist" argument which provided the basis for all English claims to land-rights in America rested precisely upon the claim that the European, unlike the Native Americans, had exercised *dominium* in the form of mingling their labour with the land' (Pagden 1998, 49). The linking of internal sovereignty with a prerequisite condition of political community defined in European terms is interesting, as is the British claim to sovereignty over land in America in terms of internal rather than external sovereignty.

We should not underestimate the extent to which the notion of (state) sovereignty has been used to enforce, coerce, and justify domination, and the cunning use of a European definition of sovereignty to ensure exclusion for non-Europeans. Koskenniemi discusses an interesting example of internal/external when he describes the use of the notion of sovereignty in the late nineteenth century in Africa by lawyers acting for imperial states. He quotes the logic of one such lawyer, that 'International law has to treat natives as uncivilised. It regulates, for the mutual benefit of the civilised states, the claims which they make to sovereignty over the region and leaves the treatment of their natures to the conscience of the state to which sovereignty is awarded'. Koskenniemi comments that, according to this logic, 'it was absurd to think of native possession in terms of sovereignty, or colonial expansion, as conditional upon treaties with native chiefs'. Sovereignty, he observes, was taken to be 'a purely European notion. Just as a person cannot transfer what he does not have, the chief cannot transfer a sovereignty of which he has no concept'. Such lawyers made a key, and self-serving, distinction between ownership and sovereignty. They agreed that 'natives did possess the concept of occupancy, or of private ownership, and were thus perfectly capable of holding or disposing of property'. However, 'in European eyes this could be only a private law matter'. According to this logic, treaties over native territories 'could create acquired rights under Article 35 of the Berlin Act, but they could not transfer sovereignty'. The crucial consequence was that colonial title 'was always original and never derivative; it followed from European law's qualification of the acts of European powers, not from native cession'. He sums up that while such lawyers 'discussed colonial problems form a variety of perspectives', with some more critical and others less, 'their discourse provides a uniform logic of exclusion-inclusion in which cultural arguments intersect with humanitarian ones so as to allow a variety of positions while at every point guaranteeing the controlling superiority of "Europe"' (Koskenniemi 2001, 127–8).

Koskenniemi reveals in detail how the notion of sovereignty was used to create a fabric of hypocrisy among European colonial powers, through the 'myth of the inseparability of European public law sovereignty and civilisation' (Koskenniemi 2001, 166). The effect of colonial powers using their definition of sovereignty to exclude any possible claims by native groups, and their deployment of the idea of the occupation of *terra nullius*, was also to ensure that 'non-European communities became a passive background' to clashes between imperial powers on their soil (Koskenniemi 2001, 148).

Reconceptualising internal/external

Rethinking sovereignty beyond the state form necessarily involves developing a new understanding of international politics. What emerges most strongly from the previous two sections of this chapter is the importance of disentangling the discourses about internal and external sovereignty from the dominant realist *practice* around the sovereignty convention in international relations, the de-naturalised historicity of the modern state sovereignty model, and the rethinking of 'international political space'. The examination of the myth of 1648 allowed us to recognise the constructedness of the reality which the mainstream discourse poses as foundational. Deconstructing the consciousness produced by the realist tradition (and disclosing its socially constructed character) is to deconstruct the power of that consciousness to some extent, and opens the way to a positive reconceptualisation. Claims about the state and about international politics can now be recognised as responses to problems rather than being simply givens. As Huysmans notes, 'sovereignty has been denaturalised by demonstrating its historical contingency' by those working in international relations critical of the realist stance. As a result the idea of sovereignty 'changes from a descriptive category to a category which is part of a political history characterised by a struggle between different imaginations of the political' (Huysmans 2003, 221). This section builds on those points to rethink the internal/external orthodoxy.

We turn now, then, to the reconceptualisation of sovereignty and the international sphere beyond the problems associated with the barrier conception of sovereignty, and to the contributions of theoretical developments within international relations, particularly from postmodern, critical theory and feminist perspectives. This section addresses the way sovereignty as political has fallen into a gap between the social (the focus of the internal discourse) and national interests and diplomacy (the focus of the external discourse). This reconceptualisation represents an enormous shift of perspective, for the modern realist sovereignty orthodoxy claimed not only that a particular notion of sovereignty was true, but that its abstract and ahistorical character exercised a sovereignty over the past, present, future, and our knowledge of them. Just because sovereignty has been taken as a defining characteristic of the modern state (resulting in the tautology of the phrase 'sovereign state') does not mean there cannot be other conceptions of sovereignty. What is proposed here is a relational conception of sovereignty that both overcomes the exclusionary barrier and seeks to account for more actors in international politics. As a result the three views that are all tied to the state sovereignty model are all superseded – the realist instrumental interest paradigm, the normative rights and cosmopolitanist and legalist institutions paradigm, and the depoliticised normative political theory view.

In developing the reconceptualisation, it is worth recalling that resources also exist within the mainstream tradition to shift and rethink some of its parameters. For instance, Williams's interpretation of Morganthau seeks to reform the realist tradition by bringing out resources overshadowed within the heart of its own tradition. Williams, developing a revisionist reading of Morganthau and his contribution to realism, argues convincingly that Morganthau's realism is 'marked by an attempt to recognise the centrality and complexity of power in politics while avoiding the extreme conclusion that politics is nothing but violence. In this endeavour, political judgment – the impact of ideas – is crucial'. In particular, Williams argues, 'a correct understanding of the concept – the very idea – of "politics" is an essential element of the ethical and evaluative stance at the heart of Morganthau's realism'. In particular, for Morganthau, 'realism required a capacity to make critical normative and political judgments about collective identity formation' (Williams 2004, 634). For Morganthau, politics is 'the sphere of contest over the determination of values and wills' (Williams 2004, 643).

The reconceptualisation proposed here centres on the notion of post-states, and is approached from the external sovereignty side. The post-state proposal has three features – inter-dependence, pluralism, and politics – and is a vehicle to overcome the gap between political theory and international politics. Post-state sovereignty is to be recommended because it can get beyond the stubborn and intractable internal/external construction, and is a better alternative to using normative notions like a human rights regime. 'Inter-dependence' captures the relational, inteactive, and porous quality of post-state political units. It also opens the way for cooperation rather than competition as the standard form of relation between post-states. 'Pluralism' refers to the presence of actors in international politics in addition to polities, and to overcoming the monopoly of the state form in international politics, issuing in the recognition of a diversity of forms of polity. 'Politics' emphasises the denaturalisation of state sovereignty, and acknowledges the political rather than moral work of sovereignty, in the context of a recast international sphere. As discussed earlier, the term 'international political space' captures the idea of multiple actors (not just states) negotiating, related and connected in a space which is not just defined by territory.

In contrast with the realist tradition, this perspective on sovereignty emphasises the importance of sovereignty rather than the kind of polity it describes. This is one of the ways in which this proposal overcomes the internal/external dichotomy. For the realist tradition it is the state that matters in the term 'state sovereignty', the state being the prize and the heart of the matter and sovereignty being the idea and practice that protects the integrity of the state, the icing on the cake indeed. The realist view was that states matter and that only states matter. As Walker (2002) notes, state sovereignty was constructed to provide the proper solution to all problems of authority in a secular modernity.

Inter-dependence

The inter-dependence of post-states stresses the relational, interactive and porous nature of these political collectives. The emphasis is no longer on an internal/external exclusionist boundary and on territoriality. The 'moral standing of insiders and outsiders' (Rosenberg 2000, 79), citizens and foreigners is no longer conceived in strict either/or terms. The claims of refugees and forced migrants, and of those in other countries who wish to sell us goods and make calls on our redistributive justice, are political and subject to negotiation, framed in relational terms rather than dismissed outright and ignored. This is also a less state-centric view of the component players in international relations, acknowledging instead positive aspects of the medieval pattern of overlapping and multiple forms of connectedness, 'boundaries as a permeable skin rather than impenetrable wall' (Hoffman 1998, 102). The emphasis moves from sovereignty as possessive ownership to sovereignty as inter-dependence. In a relational post-state sovereignty, the claims of both citizens and international issues are recognised as negotiated and as political rather than being a dichotomous predicament in which either the claims of internal sovereignty override international obligations or a universalised moral duty is given priority over domestic demands. The relational post-state proposal successfully avoids both the unpalatable play of naked self-interest and the unsustainable 'sovereignty of morality over the political' (Franceschet 2002, 31). As well as emphasising the political nature of interaction, the inter-dependence aspect of the proposal also provides a cooperative motive and intention for relations with other actors which supplants both calculative interests and duties and rights.

Rob Walker's work lays the groundwork for the inter-dependent post-state idea. It undermines the dualism, the hierarchical opposition between internal and external, and also deconstructs the story we have constructed through which we understand our nation-state community as safe and 'others' outside it as alien. Both Walker and Bartelson call for a root and branch reformulation of their discipline, in the light of the 'increasingly blurred...divide between the domestic and the international spheres' (Bartelson 1995, 9). Walker analyses the root of the problem as the way in which the story we tell ourselves about sovereignty, and the lense this creates through which we understand other political and social categories, marginalises other views and is perpetuated even when at radical variance with developments in the 'real' world (or 'empirical tendencies'). Bartelson in similar vein identifies the 'conditions of knowing' during the modern period as key to understanding the grip of the state sovereignty conception on the discourse of the sovereignty concept.

Despite the fact that Walker's view is driven in part by the spectre of globalisation, and Hirst and Thompson are impelled by the refutation of globalisation, significant common ground can be drawn from them on the importance of inter-dependence in reframing sovereignty. The common ground is not immediately apparent. Hirst and Thompson argue that sovereignty still crucially hinges on the state, but recognise that a vital role of the state is now in making choices, legitimating and sanctioning practices above and below the nation-state, rather than just in governing directly from the centre. Governance processes are neither quite shared and dispersed, nor controlled in the old way from the centre, but the centre fulfils a unique role in the process. Walker wants to do away with (state) sovereignty, and wants the 'outside to come in' (Walker 1993, 174). Nevertheless, the two views are critical of the traditional construction of sovereignty as absolute, indivisible, autonomous and independent, and both seek to overcome the notion of sovereignty as a barrier concept. Hirst and Thompson provide empirical support for the bankruptcy of the traditional construction, while Walker offers a thoughtful theory in which sovereignty is an overarching metaphor for identity that has exercised potent explanatory force.

There are also two compelling elements of Walker's thesis which are useful in helping to construct a new combined (internal/external) inter-dependent definition of sovereignty. The first revolves around his concern that the dominant conception of community and culture imposed by (the internal dimension of) state-centric sovereignty, has 'read out of the script' many groups including women (Walker 1993, 181). This view of culture, says Walker, 'read through the principle of state sovereignty', leads to dam-aging consequences (Walker 1993, 180). For community, according to state sovereignty, refers to 'the geometry of territorial exclusions' and can only foster 'a relativity of values and a clash of different ways of life' (Walker 1993, 180–1). National exclusionist cultures are incompatible with parti-cipation in wider social, cultural and political processes (Walker 1993, 181). The second element concerns Walker's central vision of the effects of inter-nal/external as a problematic dualism. Walker argues for instance that because of this dualism, the question of how to be both a citizen and a member of humanity remains an irresolvable conundrum (Walker 1993, 176). These two elements of Walker's work combine in his argument that the traditional conception of sovereignty, based on 'supposedly autonomous states in an unregulated contest of wills' in a supposedly apolitical and mechanistic neutral system, set up patterns of inclusion and exclusion. These patterns defined personal as well as political identity, and also defined a fixed view of the range of alternatives open to us. These patterns of inclu-sion and exclusion have constrained and limited theoretical discussion about identity both within the nation state, in political theory, and in inter-national relations theory (Walker 1993, 179). Linklater also explores the notion of states and state systems as patterns of inclusion and exclusion (Linklater 1992).

Feminist writers have also developed sources of theory arguing for a reassessment of the internal/external relationship, or indeed establishing a relationship, to replace the previous gap between what political theorists and what international relations theorists did with sovereignty. Feminist political theorists have criticised the public/private dualism within western liberal political practice and theory, and now ask whether and how a re-formulation of the public/private divide might map onto the re-evaluation of a domestic/international, internal/external distinction (Sylvester 1994, Ashworth 1995, Weber 1994, Krause 1994, Hutchings 1996, Chapter 8). The most convincing feminist reformulation of the relationship between public and private spheres does not seek to do away with the distinction, but only to establish a different relationship, of connection and interaction rather than of opposition and hierarchy. Similarly, the most convincing reformulation of the internal/external relation is one in which the state still has an active and unique role to play in mediating between levels of politics (local, regional, national, area, global), while recognising that the simple split between internal and external, marked by the 'horizon' Walker criticises, is superseded by a relation of connection rather than of opposition and hierarchy.

Feminists and communitarians have also criticised the Western, liberal, rational, abstract basis of the notions of autonomy and independence of the individual, on the grounds that the concrete lives of people are constituted also by ties of connection and relation. Just as the meaning of the autonomy and independence of individuals needs to be reassessed in the light of feminist and communitarian criticism, so it may be possible that the meaning of the autonomy and independence of states can be redefined without being abandoned. As Hoffman notes, 'Reconceptualising sovereignty involves...building upon and thus transcending the liberal tradition so that sovereignty becomes a relational concept. Sovereign institutions like sovereign individuals need to be conceived as agents who can only increase their own autonomy by empowering others' (Hoffman 1996, 631). Underlying the post-state proposal is a move from 'human nature' to interconnectedness, replacing the narrow instrumental rationality and competitiveness of a fixed view of human nature with a recognition of inter-dependence, intersubjective meaning formation, and the moral claims, obligations and agency-responsibility that we can make on each other. This move also involves an emphasis on the relationality of post-states, rather than the relationality of individuals, as Hoffman affirms as the basis of his notion of a post-statist sovereignty (Hoffman 1998, 96).

The recognition of inter-dependence between post-states also leads to a revision of the realist tradition's view that 'international politics is permanently conflictual because of the structural constraint that arises from the enduring absence of central authority' (Fischer 1992, 389). Acknowledging inter-dependency provides an alternative to an essentialising view of human nature as competitive and interest-based, and empirical evidence such as the setting up of bodies like the UN indicates, along with other motives, a desire for cooperation and sharing alongside conflict. Moreover, we have seen that the 'international' (and what it means to conquer territory, conclude alliances, etc.) changes over time, and that the international sphere as an anarchy is constructed.

Pluralism

The pluralism aspect of the post-state proposal registers more successfully than other schemes a fuller recognition of the presence of actors in international politics in addition to conventional political units, to overcoming the monopoly of the state form in international politics and so the 'unbundling' of sovereignty in various ways (described in detail in the following chapter), and to the recognition of a diversity of forms of polity below and above the state paradigm, including regions in the form of segments of states such as Scotland or Quebec and cross-state regional bodies such as NAFTA and the EU. It also takes into account the fluid rather than fixed and static quality of international politics such that an actor's position in international relations is not stable, but may need to be constantly reordered against a backdrop of shifting experience. It also represents a successful intermediate position between clinging to the state sovereignty system and jumping to a commitment to global politics. For instance, it offers a sound alternative to Hardt and Negri's theorisation of the inevitability of the global reach across conventional borders of flexible de-territorialised flows and apparatuses of biopower and of socialised and mediatised production, and of the postmodern multitude as an active multiplicity and as an ensemble and network agent of change with ontological power generative from below to effect global revolution, in the face of a decentred (imperial) sovereignty with national and supranational aspects which outstrips conventional state sovereignty (Hardt and Negri 2000, 2004).

It is clear that the integrity of the state sovereignty model is challenged by, as Huysmans indicates, 'transnational developments' that 'fragment the international system into functionally defined arenas of politics', and so undermine the 'unity of the international system of sovereign states' (Huysmans 2003, 226). What is proposed here is a pluralistic conception of multiple 'post-states', and multiple and diverse actors, recognising that international politics involves not just political communities but also major economies, corporations, NGOs, the UN, the World Bank, G8, international legal instruments, functional differentiation, governance networks of groups involved in sectoral areas, groups of transnational political activists, and movements of groups of refugees in response to war, famine, or the appeal of sweatshop wages. This view does not privilege states as the primary political actors (thereby overcoming the hypocrisy whereby economic and power considerations are masked behind states), but also does not necessarily celebrate this situation as in itself political or democratic. While the state is no longer a universal category in international relations, post-states continue to be the 'communities of fate' for most people. However, the pluralism of political actors is qualified in that Schmitt's observation remains true that amongst the plethora of actors on the stage of international politics, 'states wage wars only against states and... only states can face one another as enemies' (Schmitt 1996, 48).

Huysmans makes the important point in this regard, that by 'focusing on co-operation between states, most of the literature on international regimes in a functionally differentiated international system does not really raise the question of the political' (Huysmans 2003, 227). The order that established the principle (whatever anomalies were allowed to co-exist with it) that only sovereign states were the proper members and participants in international society, is being radically challenged. The realist 'fix' on international relations cannot acknowledge the real significance of other players than states. The view proposed here is a post-state one in the sense of reconceptualising the political entity as more open and interrelated, and in the sense of recognising the role of other international actors as players, thereby challenging the resistance of those in the realist tradition to recognising the effect of economic activity on the 'purely political' realm of international relations, for understanding the international system in a structural sense.

Huysmans argues that transnational flows and developments affect public political authority not in that they 'may trigger cooperation between public authorities and political communities which otherwise would not have existed'. The internal/external construction and the way of understanding the political that it enables, are both left intact. What transnational flows and developments do lead to, Huysmans signals, is 'a fragmented public authority in international politics', which is now 'spread over different, not necessarily related, institutionalised policy arenas and policy networks'. Such flows and developments have the effect of fragmenting 'the international society of sovereign states into functionally defined arenas', and so 'challenges the neat fix that territorialised the tension and the gap' between internal and external sovereignty (Huysmans 2003, 220).

The idea of transnational social and political movements as an alternative to state-centred national and party politics has gained credence over recent years. This idea signals a move that is radically transgressive, regardless of whether the attempt is effective, or of its success or failure to develop a thriving politics. The modern realist settlement figures the domestic alone as the sphere of rational community where morality and law have a place, whereas transnational groups seek to project a version of that politics (albeit in a committedly unstructured and fragmented form, without party hierarchies and leaders) onto the international sphere as an alternative to the realist context of struggle and competition between national self-interests. However one limit of this idea, as Ashley points out, is that the sphere of domestic politics remains the domain 'in which community is most fully realised'. Not only is this 'the domain wherein the intersubjective foundations of action lend authority to the state as the monopolist of coercive means', it is also 'the primary arbiter of social conflict, and the ultimate agent of social action on behalf of society as a whole' (Ashley 1987, 412). Chandler (2004) also identifies other limits, in the elitist tendencies of global civil activism, and in the derogation from collective political engagement that derives from the commitment to no higher political allegiance beyond one's moral conscience. Such an approach amounts to a retreat from politics and avoids political responsibility and accountability.

Relatedly, Connolly imagines 'a transnationalisation of the political within a democratic framework', in the 'daily politics' of social movements, civil servants, and companies competing for the definition of 'a common good across the traditional boundaries of states'. Connolly's aim is to 'imagine a politics which emphasises the nurturing of difference rather than the need for unity', which has been a key focus of state sovereignty. Here the focus is on, as Huysmans notes, 'transnational agencies acting politically', in a transnational political space (Huysmans 2003, 221). Transnational politics, on this reading, 'is presented as a politics that sustains radical antagonism between beliefs and uncertainty about outcomes and ways of reaching those outcomes'. Connolly's theory turns upside down the role of orthodox state sovereignty. Politics is about 'sustaining a contingent unity in a condition of radical plurality', rather than about 'sustaining plurality and difference in the face of unifying pressures'. Also, it 'shares with political realist views an emphasis on power politics and on the need to make decisions in situations of conflict between competing views and interests'. Like realist views too, it criticises 'concepts of the political that focus on the declaration and implementation of universal rules'. Politics for both is about competition between beliefs and views rather than about the implementation of rules. Furthermore, both realist and post-structuralist views argue against a 'procedural understanding of politics' in which politics is regarded as 'the production of legitimate consensus by the following of particular procedures'. As Huysmans indicates, whereas the Schmittean authentic sovereign practice 'is always an act of closure, of re-establishing unity and order', the post-structural concept of the political focuses on 'the need to create and maintain radical difference' (Huysmans 2003, 222).

This proposal also recognises that these 'post-states' are distinct from each other having incommensurable sets of beliefs and principles. While this view is secular it allows for other, religiously-based ideas of political form too. The diversity of forms of polity that this proposal depicts reinforces the importance of respect for difference and of non-intervention, threatened for instance by the exercise of a US unilateral single-imperial sovereignty. However this proposal retains the modern idea of equal status between, now, post-states, which is an aspect of the modern state system with important egalitarian potential.

Politics

The 'politics' aspect of the post-state proposal highlights the denaturalisation of state sovereignty. It also acknowledges the political rather than moral work of sovereignty, in the sense that the key principle, or practice, of inter-dependence acts as a kind of secondary norm like diplomacy, rather than seeking to be like a big heavy normative ideal like justice. It is a mechanism that keeps things going rather than a moral aspiration or intention which necessarily contains culturally-specific values. These elements of the 'politics' aspect of the post-state proposal are also understood in the context of a recast international sphere, positing domestic politics and international *politics* (or rather inter-post-state politics), rather than international relations, let alone international community. In addition, whereas Bartelson despairs of being able to dissolve the state from the outside in and from the inside out simultaneously (Bartelson 2001, 181), this reconceptualisation can do exactly that, because it concentrates on the political functions of sovereignty in both domestic and international politics.

'Politics' here refers to the challenges and contestations that occur to instances of government rule or state policy; protest against the things off the political agenda due to dominant social norms (for instance feminism, disability politics); the uncovering and dissecting of power relations (the politics of the meeting); as well as referring to the Schmittean exception that requires political rather than legal judgement (or a political judgement on a legal norm). In Chapter 4 another meaning of politics is developed, whereby it is authoritative claims to sovereignty which establish (and this is contingent – there is no universal substantive meaning for politics and this is precisely why sovereignty is needed) on the content of those four areas identified above, decide on the limits of politics, and the boundary between the political and the unpolitical. What is beyond the political is significant both because, for example, eye colour is taken to be un-political, and because one end of politics is when violence replaces talk.

The political aspect of the post-state proposal also encompasses a more fluid sense of the changing meaning of sovereignty over time. Teschke, for instance, recognises the changing reference of sovereignty when he posits three phases of transformation rather than the realist pre-Westphalia/ Westphalia formula. Neil Walker proposes Westphalian and post-Westphalian states in the face of pressures from 'globalisation on the one hand and multi-dimensionality and constitutional pluralism on the other' (Walker 2003b, 10). The 'post-state' conception put forward here differs from Neil Walker's in emphasising more the move from an internal/external dichotomy to an internal-external relational, fluid and more permeable boundary.

Huysmans highlights the political meaning of sovereignty persuasively when he argues that a challenge in the international sphere (for instance from 'globalisation', functional differentiation, transnational protest movements, transnational democracy) is only a challenge to *sovereignty* if it is capable of transforming the meaning of the political. Moreover, these are only challenges to the particular conception of state sovereignty if they are capable of radically reconfiguring the meaning of the current set-up and fixing in place of international politics. Although the realist tradition constructs the international realm as outside the realm of governance, institutions and rules constraining the actions of states, nevertheless the international realm operates, in the realist view, with a system of diplomacy as a prevailing practice, rules of engagement, protocols, and norms of warfare. It is just that these do not add up to a systematic and comprehensive moral, legal, normative, or procedural institutional framework. Diplomacy is well suited to the realist model for it is a practice without having to normatively constrain action.

Huysmans asks to what extent introducing radical antagonism 'moves the concept of the political beyond' the state sovereignty definition (Huysmans 2003, 222). In particular, Connolly's separation of a democratic ethos from democratic institutions, does not resolve the question of 'institutions within which the democratic ethos articulates itself in an antagonistic practice for defining a common good'. Specifically, Connolly's idea of a democratic ethos leaves open the answers to questions such as, does it 'rely on a rule of law implemented by states and/or international organisations? How are the arenas of struggle constructed? Who can participate and who cannot?' (Huysmans 2003, 224). Huysmans also questions who 'defines and protects the community of those who share a democratic ethos when the community faces a fundamental challenge that cannot be dealt with within the confines of an antagonistic respect for difference?' In other words, it is not clear how Connolly deals with 'the gap between normal political practice and exceptional political practice', a gap that is crucial to his definition of the political because for him the political involves 'breaking open existing unity'. It is not clear whether Connolly's position leads to two transnational political spaces, one of the democratic ethos articulated in 'peaceful antagonistic politics' and one in which 'the democratic ethos is radically challenged and therefore needs to be defended'. More broadly, the spectre of sovereignty as the pressure towards unity re-emerges when the question of a system of governance institutionalising this democratic rule is introduced (Huysmans 2003, 225).

Biersteker and Weber effectively denaturalise state sovereignty by demonstrating aspects of its constructedness. They develop the point that the neo-realist conflation of state and sovereignty enabled them to see sovereignty as unproblematic. Such writers failed to see how 'socially constructed practices of sovereignty – of recognition, of intervention, of the language of justification – contribute to the structures of international society' (Biersteker and Weber 1996, 5). The traditional definition saw sovereignty as a given, the 'basic rule of coexistence within the states system, a concept that transcends both ideological differences and the rise and fall of major powers...[as well as being] the basis in international law for claims for state actions' (Biersteker and Weber 1996, 1). But Biersteker and Weber argue that all components of state sovereignty – territory, population, authority and recognition – and the modern state system itself, are all socially constructed (Biersteker and Weber 1996, 3). Reus-Smit quotes an early statement of the social constructedness of sovereignty by Richard Ashley, that 'sovereignty is a practical category whose empirical contents are not fixed but evolve in a way reflecting the active practical consensus among co-reflective statesmen'. Reus-Smit continues that sovereignty is 'above all else a set of norms concerning the legitimate organisation of political authority, the content and implications of which vary from one historical and practical context to another'. The challenge is 'not to arrive at a universally valid definition that fixes its meaning and content, but rather' to explore the way the meaning of sovereignty is constructed in particular cases (Reus-Smit 2001a, 526).

A further theoretical element that is useful in the reassessment of the internal/external relationship in an integrated discourse on sovereignty, takes up the characterisation by Biersteker and Weber of sovereignty as dynamic and historical rather than static and universal. They propose a convincing view of the relation between the state and sovereignty as dynamic, mutually constitutive, as concepts defined in terms of each other. They say that instead of 'proceeding from the assumption that all states are sovereign, we are interested in considering the variety of ways in which states are constantly negotiating their sovereignty' (Biersteker and Weber 1996, 11). The value of this view lies in the consequence that, because states 'can be defined in terms of their claims to sovereignty, while sovereignty can be defined in terms of the interactions and practices of states' (Biersteker and Weber 1996, 11), the future of the concept of sovereignty is freed from its thrall to the specific state form found in the modern period. This inflexible link has been adhered to by both neo-realists and theorists of globalisation. Reinforcing the way in which the understanding of both sovereignty and the state are socially constructed and change over time, Biersteker and Weber reason plausibly that identities or 'agents like the state, then, are never the product of any one institution or discourse; their meanings arise out of interaction with other states and with the international society they form' (Biersteker and Weber 1996, 13).

Reus-Smit identifies an important political dimension of sovereignty when he describes the different, often unacknowledged, 'moral purposes' that have governed the meaning of sovereignty over time in the realist tradition, including the 'standard of civilisation' and culminating in the progressive development in the post-war period of human rights instruments formally enshrining 'modern ideals of legitimate statehood in the normative fabric of international society' (2001a, 531), that is, in the dominant norms of international relations. In this way it has been norms established for external sovereignty that have prescribed the conduct of internal sovereignty too, in the form of circumscribing the state's domestic jurisdiction.

Sovereignty is designed to supply a settled order, and within the realist tradition this occurs in the context of a balance within a Hobbesian anarchic state of nature and by the use of an instrumental reason of state devoid of moral character. But as Reus-Smit shows, this understanding was always underpinned by a normative conception, always accompanied by the 'morally appealing idea of adherence to shared standards of justice as a condition for full membership in international society' (Reus-Smit 2001a, 525, quoting Jack Donnelly). At different times this has been the divine origin of natural law, the standard of civilisation and, since WWII, the development of an extensive body of international human rights law.

Simpson argues for a political rather than moral deployment of sovereignty. He uses the distinction between sovereignty as 'territorial ideal' and sovereignty as 'organising principle' to argue for a post-Westphalian legal order based on the latter and abjuring the former. He identifies sovereignty as 'territorial ideal' with the impulse that 'states are free to do as they wish...at liberty to project power, dominate rivals and annex territory', together with the idea that sovereignty is supreme over international law, associated with nineteenth-century German scholars of the state and German history under the Kaiser and in the fascist period. Sovereignty as 'organising principle', by contrast, is a doctrine of 'both liberty and restraint', according to which it is equality that generates co-existence and security, structures relations between states as well as being something states possess, and so provides a 'relative sovereignty' (Simpson 2004, 40–1), a sovereignty measured against that of other states and a sovereignty formed through relations with other states. This notion of sovereignty constituted by a politics of negotiation of inter-dependence rather than by moral value, provides a basis for rethinking sovereignty beyond the realist paradigm that centres only on states as key players on the international stage.

Sørensen offers another insight into the politics of sovereignty when he distinguishes between stable constitutive rules (primarily the constitutional independence of states) and regulative rules (the most important or 'grund-norms' being non-intervention and a reciprocity that ensures symmetry). According to Sørensen, both constitutive and regulative rules are played out in three ideal type 'sovereignty games' concurrently in the present international system. They are the standard Westphalian game between nation-states, the Post-Colonial game, and the Postmodern game. In the Post-Colonial game weak, dependent, decolonised states rely more than do traditional nation-states on the international community to provide the guarantee of non-intervention. The Postmodern game is exemplified in the intense cooperation demonstrated by states in the European Union. Sørensen identifies tensions in the Post-Colonial game, to either reduce the legal status of 'failed states' so that they are no longer ascribed sovereign constitutional independence, or to bolster the substantial statehood of weak states. He also perceives tensions in the Postmodern game, pushing towards either a more genuine federal structure or a reversion to conventional inter-state cooperation. Sørensen argues that such tensions are likely to remain in balance for the foreseeable future and that change in sovereignty is more likely to emerge from changes in the Westphalian system that we cannot presently envisage (Sørensen 1999, 604).

One valuable outcome of fully engaging with the international politics internal/external sovereignty debate is that it allows us to see the limits of the use of the law discourse. Rather than extrapolating and imposing from the moralised and depoliticised political theory idea of sovereignty in the form of international justice or an international rights regime, or stipulating a notion of international law, law is put in its place. Its overarching character in the political theory sovereignty canon in the form of the *Rechtstaat* can be recognised for what it is. This position is also valuable in offering an alternative to Foucault's scorning of the role of law in sovereignty as a mere masquerade and sham.

The politics dimension of the post-state proposal also recognises that implementation of the reconceptualisation may need to be made in stages, pushing the limits of where we are at present, acknowledging the historical specificity of the rethinking, rather than being discouraged that traces of the state sovereignty political imagination remain. Whereas some critical IR theorists are haunted by the constraints placed on the political imagination by state sovereignty, this theory steps back from that predicament and focuses on the political and the function sovereignty claims have in relation to it.

Where does this proposal leave sovereignty, then? What work can sovereignty do if it is not policing the boundary between the unity of the internal, legal, ordered, territorial domain on the one hand and the unregulated, unterritorial, non-legal, disordered sphere of the assertion of national interest on the other? Sovereignty in its post-state shape still has a number of important roles to play. In 'international politics' there remains an important function for sovereignty in setting out the norms and rules for governance and regulation of the actions of post-states and other actors (corporations, NGOs, World Bank, etc.) in their inter-dependence, and in managing the idea of migratory and other flows across the boundary. In political theory there remains an important task for sovereignty in showing the politics of authority and obligation, and in dealing with the idea of flows across the boundary. In both arenas, sovereignty is like the 'secondary norm' discussed above – these things are best performed by a conception of sovereignty rather than by international institutions or legal regimes or a rights culture, which come with too much western baggage and can end up dominating the practice they are meant to serve.

Krasner points to another important role for sovereignty in the way the very idea of sovereignty exercises a powerful influence. Yeltsin's declaration of Russia as a sovereign state was a strategic choice among several alternatives, and in the disintegration of Yugoslavia the aspiring leaders of Croatia and Slovenia utilised the ready-made script of sovereignty to appeal for support to leading European Community countries. Palestinian claims derive their power in part from the appeal to be a sovereign state in a world of sovereign states (Krasner 2001, 13–14). This suggests the ongoing potency of sovereignty as a political concept, the importance of the appeal to sovereignty in structuring international politics, and also the constraints upon implementing a reconceptionalisation of sovereignty.

Jackson describes a value continuum, at the conservative extremity of which 'sovereignty is seen as upholding the value of freedom, i.e., political independence, and as fostering international order', contrasted with the progressive extremity where sovereignty 'is seen as denying justice to countless individuals, organisations and identities that cannot fit into the territorial logic of sovereignty' (Jackson 1999, 427). However Jackson is trapped in the state sovereignty logic. It is possible, in a post-state sovereignty world that progressive politics does not have to be allied to the abolition of sovereignty.

Where does this leave the scope of political theory and international relations/theory? It is not enough anymore for political theory to concern itself with the good life and with politics and good governance in liberal democratic states, with international relations as an afterthought. Political theory needs to be more political (not just about liberal democratic states), thus less insular, and more aware of others. Indeed the answer is not for political theory and international relations/theory to merge but for them both to concentrate on the political within their spheres. Political theory and international relations both need to become more political, dealing with political issues and recognising the impact of political power relations. The context in which politics is played out in the two realms, while overlapping, is not identical. And while the unity of the political unit that realism assumes does not have to be agreed with, political and economic and other units in international relations do have a less disaggregated form than they do for political theory. Like the optician's short and long visions, so the political theorist and international relations theorist focus on different perspectives.

Conclusion

The consensus of the previous generation of international relations scholars can be summed up in Benn's conclusion, in 'The uses of "sovereignty"' that there was 'a strong case for giving up so protean a word' (Benn 1955, 122), and in Morganthau's statement that the 'sovereign nation-state is in the process of becoming obsolete' (Morganthau 1964, 116). Camilleri and Falk echo this view, referring to 'the ambiguities which at every level now surround the principle of sovereignty' (Camilleri and Falk 1992, 39), as did Walker and Mendlovitz in their assertion that 'state sovereignty offers only a misleading map of where we are' (Walker and

Mendlovitz 1990, 2). James (1986) argues that formal academic definitions, based on unsubstantiated claims of sovereignty, are not helpful in discussing and making sense of what happens in international relations between states. He also sees the ambiguity of the term as a reason to discard it in political discourse. Hoffman (1997, 54) notes that David Easton argued in 1953 that the state is 'disqualified as an "orienting" concept within politics because of the elusive nature of sovereignty', and that sovereignty has continued to enjoy a 'foundational' status because 'the state has led a "double life". Contestable domestically, it has remained uncontestable internationally'.

There is emerging, however, amongst the work of some of the most recent writers on sovereignty, a view that gives more hope for the resilience of the concept. Paradoxically it has been the recent challenges to the conception of (external) sovereignty, which Rob Walker convincingly argues was based on taking the territoriality of the state as a general metaphor of barrier, that have led to the possibility of a more fruitful combined discourse about sovereignty. Indeed internal and external sovereignty need to be recognised as relational, not because the nation-state is now irrelevant but because a range of post-states actors are crucially important in international political space. The redefined concept no longer emphasises sovereignty as state sovereignty in terms of the territoriality of the state. Spatiality remains a condition of, but is no longer the defining feature of political life on the world stage. An integrated conception of sovereignty also has important consequences for the internal relationship that has been the subject matter of political theorists. For instance, it is better equipped to acknowledge the uncomfortable relationship between rulers and ruled as both the source of stability and self-realisation, as well as the source of coercion (Harding 1994, 58).

In sum, the reconstructed conception of sovereignty is no longer dominated by the underlying metaphor of barrier in its internal and external forms. It emphasises instead the unique role in an integrated discourse of sovereignty played by post-states in mediating processes of governance above and below themselves, in a way which does not automatically marginalise women and minorities within the polities and does not condemn other communities as 'other'. By recognising the inter-dependence, pluralism and politics of post-states and other actors in international political space, it may be possible that the 'political' can be recovered from the gap between the internal realm of the social and the external realm of interest politics and diplomacy.

2
The Liberal and State Character of Modern Sovereignty

In the previous chapter we noted Bartelson's despair over dissolving the state from the outside in and from the inside out simultaneously (Bartelson 2001, 181). While the proposal for 'post-states' and other actors in a recast international realm in Chapter 1 sought to tackle the 'outside in' rethinking of the state, this chapter broaches the reconceptualisation of sovereignty from the 'inside out', by investigating the powerful analogy at work between liberal principles focusing on the individual on the one hand and the orthodox state form on the other in the modern conception of sovereignty. The aim of this chapter is to counter the claim that sovereignty is a bankrupt *concept*, by demonstrating the specifically liberal character of the *conception* that has dominated the modern period.

The chapter analyses the liberal principles at work in modern state sovereignty, and examines the force of the individual and domestic analogies on which it hinges. Then the argument explores the inherent contradictions in liberal state sovereignty, highlighting the tension between state and individual mirrored in the tension between ideas taken from Locke and Hobbes. Finally, the reconceptualisation of sovereignty begun in the previous chapter is taken forward, through the scope for politics which is opened up by the constructedness of the state sovereignty conception, which is denied by the universalism of that conception.

Liberal principles

In the chapters in this Part of the book especially, the term 'liberal' is used to describe certain features of the modern Western state-centred conception of sovereignty. While the contemporary debate within liberal political theory is rich and broad, this book does not attempt to take account of the diversity and nuances of liberal positions and their potential compatibility with other points of view but focuses instead on the key liberal principles that have informed the development of the modern state-centred model of sovereignty. Thus, it is Reformation Protestant voluntarist ideas and the ideas about contract that later took on particular pertinence in accounting for political community, the investment in the belief in man's rational capacity later developed by Enlightenment thinkers, and Locke as expressing a political theory taken up in a newly individualist and secular political environment, that primarily inform the meaning of liberalism used here. These are some of the ideas that were radical and progressive at the time of the development of modern sovereignty and which seemed to offer it explanatory power, and which came to be called liberal.

'Liberalism' has had a range of intersecting meanings since the term was coined in the eighteenth century, from the principles derived from Locke, through the slow process of grafting them onto democratic ideas (for instance from Rousseau) and capitalist ideas (for instance from Adam Smith), through an orientation reinforcing the idea of individual freedom in J.S. Mill and opposing the anti-individualist collectivist aspect of Marxism, through the 'new' liberalism of the British idealists, through the 1920s and 1930s when European liberalism was unable to meet the crisis precipitated by fascism and communism, through Isaiah Berlin's dichotomous formulation of negative and positive liberty, through Rawls's *Theory of Justice* and *Political Liberalism*, to Fukuyama's claim in the 1990s about the triumph of liberal democratic capitalism. In 2007 liberal ideas about individualism and free speech are again drafted in, seen by some influential political actors in the West as potent rebuttals to supposed enemies and threats. Such ideas and justifications draw very strongly on a vastly influential classic meaning of liberalism, primarily derived from Locke. The meaning of liberalism here focuses in particular on Locke's influential definition of the pre-political rights of the individual, and the assertion summed up so well later by J.S. Mill that 'over himself, over his own mind and body, the individual is sovereign' (Mill 1974, 68). In the current context for discussing sovereignty Lockean liberal tenets are still very much a living force.

What has been taken from Locke, then, is a sense of the pre-eminence in political life of the individual, in the cluster around the pre-political individual, his rights, his agency and capacity to make choices, and his acceding to government only through a voluntary contract. The idea of individualism is taken to be universal and abstract, and to comprehend self-ownership in a strong sense. This methodological individualism has been taken to crucially distinguish liberal theory from communitarian theories that accent the embeddedness of the individual in social meanings, intersubjectivity and networks of interdependence, and the embodiedness of the individual in different forms of particular identity and cultural specificity and so the importance of history in understanding the individual. While some contemporary liberals have sought to embrace some elements of the communitarian critique, in its purer mainstream form the sovereign liberal individual remains, as O'Connell Davidson articulates, 'imagined as unencumbered by "his" social relations' is rather 'a person incapable of constitutive attachments'. The 'ideally free and rational agent' of liberal theory is, in Sandel's words (quoted by O'Connell Davidson), 'a person wholly without character, without moral depth' (O'Connell Davidson 1997, 172).

It follows that what is crucially prioritised for the liberal individual so described, on moving to the polity, is his rights rather than either his duties to others or to the polity. In liberal theory the idea of the individual derived from Locke builds upon Hobbes's technical and hypothetical notion of freedom as unimpeded action. When this is joined with the notion of the abstract individual, liberal theory depicts as enormously significant a literalised individual with a right to unhindered action and choice. The term 'liberal' also denotes, not just pre-political and individualised rights, but also rationality, man as a transcendental subject, and man as a condition of knowledge, man as producing abstract and universalisable truths. There is in the liberal view a close connection between individualism and secularism, which come together in the notion of rationality. Liberal sovereignty necessarily specifies a secular relation between rulers and ruled, reliant on the judgement of individuals using their individual reason, rather than ruling being based on either divine warrant or mere power and coercion. The idea of 'liberal sovereignty' crucially includes a strong belief in and reliance on reason, such that disagreement is regarded as a failure of reason.

A key feature of liberalism that follows from its universalistic and abstract self-definition is that it sees its principles as outside debate, interpretation, culture, contestation, and politics. Liberal political principles are presented as universal rather than as culturally framed. One reason why it is so difficult to disentangle the meaning of sovereignty from the liberal state sovereignty form is that this conception, in a very distinctive fashion, equates itself with the concept. Thus it is not just that over time the state form has come to seem commonsensically given. The claims of liberal principles act to reinforce that trend very strongly. Loughlin identifies two sources of confusion about sovereignty that can be seen to originate in the abstract and universalising character of liberal theory in this way. These misapprehensions arise from scholars attempting, 'to fix the concept of sovereignty within a formal, analytical and positivist frame', and from 'the efforts of political and legal theorists to devise some transcendental principles of right conduct to which legal and political behaviour must be subject' (Loughlin 2003, 56). Similarly, Simpson identifies a weakness in the establishment of the International Criminal Court, in the fear that it 'may become another particularistic institution and part of the deepening constitutionalism of the liberal project; aspiring to universality but remaining relevant only to the [self-identified] good citizens of the international order' (Simpson 2004, 8).

The kind of authority relationship that is central to the modern liberal conception of sovereignty mediates uneasily between the 'sovereign' individual and the legalised sovereignty of the state. The effect for politics is to minimise the role of collective action. Sovereignty has been closely connected with the question of the 'founding' of the nation/state, and alongside this question of the founding of the state, whether by republican, nationalist or other means, the issue of who or what authorises the state to act as a system of mutual guarantee for 'its' people involves the notion of sovereignty. Sovereignty is enlisted to bear on that which *continues* to authorise the nation to act as one. That is, continuity is provided in part, and crucially, by the notion of sovereignty. It is also inherent in the notion of liberal sovereignty to be monolithic, to impose order and stability, to erase politics as disagreement and contestation and dissent, for authority to hold sway. At the same time it accommodates difference in the private sphere and a thin notion of toleration. In addition, the settled order of a polity is understood in secular terms, and it is part of the sovereign settlement which began in the seventeenth century that the state is understood as governed by considerations of national interest, and that relations between states are similarly governed by reason of state.

The case for identifying the liberal features of the modern state-centred conception of sovereignty is strengthened by Walzer's argument about the explanatory force of mapping ideas and values in wider social contexts onto the political realm. With respect to politics the term 'liberal' also refers, then, to a set of principles which underpin an overall shunning of normative value given to politics and which are, at the same time, saturated with unacknowledged, culturally-specific values with discriminatory effects. These principles include a depoliticised individualism decontextualised from community and inter-subjective understanding, and the supposedly 'neutral' state created by the social contract tradition. They also include the lack of a moral dimension in the instrumental rationality of a society dominated by the capitalist marketplace, and an unacknowledged, abstract and universalising logic, masking its own Western and modern cultural specificity and denying respect for the cultural specificity of others. In addition these liberal principles include the conservative interpretation given to the priority of the right and of freedom over equality and emancipation, and the conservative consequence of the elimination or foreshortening of politics as a legitimate arena of the play of contestation and a more than tolerated pluralism, leading to a reliance on law and constitutionalism.

Feminists amongst others have, in Smith's words, 'argued that law is not neutral but is established and maintained by dominant political interests'. Moreover, because the liberal law is supposedly neutral, 'it must fail to acknowledge relative disadvantage and fail, therefore, to deliver substantive justice'. In consequence, liberal law and the liberal democratic state are implicated in 'establishing and maintaining, under the guise of popular sovereignty, social arrangements which are inherently unjust' (Smith 2000, 287).

We noted in the Introduction Keal's identification of an important way in which sovereignty is political, in the distinction utilised by nineteenth-century European states between civilised and uncivilised polities. Keal also makes explicit the political link (drawn by Dianne Otto) between law, liberalism and sovereignty. Keal notes that 'Otto argues that liberalism and law have mutually constituted each other in ways that tie sovereignty to the state'. Crucially, Keal maintains, the 'liberal state places personal liberties and rights "above religious, ethnic and other forms of communal consciousness"'. It follows that 'the liberal conception of sovereignty enshrined in law is thus an obstacle to re-defining sovereignty in ways that would enable it to be a foundation of indigenous cultural identity' (Keal 2003, 198–9). Keal also points to the way that indigenous peoples 'reject European notions of sovereignty in which the state exercises authority over civil society' (Keal 2003, 147), thus indicating wider political contexts in which the meaning of sovereignty is placed.

Keal goes on to describe the argument put forward by Otto for 'indigenous sovereignty', by which she means 'the power for indigenous communities to imagine themselves', to be 'creators of themselves as subjects rather than objects of law and history', 'as agents of their own destinies' (Keal 2003, 147), to move 'from being objects to being subjects of international law' (Keal 2003, 114). Keal notes the important but widely unacknowledged point that the term 'indigenous peoples' is defined in part in terms of the loss of sovereignty by original inhabitants and domination by others, as well as through cultural identity (Keal 2003, 9). Otto, theorising sovereignty in terms of elements of imagination and agency in a highly innovative fashion, regards 'indigenous sovereignty' as going beyond self-determination, now in the light of self-definition by the indigenous group rather than 'white constructions', in terms of access to international legal processes 'beyond the derivative personality of individual standing accorded by some human rights instruments', and in terms of providing a foundation for land rights and responsibilities beyond the 'human rights paradigm' (quoted in Keal 2003, 147). Keal highlights that Otto's 'case for reconceptualising sovereignty is that the power to define, shape and maintain identity is fundamental to all indigenous rights'. He emphasises, bringing out again the political dimension of sovereignty and in ways that resonate with the argument outlined in Chapter 4, that sovereignty 'is constitutive of identity, and consequently if indigenous rights are to be fully realised sovereignty must be invested in indigenous peoples' (Keal 2003, 152).

The individual and domestic analogies

The traditional conception of sovereignty has operated in a comprehensive manner as a distinctively liberal form of political order, in part underpinned by a complex of analogies between the individual and domestic realms with the domain of the state in international affairs. This conception has emphasised the autonomy of the individual, both person and state, replacing the looser hierarchical network of interconnected jurisdictions of the older idea of order, accommodating an Emperor, monarch, feudal lords, local privileges and liberties. Several scholars have highlighted how the liberal conception of sovereignty mirrors liberal individualism in asserting the sovereignty of the sovereign rights of the 'individual'. At both the individual level and the level of state sovereignty, liberal principles are predominant. There is a strong, constructed, correspondence between the liberal individual and the liberal secular state. Hutchings argues convincingly that in our liberal tradition, the 'sovereign individual is rational and exists in abstraction from both its own body and from other selves/bodies'. She notes that this 'abstraction is fundamentally related to the sovereign individual's capacity for both moral knowledge and moral autonomy, both of which rely on independence from external influences'. Hutchings reasons that the 'sovereign individual is sovereign in the sense that it has rights over itself and rules itself, whether through rational self-interest or access to the moral law' (Hutchings 1996, 2).

Onuf also registers that a key element of the liberal character of state sovereignty has been the complementarity between the territorial sovereignty of nation-states, which 'has been a central, indeed a constitutive, feature of the modern world', and the 'Kantian faith in the moral autonomy of individual human beings, as manifest in their practical ability to act, by themselves and in concert, for ends they have chosen'. Onuf makes a convincing case that a very strong analogy holds here between state and individual. 'Made for each other', he argues, 'the sovereign state and the autonomous individual decisively contribute to making the world what it is – and to making it seem naturally, inevitably so' (Onuf 1995, 43). The link between the modern state formulation and the conception of the individual as pre-eminently autonomous can also be taken a step further, by identifying some of the ways in which state sovereignty is characterised by liberal principles.

Krasner refers to the way that international lawyers, in one of the key discourses of international politics, have 'conceived of sovereign states as analogous to the individual in liberal political theory. Sovereign states are autonomous actors'. In consequence, Krasner identifies, sovereign states in the liberal paradigm, 'have the right and the ability to enter into contractual relationships. These contracts, even though they are promises that may limit freedom of action, are an indication of the sovereignty of the state, not a curtailment of it' (Krasner 2001, 5). At the heart of both the conceptions of the 'individual' the consequences of the idea of sovereign autonomy are crucial. In both, equality means a sense of a mutual recognition of equal formal rights and not of substantive equality. In both there is the fiction of equal opportunity to pursue a self-defined liberty. For both forms of the 'individual' liberty means negative liberty, restrained only (and ambiguously) by the harm principle. For both forms of 'individual' abstract autonomy and universal rights are independent of culture, community and history. For both involvement is only by choice, in voluntary contract, rather than as emerging from constituted embeddedness. And in both the internal/external or public/private divide distinguishes a morally sacrosanct, autonomous private sphere from a public sphere of moral pluralism, competition and independent individual achievement. The same logic is apparent in the condition of coexistence, not relationship, that is designed to exist between Westphalian states, which mirrors the liberal theory of toleration.

In sum, state sovereignty trades on three vital aspects of the liberal sovereign individual, as summed up succinctly by Hutchings. She identifies 'the sovereign individual as the disembodied owner of property in his own person...of Hobbes and Locke', the 'Kantian autonomous agent central to the voice of justice', and the 'Cartesian conception of the self at the heart of modern epistemology' (Hutchings 1996, 2). In addition, Kratochwil describes how crucially with the introduction of the modern liberal notion of state sovereignty, 'the notion of politics as balance and collective legitimisation gave way to a conception of politics' (Kratochwil 1995, 32) modelled on the actions of liberal competitive individuals in a market environment. Hoffman points to classical liberalism as having 'identified the "sovereign" capacity of individuals to govern their own lives' (Hoffman 1997, 57).

Smith explores another aspect of the liberal analogy when she outlines the liberal dichotomy between civil society and the state such that social relations in the civil realm are thought to be 'governed by private transactions between individual actors' while in the political realm 'citizens are governed through their relations with the state'. She cites the view that liberalism theorises 'power as sovereign power, and sovereign power as the relationship between abstract subjects – each characterised by an autonomous, responsible will – and the law'. Smith concludes that liberalism 'must necessarily fail to incorporate any recognition that power is dispersed and government practised other than through the state' (Smith 2000, 287). Smith's point is interesting for two reasons. First it highlights liberal sovereignty as a relation between *abstract* subjects, and second it highlights liberalism's constitutional inability to recognise other forms of power.

Moreover, the political concepts of the liberal 'package' such as liberty, rights, or equality are both conceptually and analogically related. Conceptually each concept in this particular conception is interrelated, reciprocally meaningful, mutually reinforcing. But the summing up, hanging together of these concepts also takes place analogically, metaphorically, symbolically. What is being asserted here is not a cause and effect connection between ideas about the individual and ideas about the polity, or between Protestant theology and secularism. The connections are much too complex and two-way to make a causal logic convincing. But more importantly, what is being made explicit here is an analogical logic, which the following chapter explores in more detail. Other scholars have also pointed to the significance of liberal analogical reasoning. Inayatullah and Blaney (1995) examine the fertile idea of a correspondence between the liberal individual and the sovereign state, as the basis for a Marxist political economy critique. Neack and Knudson emphasise the importance of recognising the link between 'a delegitimising of the sovereign, autonomous state in international relations...and the rethinking of the hegemonic self or person' (Neack and Knudson 1996, 135).

The analogies at play in liberal sovereignty are further complicated by the way in which political theorists see the state as an amalgam of components, whereas for mainstream international relations the state is analogous to an individual agent. Therefore, for the realist tradition, international relations definitionally requires an Hobbesian-type sovereignty because the state as agent equals a sovereign man. Brown, for instance, describes neo-realists working within a framework of 'a world in which egoists seek to survive under conditions of Hobbesian anarchy' (Brown 2002, 13). Thus the realist conception of politics on the world stage rests solely upon the dynamics produced by the external sovereignty of states (protecting self-interest from the basis of strict territorial boundaries, war as an instrument of policy, non-intervention as the basis of international law). For the realist conception, a sovereign is equated with the ability to raise an army, to make war and peace, and to get subjects to bear arms. This conception ignores the possible significance for the international realm of the nature of authority, legitimacy, and power in the relationship within the polity between rulers and ruled. Thus in the splitting up of sovereignty into separate discourses of (internal) sovereignty and (external) sovereignty, something of the political has fallen through the gap, between concern with the political as social and concern with the political as diplomacy.

It is a commonplace among international relations scholars to regard Hobbes as sanctioning the idea of the relation between actors on the world stage in terms of states in a state of nature, and to anachronistically take him as 'an archetypal proponent of "Realism"' (Malcolm 2002, 432). Brown *et al* perpetuate the misrepresentation of Hobbes. They argue that 'Hobbes's view of international relations is, then, one we would call "realist" or

Machiavellian. Within civil society, law rules; between civil societies "policy" (expedience) comes to the fore. The eighteenth-century theory of the balance of power illustrates how far international political theory can go on Hobbesian principles' (Brown *et al* 2002, 317). This realist misconception of Hobbes's theory (see Prokhovnik 2005) is put forward even by Wendt, when he refers to '[c]lassical realists such as Thomas Hobbes, Reinhold Niebuhr, and Hans Morganthau...' (Wendt 1992, 395). They read into Hobbes a simple analogy between the individual in the state of nature and states in a state of nature, without taking into account the flaws in the analogy. As Malcolm notes, 'states are not vulnerable in the way that individuals are', there is 'no real equality between states great and small', and there is no 'national right of self-preservation analogous to the individual one' since 'the "death" of a state need not involve the death of its citizens' (Malcolm 2002, 434). But more seriously commentators in the realist tradition fail to note that Hobbes's description of the state of nature is not meant to have ontological status, and that the 'Hobbesian state' is not 'Hobbesian man writ large' (Malcolm 2002, 434). For Hobbes the state of nature is only the logical prelude, a fictional hypothesis that shows the importance of and leads to the analysis of the laws of nature, all of which follow from the first law of nature, to seek peace. The state of nature is not meant by Hobbes to be a freestanding reality, but rather a logical point in the development of the resolutive-compositive method.

Thus while Hobbes makes it plain that commonwealths are related to each other through the same laws of nature (laws whose role in Hobbes's theory need to be taken seriously since, as Malcolm (2002, 437) observes are 'neither subjective nor determined by the sovereign's will') as apply to individuals, there is no simple analogy at work. At the end of Chapter 30 of *Leviathan* he says, 'Concerning the Offices of one Soveraign to another, which are comprehended in that Law, which is commonly called the *Law of Nations*, I need not say anything in this place; because the Law of Nations, and the Law of Nature, is the same thing'. Indeed, as Malcolm notes, there is no analogy at work for Hobbes here, since there is 'a single Law of Nature, "the same Law", applying to actions undertaken at both levels' (Malcolm 2002, 436). Covell also adds weight to the argument that Hobbes was a natural law theorist who identified 'the first laws of nature as embodying the essential principles of the law of nations' and so who cannot without severe misrepresentation be appropriated to the realist position (Covell 2004, 6). Hobbes has also been taken to be sanctioning the right of states to pursue self-interest in international anarchy, but this is again anachronistic since the understanding of the relations between commonwealths and of the 'international' current at the time Hobbes wrote does not correspond to the later realist construction. Hobbes in fact goes on explicitly (and there is a strong case for arguing, sincerely) to recommend states to seek a condition of reciprocal peace, and so translate the moral level of the law into the jural (Malcolm 2002, 437). Hobbes appeals to his readers, fully aware of the social constructedness of positive law, 'the same Law, that dictateth to men that have no Civil Government, what they ought to do...dictateth the same to Common-wealths, that is, to the Consciences of Soveraign Princes, and Soveraign Assemblies'. Contrary to the realist position, Hobbes maintains, as Malcolm indicates, that 'morality remains an objective standard', such that 'it is simply not true that the Hobbesian sovereign "creates morality as well as law"' (Malcolm 2002, 437).

Chandler gives a good example of the failure of the domestic analogy in its own terms. He points cogently to the problems and dangers associated with the asymmetry which results from cosmopolitan schemes for global democracy. He notes that the 'new "rights" of global citizens are not exercised by the rights-holders but by international institutions'. But, he underlines, the 'duties and rights created in the cosmopolitan discourse are of a qualitatively different nature to those establishing under the domestic framework of the rule of law and enforced through the police and the courts'. The effect is that the 'equation of the "right" of the global citizen or global civil society with the "duty" of international institutions creates a new level of rights on paper but is problematic in practice', for instance in the case of the prevention of wide-scale human rights abuses (Chandler 2003, 337). Chandler also argues that, in consequence, the 'rights of the [proposed] cosmopolitan citizen are outside the control of their subject in much the same way as animal rights or environmental rights can not be acted upon by their subjects'. He contends that the 'problem with rights without subjects is that they may become a licence for undermining...existing rights, such as those of democracy and self-government' (Chandler 2003, 341). The outcome of the cosmopolitan thesis is that non-citizens of the major Western states 'have gained no more power to influence the policy-making of' those states, and at the same time 'they have lost the right to hold their own governments to account'. Thus, rather than 'furthering democracy, the premature declaration of a framework of universal cosmopolitan rights can, in fact, result in rights that people did have being further restricted' (Chandler 2003, 347).

Simpson also discusses the unhelpfulness of the domestic analogy, with its strong liberal flavour. He argues that modern liberal conceptions of sovereignty have tried to give the term stable meaning by 'positing states as analogous to individuals in the liberal state'. In this context the key dimension of sovereignty is that it provides 'a form of liberty or immunity from interference, while state equality corresponds to notions of equality found in constitutional orders or in some liberal theory'. According to this view, 'states become moral persons or collective personalities capable of enjoying the same rights as human beings (within the bounds of reasonableness)'. However, the analogy breaks down, Simpson contends, for several reasons. There is 'little agreement on the meaning of equality as it refers to citizens in liberal systems'. The question of 'equality of what?' is central. There is no consensus about whether opportunities, resources, income, respect and concern, or some other criterion are to be taken as the basis of equality. Even juridical equality, Simpson reminds us, 'remains susceptible to disagreement over its precise contours'. Moreover, on the international stage there is no consensus about to whom or what equality applies. World citizens, entities, states, or civilisations are all candidates. Furthermore, Simpson notes, all societies invoke some principle of exclusion, defining membership and citizenship, which is more fundamental than their equality rights (Simpson 2004, 37). In addition, the potential for tension and conflict within the set of equality rights, separate from states' rights to independence and sovereignty – between a state's right to protect citizens even when they are situated in other states; the right to recognition from foreign states; the right to respect from other states; and the right to enter into treaties – prevents the construction of agreed meanings. The problem is further compounded by instability in the meaning of 'statehood' and its definition, in circular fashion, through the conception of sovereignty (Simpson 2004, 38).

The inherent contradictions of liberal state sovereignty

The modern liberal state paradigm of sovereignty has two interrelated tensions at its core, between the individual and the state, and between the top-down impulse of the state and bottom-up demands for democratic participation. These tensions have been held in place over time by the ambiguity within liberal sovereignty over whether the counter-productive quality of the tensions or the positive benefits of the tensions are predominant. The rights of the liberal autonomous individual clash headlong with the requirement for state sovereignty to create a settled order at polity level, expressed in the way the pre-political individual drawn from Locke conflicts with the need for order (and so the constraints imposed upon the individual) identified in Hobbes's analysis. Reus-Smit notes, for instance, 'the justificatory role that human rights principles have performed in the constitution of the modern sovereign order'. He argues that the 'organising principle of sovereignty has never been a self-referential value: it has always been justified with reference to particular conceptions of legitimate statehood and rightful state action'. Over time the notion of legitimate statehood has been 'increasingly justified in terms of the state's role as guarantor of certain basic human rights and freedoms, supplanting the... principle of divine right' (Reus-Smit 2001a, 520).

Individualism is not best served by the leviathan state, and yet a less highly regulated polity may not be able to enforce individual rights so successfully. In this sense the liberal conception of the state has always been in trouble. Since Locke, and reinforced by Berlin's dichotomous formulation of liberty, there has been a contradiction between, on the one hand, the primacy of pre-political interests, together with the liberal principle of an (in a crucial sense) inviolate individualism, and on the other hand, the idea of the constraints necessarily imposed by a compulsory state. This disjunction has created, in Kratochwil's words, a 'negative community' (Kratochwil 1995, 40) at both state and international levels. The immensely powerful but only partially successful liberal state answer to this problem has been the morally-driven rule of law in the *Rechtstaat*.

When the 'normal and neutral' conception of sovereignty is identified as in fact neither normal nor neutral, but as partial towards specifically liberal values, the tension in it between democracy and absolutism can be clarified. The ambivalence of liberal theory and practice towards both democracy and human rights (both are most developed by liberal states but at the same time both are restricted – liberal practice favours representative not participatory democracy, and favours civil, legal and political rights but not a substantial acknowledgment of social and economic rights) is mirrored in its model of sovereignty. Thus 'sovereignty' in the sense of 'self-rule' is profoundly ambivalent for liberalism. Liberal sovereignty has to mean self-rule by the state, non-intervention by other states in a free market version of international relations involving states and other players. But liberal principles also require that sovereignty be or incorporate self-rule by individuals. The two may coincide, but may also conflict and when they do it is the state that wins. Liberal principles exhibit a fundamental antipathy to the state, but cannot do without it.

Thus the liberal tradition of sovereignty, even of popular sovereignty, has provided liberalism with a tension at its heart. Weiler (1996, 528) usefully outlines the role of the constitution in popular sovereignty, and Preuss (1996, 539) discusses the tension in Rousseau's and in all notions of democratic citizenship and popular sovereignty, between citizen defined as law-maker and citizen defined through representation, universal suffrage and assembly majoritarianism. There is an inherent contradiction between the requirement that any modern version of popular sovereignty must be grounded in democratic rights and claims and yet sovereignty as the identity of the whole cannot be derived from the bottom up. This tension can be expressed in terms of the derivation of principles of liberal sovereignty from Bodin and Hobbes on the one hand and from Locke on the other. A key aspect of the liberal conception of sovereignty refers to the relationship between rulers and ruled which defines the locus of legal and political authority, the exercise of political power, and the independent status of the body politic on the international stage. This relationship is a central feature sustaining the stability of a polity and its equality with other self-governing political communities. While liberal theory has taken the crucial notion of a settled order from the theories of Bodin and Hobbes, both of these theories are also associated with absolutism, the apology for the rule of absolute monarchy, and rule over a centralised system of administration. As a result there is an absolutist core at the centre of liberal theory. Some of the consequences of this situation are not unwelcome to liberal theory. For example, liberal sovereignty is a theory which minimises the meaning of citizenship. It promises citizens active involvement in (notionally pre-political) *economic* activity and in the non-political civil associations of civil society, but even now the discouragement of an active interest in (state) political life has a powerful resonance.

The absence of a theory of sovereignty (and citizenship) in the political theory of the exemplary theorist of liberalism, Locke, is no accident and is indeed part of the problem. Locke's abjuring of the term 'sovereignty' in the *Second Treatise* is unsurprising since for him it would express a dangerously collectivist idea. Locke can most plausibly be understood to have deliberately avoided the term 'sovereignty' and to have done so because he identified it with 'absolute power', which he defined in turn as 'arbitrary power'. Locke does propose a notion of 'supream power', which has some but not all the features of sovereignty. 'Supream power' antecedes government, derives (although Locke does not spell out how) from the people, and clearly has the role of legitimising (and delegitimising) 'legislative power'. However the 'supream power' implies neither a moral identity nor a common purpose of 'the people' as a whole, upon which a full theory of popular sovereignty would depend. Moreover the 'supream power' is a stringently diffused concept. It only operates under conditions supplied by an extensive phalanx of other measures, all of which are carefully designed to guarantee individual, not collective, natural rights. These include natural law, pre-political private property, the moral precedence of the definition of individuals in the state of nature over any additional definition in civil society, social contract, consent, the moral precedence of the definition of individuals in civil society over government and over the definition of individuals in political society, trust, the rule of law, limited government, separation of powers, constitutional government, and the right of resistance. While the role of majoritarianism has an uneasy place in Locke's theory, it is clear that its role is instrumental only; it does not represent an enthusiastic collectivism, and it does not take moral precedence over the phalanx of individualistic measures Locke outlines. Furthermore the functions of a sovereign are dispersed between the magistrate, the legislative and the executive. But most importantly, individuals crucially retain their full right of conscience and judgement of political matters. Thus, in sum, the term 'sovereignty' is absent from Locke's political vocabulary because in the end the categories of political society (of which sovereignty would be one) cannot override the categories of the state of nature. The fundamental order which sovereignty establishes in other political theories, is transferred unchanged in Locke from that which reigns naturally in the state of nature, in natural law. This view is developed in Prokhovnik (2008 forthcoming).

While there is a commonplace view that sovereignty is about absolute power and liberal principles are about the opposite, about the freedom and autonomy of the individual from state power, nevertheless these two have gone hand in hand. The ideas that sovereignty is about absolute power, that sovereignty cannot be reconciled with constitutionalism, that sovereignty is anathema to democratic power, stem from a logical confusion between the history of the development of absolutist states in early-modern Europe with their centralised power, and the meaning of the concept of sovereignty as being concerned with the distribution, content and limits of powers at the most general (absolute) level. Despite the logical confusion the subsequent history of state sovereignty did nothing to de-couple absolute and centralised power from the general notion of the distribution of power. This chapter is about how certain liberal principles have been crucial to the development of modern state sovereignty. Liberal sovereignty has not been about respecting plurality and celebrating difference: while these are also liberal principles they are not ones which have been prioritised. Liberal sovereignty has crucially been focused upon protecting the unity and integrity of the individual by excluding others and refusing to recognise the claims of interdependence.

The problem of the tension between individual and polity in liberal sovereignty has been compounded by the development at the same time of the state form, expressed in the conflict between the particular repressive tendencies of the state form and the development of ideas about democracy, representation and popular sovereignty. This is the tension between on the one hand (state) sovereignty as autonomy to act, independent of both external and internal undue influence, and on the other hand the demand by democratic citizens for political scrutiny and accountability. A shifting balance between the state and popular sovereignty has been an enduring feature of democratic politics. Another expression of this tension, identified by Schmitt, has been between the claim to freedom of action by (state) sovereignty and the impulse towards legalism and a (written or unwritten) constitution. Sovereignty is sanctioned by the constitution but is also in one sense prior to it.

As Deudney expresses, the notion of state sovereignty holds that sovereignty refers to 'the ultimate source of all legitimate authority in a polity' (Deudney 1996, 195). It also involves, on the basis of the Weberian definition, which is taken as paradigmatic, that the state is centralised such that it has a monopoly of (coercive) power and (legitimate) authority. Thus as conventionally understood, sovereignty is, as Onuf notes, 'an exclusive and defining property of states' (Onuf 1995, 44). According to this conventional construction, the development of modern sovereignty as abstract, absolute and indivisible, coincided with the definition of the modern state as the model of the autonomous, independent and self-determining political unit. State sovereignty also establishes a fixed order, by instituting an inflexible hierarchy within the integrity of the whole, and within which the holder(s) of sovereignty form an indivisible unity, whose rule is subject to no other. Lyons and Mastanduno underline the historical continuity in state sovereignty, 'developed as an instrument for the assertion of royal authority over feudal princes in the construction of modern [centralised and later industrialised, mass, liberal democratic] territorial states' (Lyons and Mastanduno 1995, 5).

Once the modern polity had developed into its mass-industrialised bureaucratised state form, expressed in an array of practices and institutional mechanisms for regulation and control, then the meaning of sovereignty became quite specific and highly charged. For here sovereignty functions explicitly to cohere and unify the state as a dominant and potentially repressive and inhibiting entity. There has been an explosion of policy-making as the key work of government and ruling and absorbing much of the time and energy of governments. The practice of policy-making is also crucially tied to the important symbolic as well as literal power of legislation. Announcing policy initiatives, implementing and delivering in high profile ways, and enacting legislation, all play a vital symbolic role. They reassure voters that governments are active and that democracy, the people's will in parliament, is being *seen* to be done. It also enfolds citizens into the ruling and governing process. At the same time it is not that there was a golden age of sovereignty prior to the state for sovereignty functioned before the state in part to confirm status hierarchy and reinforce social and political order. But the experience as a citizen of coming up against the sovereignty of the modern state is formidable, and jars with the rhetoric of living in a liberal democracy. However, state sovereignty and liberal democracy are closely implicated in each other, since liberal democracy is made possible by the ordering provided by state sovereignty, and the control exercised by the state is legitimised by the liberal democratic process.

As Onuf notes, the liberal sovereign state is also a 'regime of laws', 'composed of individuals who have assigned agency to the state for a broad range of activities, including dealings with other states' (Onuf 1995, 44). Onuf's formulation, that states 'have rules reassigning responsibility for particular activities to agents collectively known as governments', highlights the tension between absolutism and legitimacy in state sovereignty. Within a 'state's territorial limits, governments monopolise agency for assigned activities. Beyond those limits, other governments enjoy similar monopolies' (Onuf 1995, 44). Kratochwil underlines this point, noting that, according to the notion of state sovereignty, 'the "rights" to sovereign dominion – territorial integrity, autonomy, and non-interference – belong to the state qua participant in the international sovereignty game, rather than to the people who have delegated specific powers to the government' (Kratochwil 1995, 34). Onuf reinforces the same point, arguing that the idea of state sovereignty 'links a bounded territory to the people taken as a whole, but does not link the people directly to each other. Instead, the land and the people are each linked to those agents empowered to act at home and abroad in the name of the state' (Onuf 1995, 49).

The application of the critique of liberalism to the debate on sovereignty also shows that the paradigm of state sovereignty, drawn from the dominant liberal tradition and developed from the theories of Bodin, Hobbes, and Locke has excluded serious consideration of other conceptions. For example, the theories of sovereignty advanced by Rousseau and Hegel, according to which more active senses of citizenship and richer ideas of common good are entailed by sovereignty, have been sidelined. Hegel's idea of the primacy not of states but of history has been recessive, whereas the historical perspective helps provide judgement and a wider vista on the actions of states. Spinoza's conception of sovereignty, in which republican citizenship supports a balanced but dynamic tension between provinces (or even towns) sharing sovereignty, has been marginalised. In terms simply of intellectual strengths and weaknesses, the conceptions of sovereignty of Rousseau, Hegel and Spinoza are just as plausible as those of Bodin, Hobbes, and Locke. These ideas are developed in Prokhovnik (2008 forthcoming).

The inherent tensions within liberal state sovereignty have produced paradoxes, lacunae, and anomalies in the conventional paradigm. The first example refers to the way in which, since Locke there has been an issue about the division and sharing in sovereignty between the lawgiving person/assembly and the constituent power of the people, but this issue has recently been given added force. For the mainstream political theory discourse this question has been identified as the mechanism through which either the dormant constituent power of the people can be invoked if the legitimacy of government is seen to be broken, or the active democratic power of the people is exercised. This division and sharing of sovereignty was regarded within the international relations discourse as a purely internal matter, so long as it did not challenge the idea that it is the government that matters – those authorised to do business on behalf of the state. However, with the growth of transnational political groups such as anti-globalisation protesters, human rights groups and ecological issues protesters, this 'purely' internal matter does start to impinge on the meaning of 'external' sovereignty. Such protesters claim to act in the name of the constituent power of the people, thereby bypassing their national governments. Even if the claim cannot be endorsed (and what would be the means whereby it would?), such groups do have an impact on international politics. However, the 'constituent power of the people' is a modern western liberal idea imposed and falsely universalised onto other cultures. But this doesn't amount to 'global politics'.

The second example relates to the *de facto/de jure* distinction, familiar within the conventional discussion of state sovereignty. Fowler and Bunck

(1996) provide a detailed illustration elucidating the problems associated with the *de jure/de facto* distinction. In terms of the orthodox conception of sovereignty this distinction is, strictly speaking, incoherent, because sovereignty by definition must comprise both independence (formal legal status) and autonomy (the actual capacity to act). Indeed there is a disjunction more broadly between the theory of the necessarily absolute quality of state sovereignty (a supreme power to legislate and act) and the established practice of accounting for anomalies by the conceptually unsustainable *de jure/de facto* distinction. Elshtain is representative of writers led to criticise this disjunction as 'the (phony) parity in the notion of *equally* "sovereign states"' (Elshtain 1987). Nevertheless in practice the distinction between *de jure* and *de facto* sovereignty remains an important and useful one within the state paradigm, for instance in international relations to 'explain' the patently *un*equal capacities of different 'sovereign' states to act and to maintain authority and power.

Thirdly and relatedly, while it is a criterion of sovereignty that it be susceptible to no higher authority, in practice no sovereign dominion has ever been immune from outside or internal influence to a greater or lesser extent. James's attempt (James 1986) to invalidate the use of the term on this ground does not succeed, since the utility of sovereignty in the state model depends upon a belief which is not dislodged merely by a piece of empirical evidence to the contrary. A point made by Kratochwil reinforces the refutation of James: '[i]f domestically sovereignty never meant supreme "power" but rather meant the quality of a claim to authority that could "bind" all subjects', then it can be argued that 'internationally sovereignty cannot be equated simply to power wielded by a self-interested (rational) actor', since it is important that 'part and parcel of playing the international game consists in recognising the sovereignty of others'. Kratochwil concludes that '[c]laims to sovereignty are therefore inherently limited, and differ in important respects from imperial claims to authority, or from simple "rational", or maximising, behaviour' (Kratochwil 1995, 25). Kratochwil's convincing argument that the notion of 'sovereign autonomy' need not mean freedom from social pressures, but rather the validity of *acting* in the light of them, is also important to a reconceptualised sovereignty.

The soundness of the second and third anomalies is supported by earlier critics. Bartelson testifies to the value of pluralist critics of the state in the early twentieth century such as Hobhouse and Laski, who can be acknowledged as precursors of contemporary perceptions of a mismatch between the theory and practice of the state and sovereignty. These early pluralist critics argued that developments which dissolved the sociocultural unity of the state (the intensified polarisation between labour and capital that made a mockery of the state as the focus of the interests, loyalties and allegiances of citizen subjects) also threw into question the idea of indivisible sovereignty, one of the defining features of the state and a necessary condition of state unity. Pluralist critics maintained that authority 'was no longer indivisible, but ought to be understood as profoundly and irreversibly divided between groups and institutions in society'. They also contended that 'democratisation and the enlarged franchise had effectively bridled' claims of state authority to be comprehensive and unlimited, for authority was 'no longer centralised and absolute, but ought to be understood as diluted and dispersed in the social body' (Bartelson 2001, 90). Bartelson identifies that what was new in such pluralist critiques was 'the idea that this problem was a matter of social organisation rather than a matter of constitutional checks and balances' (Bartelson 2001, 94), that sovereignty could be discussed in principally social and political terms rather than first of all in legal terms. Bartelson notes that Laski outlined the idea of the pluralist state 'as a society composed of self-sufficient groups, and in which sovereignty is partitioned on the basis of function' (Bartelson 2001, 105), but that Laski remained ambivalent about the unifying role of the state.

Military intervention, that is, cross-border coercive action, is a fourth intractable problem for the conventional liberal sovereignty form. Over the past couple of decades unilateral intervention has become more difficult to rationalise and the justification for intervention is now more commonly made in the name of, and presupposing the meaningfulness of, an 'international community'. The liberal conception of sovereignty contains a predicament here. On the one hand it cannot allow intervention, for sovereignty 'entails the right of states to be free from interference' (Onuf 1995, 49), but on the other hand intervention is the very *proof* of sovereign statehood. To act upon reflective choice, to intervene as the result of deliberation, is the exercise of the legitimate political authority bestowed by and constituting sovereign autonomy and freedom. In this way state sovereignty established both the prohibition against intervention and the grounds for intervention. So while Kratochwil notes that 'intervention raises issues of justification, given that sovereignty provides a powerful prohibition' (Kratochwil 1995, 33), at the same time the model of state sovereignty provided the conditions for aggressive intervention, encouraging states to act as competitive atomistic individuals with obligations to minimal rules of the game that could be easily ignored or overridden. What has changed is that such rules are now less readily ignored. Human rights, environmental issues and the idea of 'international justice' all constitute similar intractable problems for this kind of liberal international perspective. Hutchings's observation that it is 'the sovereign individual who is capable of undertaking contractual relations which are constitutive of both morality and civil and political rights' and freedom, applies as much to liberal state sovereignty as to liberal social contract theory (Hutchings 1996, 15, 17).

The final lacunae of the liberal model of sovereignty to be considered here concerns globalisation. The idea of globalisation can be seen indeed as the outcome of the absurdity of taking to their limit the liberal principles of abstract autonomy, rationality, individualism and economic competition in civil society. Theories of globalisation have sought to argue, or even simply now to take as an article of faith, that the alleged disintegration or breakdown of the modern nation state challenges the orthodox conceptions of both the internal and external dimensions of sovereignty. How can claims to state sovereignty be sustained, theorists of globalisation ask rhetorically, given the creation of new forms of social reality and social relations, and given the European Union's increasing derogation of the legislative, administrative and judicial powers of member states, when it has been taken as axiomatic that it is a criterion of sovereignty that there be no power higher to make law? And how can we continue to claim sovereignty if the territorial borders of states are overridden by and no longer relevant to the global economy? (See Held *et al* 1999, Held 2004, Giddens 1990, Wallerstein 1983, Robertson 1990). Some British commentators pessimistic about British sovereignty in relation to Europe echo these questions that follow from continued adherence to the liberal definition of sovereignty.

Hirst and Thompson's powerful argument still holds that globalisation is a myth (Hirst and Thompson 1996, 5) and that we still live in a world characterised rather by 'inter-nationalism' (Hirst and Thompson 1996, 8). They make a convincing case that the claims for a strong, economic version of globalisation, let alone a soft cultural and political version have been exaggerated. Crucially, they contend, world markets are neither ungovernable, nor have they been replaced by proper systemic interdependence, because there are very few transnational companies which are not nationally based, and there is very little genuinely footloose capital. (Hirst and Thompson 1996, 2). Hirst and Thompson conclude that states play, and will continue to play a role in world politics as well as in respect of their own populations, which cannot be played by any other actor on the domestic or international political stage. That role is about governance, particularly of 'inter-national' markets. The role involves the distribution and delegation of governance to levels above and below the state itself, and it involves states providing legitimacy and sanction for, and ensuring the accountability of supra-national and sub-national governance mechanisms (Hirst and Thompson 1996, 190).

Shaw provides support for this case when he argues convincingly that states 'remain central actors in world politics, but their interactions are surrounded and complemented by the ever more important interventions of transnational and subnational actors' (Shaw 1991, 16; 1994). It is also the case that globalisation appears so disastrous and decisively destructive for sovereignty because if the liberal autonomy and self-rule of the sovereign state is breached, then there seems no alternative in the liberal scheme to complete disintegration. But this appearance applies only to a liberal definition of sovereignty, and not to sovereignty as reconceptualised here.

Reconceptualising sovereignty – acknowledging constructedness

We have grown up with the view that the liberal state conception of sovereignty is normal, neutral and right, true and correct, 'inevitable and universal' (Deudney 1996, 190). In doing this we have confused conception with concept. Having identified the distinctively liberal character of the inherited paradigm of sovereignty, it may be possible to develop a different conception without having to abandon the concept. The reconceptualisation of sovereignty in the previous chapter, 'from the outside in', proposed a notion of 'post-states' and other actors in a refigured international realm of 'international political space'. The reconceptualisation here develops 'from the inside out', from the critique of the liberal and state character of the modern sovereignty form.

Rob Walker develops a strongly principled critique of traditional state sovereignty from which some very important positive pointers for a reconceptualised notion of sovereignty can be identified. Walker examines the way in which state sovereignty is a barrier concept and proposes that it should be repealed. As we have seen he argues that the barrier concept results in a discriminatory internal/external dualism, because the view of culture which is promoted, 'read through the principle of state sovereignty', is extremely divisive (Walker 1993, 180). Hutchings is pointing to the same problem at the level of the individual when she points to the value of Pateman's *Sexual Contract* in its exposure of 'the inseparability of freedom and subordination in the construction and effects of the sovereign individual' (Hutchings 1996, 21). For Walker the idea of community understood within state sovereignty, refers to 'the geometry of territorial exclusions' and can only foster 'a relativity of values and a clash of different ways of life' (Walker 1993, 180–1). Walker's central vision is to explore the problematic character of the internal/external dualism. It follows, he contends, that the traditional conception of sovereignty, based on 'supposedly autonomous states in an unregulated contest of wills' in a supposedly apolitical and mechanistic neutral system, sets up patterns of inclusion and exclusion. These patterns define personal as well as political identity, and also define a fixed view of the range of alternatives open to us. The patterns of inclusion and exclusion have constrained and limited theoretical discussion about identity both in political theory and in international relations theory. The urgency of the need to repeal the barrier conception of sovereignty derives from the incompatibility of national exclusionist cultures with a growing trend of participation in wider social, cultural and political processes (Walker 1993, 181. See also Scanlan and Kent 1988).

What emerges strongly from the critique of liberal state sovereignty are the lessons of the resilience of politics to adapt to new situations, the constructedness of the liberal paradigm, the plausibility of the application of the communitarian critique to the modern state form, the resilience of subjectivity, the possibility of intermediate positions between the hard-shelled state and fragmentation, the resilience of state functions, the potential for greater acknowledgment of the 'unbundling' of state sovereignty functions, and the interconnections between 'internal' and 'external' processes. The outcome of these lessons is the recognition that the internal and external dimensions of sovereignty can be parts of a single discourse, in which sovereignty is no longer dominated by the underlying metaphor of barrier.

Thus, instead of the political order defined, in Deudney's words, by 'hierarchy inside and anarchy outside' (Deudney 1996, 190), a reconceptualised sovereignty can describe an orderly set of possible connections in which post-states are the focus of identities rather than a definer of a single overarching identity itself. Deudney also identifies a fallacy maintained by those writers who hold that sovereignty must mean state sovereignty. They tend, he notes, 'to leap from the definitional impossibility of divided sovereignty to the mistake of thinking [that] a system of multiple authorities that are not hierarchically arranged is impossible or inconsistent with sovereignty' (Deudney 1996, 196).

Until recently the traditional paradigm of sovereignty has been regarded as both natural and neutral, simply describing the 'real' world. We have already seen in the previous chapter that the constructionist approach successfully challenges this view, demonstrating that, historically and in practice, conceptions are constituted by particular societies and cultures (Biersteker and Weber 1996, Walker 1993, Bartelson 1995, Onuf 1995), and in the Introduction that a concept may remain meaningful even though conceptions change over time (Connolly 1993, Ball 1988, Taylor 1992). We have also noted that the abstract and universalised quality of the modern sovereignty model is itself partly responsible for encouraging the conclusion that current changes taking place in political relations must herald a profoundly serious crisis and that sovereignty is in fact at a dead end.

Sovereignty in the form of modern state sovereignty has been a liberal form of political order, emphasising the autonomy of the individual. But the idea of the polity need no more disappear under the critique of sovereignty than does the self under the communitarian critique of liberalism. We can construct a relational and constituted, but still viable, conception of sovereignty, modifying the analogy between the self and the state to take account of interdependence and interconnection. One way of developing the theme of this chapter would be through the recognition that liberalism developed a theory of sovereignty from Hobbes (for whom the state and sovereignty are mutually self-defining), rather than from Locke (for whom there is – grudgingly – a state but no positive theory of sovereignty), but that a reconceptualised sovereignty could draw upon Spinoza (for whom there is a notion of sovereignty but no centralised state).

Onuf argues cogently that state sovereignty was formed from the 'bundling' of three elements, when the functions of majesty (inspiring respect), power (competence to rule, an exclusive but provisional grant of agency) and stewardship (acting on behalf of others, for the common good) became fused, and codified in regimes of laws (Onuf 1995, 48–9). He identifies ways in which these state functions have in the contemporary world come to be challenged and contested, in particular when alternative claims to majesty have developed, for instance from nationalist movements on the grounds that the nation rather than the state defines the self-governing unit. With the diffusion of majesty, and in consequence of functional growth, governments tend to lose their monopoly on agency and competence to rule, as well as their legitimacy to represent the common good (Onuf 1995, 52).

Biersteker and Weber's analysis of the social construction of sovereignty is important, comprehending recognition as a vital component along with territory, population and authority (Biersteker and Weber 1996, 3). Onuf underlines the importance of the argument that the 'co-constitution of individuals *and* societies has no beginning or end', because 'neither can be said to exist without the other'. He also argues that '[f]rom the point of view of any given individual, society is already there; from the point of view of society, at least as imagined by social contract theorists, individuals must come first' (Onuf 1995, 45).

In the light of the insights drawn from the constructionist approach to sovereignty, the traditional view that equates sovereignty with state sovereignty can be recognised as a functional fiction. Biersteker and Weber identify the way in which the notion of state sovereignty contains a tauto-logical relationship rather than a theoretically-illuminating explanation, in that 'states can be defined in terms of their claims to sovereignty, while sovereignty can be defined in terms of the interactions and practices of states' (Biersteker and Weber 1996, 11). It follows that, when state sovereignty is seen to rest upon a tautology, the future of the concept of sovereignty is freed from its thrall to the specific state form found in the modern period.

The social construction of sovereignty is also accented by Reus-Smit to great effect. He points to the 'highly categorical terms' in which sover-eignty has been traditionally understood as final, absolute, inviolable state power which 'cannot be qualified without nullification'. States are thought to have 'supreme decision-making authority within their territorial bound-aries, while being under no political or legal obligation to observe any overarching authority outside those boundaries' (Reus-Smit 2001a, 521). Reus-Smit also rehearses the familiar contrast between realists who 'treat sovereignty as an empirical attribute of the state' and the English School for whom sovereignty is 'an institution of international society, a deeply embedded organising principle that licenses the organisation of political authority into centralised, territorially demarcated political units'. Realists emphasise 'the role of war-fighting and military competition in the rise of the modern international system', while the English School 'stress the emergence of norms of mutual recognition, non-intervention, and self-determination' (Reus-Smit 2001a, 521). Reus-Smit also makes the significant point that sovereignty is not the primary bedrock international institution after all. 'Contrary to conventional wisdom', he argues, sovereignty is a 'dependent or secondary principle', a 'historically contingent prescription about the distribution of power and authority that needs to be grounded in more fundamental' historically-specific social values. Reus-Smit concludes that even constructivists have overlooked this aspect of the constructedness of sovereignty, still taking it as a basic principle, 'often writing as though sovereignty were a self-referential value that could be upheld without reference to other social values' (Reus-Smit 2001a, 528).

Bartelson underlines the extent to which 'this construct – the sovereign state – has been rendered a natural kind'. He argues persuasively that reimagining political community and international relations involves more than showing that 'the state is the outcome of undue reification'. Revealing the depth of the naturalisation also includes providing an 'account of how such an interpretation has become constitutive of political reality'. It becomes clear that the key to that construct is the timeless internal/ external distinction, 'stuck in ontological interdependence', it poses. It is 'the categorical distinction between the domestic and the international that conditions the possibility of statehood' and, moreover, it is this that 'makes modern politics modern' (Bartelson 2001, 161).

Bartelson describes two versions of this argument. For Ashley, 'the constitutive divide between the domestic and the international' is reproduced in the present, 'drawn and sustained by the discursive practices of realist power politics, and the sovereign state is situated in the narrow discursive space between these spheres'. According to this view, the depth of the 'reification of the sovereign state is ultimately based on a concealment of its constructed' character and a denial of 'the contingency of the boundaries' of the state. In this way the realist mode 'differentiates the international field of practice from the domestic one and places them in ethical opposition to each other', creates two separate kinds of political space, and 'represents the outcome of its activity as existing independently of human knowledge and practice', with the state as a 'given, both as an acting subject and as an object of investigation' (Bartelson 2001, 163).

In the second version, Bartelson relates, Rob Walker holds that 'the constitution of the state takes place through the sequential unfolding of the same conceptual oppositions', of reconciling universality and particularity, centralisation and fragmentation, and through the state's claims to universality made in a particular historical context, 'throughout the gradual emergence of international relations discourse' (Bartelson 2001, 162). For Walker, 'the most important expression of the limit of political imagination is the principle of state sovereignty' (Bartelson 2001, 164). The realist mode appears as a kind of carpenter's vice, delimiting possibilities for change and difference in the system. Even though the international is posited as anarchy with no overarching common values or institutions, it is a space in which 'pluralism itself is universalised' (Bartelson 2001, 165), constraining other potentialities. In addition, the domestic community is envisaged as a place in which ethical progress can be realised, while the basic structure of the international sphere (that is, interstate relations) is posed as a realm of 'recurrence, moral stagnation and profound immutability' (Bartelson 2001, 166).

Bartelson argues that, while Ashley and Walker successfully denaturalise the state, in both versions the political imagination remains 'imprisoned' within the state sovereignty settlement (Bartelson 2001, 167). However, he says, this does not demonstrate the necessity of the state within all politics, but rather shows only the limits of the deconstructive method. According to Bartelson, Ashley and Walker's perspective crucially precludes them from being able to dissolve 'the state as conventionally conceptualised within domestic political theory' (Bartelson 2001, 168). For these writers, says Bartelson, the state concept corresponds to what 'ideas of empire were to the Renaissance: a fiction which has not yet entirely lost its power to generate reality, or a reality not yet fully turned into fiction; a truth which remains seen as a lie' (Bartelson 2001, 168). On the positive side, such writers do signal the important point that the state 'is but one possible constellation of authority in the historical evolution of technologies of power' (Bartelson 2001, 169). Bartelson comes to the view that the state is nothing other than one possible mode of governing, with its own rationality (including that its principles should not be derived from any other, human or divine, source) and of distinguishing the realm of political power from other forms of power.

Bartelson analyses the realist internal/external settlement of the state and its sovereignty, and the way internal/external operates for it in a positive manner rather than as a tension. He observes that 'the conceptual identity of the state is conditioned by the largely implicit assumption that the political order represented by the state is distinct from the kind of relations that exist between states in an international context'. He notes that it is precisely this differentiation that 'affirms the state as a source of authority and community among a multitude of similar units, and construes the state and the international context in which it finds itself as mutually constitutive yet opposed spheres of politics'. Bartelson convincingly draws attention to the way the concept of sovereignty lies at 'the heart of this distinction between inside and outside', and captures the way that rather than 'simply being an attribute of individual states or a rule constitutive of the international sphere, sovereignty is what separates these spheres while simultaneously binding them together' (Bartelson 2001, 12).

Onuf and Inayatullah and Blaney underline the constructedness of territoriality in the modern state paradigm of sovereignty, in the form of the idea about the ability of a state to exercise effective authority over a people within a given territory. While Onuf agrees with the theorists of globalisation that boundaries are becoming increasingly nominal (Onuf 1995, 53) it is clear that what is important in sovereignty is not territoriality as such, but the significance that is placed on it. Inayatullah and Blaney (1995, 17–20) also make useful proposals for reconceptualisations of the role of boundaries and of the role of states. They suggest that 'some of the problems attributed to sovereignty may be better seen as a failure to realise sovereignty'. They contend that 'realising sovereignty necessitates, not the rejection of boundaries, but reconsidering the uses to which they are put'. In particular, they argue, 'realising sovereignty entails a state's "right" to a portion of global wealth'. The effects of implementing 'such a "right to wealth" would weaken the property rights associated with the "hard shell" of the state, but would simultaneously strengthen the state's claims as a cultural arena and agent, increasing its security as a "unit of meaning"' (Inayatullah and Blaney 1995, 4). The question of territoriality highlights the socially-constructed origin of conceptions like sovereignty. The conventional conception of external sovereignty raised an empirical condition (the territoriality of states) to the status of primary epistemological significance, in order to mark in concrete form (although the exact empirical position of the line is often ultimately arbitrary) the barrier between inclusion and exclusion. A redefined notion of sovereignty does not have to have as its aim the instantiation of a single identity defined by inclusion and exclusion and so no longer emphasises sovereignty as state sovereignty in terms of the territoriality of the state. Speciality remains a condition of, but is no longer the defining feature of political life on the world stage, because the autonomy of post-states can now be seen to involve multiple ties of relation and connection, and need no longer be expressed and signified in a material barrier or horizon.

The critique of liberalism which has been made from a broadly communitarian perspective from Marx (1975) to social democrats (Miller 1989) to liberal communitarians (Sandel 1982, MacIntyre 1981, Taylor 1990, Frazer and Lacey 1993), contains important central criticisms of key tenets of the liberal state sovereignty model, highlighting their constructedness. Particularly forceful are the communitarian critiques of the antecedently individuated self, asocial individualism, and the metaphysical conception of the person. According to this critique individuals are not unencumbered, with their identity established prior to the social context, but develop within its practices and language, values and principles, and within the good of political community. It is in this context that individuals are partially constructed and themselves construct exercise agency. The cogency of these criticisms has not been fully absorbed by liberals and their persuasive force can be gauged by Rawls's attempt to reformulate his liberal political theory in order to accommodate his communitarian critics (Rawls 1993a). In broad terms the communitarian critique of liberalism focuses on the criticism of atomistic methodological individualism. Individuals do not exist prior to social context, but develop within it its practices and language, values and principles. Individuals both construct and are partially constructed by these factors.

The broadly communitarian perspective also encompasses feminists who have developed a convincing criticism of the western, liberal, rational, abstract basis of the notions of autonomy and independence that follow from the liberal view of the individual, on the grounds that the concrete lives and subjectivity of people are constituted also by complex ties of connection and relation (Gilligan 1993, Tronto 1993, *Symposium* 1995, Frazer 1997, Lloyd 1989, Tapper 1986, Benhabib 1987). There is now the basis for recognising that persons are both interdependent, partially-socially-constructed and involved in ties and connections of reciprocity and care, and beings who choose to acknowledge in each other an idea of autonomy under abstract, universalist rules of justice which are set apart from us as particular individuals. The meaning of the autonomy and independence of individuals has been reassessed in the light of recurrent communitarian concerns. Feminism in particular offers a means by which this can be successfully achieved without the notion of the individual being absorbed by a notion of community. Likewise the meaning of the autonomy and independence of states can be redefined without being abandoned. Contemporary defenders of state sovereignty presuppose that threats to the traditional state, and the development of new political forms that affect the context in which states operate, inevitably leads to the erosion of sovereignty. But this presupposition does not follow from the logic of concepts, as evidenced by the proposal developed here for post-states and other actors in international political space.

Another point that follows from the critique of liberalism pertinent here concerns the resilience of subjectivity. It reinforces the view that a viable conception of sovereignty can be theorised as relational and constructed. Against handwringing about the imminent or already-happened collapse of the state, it is important to note that the state need no more disappear under the critique of contemporary sovereignty than does the self under the broadly communitarian critique of liberalism. Mouffe's observation that 'multiplicity and fragmentation' is not the only alternative to 'the notion of a unified and homogeneous subject' (Mouffe 1992, 10–1) applies equally to the subjectivity of the person and the integrity of the state (though this does not necessarily endorse the conclusions which Mouffe derives from this statement).

A reconceptualised sovereignty beyond the state form can also recognise that intermediate positions can be elucidated between a conception of a single unity and one of a fragmentation or dissolution, the 'other' of the state sovereignty conception. This is what Pierson means by the 'integrity of statehood' (Pierson 1996, 49), while still acknowledging that sovereignty is the recognition that a fundamental non-personalized political *order* exists. Pierson makes a strong case that to pronounce upon 'state decline' is to '(over)generalize from particular areas of the state's activity in which change has been most striking' and to underestimate '*new* functions of the state (for instance in the *regulation* of privatized industries or the *juridification* of industrial relations)' (Pierson 1996, 193). He argues that the contemporary state 'is not a single unified actor, but rather an ensemble of forces...state activity may be relocated away from the level of the nation-state without our assuming that "state-effectivity" has been correspondingly weakened' (Pierson 1996, 194). He goes on to detail the way that '[s]tates still redistribute income and opportunities on a massive scale' (Pierson 1996, 203). He also observes with some force that the 'prospect of Identity Cards being introduced for the first time in peacetime UK hardly betokens a state that is "withering away"' (Pierson 1996, 204). Werner and De Wilde also make the sound point that 'increasing international inter-dependencies, the growing power of international organisations and the globalisation of the economy has not led to a renunciation of the idea of the sovereignty of states'. On the contrary, they note, 'threats to the state's autonomy and ability to rule have reinforced the claims to sovereignty rather than weakened them' (Werner and De Wilde 2001, 284).

The idea of the 'bundling' and 'unbundling' of sovereignty functions follows from recognition of the constructedness of liberal sovereignty and points to the framing of a relational conception of sovereignty in terms of post-states and other actors in international political space. Onuf, Kratochwil, Philpott, Neil Walker, Sørensen and others all explore this idea. The 'unbundling' of sovereignty is an important part of the pluralism of the post-state proposal outlined in the previous chapter. While some of these writers interpret sovereignty only narrowly within the state paradigm, the principle of unbundling the elements of sovereignty is clear and instructive for further and more radical reconceptualisation.

Modern liberal political principles, the modern realist tradition of IR, and the dominance of modern legal discourse, all work together. For instance, it is the legal definition of sovereignty, the definition used by lawyers in domestic and in international law, which has through the canon and its *Rechtstaat* emphasis overshadowed the political dimension and condition of sovereignty, that presents the theoretical obstacle to expressing more forcefully the notion of the disaggregation or 'unbundling' of the elements of sovereignty. The notion of legal jurisdiction has come to be coterminous with territory, with independence and self-government, with autonomy and competence. The idea of exclusive legal jurisdiction (wholly competent within and bounded by clear borders) assumes a neat and tidy state form and a set of differentiated states. The dominance of this modern legal discourse in relation to sovereignty, its apparent neutrality, and the trumping of law over politics in consequence, has also been one of the factors acting to depoliticise sovereignty.

Onuf's description of the 'bundling' or fusion of sovereign functions that took place with the development of the modern state is mirrored in 'unbundling' proposals of state functions (which resonate with the 'unbundling' of states' sovereignty functions in the international realm, discussed in the previous chapter). Onuf articulates the view that, while the functions of sovereignty (majesty, agency and stewardship) have been partially hijacked away from the state, nevertheless governments have resources for protecting their monopoly of agency, 'resources...that far exceed the resources of their private rivals. Not the least are their normative resources – the capacity to make and use rules to advantage' (Onuf 1995, 57). Onuf maintains that states are still vitally necessary in the exercise of sovereignty, because they still provide the crucial link between people and their land (Onuf 1995, 58). Indeed the reconceptualisation of sovereignty can usefully draw upon Onuf's definition of state sovereignty cited earlier, once the monopoly of agency by governments for assigned activities is seen to include the agency to assign the delivery of those activities to others.

Kratochwil's suggestion for the 'unbundling of sovereign rights' (Kratochwil 1995, 28) on the model of sovereignty as a corporation is also an important contribution to a reconceptualised sovereignty. Krasner makes a similar claim for the 'uncoupling' or 'unbundling' of domestic sovereignty (public authority and its effective control), interdependence sovereignty (control over transborder flows), international legal sovereignty (mutual recognition), and Westphalian sovereignty (no higher or external authority) (Krasner 2001, 6). Bader (1995, 212) also discusses the need to conceptualise sovereignty as a 'bundle' of powers that can be divided, limited, delegated. Kratochwil suggests that the notion of 'ownership' involves a set of functions – to control, to manage, and to derive benefits from – that can be separated without sovereignty becoming dissolved. According to a model of corporate ownership, he argues, 'the right to control is divorced from the right to manage, and from the right to receive an income from the activities of the firm'. However, he notes, 'since these rights are vested in different persons, it is difficult to locate the "owner"' (Kratochwil 1995, 28). Kratochwil discusses an important example of what a reconceptualised sovereignty might mean in practice, in the process of European integration. He argues that the process 'would be comparable to control of and access to intangible assets rather than a process in which sovereignty 'moves' from national to supranational loci of "power"'. This line of thinking is important in reconceptualising a more flexible notion of sovereignty, because, understood in this way, assets such as sovereignty 'denote legal relations that regulate a person's access to and control of resources without making him or her the owner (sovereign) in the sense of the Roman conception of dominium' (Kratochwil 1995, 28). We return to this example and the question of unbundling sovereignty in Chapter 5.

Philpott (1999) identifies three 'faces of authority' which he perceives as already present in the orthodox Westphalian international relations under-standing of sovereignty, which constitute a form of unbundling. The first refers to characteristic and settled ideas based on mutual recognition about what count as legitimate polities. In other words, states as polities having autonomy *vis-à-vis* other polities, and having supreme authority within a territory. The second face consists of membership criteria to the society of states. Philpott has in mind here criteria such as granting member-ship, diplomatic immunity, commitments, restraint, capacity to maintain a viable government and to enter into treaties. The third face comprises the rules establishing prerogatives for actions by equal sovereign states by virtue of their membership, for example the principle of non-intervention, sending diplomats and entering treaties, and the obligation not to invade.

Neil Walker provides a measure of 'unbundling' in the course of his strong argument opposing the realist 'mirror-image' view of internal and external sovereignty. He makes the case that the locations of internal and external sovereignty need not necessarily coincide at all. He argues that the 'source and agency(ies) of ultimate legal authority within the state are quite distinct from the source and agency(ies) of the ultimate legal authority of the state'. The way in which the executive branch of govern-ment is usually the location for external sovereignty 'implies nothing about the location of authority for the purposes of internal sovereignty', he contends, and we can see this more clearly in the American checks-and-balances system than in the UK fused and centralised political order. Moreover, the capacity to exercise external sovereignty 'means no more than that the independence of the state and its capacity to participate in international decision-making is unchallenged'. It does 'not also imply ulti-mate authority over the content and operation of the relevant legal order' as with internal sovereignty, since the 'international legal order is a product of negotiation between formally equal states' (Walker 1998, 359).

Sørensen (1999) unbundles sovereignty in terms of 'constitutive rules of sovereignty', 'regulatory rules of sovereignty' and 'substantial empirical statehood'. The first are foundational, constructing the very possibility of some activities, such as that only a certain type of player counts. Examples include the constitutional independence of states with territory, people and government; states within a society of dialogue and consent and not merely a system of interaction; states and not transnational corporations, churches or football clubs. Sovereignty as the legitimate foundation of state authority is contrasted with its dynamic secondary, regulative rules. Sørensen sees a strong continuity in the constitutive rules of sovereignty, but regards regulative rules (such as the expansion of the rules of admission beyond a European game, and a denser regulation of relations between states over areas such as intervention practices, international law and human rights) as having changed over time.

In a sense the 'unbundling' characteristic of this new formulation of relational sovereignty, overcoming the barrier concept, can be seen as simply accenting a feature of sovereignty that can be found in Bodin and Hobbes. As Harding observes, what 'Bodin's sovereign does, and alone has the power to do, is allocate status to those within the compass of the state's authority' (Harding 1994, 69–70). Likewise, Hobbes's sovereign is, fundamentally, the source of political authority. It can plausibly be argued that the delegation of governance is not incompatible with his theory. According to Hobbes in Chapter 23 of *Leviathan* the delegation of governance powers but not of authority is stipulated, for instance through the wide-ranging category of Publique Ministers.

As well as disclosing the constructedness of the liberal sovereignty model and outlining proposals for unbundling, this reconceptualised sovereignty also emphasises relational processes across the internal/external divide. Hirst and Thompson make an important contribution in recognising that a contemporary theory of sovereignty needs to take more account than has previously been done of the greater interconnectedness of internal and external issues and processes. They argue that the days are over when sovereignty could be represented as a state monopoly of power and authority, and that sovereignty now needs to be envisaged as shared and dispersed, though this function can only be sanctioned by the state (Hirst and Thompson 1996, 190). Thus Hirst and Thompson's view is of a plausible form of sovereignty which, while still hinging on the state, recognises that the role of the state is now in making choices, legitimating and sanctioning practices above and below the nation-state, rather than in necessarily always governing directly from the centre.

A reconceptualised sovereignty recognises that the function and value of politics can neither be reduced to nor eliminated by computer-run global markets, because questions of who profits from markets and who loses, who regulates them (for regulation is always necessary), the social relations of power that are expressed through them, and contestation over these results, remain as political questions with political answers. The polity and the conceptualisation of sovereignty are likewise resilient and adaptable. The alternative conception of sovereignty that this chapter seeks to contribute to, does not deny that changes in and between states are occurring. But, on the basis of arguments concerning the 'naturalisation' of the traditional view and about the role of recognition in the concept of sovereignty, a case is made here for a different assessment of the significance of the changes. Instead of holding that sovereignty has been lost or become impoverished, the view of sovereignty in the contemporary world put forward here is a positive one.

Conclusion

This chapter has examined tensions within liberal state sovereignty that have helped to render this model unworkable. One way of expressing the tensions is to note the paradox involved in linking a Hobbesian-derived notion of the state's sovereignty modelled on individual negative liberty over individual political subjects, with a Lockean notion of pre-political individual rights against the state.

The reconceptualised sovereignty proposed here is, in important respects, neither illiberal nor non-statist, but now recognises a relational and constructed polity in both its (intersecting) internal and external dimensions, and accepts a diversity of state forms. This reconceptualisation still also in important respects trades on an analogy between individual and state, but now the correspondence is between embedded, embodied and inter-subjective personhood and a polity characterised by some communitarian and republican values.

On the question of whether the link understood here between the state and sovereignty is conceptual or historical there is a plausible sense in which it is both. It is clear on the one hand that the conceptual link derives from Hobbes's reciprocal definitions of the terms, and that a link remains (although not the exclusive one Hobbes envisaged) if the stretching of both concepts, undertaken here, is accepted. On the other hand, the characters of the two terms and of the link between them are all also necessarily subject to the principles of historical explanation, and so the terms and the nature of the link do certainly change over time and are contingent. The significance of this question, and the force of this chapter, lies in the need to argue that, contrary to Hobbes's paradigmatic definitions of the state and sovereignty, the link between the terms can survive a radical reconceptualisation in terms of post-states as the focus of multiple identities and sovereignty as shared.

Moreover, recognising with Foucault the inadequacy of the transcendent, normative Enlightenment mode of theorising found for instance in Habermas, which seeks to elide difference in favour of some fundamental sameness that is an end in itself and then spawns myths, we do not have to fall into Foucault's view that strategic responses are all that is left, combined with the necessity of subjecting any new myth to resistance, in the context of a permanent ongoing war against incorporation. The idea of relational sovereignty is open because it does not say what the relation has to be and because it does not reify relationality into a new transcendent category.

This reconceptualised sovereignty remains liberal since, as Halley remarks, liberalism is 'the mode in which all our politics are waged' (Halley 2006, 79). In going beyond the liberal sovereign individual, the autonomy and rights of that individual are not being dismissed as illusory. They are retained but are now understood as enhanced and embedded. Hutchings articulates the problem of these alternative futures for autonomy and rights, in going beyond the liberal sovereign individual. Her discussion is as relevant to a reconceptualised sovereignty as it is to personal subjectivity. In addition, the proposal developed here still focuses to some extent on the state, because rather than being dismissed, the 'post-state' (now incorporating as a positive principle the idea of 'central-state incapacity', or the diffusion of governance functions, to a greater or lesser degree) remains important as the focus of multiple identities. Liberal state sovereignty was very effective in providing a strong expression of identity, but has been unable to accept challenges to that identity. The idea of reconceptualised sovereignty presented here contains the acknowledgment that the single, unitary, and hierarchical model of the state form is in the process of giving way to the recognition of the interaction of a variety of more flexible forms.

At a general level, one of the things that sovereignty involves is a particular kind of recognition of an identity as a whole. But 'wholes' come in different forms, with different permeabilities, and can now be understood to include a form that is loose, ragged-edged, with and overlapping set of identities, as well as a form which is a single unified hard-shelled identity. The integrity of identity remains, as a constant feature of the variety of forms of post-state, even if its functions are separated. The concept of sovereignty functions to account for, and to sustain the stability of the polity and its equality with other political communities. The liberal and state paradigm of sovereignty is modelled not simply upon the individual person but upon a narrow individualism whose abstract and universally-defined independence and autonomy alone constitutes the source of their freedom and their moral capacity, with pre-political rights against others and against the state. This conception can now be seen as the basis of only one, and not the most convincing, of contemporary ways of envisaging the relation between rulers and ruled, defining the locus of authority and the exercise of political power and establishing the equal status of polities in international terms.

This alternative conception of sovereignty recognises, as the abstract nature of the liberal conception cannot, that conceptions of sovereignty are inherently conditioned by their connections to a contemporary and historical context. The aspect of liberal state sovereignty that is being discarded is the idea, indeed the myth that the autonomy that sovereignty confers has to mean absolute negative freedom to act.

3
The Metaphor of Sovereignty

This chapter has two purposes. The first is to build upon the argument in the previous chapter that modern state sovereignty identifies a symmetry between state and individual but takes an analogy between the liberal individual and liberal state as an ontological reality. The second is to use that analysis to examine the economy of explanation that discloses the metaphorical architecture of modern sovereignty more generally, and thus to discuss, as a case study, the implications of metaphorical thinking for our conceptualising of gender relations.

The previous chapter criticised the vision of the universal, rational, rights-bearing, free and choosing, and so figured as male, person of mainstream liberal political theory. The modern liberal conception of sovereignty has contained a strong gender coding, and the liberal public/private split has identified the public with male qualities, and the private with bodies and child-rearing. The picture is made more complex by the resurgence of liberal, now neo-liberal ideas and processes in the private realm of work and economics, and by the way the welfare state straddles the public and private divide. By a metaphorical process the public realm is associated with gender (choosing, separate from bodies) and the private domestic realm is associated with sex (biology and corporeality typified by child-bearing). What this chapter adds to the post-state proposal developed in Chapters 1 and 2, is to reinforce the relational rather than dichotomous character of post-states.

The chapter first outlines and celebrates elements of the philosophy of metaphor within an interpretivist framework which forms the basis for the discussion of the metaphorical status of sovereignty. Then, after setting out three forms of mapping, the chapter argues that in the modern conception, sovereignty has operated concurrently and interactively at three distinct levels – to define the state form of the political community, to signal liberal democratic citizenship, and to indicate the inviolability of the private individual. This section of the chapter revisits some of the line of argument discussed in Chapters 1 and 2 but from a different perspective. The consequences of Locke's description as literal of what Hobbes took crucially to be metaphorical, plays a key role in the argument. The chapter then goes on to critique and reconceptualise the covertly gendered dimension of the metaphor of sovereignty. In introducing the idea of metaphor, the argument here does not thereby psychologise politics nor reduce politics to psychology. Metaphor is an important general mechanism for the way socially and culturally constructed values underpin political ideas, concepts and practices. Neither does this insight detract from the critique of the specific way liberal principles have reinforced the orthodox modern conception of sovereignty, described in the previous chapter.

The possible scope of the metaphor of sovereignty in politics and epistemology is very broad, from sovereign as identifiable person, king, or ruler (personal sovereignty), to sovereign as office-holder (impersonal sovereignty), to a sovereign meaning setting up a general A/not-A dichotomy as a thinking strategy, to a sovereign meaning which performs a dominant, hegemonic, or absolute role (for example, 'sovereign definitions'), to sovereign knowledges which exercise a certain kind of power (for instance as found in Foucauldian discourse). Ashley and Walker are referring to the potent metaphorical force of the idea of sovereignty in these latter meanings when they warn us to regard 'every historical figuration of sovereign presence – be it God, nature, dynasty, citizen, nation, history, modernity, the West, the market's impartial spectator, reason, science, paradigm, tradition, man of faith in the possibility of universal human community, common sense, or any other – as precisely a question' (Ashley and Walker 1990, 368). The target of Ashley and Walker's attack, quite validly, is the unacknowledged metaphorical reach of (modern state) sovereignty expressed in grand theories, totalitarian interpretations and universal explanations.

Edkins and Pin-Fat outline the insight that the notion of sovereignty acts as a key concept to fill the gap between the messy world of social antagonisms and the constructed world of social reality, achieved through the imposition of meaning. Thus, sovereignty 'informs conventional notions of what political power might be', and the examples they give are 'the relationship between sovereign and subject within the absolutist kingdom, or the sovereignty of a government over the lives of its citizens in the modern nation-state', and in international politics sovereignty 'also plays a foundational role in discussions of international autonomy: the sovereign state is a bounded unit in the international system'. The centrality of the concept of sovereignty leads Edkins and Pin-Fat to attribute to it the place in the social order of 'master signifier around which a particular symbolic order is constituted' (Edkins and Pin-Fat 1999, 6). Further, they refer to 'the totalising part played by sovereignty in stabilising the semantic field' (Edkins and Pin-Fat 1999, 12).

In a later work Edkins and Pin-Fat go further, arguing plausibly that sovereignty is not 'a form of power relation [to which resistance is possible] but rather a relationship of violence', on the grounds that because 'it seeks to refuse those whole lives it controls any politically valid response, it operates as a form of technologised administration' (Edkins and Pin-Fat 2004, 18). Dillon goes further still and presents a picture of sovereign power '[n]ewly allied with proliferating forms of biopower, networks of disciplinary power knowledge and surveillance as well as with more cybernetically organised public/private control systems'. For Dillon this new sovereign power has 'become re-engineered as one powerful modality of power in an emergent and complex network of powers that has increasingly come to characterize power at the beginning of the Twenty-first century, at one and the same time both global in its reach yet also penetrating deep into the very structure of cellular life' (Dillon 2004, 58). Walker takes an additional step in this line of reasoning and contends persuasively that once 'we start messing with sovereignty' and see it as a problem rather than as a solution, 'as the site/event demanding engagements with the authorisation of authority rather than the necessary ground of all authority, whether in politics or in scholarship about politics', then 'knowledge must also be understood to be a problem' (Walker 2004, 244).

It is clear that conceptions of sovereignty can and have operated to entrench inequalities and discriminatory practices, and indeed to conceal social antagonisms. However, this book seeks also to highlight the opportunity for positive reconceptualisation which is found especially in the distinction between the concept of sovereignty and its different historical conceptions, some of which, like the liberal state conception, have operated with negative effects, and others of which offer resources for rethinking. Indeed, because none of the historical conceptions of sovereignty from Bodin to Hegel in fact corresponds, on detailed inspection, to the modern state realist liberal model (see Prokhovnik 2008 forthcoming), we can see that the resources for reconceptualisation and the historical specificity of the modern model open the way for further distinctive conceptions. The dichotomous thinking and practices which have characterised the modern state conception have rightly been criticised for effecting an inherently unjust and oppressive social order, and for expressing a master signifier of oppression in which sovereignty replaces other blanket 'explanations' like divine providence, the invisible hand of the market, or the objective logic of history. However, the negative effects of that conception of sovereignty do not prevent the positive theorisation of sovereignty now in relational terms. For instance, while Edkins and Pin-Fat correctly identify ideas that fill the 'place of constitutive lack' in the social structure (Edkins and Pin-Fat 1999, 7), it is also possible to recognise the feasibility of turning from critique to framing a new conception of sovereignty.

In political theory the dominant meaning of sovereignty is that of a relation establishing social order, but sovereignty is also about the integrity and identity of the whole. It is this second sense that is initially active in the metaphorical relation between liberal individual and liberal state being explored here. In political theory and international relations sovereignty belongs very much on the public side of the liberal public/private divide, and very much on the state side of the liberal state/civil society divide. However, Neocleous's *Imagining the State* (2003), taking the metaphor of body to body politic seriously, is a fine example of showing how a strong resonance has been present from individual up to political concept.

This chapter is concerned with the crucial importance of metaphor, metaphorical shifts, and metaphorical meanings to the concept of sovereignty, both conceptually and historically. It therefore attends to metaphor in sovereignty for its political effects and not just as a linguistic phenomenon. The argument here is also that while metaphor is vital to organising thinking in general, and while every successful conception of sovereignty will trade on and so generate metaphorical meaning, the conception of liberal state sovereignty deserves special attention. Metaphor is a key concept in the cluster around sovereignty, but the metaphor in the modern liberal paradigm of state sovereignty between the autonomy of the polity and the autonomy of the individual is largely unacknowledged by the modern narrowly-rational mode of explanation. The metaphorical force of this specific connection is deeply political in that it is one of the sources of the power of the state conception of sovereignty and its resistance to change.

In the previous chapter we saw how potently and cogently the metaphor of sovereignty operated from the individual to 'explain' political relations at the level of the polity and between states. The idea of the metaphor of sovereignty is also already familiar from the history of political thought. For instance, the engraved frontispiece of Hobbes's *Leviathan* conveys the idea of the authorisation of the sovereign that serves as the key to the coherence of the polity and the power of the sovereign. Also, Hegel posited a strong analogy between person and state in his theory of sovereignty. We can also observe that Kant uses the sovereignty of the moral law as the basis for the metaphorical relation between autonomous individuals and autonomous states. He uses metaphor again when mapping (internal, state) sovereignty onto the realm of international politics to provide the principles of external sovereignty. Foucault also extensively uses a metaphorical method to approach sovereignty, in regarding the tradition of state sovereign power as a metaphor for the absence of individual freedom, in regarding sov-ereign power as analogous to disciplinary power, and in making a metaphorical shift from the formal political level to the social level of social power relations. In each case the use of metaphor enriches the theory that is developed. See Prokhovnik (2008 forthcoming) for a fuller discussion.

Moreover, Dufour notes that Pufendorf is not the only political theorist to see a metaphorical relation between the 'highest and absolute liberty of individual men' and the absolute sovereignty of the state. Dufour cites *On the Law of Nature and Nations*, in which Pufendorf argues that the state has 'the same liberty, or faculty to decide by its own judgment about the means that look to the welfare of the state. And this liberty is attended with absolute sovereignty' (Dufour 1991, 576). Pufendorf, contends Dufour, 'sees the moral persons constituted by states as partaking in the same rights as physical persons in the state of nature. Just as with individuals, the principle of sociability is compromised by the right to act in our interest, where there is no common sovereign arbitrator' (Dufour 1991, 585–6).

Likewise Keal alludes to the metaphor between sovereign individual and sovereign polity when he discusses seventeenth-century views about whether men living in a state of nature possessed natural rights. Property rights, notes Keal, were 'active rights expressing their possessor's sovereignty over his world', which could be 'defended against other men...and transferred or alienated by [their] possessor' (Keal 2003, 78). It follows, says Keal quoting Tuck's argument, that 'the rights individuals possessed "*vis-à-vis* one another (outside the arbitrary and contingent circumstances of their civil arrangements)" could best be understood "by looking at the rights which sovereign states seem to possess against one another"' (Keal 2003, 79).

However, an important example of an unacknowledged and unjustified metaphorical shift described later in the chapter concerns the tradition of realist international relations which has taken aspects of Hobbes's theory of the *individual*, namely his conceptions of rational autonomy and freedom, and applied it to their conception of the sovereign *state* in the international context. Wendt points explicitly to the explanatory force accorded to metaphorical reasoning in the meaning of state sovereignty in the modern realist tradition. He describes the 'productive analogy...between individuals and states' that 'is an accepted practice in mainstream international relations discourse' (Wendt 1992, 397).

The key role of metaphor in epistemological mapping

Turning now to the first part of the argument of this chapter, Walzer describes well the way analogical reasoning overcomes the separateness of things. He argues that '[p]olitics is an art of unification; from many, it makes one. And symbolic activity is perhaps our most important means of bringing things together, both intellectually and emotionally, thus overcoming isolation and even individuality'. Walzer underlines the importance of the symbolic when he notes that 'the union of men can only be symbolised; it has no palpable shape or substance. The state is invisible; it must be personified before it can be seen, symbolised before it can be loved, imagined before it can be conceived' (Walzer 1967, 194). Walzer also underlines the way 'changes in the way men conceived the cosmological reference-world did undermine conceptions of the polity'. Consequently, 'the new science had its subversive effects, for it called into question the very vocabulary with which fame and opinion work and the crucial symbols through which authority inspires consent' (Walzer 1967, 197). It stands to reason that a conception of sovereignty has analogical and symbolic meaning, as part of a whole package of political concepts meaningfully interrelated. It could do no other.

An interpretivist approach drawing on the work of Gadamer, Geertz, Ricoeur, and others, goes further than Walzer and is a valuable starting-point for understanding how metaphor is so important for a concept like sovereignty. The interpretivist approach regards as impossible the idea that we can gain an objective, neutral and superior God's-eye vantage point outside our societies and their presuppositions from which to study human subjects, or that we ever start simply with 'raw data'. It looks instead to use the way we are 'always already' steeped and drenched in social meaning, our ability to actively engage with the meanings of the past and its continuities and discontinuities with the present, and our capacity to reconstruct the contexts in which meaning has operated, to develop reasons for a particular interpretation of human conduct, dialogical communication, and conceptualisation. This sense in which interpretation is an 'ontological necessity' is what Ball refers to as the 'inescapability of interpretation' (Ball 1995, 7). The key to the method is inter-subjective meaning rather than a subject/object dichotomy. At a very general level interpretivist theorists would subscribe to the importance of attending to the way in which a society is a consolidated network or arrangement of social meaning, value, explanation, interpretation, assumptions, conventions, power relations, claims, and contestations as well as being taken to be a physical entity in territory and population. No interpretation can be neutral or value-free (Ball 1995, 10) but one can examine and so debate some of the presuppositions of the perspective from which one's interpretation is made. Ball also makes the important point that a 'text is not merely an artefact produced by an author; it is also a communication received by a reader. Its meaning must in some part be the product of a "negotiation" between the two' (Ball 1995, 14), including both the author's intentions and the unintended consequences of the text's ideas, and misunderstandings and misrepresentations of it, as well as the product of examining the context of a text's composition and the contexts of its reception (Ball 1995, 32).

In societies that are regarded as corresponding to political units the fit between what is understood as the physical entity (whether in terms of territory or of space more generally) and the economy of meaning may be particularly close. As Reus-Smit notes sovereignty, like all social norms, rules and principles is 'subject to the same constitutive processes'. These things are 'social artifacts, the normative products of moral debate and dialogue' about conduct (as well as the product of social power relations, we might want to add), 'products that are reproduced through routinised communication and social practice'. He emphasises that all '[n]orms, rules, and principles thus have histories, they emerge out of complex processes of communicative action, and they are maintained through the conscious, and at times unconscious, application of taken-for-granted canons and repertoires of appropriate' conduct (2001a, 526). To support this argument Reus-Smit invokes Habermas's notion of the 'lifeworld', the 'storehouse of unquestioned cultural givens from which those participating in communication draw agreed-upon patterns of interpretation for use in their interpretive efforts' (Reus-Smit 2001a, 527).

Teschke argues strongly that the 'modern self and the concentration of political power in an indivisible notion of sovereignty over a spatially demarcated territory are historically parallel phenomena' (Teschke 2003, 29). Societies need to be understood not just in terms of 'given facts' about physical entities in territory and population. They are also in an important sense interlocking patterns of meaning, value and explanation, expressing and expressed intersubjectively by persons understood as meaning-seeking creatures. As Geertz remarks, humans have an 'extreme dependence upon a certain sort of learning: the attainment of concepts, the apprehension and application of specific systems of symbolic meaning' (Geertz 1973b, 49). Each society or group of societies can, especially with hindsight, be characterised by distinctive principles by which explanation in different areas of social practices, understandings and values are mapped onto each other. Such principles are not simply 'rational' but they are regarded as forming a meaningful rationality or coherence. All societies are at least partially-coherent 'patterns' or imprints of social meaning which are expressed dynamically in concrete form in language, social interaction, social practices, norms and presuppositions; clothes, accents and other concrete symbols denoting social positioning; and in specialised and technical discourses. At the same time societies are constructed and reconstructed through those dynamic social practices and their perceived understandings. There is thus always a two-way and interdependent process going on between the inherited construction and meanings of a society (with its entrenched inequalities and structural power relations) and the actions and constructions of persons understood as meaning-seeking and meaning-constructing creatures. This two-way process follows either or both a conservative impulse to reinforce the value of traditional meanings or an emancipatory impulse to challenge and reform them.

In many societies, more than one available pattern of social meaning is taken to be meaningful and valuable, and Western liberal democracies purport not only to celebrate plurality or even difference in this respect, but also to encourage contestation, so long as such challenges are not directed at the foundations of liberal theory and practice themselves. Nevertheless the internal stability of a society depends in part upon the existence of a consensus about or legitimation of, though not necessarily a close self-conscious subscription to, a dominant 'map' of social meaning. This consensus, at its loosest, may be no more than a tacit agreement to tolerate the dominant map. A dominant map need not necessarily be an overtly oppressive map, but all contain ways of excluding and of defining inequalities that may or may not be politically relevant. One of liberal society's significant weaknesses follows from its denial of the way liberal principles themselves form a dominant, naturalised, and oppressive map. It is partly because of this very denial that the dominant liberal map has operated oppressively (Tapper 1986).

This map operates to provide a relatively coherent intersecting framework of meaning and explanation of the major institutions of social life (the family, education, work, the state, the self), thereby anchoring meaning in a generalised pattern of explanation and interpretation. The framework of meaning is only ever more, or less, relatively coherent, both because its sedimented meanings – like Geertz's theories, which 'grow increasingly awkward, unproductive, strained, or vacuous' but 'persist long after all but a handful of people...have lost much interest in them' (Geertz 1973a, 27) – are challenged and augmented by marginalised, recessive ideas and practices, and because the framework is dynamic and flexible, built up and changing over time.

But the map also generates and is generated by explanations of our categories of thinking which provide, for instance in the political realm, conceptualisations of authority, obligation, power, democracy, and sovereignty. As Geertz observes profoundly, 'a country's politics reflect the design of its culture' (Geertz 1973c, 311). The metaphorical depth, picking up on social and cultural explanations and values, which invests sovereignty with meanings and resonances and so contributes to its success and social import in functioning as a political principle, combines two kinds of meaning – constructing human cultural meanings in the absence of given meanings from nature or God (and so the sense in which meaning is always attributed meaning, or significance), and meaning in the sense of value as a moral and normative concept.

Moreover we can see, especially retrospectively, that an epistemological map (a map taken to provide a template and conceptual framework to 'explain' social reality) gains its level of coherence, through a principle of economy, by the 'mapping' that has taken place through either consensual or imposed shared understandings. In this way the general form of the dominant explanation in one domain of social explanation is understood and accepted as illuminating in other areas as well, such that metaphorically-related explanations are constructed through the potency of such resonances. The ideas of 'mapping' and 'patterning' used here refer to systematic networks of metaphorical meaning. Lakoff and Johnson make a similar point when they affirm that the 'most fundamental values in a culture will be coherent with the metaphorical structure of the most fundamental concepts in the culture' (Lakoff and Johnson 1980, 22).

Skinner's descriptions of interpreting a text 'within a field of assumptions and conventions to which it contributes and from which it derives its distinctively meaningful character' (Skinner 1975, 210), and of aiming 'to recapture the presuppositions and purposes that went into the making of it' (Skinner 1988, 274), also contribute strongly to understanding this mapping process. Ricoeur's emphasis on the openness of a text's meaning, which is, 'considered as a whole, open to several readings and to several constructions' (Ricoeur 1973, 107), and the need to select and interpret in the face of indeterminacy, is also helpful in accounting for social meaning. Metaphorical meaning is established by and is the product of effective and successful mapping. The metaphor acts to hold together the continuity of explanation from one area to another, and to 'graft' a further claim onto prevailing views. The metaphorical process structures thinking through a condensed analogy, and both reduces complexity and fuses complex meanings together. As Lakoff and Johnson articulate, not only is metaphor a matter of 'understanding and experiencing one kind of thing in terms of another', but of using one thing to conceptualise another, grounded in a recognition of a correlation (Lakoff and Johnson 1980, 5, 9, 155). Chilton confirms that 'metaphorical processes are one of the most important means by which human minds form concepts…and reason'. This is especially the case, Chilton notes, 'for conceptualisation of abstract, unfamiliar, or complex domains' (Chilton 2004, 48). It follows, as Gadamer argues, that the metaphorical process also enables the 'anticipation of meaning' (Gadamer 1975, 261).

Three kinds of mapping

There are three meanings of 'map' which are utilised in this chapter. The first sense of 'mapping' refers to the schematic plan of social meaning and reality which in some respects is like the London Underground map, a shorthand depiction of a more complex picture. 'Mapping' in the second sense is concerned the interconnecting and interdependent links between ontology and epistemology in the social world. The third sense of 'mapping' refers to a society's historical development. Over time some of the social values and explanatory categories of a society alter, whether abruptly as in the adoption of democracy with the French Revolution, or more gradually as with the incremental expansion of democratic rights in Britain. Disclosing these three forms of mapping highlights the limitations of the general principle of the rational agent to which the modern form of explanation attaches such importance.

What has been described so far falls under the second of the three meanings of 'map'. This palimpsest mapping is not the only way that new ideas are incorporated. But the overlaying of old meanings and old ways of understanding onto new ideas, phenomena and practices, is a key way of making them intelligible, relating new ideas and practices to old ones. New ones will be more successful if they can be shown to map onto and trade upon older valued ones. In this way metaphorical meaning, which at a general level is a necessary aspect of living in society, is never merely neutrally rational but is always loaded with normative import (Prokhovnik 1991, Chapters 1, 2). An example where meaning is successfully formed (but which has proved unsuccessful in constructing a new meaning) is given by the successive efforts of the Blair government in Britain to reform vocational secondary school qualifications in relation to academic ones. All attempts to revalue and upgrade vocational qualifications (however good those reforms in their own terms) *vis-à-vis* 'A' levels have failed to budge the potent undertow of meaning patterned in important respects onto among other things class divisions, whereby 'A' levels are regarded as respectable and vocational qualifications disdained as second-rate. This process of meaning construction tends to operate except in the case where the old meaning is seen as moribund and where fresh ideas are thought to be needed, for instance (at least on the face of it) with the French Revolution.

So for instance in modern, Western liberal democratic society, particularly in its Anglo-American form, one important aspect of this map and the mapping process has been the explanatory force in societies still patriarchal in their underlying values and practices of the mind/body dichotomy, not only onto the man/woman distinction, but also onto the heterosexual/homosexual dichotomy, and more recently onto the sex/gender distinction. This case study is discussed later in the chapter. The disposition to explain in terms of self/other dualisms, to find explanatory force in these dichotomies, is a strong feature of the modern rationalist tradition. The key features of dichotomous thinking and explanation are the twin principles of polarised opposition and hierarchy, thereby classifying patterns of dominant and subordinate categories (Prokhovnik 2002, Chapter 1). Now that some of these mechanisms of dominance and subordination are being challenged, we can start to get a clearer perspective on the way they work by reinforcing concrete social inequalities and investing and explaining fresh experiences with self/other meaning through the mind/body dichotomy. An example here might be the dominant social response to West Indian immigrants to Britain after World War II, in terms of a racist self/other mind/body explanation.

According to this meta-explanation all stable societies (where 'stable' refers to both internal social order and to stability in the society's self-understanding) contain a map and a mapping process. The use of metaphorical explanation is a necessary feature of a society, providing a line of coherence in social understanding as well as a short-cut way of constructing meaning. Richards argues convincingly that metaphor is not only a 'verbal matter, a shifting and displacement of words', but is fundamentally an account of what takes place in thinking itself. Thought, he says, is metaphorical, and 'the metaphors of language derive therefrom' (Richards 1967, 94). Lakoff and Johnson agree that metaphor is pervasive in language and thought (Lakoff and Johnson 1980, 3). This means, and this is an important point, that the understanding attached to the concept and practices of sovereignty indeed *must* trade on a dominant metaphorical meaning to be successful in 'explaining' social reality and meaning. The explanation of social reality and meaning, and the practices through which they are expressed, are both inherited and constructed (and perhaps reconstructed) by persons and groups. But the specific dichotomous self/other principle which underpins the dominant values and categorisation of the map and mapping of modern western society, is contingent. Other guiding ideas are possible, including different forms of relational principle. This remains a radical statement, not only because the grip of the rationalist mind/body split is still very strong, but also because both traditional and 'modern' societies have tended to naturalise (Plumwood 1993, Grosz 1994) their dominant maps, making it appear that the particular map whose organising principle is self/other dichotomies is 'normal and neutral', a self-evident assumption, a given. Moreover, while the Western liberal metaphor for the sovereign polity is based on the individual – the rational, autonomous, self-governing and rights-bearing individual – it is possible that in other cultures the metaphor for sovereignty could have some other source, and that the metaphors for understanding both the polity and the person could both derive from another source.

However, while operating with naturalised values and concepts may make life easier, by analysing the basis of the naturalisation it is possible to identify two important features of the dichotomous self/other principle. The first is that this particular principle need not be taken as part of a given natural fabric, and so is not a *necessary* principle. The second is that because the dichotomous self/other principle is not a given it can be recognised as socially constructed in a complex sense. Thus, while repudiating reductionism to either biological and social determinism or to the extreme form of liberal agency, social constructionist theory can acknowledge three interacting contributions to social explanation – of (mediated) material and physical imperatives; of the habits and values (some of them reflecting structural power relations and entrenched inequalities) produced by socialisation and its roots in history and memory, and the meanings attached to a vocabulary to express them; and of reflection and collective and individual agency.

As we noted earlier, the mapping of ontological and epistemological maps goes hand in hand. At a meta level it can be discerned that social values and explanatory meanings – the ontologically given concrete practical social reality and the epistemologically given theoretical framework – have combined in a stable society's relatively coherent self-understanding. The *dominant* social values and explanatory meanings mesh together to form a relatively coherent political identity. Through this process of mapping we use metaphor to structure our thoughts and conceptual systems, understanding one thing in terms of another, and we give coherence to our notion of rationality.

The third sense of 'mapping' referred to a society's historical development. But while values and explanations change over time (but according to no particular grand logic), new ones tend not wholly to supplant or replace the old, but simply to suppress them by 'mapping' onto them in complex fashion as a palimpsest, over discredited, discarded, or disused values or explanations. The third sense of mapping, then, describes the way that new values and explanations are superimposed over the top of the old ones which remain in reserved or latent form. Indeed, this is part of what Weber recognised as 'the perpetual reconstruction of those concepts through which we seek to comprehend reality' (Weber 1949, 105). Good examples with respect to values are the resilience of underlying older cultural and social values (including the mapping of Stalin and Mao onto older imperial and semi-mystical understandings of leaders) in Russia and in China in the last century, despite the enthusiastic embrace in those countries of the Communist system and despite the root and branch attempts to eradicate pre-Revolutionary elites and thinking. Good examples with respect to explanations, in the western tradition, are Ancient Greek and Roman, and medieval and renaissance theories, periodically resuscitated for instance in Nussbaum's use of Aristotle, Skinner's cogent use of renaissance and Roman republicanism, or the enduring power of Augustine's loathing of the body.

Mapping sovereignty – self, citizenship, and polity

The location and character of the category 'sovereignty' is an important feature of a society's explanatory map (in the first sense) because one of the things that a conception of sovereignty spells out is the particular form that the principle of order takes, both in the relation of rulers to ruled and the identity of the polity, which governs that political community. In addition a normative status is attached to sovereignty as a good, in that value is placed on it. Furthermore we take sovereignty to play a role in providing the meaning of the relation between the parts of the society and polity and the whole. Hegel and Kant both consider this an important aspect of sovereignty, and it also relates to Skinner's description of interpreting a text 'within a field of assumptions and conventions' referred to earlier. The role sovereignty plays here is deeply metaphorical.

The meaning of sovereignty is found in at least three interlocking levels (using mapping in the second sense), in the state, in citizenship, and in the individual and family. At the beginning of the twenty-first century there is now a disjunction between on the one hand the longstanding dominant

modern Western meaning of all three levels of sovereignty, as a principle of order expressed here as a hard-shelled unity and hierarchy and as
a barrier concept defining inclusion and exclusion, and recent developments of political theory and practice on the other. Currently, for
instance, there are a number of serious efforts being made to extend
the meaning of politics, in order to fragment some of the self/other
and mind/body social values at play – for instance in the areas of post-
colonial multiculturalism, gender equality, sexual preference, the reimagining of the state, and children's rights. One of the major problems
with the metaphor of state sovereignty understood as mapped onto the
autonomous individual has been that, as Lakoff and Johnson observe,
using one metaphor to understand something else rules out other understandings of it (Lakoff and Johnson 1980, 10). The disjunction between
the dominant meaning and recent relational understandings exacerbates
this problem. Moreover the modern western elevation of scientific explanation has reinforced this state of affairs. Lakoff and Johnson observe
that in our 'culture where the myth of objectivism is very much alive
and truth is always absolute truth, the people who get to impose their
metaphors on the culture get to define what we consider to be true –
absolutely and objectively true' (Lakoff and Johnson 1980, 160). They
suggest persuasively that, instead, 'truth is always relative to a conceptual
system, that any human conceptual system is mostly metaphorical in
nature, and that, therefore, there is no fully objective, unconditional, or
absolute truth' (Lakoff and Johnson 1980, 185).

In consequence of observing these developments a growing group of
writers is addressing the reconceptualisation of sovereignty in line with this
movement. Many of these writers have in common the proposal and analysis of an alternative relational and interactive dynamic for sovereignty.
The re-theorisation of sovereignty in terms of now a relational and interactive principle of political order, in contrast with the unitary and dichotomous principle of state sovereignty, is already underway, as described in
the last two chapters. This process represents a form of mapping in the
third sense, in the supplanting of a conception but not of the concept. In
doing so the argument draws upon the well-established concept/conception
distinction (Ball 1988, Connolly 1993, Taylor 1992) discussed in the Introduction and shows how these two have been conflated. It follows, inci-
dentally, that the limits of the enterprise, in terms of rational re-theorisation,
are clearly indicated, both by the superimposition principle along which it
operates, and in the absence of any convincing reason to believe in overall
historical progress. What this chapter seeks to offer to this development is
to make explicit the link between the state, citizenship and individual/
family levels in the character of sovereignty in the modern period, and to
point to some aspects of the relational reconceptualisation of sovereignty at
these three levels.

It is clear from recent work on the concept of sovereignty that the dominant conception of sovereignty in the modern period has both operated metaphorically and has contained a gendered character (Hutchings 1996, Gatens 1996, Neack and Knudson 1996, Hoffman 1998, Biersteker and Weber 1996, Bartelson 1995, Sawer 1996, Molloy 1995). The gendered character of the conception has been sustained by a governing self/other principle (Walker 1993). This chapter will examine further the metaphorical and gendered aspects of the dominant 'modern' conception of sovereignty. The chapter will also demonstrate the crucial link between the metaphorical and gendered aspects of 'modern' sovereignty, a link which has helped to reinforce the stability of the conception over the last 300 years. The chapter will go on to indicate how feminist and other scholarship on sovereignty, citizenship, sex and gender, dichotomous thinking, and the body, is brought to bear to reconceptualise sovereignty in a positive manner on a relational and non-dichotomous basis. The work is feminist because feminist theory has made important contributions to the critique of rational individual, the critique of an identifiable 'male' norm, which has defined the dominant mainstream position and value, and has developed theoretical challenges and amassed empirical evidence concerning women which has a larger reference for other forms of marginalisation. But the current argument is not 'feminist' in a sense which is designed to exclude men.

The modern conception of sovereignty is not only richly metaphorical, but has also depended upon a complex interplay of literal and metaphorical meanings. In the modern conception, sovereignty has operated concurrently at three distinct levels – to define the state form of the political community, to signal liberal democratic citizenship, and to indicate the inviolability of the private individual. Normative status attaches to sovereignty at each of these three levels and reinforces the status of the others. Indeed, Rob Walker makes a strong case for recognising a tight metaphorical link not only between the modern sovereign individual and the modern sovereign state, but also with the modern state system as well, and for recognising that the character of modern sovereignty is profoundly shaped by what modernity rejected (Walker 2004, 248, 249).

Wendt argues that sovereignty applies not only to states but to other associations too. He contends that 'all organisations, not just states, have an interest in autonomy, since without it they will be constrained in their ability to meet internal demands or respond to contingencies in the environment' (Wendt 1999, 235). The strength of the perceived correlation between state and individual in particular has meant that the distinctive power or sovereignty of the state as the paradigmatic form of political unit, is metaphorically transposed back again to explain the independence and autonomy of the individual and the citizenship relation between individual and state. Support for this argument comes from Reus-Smit, who notes that '[h]istorically, the identity values defining ideal individuals and states have been closely linked, with the latter usually being cast in the service of the former. Furthermore, domestic and international identity values have changed over time' (2001, 527).

Edkins and Pin-Fat (1999, 2) draw out how 'the rational Cartesian subject and the search for certainty' have gone hand in hand. The mutually-reinforcing reciprocal metaphor between the modern subject and state sovereignty have claimed between them not only rational action and choice but also certainty, knowledge and truth. They also quote Ashley's insight that 'Reasoning man...is the modern *sovereign*' (quoted in Edkins and Pin-Fat 1999, 3). They describe the decenterings by linguistic philosophers about language, by Freud and others about the unconscious, and by Marx and others about the role of economics. They conclude that the 'picture of the rational, conscious, autonomous individual' has been replaced with a notion of 'subjectivity that is bound up with the social or symbolic order. The constitution of the subject and the social order seem to implicate each other' (Edkins and Pin-Fat 1999, 4).

The tight metaphorical relation between man and state characterises, indeed defines – the notion of sovereignty in the modern conception. Walker, for instance, remarks on how the 'twin absolutes of a unitary sovereignty and a unitary individual' (Walker 1999, xiii) seemed to be the modern answer to questions in modern politics. Bartelson makes the case that the international becomes intelligible at the same time as man himself becomes regarded as 'the source of all intelligibility and himself intelligible; he is sufficiently analogous with his own construct', and that this correspondence in the modern period is not an accident. Now, 'man is not only the author of his own deeds, concepts and representations, and creator of his own history and self-knowledge; his sovereignty is no longer confined to nature and culture, but also encompasses the source of his finiteness and the limit to his creative powers; having usurped Time, man is not only king, but also God' (Bartelson 1995, 236).

Wendt also highlights the tight fit between individual and state for the metaphor between them in liberal thinking, in that an important aspect of the emergence of the state form was its specification as a distinctive kind of corporate actor (Wendt 1999, 215). In consequence, Wendt argues, while 'concrete individuals play an essential role in state action, instantiating and carrying it forward in time', state action is not 'reducible to those individuals'. In his words, insofar as 'the state is ontologically emergent... anthropomorphizing it is not merely an analytical convenience, but essential to predicting and explaining its behaviour' (Wendt 1999, 221). It is precisely because the metaphor holds that such reductionism does not occur. Moreover, it is because of its notably secular and impersonal, and later rational and modern form, that the state mirrored the rational, autonomous liberal individual in a way that, for instance, a theologically-inflected state could not do.

Wendt also makes the interesting point that the limit of the metaphor, or 'anthropomorphizing' as he puts it, between the individual and the state is seen in the alternative forms of action to the interaction between individuals that are available to the state. In addition to interaction, states can divide (for instance in Czechoslovakia's 'Velvet Revolution'), merge (as in German reunification), grow in the form of conquest, and specialise (for example delegating the issue of security to another state, as is the case in sphere of influence) (Wendt 1999, 223). This point reinforces the case for regarding the international sphere as a distinctive realm, non-reducible to the criteria of domestic politics.

Bartelson describes the view that the modern, realist definition of internal and external, the domestic and the international, mutually exclusive and together exhausting the realm of possibilities, is actively sustained by the image of the sovereignty of man. In this way, 'the state is man writ large as much as man is the microcosm of the state, since both instantiate the rationality and autonomy intrinsic to all modern subjectivity'. The state is presupposed as a sphere of rational action in both law and violence, whose justification is that it provides the conditions in which sovereign man can flourish, and which stands as a bulwark against the irrationality of the outside. Cartesian dualism has been mapped onto the political, such that the inside is aligned with the mind and the outside with the body, and the two are radically split from each other. As a result, as Bartelson notes, 'sovereign man and sovereign state go hand in hand' (Bartelson 2001, 162).

The following interpretation rests upon a reading of intellectual history that highlights as paradigmatic the roles attributed to Hobbes and Locke in the development of the 'modern' sovereign state and sovereign individual respectively. The levels of the state, the individual, and citizenship will be considered in turn.

Hobbes's mutually-defining analyses of sovereignty and the state have been taken as the primary theoretical warrant for the development of the notion of the sovereignty of the modern non-personalised nation state. His figure of the Leviathan represents graphically and accurately his theory of the fusion of state and sovereignty (Prokhovnik 1991, Chapters 5, 7). According to Hobbes the state is an artificial body, which derives its integrity, and so its sovereignty, from being knowingly constructed through the process of authorisation and representation agreed upon in the multitude's transfer of right. For Hobbes this process of construction, by artifice, of the relationship between ruler and ruled, is a cause for celebration, a pre-eminent example of the art of man imitating and superseding the art of God in natural construction.

The metaphor of the generation and representation of the sovereign state as unitary and centralised encapsulates the theory whereby the modern sovereign state is taken to be the appropriate expression of political order. It provides the model for a political community with the following characteristics – it is internally stably-constituted; independent of all other states and so free to act; autonomous and so having the capacity to act; making law without interference, and so being self-governing in a self-determining manner. Furthermore it provides the model for a political community conducting itself on the basis of fundamental equality with other states. This stable, independent, autonomous, and self-governing political unit thus describes the literal meaning of the modern theoretically-inviolate sovereign state in both its internal and external dimensions.

However, upon further inspection, this literal meaning also rests upon a richly metaphorical understanding, for as noted in the Introduction sovereignty is intangible. Sovereignty is not an observable fact but a practice for assessing observations in terms of certain normative criteria (Kratochwil 1995, 21). It follows that the binding force of sovereignty, as well as its connection to literal references (the activities of the state), must be made by a process of recognition or acknowledgement which is prepared to equate sovereignty with specific literal, substantive, references. Sovereignty does not refer directly to something relatively tangible such as an institution, but relies upon this act of recognition on the part of others in order to close the gap and so become operational. Recognition entails acceding to the view that the abstract construction is to be taken as a given, and as a given and binding feature of political reality, and in this way recognition is thus a key feature of sovereignty (Fowler and Bunck 1996, 400–4, Kratochwil 1995, 40–1). However, the combination of metaphorical and literal elements in the 'modern' conception of the sovereign *state* is not the only source of metaphor in the modern conception of sovereignty.

Coming to the level of the individual, we can note that Locke's redefinition of the sovereignty of the individual in terms of a personhood which is crucially pre-political, radically extended the notion of individual rights and power in the secular and temporal world. Locke's rational, free, rights-bearing, independent, autonomous, unencumbered, inviolate, and self-governing individual, expresses a second form and level of modern sovereignty. In an important sense Locke's conception is achieved by taking as literal the outlines of Hobbes's figure of the Leviathan, and thereby supplying a direct reference to the individual. By describing as a literal human figure the image that Hobbes meant to be taken as metaphorical (that is referring to the state), Locke derived conclusions about the person which were the opposite of those which Hobbes had intended. Hobbes's individual can only be redeemed *as* an individual in the social world provided by political order (Prokhovnik 2005).

In the modern period Locke's definition has been importantly developed, especially by J.S. Mill and Kant, to specify the theoretical basis of both the 'private' individual within the family, and the individual within the limited scope of 'public' life. As a result, as Hutchings notes, as we observed in the previous chapter, 'the sovereign individual is sovereign in the sense that it has rights over itself and rules itself, whether through rational self-interest or access to the moral law' (Hutchings 1996, 2).

The two most influential modern theories of the state, the liberal and the Marxist, are both highly suspicious of the state. For both these traditions there is a tension between the definition of the sovereign state and the sovereign individual in the modern period. Liberal theory has concentrated its attention on specifying universal and absolute rights held by the individual as inalienable property, and on arguing for a limited state whose legitimacy ends where the scope of individual rights begins. The Marxist tradition has attacked what it has regarded as the triple claims of the modern state – to a legitimate monopoly over the instruments of coercion, to an exclusive right to exercise power within a defined territory, and to sovereignty over the lives of subjects. Both the liberal and Marxist traditions juxtapose and see as irreducibly in conflict (though in very different ways) the absolute sovereignty of the modern state, equated with domination and repression, with the absolute sovereignty of the modern individual, equated with self-determination and control over one's choices. Furthermore both traditions naturalise this juxtaposition.

Between the levels of the state and the individual, the modern notion of citizenship as equal membership of the political community was articulated as part of the development of democratic theory and practice in Europe. Influential markers in this process include the republican conception of active citizenship developed by Rousseau, the tradition of democratic theory and practice subsequent to the French Revolution, and T.H. Marshall's extension of a rights-based perspective, in an influential specification (Marshall 1950) of the civil, political and social rights of citizens in the context of European welfare state social democracies. Citizenship in modern liberal democracies entails the idea of its being grounded in popular sovereignty, in a degree of civic virtue that restrains individual self-interest, and in a constitutionalism that ensures the impartial rule of law if not the entrenchment of rights. Citizenship expresses a third level of sovereignty, a third kind of inviolable self-ownership, and a third means of sovereignty's social contexualisation. The modern notion of citizenship not only occupied an intermediate position between the state and the individual, but also came to mediate between, to accommodate, and to hold together the inherent tension between state and individual, as well as to justify the twin but opposed claims of state and individual.

Although the concept of modern democratic citizenship is more emancipatory and politically progressive than either of its modern sovereignty correlates (state and individual), it nevertheless asserts membership of the political community primarily on an individualistic basis. Political identity, rights, and political obligation arise from this individual membership, and citizenship also expresses the legitimacy in the political community of the interests, rights, aspirations of individuals as peers. While citizenship bestows meaningful powers, articulated in terms of the speech and action of political participation, just as important is citizenship in terms of economic independence through formal paid employment (or, more and more grudgingly given, entitlement to make a claim on the state for welfare provision). Citizenship is thus contrasted with sham instances which do not grant meaningful powers, such as John Major's citizens' charters.

The metaphorical architecture of modern sovereignty is now clear. The three levels of modern sovereignty are distinct but interdependent, composing together an architecture of explanation which is both ontological and epistemological. The theory and practice of the sovereign state, of citizenship, and of the sovereign individual are connected to each other by tight metaphorical relation.

Drawing on the language of mapping outlined earlier on, the metaphorical dynamic at work here operates by a process of mapping in the second sense, the mapping of an explanation in one area onto other domains, because the general form of the explanation is taken to illuminate the meaning of practices and values in other areas as well. Retrospectively and at the meta level it is clear that a theoretical explanatory fit was attained in liberal political theory by laying the outline of the sovereign state back onto the notion of autonomous personhood, or through the mutually-reinforcing 'fit' between the two, with the later development of the citizen being achieved by superimposing upon both the notion of the politically-active individual. But because of a 'whiting out of meaning' through overuse of a metaphor, in Richter's memorable phrase (Richter 2005, 230), the metaphor functions to sustain itself by operating simultaneously in both a top-down and a bottom-up direction. This process was sustained theoretically by Locke's adoption as literal what Hobbes had intended as metaphorical. The consequent loss of metaphorical character of the liberal metaphor of sovereignty and its coming to be regarded as literal, was thus due to the whiting out process so characteristic of liberal principles, but also to the liberal tendency towards depoliticisation, as well as being due to the ageing and loss of metaphorical import that is a general feature of the use of metaphors (for example in 'the leg of the table', or 'he's been sidelined').

The gendered dimension of the metaphor of sovereignty – critique and reconceptualisation

In this process of mapping, which delineates an economy of explanation in the modern period, the mind/body dichotomy operating through the bipolar male/female distinction is one of the most important expressions of the map's self/other principle. The mind/body split on which the male/female dichotomy rests has played a crucial role in sustaining the meaning, potency, naturalisation, and longevity of the triple metaphor describing the three levels of the meaning of sovereignty. Moreover, over the last 30 years one of the primary effects of the sex/gender distinction has been, not to effect women's emancipation as promised, but to become absorbed into the self/other mapping order. As a result young women are once more encouraged, through harsh disciplinary practices, to conform to strictly-prescriptive norms of body shape, clothing and behaviour in order to attract men still defined as 'the opposite sex'. Sex and gender have been significantly mapped onto the underlying dichotomies to further sustain the 'modern' triple meaning of sovereignty. This case study is explained more fully in Prokhovnik (2002).

The tools used to construct an alternative, relational and interactive, conception of sovereignty include, as well as the exposure of the naturalised basis and gendered character of the 'modern' conception, the disclosure of the false dichotomy set up by the sex/gender distinction.

The critique by feminists and other theorists of the liberal, rational, autonomous individual (which are the primary qualifications for 'modern' sovereignty at all its three levels) has very effectively challenged the narrow and particular basis of the modern sovereign person which was made along gendered lines. Lloyd's classic work, *The Man of Reason. 'Male' and 'Female' in Western Philosophy* (Lloyd 1993), outlines conclusively the historical association of reason with men and body and emotion with women. Pateman (1988) makes a strong case for the liberal self-owning individual as a necessarily patriarchal conception. Wendy Brown criticises the individual rights discourse and argues strongly that 'rights consolidate the fiction of the sovereign individual' and that 'the terms of that individuality are predicated upon a humanism that routinely conceals its gendered, racial, and sexual norms'. She shows how rights language for women is unsatisfactory because it 'promise[s] increased individual sovereignty at the price of intensifying the fiction of sovereign subjects' (Brown 2000, 238), and because 'rights in liberalism also tend to depoliticise the conditions they articulate' (Brown 2000, 239). Hutchings sums up succinctly the important insight, noted in the previous chapter, that in the modern period, the 'sovereign individual is rational and exists in abstraction from both its own body and from other selves/bodies' (Hutchings 1996, 2). This critique has also had an important impact in problematising the givenness of the narrow basis of both the modern sovereign state and the modern citizen (Prokhovnik 1996, 1998, 1999).

The reconceptualisation of sovereignty undertaken here develops a relational and interactive principle, in contrast with the dichotomous, exclusionary character of the modern conception. But while the first step was to identify modern sovereignty as gendered, a further step can be taken to undermine the very gendering of the basis of sovereignty. A relational principle for sovereignty can be developed by exploring the consequences of the way in which gender has been determined by a given and natural biological sex. Feminists and others have disclosed that sex as well as gender is socially constructed. There is still room for biologists to study 'sex difference' and for sociologists to study 'gender roles and practices', so long as practitioners in both disciplines recognise the socially-constructed basis of their objects of study. But it follows that the basis of the sex/gender *distinction* and the exclusionary practices it has sanctioned, is shown to be invalid, because there is no meaningful category distinction involved. While it is recognised that this reconceptualisation replaces one metaphor with another, the relational and interactive metaphor has clear advantages over that associated with hard-shelled autonomy and dichotomy. It fosters the acknowledgement of the inter-subjective, historical, and culturally embedded character of meaning and social practices; it sanctions the validity of multiple interpretations; and it leads to an emancipatory politics.

The sex/gender distinction has a wide assortment of references, some of which are overlapping, covering a whole range of practices, all involving mediated understandings. But the list of the meanings of 'sex' – sex as psychological mainspring, as reproductive capacity either defined by anatomy or by biology more broadly, as a drive, as sexual orientation, as sexual activity, as love and intimacy, as power, as identity, and sex representing body – as well as the taxonomy of 'gender' – gender as sexed embodiedness, sexuality, sexual identity, gender identity, gendered division of labour or social relations, and gender symbolism – have all been mapped onto a man/woman dichotomy that has been read through, and interpreted in terms of, an underlying mind/body disjunction.

The idea that sex as well as gender is socially constructed contains several strands of argument. For instance, Nussbaum recognises one important aspect when she observes that the manner in which 'the difference in external genitalia figures in social life...is interpreted by human cultures; thus we are never dealing simply with facts given at birth, but always with what has been made of them' (Nussbaum 1995, 62). It follows, she elucidates, that even the 'common distinction between "gender", a cultural concept, and "sex", the allegedly pure biological concept, is inadequate to capture the depth of cultural interpretation in presenting even the biological "facts"' (Nussbaum 1995, 62). Lloyd builds upon this insight into the absence of a clear categorial distinction between sex and gender when she observes, 'our bodies, as they figure in our self-consciousness, are always already socially constructed' (Lloyd 1989, 20). Kaplan and Rogers take up another element of the argument when they demonstrate that 'biology is not value-free' (Kaplan and Rogers 1990, 205). Hood-Williams provides additional support when he argues that despite the fundamental assumption in much of the social sciences that 'what is called culture is variable and what is called nature is obdurate', it is clear that 'sex cannot operate as a sort of material base to the superstructure of gender. Gender is always already implicated within the attempts to define sex – whether as difference or similarity' (Hood-Williams 1996, 13).

Hood-Williams also recognises the cultural and historical specificity of the notion of sex found in the sex/gender distinction. Sex in the sense of reproductive organs as the 'foundation of incommensurable difference', was only 'invented' in the eighteenth century, he notes (Hood-Williams 1996, 12). Previously women had been considered to be imperfect men. Laqueur confirms that before the seventeenth century, the sexed body 'was still a sociological and not an ontological category' (Laqueur 1990, 8). Moreover, the bipolar definition of sex was consolidated only in the twentieth century with the entrenchment of a biological notion of a natural sex difference based on the presence of X and Y chromosomes, taken as providing explanatory force. Recent biological evidence, however, presents such a complex picture of sex difference that a simply bipolar definition on the basis of genetic chromosomal and hormonal criteria cannot be maintained. In addition the extent of cases of 'deviance' from the 'norm', as well as the normative exclusivity of the norm/deviance dichotomy, calls into question the utility of those criteria. Laqueur makes the case that science 'does not simply investigate, but itself constitutes, the difference...of women from man' (Laqueur 1990, 19), and Haraway condemns as 'bad biology' the widespread 'fetishisation of the gene, where the gene is seen as the blueprint and makes everything work'. DNA molecules 'are never working in isolation', she says. They 'are always working in inter-action with other cell structures...the smallest unit of life is the cell, not the gene'. The gene is not 'a simple, concrete thing', but 'always in process', a 'name for an observed process' (Haraway 2000, 95, 91).

Moreover it is now clear that biologists rely upon assumptions about sex difference which go beyond the scope of their scientific method and evidence, and that this further undermines the scientific claims about sex difference made by them (Hood-Williams 1996, 9–11, Segal 1994, 219–20). Furthermore a decisive specification that conclusively resolves the basis of the criteria for the biological basis of sex determination has yet to be provided: candidates include observable genetalia, reproductive capacity, genetic chromosome formation, hormonal makeup, all of these, or some of these. In addition the proportion of persons designated as 'women' who are actually fertile at any time is perhaps only half of all women, due to physiological problems, or malnourishment, or simply because even without these factors women are fertile only between the ages of approx-imately 15 and 45 and only within a part of the menstrual cycle (Hood-Williams 1996, 5).

A medical model of human sexuality, in terms of anatomy and disease, has been used to reinforce the belief in natural bipolar sex difference and its heterosexual/ist consequences (Kaplan and Rogers 1990, 223). In the light of the complexity and variations found in the biological evidence, the 'rigid either/or assignment of the sexes is only a convenient social construct, not a biological reality' (Kaplan and Rogers 1990, 214).

One of the consequences of the reductionist biological explanation on which the sex/gender distinction rests has been the idea of strict bipolar sex assignment, and the 'natural' attraction of the 'opposite' sex (Kaplan and Rogers 1990, 217). It is this naturalised explanation, and the imposition of the heterosexual/ist norm which assumes the complementarity of the (two) sexes, such that the conventional idea of 'sexual preference' (which can only mean between men and women) is coeval with sex difference, and with gender difference, that gay, lesbian, and queer theories have challenged very effectively.

Hood-Williams provides a range of valuable evidence for the view that the sex/gender classification is 'wrong in its apparent assumption that a straightforward distinction may be made between these two terms' (Hood-Williams 1996, 13). Once the dichotomous force of the sex/gender distinction (biology/social) construction is exposed as false, then it can be seen that there is only (multiple) thing at issue here, that is neither sex nor gender, and that its character and features need to be retheorised.

There is only one (multiple) thing, not a plausible sex/gender distinction. It follows that in the complex multiplicity of identity, a 'natural' identity cannot plausibly be isolated from constructed elements. We only know 'natural' elements of ourselves through actions and behaviour which occur in a constructed world of social practices and their multiple and contested meanings, and thus have no access to any separately 'natural' base. For instance, from hunger alone we cannot construct the meanings which eating has for us.

The sex/gender distinction was taken up by feminists in the 1970s to specify an area of choice and agency for women in the social world distinct from the biological definition of sex. But one of the major effects of the sex/gender distinction has been to reinforce the dichotomisation of sexual difference. Butler, Grosz and Gatens have outlined two linked dichotomies generated by the dichotomisation of sexual difference. These are the bipolar male/female dichotomy (based on anatomy) and the bipolar heterosexual/homosexual dichotomy (based on sexual orientation). As a result of the dichotomisation of sexual difference, which underpins the specific dichotomies of man/woman and heterosexual/homosexual, it is clear that the sex/gender distinction also operates dichotomously. In effect these three dichotomies operate as a cluster. They are interrelated and reinforce each other. Indeed, Brown makes a strong case that the attempt to provide the category women with rights has resulted in the consolidation of 'the regulative norms of gender', such that 'sexuality and gender have been folded together in the rights designed to protect women from injuries sustained on the basis of heterosexually defined gender'. The outcome is that the 'heterosexual designation of women, is reinscribed in the formulation of rights promising redress' (Brown 2000, 234, 235).

In consequence, while being designed to distinguish (mistakenly as it turns out) between the natural and constructed aspects of identity, the sex/gender distinction has operated socially to map onto the binary pair between anatomical sexes, and onto the mind/body split. Brown analyses how 'gender itself is the effect of the naturalised sexual division', with the result that 'rights oriented toward women's specific suffering... have the effect of reinforcing the fiction of gender identity' (Brown 2000, 237). In this way, since the 1970s man has equalled gender, which is associated with mind and choice, freedom from body, autonomy, and with the public realm, while woman has equalled sex, associated with the body, reproduction, 'natural' rhythms and the private realm. The sex/gender distinction, instead of giving women their promised liberation through gender role choice, has actually functioned to reinforce their association with body, sex, and involuntary 'natural' rhythms. The sex/gender distinction has acted to consolidate the man/woman dichotomy.

The upshot of this argument, taken with the critique of the heterosexual/ist norm, is that not only the parts but the whole distinction between sex and gender no longer works, once the value of a relational social constructionist viewpoint is recognised. The first step in the reconceptualisation of the things described and misdescribed by the terms sex and gender is the crucial recognition of two suppressed groups – the visibility of women and the visibility of those with marginalised sexualities. The second step is the conceptualisation of corporeal subjectivity. This involves a reimagining of personhood which crucially recognises bodies not just as material, biological, physical and sexed objects in terms of the mind/body split mapped onto the man/woman dichotomy, but as crucially interconnected centres of embedded thought and feeling. These two steps, of visibility and corporeal subjectivity, need to be taken in sequence, for the assertion of the second step taken on its own would only dissolve into the familiar male-defined notion of gender neutrality. On this basis the problems of essentialism and the equality/difference dilemma that have plagued second wave feminism, can be shown to rest on adherence to a misplaced mind/body dichotomy.

In sum, then, this argument goes beyond 'sex and gender'. It goes beyond 'sex' because it identifies some of the extended implications of what it means to say that biology is not neutral, and shows how the dichotomy between sex and gender on this basis is flawed. There have always been and always will be men and women, but the categories of man and woman and whether and how their definition is dichotomous or not, have been constructed differently at different times. In a non-dichotomous relational mode of theory and pactices the man/woman distinction would cease to operate as the key which genders reason, work practices and social practices and values in an exclusionary manner.

The argument goes beyond 'gender' by showing that having demonstrated the social construction of sex as well as gender, it follows that the ground is cut from under the uniquely social definition of gender. The sex/gender distinction referred precisely to an invalidly constructed natural/constructed contrast. The theoretical distinctiveness of gender from sex is untenable once it has been shown to share with sex a complexly constructed basis.

The argument goes 'beyond sex and gender' by contending that it has not been sufficiently recognised that the significance of having bodies extends beyond what anatomical sex they are. The sex and sexuality of bodies, as understood in biology and medicine, has colonised and transfixed the whole recent discussion of bodies. Bodies are sexed but perhaps even more importantly bodies are used to express a range of other things as well – they are the tangible location of personal narrative and social identity, family history and social genealogy. They are ethnically coded, inscribed with social and cultural meanings and generational values, and are centres of lived experience. Within this range the 'fact' of biological sex difference cannot be taken as foundational. Bodies as lived and experienced in culture are not reducible to an explanation which is biological, materialistic, deterministic, and causal. The meaning of materiality is also and always socially mediated. The modern mind/body and culture/nature dichotomies still powerfully at work in our culture prevent us from recognising how radically body, intellect, emotions, character, identity, and memory are interdependent and are integrated in experience.

Having outlined the reasons for a relational and interactive conception of the link between man and woman, mind and body, gender and sex, rather than a dichotomous conception that trades on the modern metaphor of autonomous state sovereignty, we turn again to the state level of the metaphor. A conception of sovereignty among other things spells out the particular form of the principle of order, the relation of rulers to ruled, which governs that political community. At the beginning of the twenty-first century there is now a disjunction between the longstanding dominant modern western meaning of sovereignty and recent innovations of theory and practice. The reimagining of state sovereignty also takes place concurrently with other developments, in the context of a world now defined as post-Western, and conceived as containing more than just the one modern nation-state political form. The view of the world as simply composed of Westphalian states, with a monopoly on the definition of the unit of political community, has passed. In consequence the notion of indivisible and absolute sovereignty as the exclusive, exclusivist and defining property of the Westphalian state, is losing its centrality. Feminist and other theorists have identified certain of the gendered characteristics of the modern sovereign individual. They have undermined the very gendered basis of modern sovereignty, and are now re-theorising sovereignty as a relational and interactive principle of political order in a variety of ways.

A key insight underlying these contributions has been the exposure of the naturalisation of the modern conception of sovereignty (Hoffman 1998) as normal and neutral, 'inevitable and universal' (Deudney 1996, 190). The process of naturalisation, which describes the confusion of conception with concept, occurred on the basis of the naturalised biological definition of bipolar male and female persons (Grosz 1990, 334–5, Haste 1993, 61, Plumwood 1993). Accordingly the identification of women with body and the natural, was contrasted with the naturalised freedom of men from body (Brown, 1987). In this way attempts to extend the liberal theory of autonomous individualism, especially to include women, is persistently undermined by the unacknowledged tie to a biological sexed body.

The contributions of feminist and other theorists also contain another central insight, the notion of the reconceptualisation of sovereignty in terms of the achievement of identity as a form of the integrity of the whole. This notion contrasts with the idea of sovereignty in the modern period as either an absolute and abstract rights-bearing unity or as absolute domination over subjects. The sovereignty of a political community, citizenship, and the sovereignty of the person, are all now being explored in terms of overlapping and multiple identities engaging with others and groups. All three levels of sovereignty are also being explored as constructed (constituted within particular societies and cultures), malleable, contestable, and open to self-reflection (Walker 1993, Biersteker and Weber 1996, Bartelson 1995). In addition all three levels of sovereignty are being explored as conditional, limited, constrained, permeable and modified rather than as absolute within an exclusivist boundary. The fusion that took place in the modern period of the Westphalian state form with the idea of sovereignty, is now widely recognised as historically contingent rather than as necessary to the logic of the concept of sovereignty.

Among promising recent contributions to the consequent flourishing debate have been the proposal, against the backdrop of coercive state sovereignty, to reconstitute sovereignty through the relationship it poses between ruler and ruled, through the recovery of the sovereignty of the individual in relational terms (Hoffman 1996, 1998). Further promising proposals include the idea of devolved sovereignty embracing in positive fashion 'a toleration of diversity and central-state incapacity' on the Philadelphian model (Deudney 1996, 229); the 'unbundling of sovereign rights' of ownership and access (Kratochwil 1995, 28); and the 'uncoupling' of 'citizenship from sovereignty, shared nationality and territoriality' (Linklater 1998, 200), in the light of the barriers of exclusion effected by the fusion of these four components in the modern conception. In many of these recent proposals the reconstituted state acts as the focus of multiple identities rather than as the sole definer of and instantiating a single and fixed identity. Furthermore, it is now possible to rethink internal/external, the defining dichotomy for the state form, corresponding to public/private as the defining dichotomy for liberal political society. Alternative conceptions to the bipolar one envisage internal and external as on a continuum, in terms of a blurring around an internal-external boundary or overlap between them, the forging of connections between internal and external, internal and external as interactive, and internal and external as helping to constitute each other's meaning.

Rob Walker is also deeply insightful about the metaphor of sovereignty. For him the issue is the way state sovereignty is a spectre over political life, due to the way sovereignty has worked as a master concept in the modern period designating relations between self and other, inclusion and exclusion, internal and external in terms of given dichotomies. According to this view the default position for our thinking and our ideas is to perceive ranking, hierarchy and opposition, and the default position for our practices is to construct unbridgeable boundaries and borders. This view holds that the dominant strain of our inherited tradition of ideas, practices, ways of valuing, and ways of organising the world is to use these patterns of superiority and inferiority, domination and subordination, civilised and uncivilised, together with the gulf between them and the idea of an edge or rim or brink of civilisation beyond which is unfathomable in the same terms, to explain and provide exemplary meaning. In seeking to explain and understand events and phenomena in social and political life and especially in international relations, our first recourse is to find significance and explanatory force, and answers to questions about purpose and intention, in these patterns, to immediately and lazily translate self-other relations into an us/them dichotomy. The metaphor from the individual person and the edge provided by their skin, to the state form of sovereignty with its fixed territory and boundaries, is particularly cogent here.

Turning again to the level of the person, the contribution of feminist and other theorists to a reconceptualised conception of sovereignty, develops the relational sovereignty of *personhood* by exploring the potential of the metaphor of the self, no longer seen as the unsocial and self-interested individual radically abstracted from others. Between the isolated self of methodological individualism and the absorption of the self into community, there is a broad range of relational and interactive possibilities. In Hutchings's terms, noted in the previous chapter, the 'sovereign individual as the disembodied owner of property in his own person...of...Locke', the 'Kantian autonomous agent central to the voice of justice', and the 'Cartesian conception of the self at the heart of modern epistemology' (Hutchings 1996, 2), is now supplanted by the relational personhood of constituted embeddedness within a 'family' dynamic. The antecedently individuated and unencumbered self gives way to a subjectivity which is understood as developing interdependently within a particular society's concrete practices and languages, values and principles, tensions and mappings. In a radically relational way, Coole outlines a valuable theory which identifies individual and collective agents in the middle range of a spectrum of agentic capacities and processes centred on the body (that runs from corporeal processes to transpersonal intersubjective practices) that emerge and operate in a shared lifeworld. Such a theory provides, as Coole shows, a plausible alternative to the problems associated on the one hand with the modern 'ontology of rational agents whose freedom and responsibility are related intimately to their interiority' (Coole 2005, 126) as well as to those associated on the other hand with the disappearance of political agency in Butler and Foucault.

Coleman criticises the idea of self-ownership as an 'intensely individualised' concept (Coleman 2005, 128), that constructs individuals as sources of rights on the basis of a negative freedom that 'excludes any duty to help others' (Coleman 2005, 127). Contemporary liberal discourse uses, she notes, a very distinctive and 'impoverished, definition of what it means to be a person...collapsing "person" into private, self-conscious, self-identity of self-owners' (Coleman 2005, 128), which ignores the important older meaning of 'owning' as taking responsibility for. Coleman's portrayal of the pre-modern picture, 'not of exclusive rights over one's being and powers, construed as self-ownership, but rather of one's moral relations with others as certain kinds of social agents from the beginning' (Coleman 2005, 140), of '*dominium* as collective sovereignty' (Coleman 2005, 142) is also fertile ground for rethinking. Pointing to the broader historical resources at our disposal, she argues that in Aristotle as well as in the pre-modern natural law traditions, individual rights claims were considered only after 'a collective commitment to ensure that all people, whether poor or rich, educated or not, get treated with humane concern for their well-being by a public sharing in collective goods' was fulfilled (Coleman 2005, 141).

Brace's work on how classic liberal notions of self-ownership and self-sovereignty co-existed with women's servitude and a range of forms of slavery and bondage, brings out the resilience of the modern metaphor of sovereignty and its high tolerance of inequalities and anomalies. This corresponds to the tolerance in realist international relations of anomalies where states do not qualify as sovereign, autonomous, and self-determining. The symmetry between conceptualising individuals in terms of boundaries and perceiving differentiation in international politics in terms of territorial borders is powerful and self-fulfilling. The modern liberal conception of sovereignty and its metaphorical reach is tolerant of anomaly for three reasons – it is self-proclaimedly tolerant (up to a point) of difference; the abstraction of its own story of individual empowerment has the effect of denying a problem; and its dichotomous thinking (looking to organise the world in terms of self and other) actually produces anomalies.

The reconceptualisation developed here mirrors the change by which the inflexible hierarchy of the fixed conception of order of Westphalian state sovereignty gives way to a dynamic intersubjectivity. In the modern period the sovereignty of the individual in the private realm of the family closely resembled in miniature the hierarchical and exclusionist (that is dichotomous) character of modern state sovereignty. This supposedly gender-neutral individual who had the characteristics associated with male gender (Carver 1996, Brown 1987), fulfilled the role of patriarch in the hierarchical family. It is ironic that in successfully undermining in their different ways the claims of natural patriarchal political rule, Hobbes and Locke helped to reinforce the claims of the patriarchal family.

Brace (1997) usefully compares Hobbes's and Winstanley's conceptions of the metaphor of self-sovereignty in terms respectively of territory and domain. Hobbes's theory, she argues, creates the image of a fortress with boundaries which exclude rivals, and uses a boundary metaphor that implies a masculinist sense of separation and dread of engulfment, where any relationship is based on struggle, distrust, vulnerability to invasion, and competition for mastery and dominion. According to this conception the aim of sovereignty is about 'fixing the territory, staking a claim to ownership and enforcing a monopoly' (Brace 1997, 144). In contrast, for Winstanley the sovereign self identifies with wholeness, and he regards the Fall as the source of the creation of division and private property. For Winstanley, relationships imply individuality within wholeness, and sovereignty requires the acceptance both of boundaries and of community. As Brace puts it, from Winstanley we can draw a vision in which each person 'inhabits her own domain, but is also partially constituted by her relationship with others', tied together 'by their common interests and by the world' (Brace 1997, 149). The contrast between Hobbes and Winstanley makes it possible to visualise a space between engulfment and conquest, a chance to be neither enclosed nor excluded, and a chance to move beyond sovereignty primarily expressing social relations of power. Sovereignty understood through the static metaphor of boundary structures relationships only through contract, as 'restraints on our natural proclivities' between 'separative' selves, where the best one can hope for is to draw a line in water. By contrast sovereignty understood as dynamic and relational provides a means to 'meet others morally' as interdependent selves, and a means of 'clearing a space' for the self that is subject to neither conquest nor engulfment (Brace 1997, 153).

The relational sovereignty of personhood crucially recognises that the integrity of personhood is established in sounder and more grounded form by drawing upon the individual's complex ties of attachment and interdependence, complex connections of reciprocity and care, as well as in the acknowledgement in each other of an idea of autonomy under rules of justice set apart from us as particular individuals. Rather than attempting to isolate an abstract and universal idea of the individual, this conception acknowledges the importance of ties that are found through family, and significant others, as well as by engaging with cultural constructions of ideas, and social practices and norms. The recognition of the integrity of personhood in dynamic inter-subjective interdependence is one of its constituent features. But giving up the conception of the abstract unencumbered subject does not mean 'drowning the sovereign subject in the ocean of non-differentiation', as Brace puts it (Brace 1997, 137). Relational and interactive sovereignty at the level of personhood also views the family not as hierarchical and exclusionary but as polycentric, and thus as a fit site for democratic relations. Relational personhood within a family dynamic refers to a family both in the sense of variously-composed family groups (formal or informal, traditional or one-parent or single-sex), and as a metaphor for the chosen and unchosen networks or clusters of persons within which we each live.

The move away from the subordinate role of women and children in traditional hierarchical families, leads to a new emphasis on children as persons worthy of respect and to the possibilities of democratic relations with children in the family. The relational sovereignty of both the family and of citizenship has the capacity to recognise children as persons more fully. It also leads to a reassessment of women in the roles of wife and mother, and a reconstruction of those roles. The use of the term 'sovereignty' in relation to the family gains credence from the perspective that all stable family groups can be characterised by the operation of some identifiable principle of order (whether it be patriarchal, matriarchal or democratic), and by the role of recognition in that order. The term 'family sovereignty' does not imply that families are states writ small or that states are families writ large. The differences between families and states as organisations are clear and important. These include their influence on politics, the basis of belonging to one and the other, their size, their impact on the social world, their purposes and aims, the kinds of obligations and commitments involved in each, and the significance of the family and the state being on different sides of the public/private divide.

Turning again to the level of the citizen, in the modern period, the notion of citizenship has defined equal membership in the political community by the individual, and the legitimacy of their rights as meaningful powers to political participation, economic independence and welfare claims. There is a strong feminist-inspired case for a citizenship (Lister 1995, 1997, Walby 1994, Prokhovnik 1998) which contests the liberal definition more radically than simply seeking to 'add women' to the current construction. Brown aptly summarises the work of feminists in disclosing 'what liberalism cannot deliver, what its hidden cruelties are, what unemancipatory relations of power it conceals in its sunny for-mulations of freedom and equality' that characterise the 'condition of entrapment' of women (Brown 2000, 230). Liberal democratic citizenship has contained an underlying opposition in which it is mind (and so freedom and a narrow rationality) that is active in the public sphere, with body (and so child-bearing and emotional connection) active in the private sphere. According to the liberal view access to the world of agency of which citizenship is a part can only be gained through transition to the public sphere, which is a public space insulated from the private sphere.

Because this notion of citizenship rests upon an abstract and universal conception of the individual, and upon a dichotomous public/private distinction, it has been unable to recognise the political relevance of gender. Its 'gender-neutrality' has had the effect of excluding women, both in practice and by the terms of the theory, in such a way that legislating for women's inclusion has not been an effective remedy. As Walby says, '[a]ccess to citizenship is a highly gendered and ethnically structured process' (Walby 1994, 391). Unless the powers that citizenship grants are underpinned by a clear sense of citizenship as a social status, those powers do not bestow citizenship. The exercise of particular powers is not in itself sufficient for the granting of full citizenship status.

A strong case has been made for an alternative conception of citizenship, grounded in the sense that persons whose freedom and autonomy are recognised as including their relational connections which originate in the private realm, and whose rationality includes their being embodied and emotion-bearing, can be active in both spheres as citizens. This view is thereby different in important respects from the maternalist feminist conception of citizenship developed from the insight that the private is political. The maternalist view derives the qualities of a redefined citizenship from the assertion of the moral primacy of the family, associated with the traditional female virtues of nurturing and cooperation. It seeks to prioritise these qualities in political debate and government policy making. The maternalist view is not only unrealistic about the prospect of the acceptance of maternal values in public life and about the character of politics. It is also in danger of resulting in 'sexually segregated norms of citizenship', and of legitimising the traditional sexual division of labour (Lister 1995, 12).

The key to citizenship in the feminist conception proposed here is defined, rather, in terms of its extension to women and other marginalised groups of a fundamental social value of equal ethical social status, which is not conditional on participation in specific activities in the public realm. Ethical association between persons in a political community may then be recognised as expressed in a diversity of practices, rather than being tied to narrowly-specified political and economic performances.

Conclusion

This chapter has highlighted and celebrated the importance of metaphorical explanation in establishing a successful form of sovereignty. In general terms metaphor acts as a mechanism ensuring continuity of explanation between the three levels of the state polity, citizenship, and personhood. The chapter has thus identified three kinds of mapping by which societies present a relatively coherent social reality and social explanation, but has argued that in the modern period a dominant dichotomous self/other mapping principle whose primary form is the mind/body dichotomy has had oppressive effects. The argument has further contended that the dominant conception of sovereignty over this period has replicated the self/other principle. The role of metaphor has been, more specifically, to effect the connection between the state and individual levels of sovereignty through the value accorded to Locke's postulation as literal of what Hobbes considered to be significantly metaphorical.

Feminists and other theorists have contributed to a relational reconceptualisation of the sovereignty of the self, citizenship, and the sovereignty of the variety of political communities. The metaphor of sovereignty as interactive, intersubjective and interdependent replaces the metaphor of sovereignty as mastery over, competition with, and distrust of. By metaphorical extension, this notion of dynamic interrelated personhood can legitimately lead to a richer conception of the basis of political communities and their relation with other polities, and to a richer view of citizenship.

A process of mapping still occurs with relational sovereignty, and still between the political community, the citizen and the person. But the character of the mapping is different in two crucial respects. The mapping is no longer simply seen as given and natural. It is now recognised as socially constructed and malleable, and as particular and culturally-realised. Moreover the mapping involved here differs from that involved in the modern conception of sovereignty at its three levels. For this mapping can recognise important differences between the forms of organisation (such as the family and the polity), as against the reductionist and homogenising, abstract and universalising impulse of the modern conception.

4
The Politics of Sovereignty

This chapter continues the work of disentangling the meaning of sovereignty from the modern state conception of it. Having outlined a relational conception of sovereignty in Chapters 1, 2 and 3, this chapter returns to the question of the political character of sovereignty. It argues that the political nature of the concept of sovereignty has been obscured in the modern state conception by the division of labour between internal and external dimensions. In the 'internal' discourse on modern sovereignty the emphasis has been either on analysing a depoliticised notion of authority or on prioritising legal over political sovereignty and promoting the *Rechtstaat*, and the discourse has largely understood political sovereignty very narrowly in terms of the highest authority to make law. The 'external' discourse has largely fixed upon political sovereignty very narrowly in terms of 'ruler sovereignty', the agency of the sovereign body acting as an individual. In consequence, full recognition of the political work of sovereignty has fallen between the legal and international relations discourses.

This chapter suggests that political sovereignty, as well as referring to the highest authority to make law and to ruler sovereignty, comprehends another, profoundly political task that we ask sovereignty to perform, beyond the legal/political distinction. Sovereignty is necessarily outside politics but it also establishes the sphere and condition of politics itself, the boundaries and limits of politics, and so the identity of the political unit. At the same time the settlement that sovereignty establishes is conditional and these functions are politically negotiable. This is part of the idea, developed in the Introduction, of the way sovereignty is not just a legal category but also depends upon the use of broader cognitive connections to recognise secondary rules. The idea of the 'mystery' of sovereignty calls attention to the way the concept of sovereignty is at the same time both political and unpolitical in this fashion.

This chapter also builds on the argument of the previous chapter. Seeing one thing in terms of another, or understanding a thing by mapping it onto an already familiar pattern of meaning, is central to the work of metaphor in our lives. To add a level of complexity we can recognise that all metaphors play with the boundary metaphor, for the boundary between the two things metaphorically related is being disrupted. To add another level of complexity sovereignty is a metaphorical concept *par excellence*, because its meaning is constituted in a complex mapping process which conditionally establishes boundaries. The potency of the concept of sovereignty lies in part in its metaphorical potential. Black describes how '[t]hose metaphors which turn out to be successful establish a privileged perspective on an object or constitute "the" object and by doing so, disappear as metaphors' (Black 1995, 15). This process whereby the metaphorical dimension of a meaning becomes invisible accurately expresses the way that sovereignty establishes the content and limits of politics as unpolitical.

The argument of the chapter is developed in the following sections. After describing the 'mystery' of sovereignty, its political character and the implications for theorising political identity are outlined. Then this meaning of political sovereignty is distinguished from legal sovereignty; attention is given to political sovereignty in this sense as a condition of the concept rather than as a new conception of sovereignty; and its conditional, contingent, unstable and indeterminate character is examined. The historical specificity of the idea is then explored, and finally other benefits of the idea are discussed.

The mystery of sovereignty

The Introduction specified some features of sovereignty as a political concept, and at different points in the book we have noted some of the ways in which conceptions of sovereignty, sovereignty claims, and discourses about sovereignty are political. Sovereignty provides the architecture within which other political concepts operate and so works as a master concept in this sense. The cluster of concepts involved in the meaning of sovereignty includes authority, legitimacy, and power; politics, law, economics, government, social values; democracy, participation, citizenship; rule of law; freedom, equality, individuals; choice, respect, autonomy, independence. Sovereignty also relies on recognition in a more complex way than other political concepts do. The successful working of sovereignty depends on the recognition of its distribution, coordination, allocation, and architecture functions, as well as on the recognition that the meaning of sovereignty is also constituted by the meaning of the things that make it up. It also depends on the recognition that all of this *does* define the political architecture. The role of recognition here also leads to sovereignty's function in greater or lesser identity formation of the 'whole'. In addition, order, cohesion, and stability follow from a successful setting up of its properties and conditions.

One of the perceptions that arises from such observations is that different conceptions of sovereignty shape political reality very differently and that sovereignty has a massive effect on the way we conceive politics. We can now identify an important attribute at the core of the concept of sovereignty, and thereby state a key 'mystery' about sovereignty. The category of sovereignty occupies a 'neutral' position outside of politics and would be invalidated if thought to be partial to or captured by particular interests, and yet it is also deeply political in regulating the negotiation of the norms and processes of political life in a particular society through a claim that is conditionally-stable. A key part of the 'mystery', then, is that all 'lived' conceptions of sovereignty, because they are maintained by the fragile mechanism of recognition and because they are political, are immanent, ongoing and highly charged. The mystery inheres in the tentativeness of reliance on recognition, in the way recognition is not given once and for all but needs regular reaffirmation, in the job of politics to negotiate indeterminacy, the way politics is conducted within rules and parameters which are partly tacit, as well as in the shadowy, not fully acknowledged meaning that sovereignty must have on a day-to-day basis.

We can use a transcendental argument as a starting point, to derive this characteristic of sovereignty from the character of politics itself. If we can take politics reasonably unproblematically to be among other things the search for social cooperation, the articulation and negotiation of contestation and difference, and the designation of political identity, then sovereignty is a condition of and for politics, in two ways. We use sovereignty to specify the boundaries of politics, for instance in the end or limits to politics in Schmitt, the condition of politics in Spinoza and Rousseau, the elimination of politics in Hobbes. In addition sovereignty helps to define (the nature of) politics and political practice in any particular society, through its links with a constitution, the kind of law and the importance given to it, the dominant political mentality, where the boundary between participation and dissent is set, customary ways of doing politics, and the sense of political identity. It also regulates norms, in social values, rules regarded as obligatory and usually practiced, customary conduct, moral beliefs, standards that constitute the identities of actors, as well as in patterns of behaviour that arise from fear of sanctions (Philpott 1999, 573).

Definitions of sovereignty which highlight 'supreme authority' only point to the extreme case, and so are only partial definitions. On a day-to-day basis sovereignty is much more importantly the repository of political values – about the nature, scope and limits of politics – which are expressed in laws, rules and policy orientations, as well as in social values and norms. This means that there are three tiers involved here rather than just two. The view that sovereignty involves a legal face in laws and a political face in the system of party politics and government, leaves out of the equation the crucial glue provided by social norms and values that in a sense express the constituent power of the people. The idea of three tiers also means, contrary to the view that popular sovereignty is dormant and secondary unless and until invoked in a crisis, that on a day-to-day basis both the constituent power of the people and governmental rule are both dormant.

The conventional meaning of political sovereignty designates a very limited notion of politics. It is a politics in terms of liberal democratic institutions and procedures (contested elections, a multi-party system, a free press, the rule of law, religion located in the private realm, a neutral public realm, liberal pluralism), focused on the legitimacy of the supreme law-making body. This narrow conception of politics leaves out of the picture of the political the still-active context out of which these institutions and processes have congealed. For instance, the changing patterns and changing impact of social values, norms, political culture, cultural reference points, controlling assumptions, ideological world views, and 'secondary rules' that sustain it (for well or ill – look for instance at the debate about voter disenchantment and the erosion of support for political parties), are all important. The volatile forms of popular energy and social movement (such as disability politics and pro-hunt campaigns in Britain) for contesting the settled channels in which established politics is conducted, the climate of opinion, and debates about the political identity of the polity, also help to form this context. Furthermore, just as different theorists who have theorised sovereignty have allowed different roles and meanings for politics, so different political societies have different approaches. Polities and theorists may enable and facilitate politics, prevent and erase popular politics, rein in and control politics in particular ways, align politics with the identity of the nation state, critique and dismiss the value of politics. The narrow conception of politics also sidesteps the way in which politics is the business of negotiating indeterminacy, and about making decisions about what counts as politics, the conditions under which politics operates, and the terms in which it is performed. The 'political sovereignty' highlighted here is about the overlooked but crucial importance of these kinds of 'background' and second-order factor.

In this way, then, sovereignty is a key means of setting out the degree of space allotted to politics (how much participation, dissent, contestation), as well as the ways in which politics is habitually expressed (the formal institutions and informal forms it habitually takes, what kind of 'street' politics is tolerated, and politics at national, regional, local, and international levels). Political sovereignty in this sense sums up the normative purpose and identity of the political form. It is also a power, in Morganthau's sense, the power of meaning imposition. Part of the meaning of the mystery of sovereignty here is that, in establishing the boundary between the political and the unpolitical, sovereignty functions as the principle beyond which there is no appeal to a more ultimate set of rules, and yet that boundary is only conditional and can be contested and re-formed.

Both of the ways in which sovereignty is a condition of and for politics set out sovereignty as unpolitical. Where a conception of sovereignty is generally accepted within a political society, its definition of the political/unpolitical boundary will be unpolitical and its specification of the definition and scope of politics within the polity is unpolitical. Moreover, the specific content of both these settlements will vary considerably from one polity to another across time and space. One of the things sovereignty enables, through a conditionally-settled claim, is the establishment of a stable link between rulers and ruled, and between the ruled, and it can do this precisely because it offers a settlement of what can and cannot be done by politics in a particular society. However (and this is the second part of the mystery), as well as functioning to specify politics, the limits of politics and the unpolitical, conceptions of sovereignty and the effects of sovereignty will at times be contested and challenged, and so become political – where meaning is no longer a given. Some kind of event triggers a feature or features of the background conditions or secondary rules to move from being unpolitical to being regarded as highly charged. As Schmitt recognised, 'we know that any decision about whether something is *unpolitical* is always a *political* decision, irrespective of who decides and what reasons are advanced (Schmitt 1985, 2, emphasis in original). By 'political' Schmitt means that this is the realm of intractability and conflict, and of priority over the legal. This point deserves to be underlined in a culture in which the meaning of sovereignty in particular is taken by many political actors and academic writers alike to have a wholly 'off-limits' fixed and universal meaning that ignores 'empirical tendencies' (Walker 1993) and that in practice acts to sustain patterns of privilege and exclusion. We will return to this point in the section on historical specificity.

Sovereignty marks out one version of the public/private distinction, in regulating the distribution of political, legal, and economic (and religious) power and the architecture of public institutions. Moreover, political sovereignty as specified here (in terms of the parameters, content, and limits of the political) is a precondition for politics to operate effectively. It is the necessary framework in which political moves can be heard, understood, responded to, or contested. This is because political activity is not a given, natural occurrence, but a human construction, and one which can be constructed according to different norms, principles and expressed in different procedures. Sovereignty in this sense thus does not provide a causal explanation but does supply a system of meaning and interpretation.

This is the mystery of sovereignty, then, something that is the case even though by normal logical standards it ought not to be so. Sovereignty is political and unpolitical at the same time, which seems contradictory but isn't. The way in which sovereignty is both political and unpolitical renders its definitive meaning elusive, mysterious. However, this mystery is not one that can or even needs to be solved. It is more like a religious mystery, a deep and half-forgotten truth, a truth that seems almost beyond reason. Fassbender (2003, 115) refers to the way that sovereignty, over 'the centuries... has acquired an almost mythical quality', and this is not just the cloaking of power that Foucault draws attention to. The mystery of sovereignty is not an ambiguity (holding two potentially contradictory things to be the case at the same time), it is not an ambivalence (uncertainty about which option to choose), it is not an enigma to be decoded nor a paradox to be resolved, and it is not a predicament to be overcome. By referring to the mystery of sovereignty neither is it suggested that sovereignty is a mere epiphenomenon or abstraction. Rather political sovereignty in this sense is a settled and stable mystery at the core of the constitution of the meaning of sovereignty (although also one which needs regular reaffirmation or reform and one which is precariously dependent on recognition, as described earlier), and it can be either or both benign and put to malign use in domination. It is part of the very concept of sovereignty itself to hold together that sovereignty is political but also outside politics. At the same time, identifying this attribute of sovereignty discloses a fugitive and transgressive quality in the meaning of the concept. As Brown notes, sovereignty contains 'multiple yet incommensurable truths' and 'challenges received authority – goes against the *doxa*' (Brown 2000, 238). We take it for granted that sovereignty at some abstract level functions to regulate politics but we also forget its own link to the political realm. In this way, the condition of sovereignty described here is also a mystery that has been here unmasked.

Whether the location of the sovereign is a prince, a queen, a parliament, an expression of the general will, the state, a constitution, a set of powers distributed to different institutions which check and balance each other, Stalin, or Leviathan, what they all do, behind the particulars of what they do, is establish (by word or deed or both) the content, character and limits of politics, and in doing so they are both unpolitical and political. This is so for both ancient and modern conceptions of sovereignty. Sovereignty is an important feature of politics itself. It is because sovereignty performs this role that we can then go on to say, for instance, that sovereignty is about establishing the relation between ruler and ruled. We have lost sight of this link between sovereignty and politics because in studying political concepts in political theory, we rarely talk about politics and the political. We take politics as a given and it gets erased. Moreover, there is a strong case for arguing that sovereignty changed in the modern period, not just because of the rise of the modern sovereign state, but also because of a change in how politics was done. Sovereignty is an effect of politics as well as acting to regulate politics. Starting with politics makes sovereignty look much more comprehensible.

It is useful to take a step back from questions of who has the power to act in the name of the collectivity, who has the ultimate legal authority, who has the power to coerce on behalf of the whole (the questions into which discussions of sovereignty are often immediately reduced), and to consider the habitual and conventional procedures and rules through which politics is conducted and which define its limits, and to note the political character of those things. By identifying how sovereignty is both unpolitical and political, it then makes sense that at the level of these questions of the locus of effective power, legal authority, and power to coerce, there can be very different conceptualisations of sovereignty, the coupling of state sovereignty with the dominant liberal popular sovereignty being only one.

The symbol of ruler sovereignty figures strongly in writers who see the state as dangerous and all-powerful and is taken up by Foucault in his conception of sovereignty as allowing a form of oppressive power relations. The idea of popular sovereignty has not banished the association of sovereignty with overpowering and tyrannical government. The notion of ruler sovereignty remains a powerful threat, from James II to Louis XIV to Napoleon to dictators of the twentieth century. The 'mystery' of sovereignty presented here focuses on something very different. Rather than aligning sovereignty with the dichotomy formed by the burden of unjust and burdensome government (or with political power inhering in 'the people'), the 'mystery' of sovereignty calls attention to the implicit but ongoing work that is done in shaping the parameters of political debate.

This function that we ask sovereignty to perform for the polity also has the effect of providing legitimisation for the polity. The way in which legitimacy is granted or achieved is often shrouded. We see the performativity of the election, the coronation, the popular assembly, but there remains a gap between such acts and the polity they are said to legitimise. With the kind of political sovereignty analysed here the gap is narrowed or eliminated for we can see the correspondence between the dominant or commonly-understood (if not universally agreed) norms and values about the conduct of politics and the settlement about the content and parameters of the political, the agreed area of (even if ever more symbolic) contestation and political negotiation.

This mystery of sovereignty is a condition that goes to the heart of the sovereignty concept. It fills in the meaning behind the definition of sovereignty as supreme authority, or as Bellamy puts it, 'some ultimate adjudicator of all conflict in a world where consensual agreement on the right and the good cannot be counted on' (Bellamy 2003, 171). Bellamy's conception, like the one put forward here, sees sovereignty as something we ask to perform a political function for us. This idea of the function of sovereignty in designating the meaning and limits of politics thus gets behind the definition of sovereignty in terms of questions about 'the proper exercise of power'. It provides a way of getting beyond the state as the concept that presupposes 'that central authority is a necessary condition for the existence of political order' (Bartelson 2001, 171).

The content, parameters and limits of the political that political sovereignty provides covers both Chryssochoou's constitutive principles, the 'conditions of shared rule', and the normative commitments, the 'search for the common good' (Chryssochoou 2002, 343). The condition for sovereignty outlined here also resembles in some ways the idea of 'normative order' that Neil Walker uses in his distinction between 'ruler sovereignty... the will to power as the source of normative order', and 'rule sovereignty... normative order as the source of power' (Walker 2003a, vii). It also represents one way of spelling out Neil Walker's contention that the different ways in which sovereignty can be operationalised (for instance identified by Krasner as domestic sovereignty, interdependence sovereignty, international legal sovereignty, and Westphalian sovereignty) gain their coherence from a 'common derivation from a deep core claim to know and order the world in a particular way' (Walker 2003b, 8).

Huysmans also sets out a political reading of sovereignty which, like the one delineated here, identifies a core function of sovereignty underlying its surface effects. He observes that (state) sovereignty is 'not first of all a principle of international law or a condition of territorially bound authority' but is rather, at a deeper level, 'a specific matrix that defines parameters that structure variations in the imagination of what constitutes proper politics'. In this scheme, sovereignty is pre-eminently 'a matrix of framing questions of the political', for 'fixing' in place the scope, meaning and limits of unity and law. It follows that issues such as 'the withering away of the state or the loss of control over societal flows by public authority' are not challenges to sovereignty if they do not defy the orthodox settlement of the political. Rather, reworking and challenging sovereignty goes much deeper than these phenomena and 'has to be interpreted as reworking and challenging the particular way in which the matrix frames the possible imaginations of the political' (Huysmans 2003, 226). Huysmans goes on to argue that the idea of the 'spectre of sovereignty refers to the difficulty, if not the impossibility, of escaping the matrix of sovereignty when imagining the political' (Huysmans 2003, 211), in other words the difficulty of rethinking politics outside the dominating state sovereignty form. Here Huysmans has in mind the specific problems for rethinking politics and sovereignty in the context of the modern state form and the realist construction of international relations.

The two key dimensions of this underlying matrix that structures the meaning of sovereignty, according to Huysmans, are the creation of unity in an inherently plural world, and the way sovereignty is tightly connected to the rule of law, a 'particular technique of governing the conduct of free individuals' (Huysmans 2003, 210–11). He notes that in the state sovereignty paradigm both these dimensions of the matrix of sovereignty are territorialized so that, for instance, the first dimension defines 'a plural international system of sovereign states'. Huysmans identifies the problematic nature of the second dimension in the context of the state model, not just in that it sets up a gap between normal rule and exceptional rule and maps this gap onto an internal/external dichotomy, but also because of the tension between legality and legitimacy, law and politics – as he puts it the 'tension between the law circumscribing the proper way of politics and politics circumscribing the proper rule of law' (Huysmans 2003, 226).

While the 'mystery of sovereignty' as outlined here looks functionalist, it much more importantly has a strong normative dimension. Determining the notional content of politics and placing the boundaries of politics at a certain point are outcomes of normative thinking about the relation between individuals and groups with the polity, participation and dissent, equality, democracy, multi-party electoral contestation, politics as progressive and transformative or conservative and constrained in the liberal sense. Answers to all such questions are the upshot of political debate within a larger or smaller group and are expressed in a dominant (either open to further contestation or exercising an oppressive hegemony) set of values.

The political reading of sovereignty advanced here also entails a freedom of action to take decisions on the nature and scope of the political (where those things are not naturally or neutrally given), and as providing a certain latitude for the expression of difference as well as of a sphere of commonality and equality. The active side of this is, as Fassbender notes, that sovereignty is invoked in practice most often in a political rather than legal fashion, when claims are being made 'for a change of the *status quo*, or claims to power', and the 'clearest manifestation' of the 'impulse to power' is still war (Fassbender 2003, 141). Sovereignty is in this sense a threshold concept, invoked when claims are being made on it or in its name. Fassbender attests to the political, 'untamed', character of sovereignty, notwithstanding the efforts of 'legal science to domesticate the notion and define it as the legal autonomy of a state under international law' (Fassbender 2003, 142).

Like Schmitt's theory, this notion emphasises the political nature of sovereignty and sees the political and unpolitical aspects of sovereignty as central to its meaning. Prokhovnik (2008 forthcoming) develops this view of Schmitt. Strong highlights this aspect of Schmitt's work. He notes that sovereignty 'is what Schmitt calls a *Grenzbegriff*, a "limiting" or "border" concept'. In other words, sovereignty for Schmitt 'thus looks in two directions, marking the line between that which is subject to law – where sovereignty reigns – and that which is not – potentially the space of the exception'. As Strong underlines, according to Schmitt, to 'look only to the rule of law would be to misunderstand the nature and place of sovereignty' (Strong 2005, xx–xxi). Like Schmitt, the performative character of the meaning of political sovereignty developed here is seen as important, though here the performativity lies in the way sovereignty is a process, constructed through specific forms of politics, rather than resting in the decisionist act of the sovereign President. However, this notion differs from Schmitt's theory in several key respects. Schmitt is committed to a state conception of sovereignty, places great weight on a dichotomous friend/ enemy distinction, and regards the nub of politics as contestation. In contrast, the mystery of sovereignty as outlined here is compatible with a relational conception involving a variety of polity forms and interrelations, and with politics understood as being as much about social cooperation as about conflict. Moreover, the key to sovereignty for Schmitt lies in identifying he who decides on the exception in the context of the threat of social disintegration. The proposal put forward here sees sovereignty more broadly, and post-theologically, and focuses primarily on challenges (such as from feminism or anti-racist politics) that fall short of the kind of political crisis experienced in Germany under the Weimar Republic. The notion developed here is also political in a more thoroughgoing way, in contrast with the perspective of Schmitt which keeps at the forefront the inadequacies of the legal order. At the same time the current proposal does not valorise liberal constitutionalism, so despised by Schmitt. As a result, the characterisation of sovereignty sketched here has the capacity to move beyond Schmitt's problematisation of sovereignty.

The ways in which this mystery is political

Faced with this mystery of sovereignty, there are logically several possible responses. Sovereignty, it could be maintained, is not political. The power given to the sovereign is non-reversible. Hobbes, Kant, and Hegel might for different reasons hold this 'denial' position. A second response could be that two senses of 'political' are being used here, at an ordinary level and a meta-level, such that the unpolitical and political parts of the mystery are not the same. Rousseau might be invoked here. A third response, and the one that seems to fit with the character of the concept of sovereignty most strongly, that both things hold at the same time, might be held by Spinoza, Locke and Schmitt in different ways.

This section of the chapter, however, draws together the historical and theoretical insights into sovereignty from the previous chapters and accents the political character of sovereignty. It is political in a range of respects. There are several aspects to the value of pointing to this mystery of sovereignty. The mystery of sovereignty discloses an important condition of sovereignty that has been overlooked in the political theory discourse. It reinstates the political as central to the discussion about sovereignty, reinvigorating the meaning of the concept and placing it at the centre of political imagination about the development of political practice and its capacity to enrich the meaning of politics. It thus reveals the extent of the depoliticisation of that political theory discourse. The way that discourse has been constructed is that it typically moves from the meaning of politics and resolves the question of the political straight away into questions of democracy, or justice, or rights, etc. This dislike and distrust of politics and the political and the haste to move the debate onto more acceptable ground is another aspect of the liberal character of our tradition of political theory. Restoring politics at the heart of sovereignty also moves us on from the way the tradition of thinking about sovereignty in the mainstream canon has been transfixed with the role of law and the location of sovereignty in a *Rechtstaat*. Notwithstanding the benefits and civilising influence of that discourse, restoring politics and the political to the centre of debate has the useful effect of qualifying the self-affirming and other-denying moralism of that tradition.

Sovereignty is political in having as its focus of attention *political* communities, political entities, polities, political societies, political organisation. It highlights the sense in which what persons have primarily in common is political relationship, rather than having an economic, linguistic, shared history, ethnic origin, birthplace, religion, or territory in common. They may have some of all of those things in common too but they are not primary. To have a political relationship in common is to live together in organised fashion alongside each other – as friends rather than enemies according to communitarian perspectives, or as strangers in the liberal view.

We have seen in earlier chapters that there is a politics of the (especially political theory and international relations) discourses about sovereignty. Sovereignty performs a very political function and establishes the source of political power – described as the 'mystery' of sovereignty. Legal sovereignty is political in being constructed one way rather than another, and the distinction between legal and political sovereignty is political in being in principle contestable. The meaning of sovereignty changes according to the values and norms of the country and over time, and the change in the meaning of sovereignty with the change in political form is political in the sense of not being derived from an uncontestable foundation. Sovereignty is an object of political knowledge, in the sense that sovereignty is not natural, normal and given, but is something whose meaning needs to be recovered as politicised and constructed by making choices for this rather than that. Sovereignty is open to political manipulation as an instrument of legitimacy, for instance by Pinochet in Chile, who in 1980 claimed that the success of instigating constitutional change through a referendum gave him a personal endorsement of his regime (Taylor 1997, 159). Sovereignty is also political in the ideological politics attached to the history of the term, especially in the liberal dominant modern state form. The self-fulfilling prophecy that we can see in the construction of the state form is political. The proposal in Chapters 1, 2 and 3 for post-states and other actors in a recast international sphere, informed by a communitarian and feminist logic that normatively advocates cooperation and the acknowledgment of interdependence, is all political in being normative. The subject of this chapter, concerning the contested ownership and meaning of the concept of sovereignty in the face of the lack of clarity about its meaning, purpose and utility, is all political.

The idea that sovereignty is exercised through claims to sovereignty points to the way that sovereignty is not just a discursive practice rather than an institutional 'fact', and is not just about the importance in authority relationships of making claims rather than asserting power. The idea of sovereignty as a claim also spells out the political nature of sovereignty, the way a claim is tentative, can be made against the grain of the dominant order, a point of contestation, a demand to be heard, or an assertion of inclusion. In addition, while a sovereignty claim is in one sense most successful when politics is depoliticised and naturalised, the conditionality of a sovereignty settlement ensures room for dynamic flexibility, both in terms of a balance of tensions within stretchy boundaries or through interrogation and reflection upon part of the background conditions which becomes recognised as highly charged.

Upfronting this political condition of sovereignty also puts into perspective the claims of those who argue that sovereignty is a malign concept, acting to exclude and to sustain marginalisation. While it is indeed true that modern state sovereignty has been used in this manner, the target should more accurately be the way the conception has been deployed and the practices it has been used to sanction, rather than the concept of sovereignty itself. Sovereignty's dirty hands do not go all the way down, and this criticism of it confuses concept and conception. The idea that sovereignty equates with a totalising form of knowledge is not a necessary claim, and re-establishing this political condition of sovereignty situates sovereignty within a wider context of knowledge. Relatedly, while sovereignty is upbraided as inimical to dialogue, persuasion, consensus and compromise, this criticism can again be seen as a function of the state form rather than inherent in the concept of sovereignty itself.

Another value of this meaning of political sovereignty is that the normative implication of reinstating the political in talking about sovereignty is to reconceptualise sovereignty where politics is envisaged in terms of the positive role of irreducible disagreements in promoting an open and inclusive political practice, rather than in terms of the inadequate Habermasian ideal of deliberative democracy. As Schmitt recognised, as Müller notes, 'even a decision on which concepts were political or not, was always already a political decision' (Müller 1999, 73).

This mystery of sovereignty also supplies a valuable political underpinning for Neil Walker's legal resolution to the problem of legal sovereignty. He argues that if sovereignty is 'simultaneously source and vehicle of the juridical order', there is 'a tension within its conceptual structure between legal and political registers – between the idea of law as foundation of the polity and the idea of law as the medium through which a non-legal or political foundation to the polity is given legal expression'. In response to this supposed incoherence in the definition of sovereignty, Walker responds that, rather than undermining the idea of sovereignty, this tension 'is actually key to the meaning and distinctive function of the *claim* to sovereignty' (Walker 2003b, 8). However, the proposal put forward in this chapter identifies a very different conditionality to the 'irreducible core, the non-negotiable given of any sovereign order', that Walker posits. For Walker, as a legal theorist, that 'core' is a sovereign order's capacity to 'assume its own continuing or self-amending sovereignty within its sphere of authority (rules of recognition and change)', along with its retention of 'interpretive autonomy (rules of adjudication)' and 'deciding the boundaries of that sphere of authority' (Walker 2003b, 28). The point is that the legal requirement does not trump the political condition of sovereignty, but in the European *Rechtstaat* tradition the legal has been given unprecedented and perhaps overstated authority in the meaning of sovereignty. However, there is overlap between the two meanings, especially for instance where Walker speaks of 'the ordering work of sovereignty...in providing an enabling normative frame for constitutional polity formation' (Walker 2003b, 32).

Political identity

The establishment of the political identity of the polity as a whole is a key feature of political sovereignty as outlined here. Sovereignty is not only about the identification and exercise of supreme authority, ruler sovereignty, the relationship between rulers and ruled set out in legal rules, state sovereignty as the expression in democratic polities of popular sovereignty, and the normative link between politics, law and morality/reason in the *Rechtstaat*. It is also about the (perhaps decentralised) symbolic unity of the polity, the 'imagined' political identity that expresses what is shared or held in common, as well as about the conditional settlement that enables the maintenance of political stability about the realm of the political and how political performance is conducted within it.

Not only states but all sorts of political entity need a clear sense of their political identity. The UN, the World Bank and other IGOs, NGOs and other agents in international politics – none of which claim to be states – all need a political identity and sense of the content and limits of their political contribution, in order to be able to operate effectively and to have a clear 'brand' in a crowded world. In that sense they all need a clear sense of their sovereignty. This claim challenges the Westphalian order based on the notion that states and only states are sovereign, but is consonant with the post-state proposal developed in Chapter 1. In the following chapter the significance of the aspect of political sovereignty concerned with political identity will be explored in relation to the conceptualisation of the European Union.

Legal and political sovereignty

In the Introduction we noted Neil Walker's definition of sovereignty as the starting point for the argument. Sovereignty for Walker is 'the discursive form in which a claim concerning the existence and character of a supreme ordering power for a particular polity is expressed, which supreme ordering power purports to establish and sustain the identity and status of the particular polity *qua* polity and to provide a continuing source and vehicle of ultimate authority for the juridical order of that polity' (Walker 2003b, 6). This definition seeks to balance legal and political aspects of sovereignty. Few commentators would support the legal perspective as fervently as Raphael does. He argues that sovereignty equates with 'supreme legal authority', and says, 'I do not think that state sovereignty can be understood as anything other than legal sovereignty' (Raphael 1990, 16, 154). Raphael's reasoning is that there cannot be a separate political or power theory of sovereignty because sovereignty is about authority and in modern states there cannot be an authority which is higher than a legal sovereignty, because the laws of the state have final authority (Raphael 1990, 155–6). The idea of political sovereignty put forward in this chapter highlights the limited nature of Raphael's perspective, underlining instead the political work that sovereignty does before legal sovereignty can be established.

One of the things that this book has sought to do is to argue that sovereignty also has a set of political dimensions which can be investigated within political theory and international relations theory but are outside the domain of constitutional and international law and invisible to mainstream international relations. Such political dimensions are necessary for understanding what the idea of 'ordering power' and the idea of 'polity' can possibly mean and how they are glued together. Articulating the 'mystery' of sovereignty thus throws new light on the relationship between legal and political sovereignty.

Brown (2005, 116) states the orthodox liberal state distinction between legal sovereignty as an unqualified juridical status setting out the legal position between states in the world, and political sovereignty as a political concept referring to a bundle of powers and capacities, the degree to which and the political nature of the actual capacities that states have to perform certain tasks. However, the distinction and connection between legal and political sovereignty is a complex and ambiguous one. The roots of the meaning of the distinction and connection are not simply 'given' but go back to the emergence of the modern model of sovereignty out of the medieval sanction of kingship by divine law, the modern secularisation of law and legal authority, and the subsequent development of the *Rechtstaat*.

The complexity of the distinction and connection between legal and political sovereignty is also compounded by the difference between the discourses in which law and politics are primarily discussed. The legal discourse is about rule-making and about a hierarchy of kinds of law. It takes the distinction between international and 'constitutional' law as natural, and has an inherently conservative social perspective in terms of security, order and legal authority. The mainstream political discourse equates political sovereignty with ruler sovereignty. Neither of these discourses capture the importance of political sovereignty as described in this chapter. There is also a close connection between the legal/political distinction and the *de jure/de facto* one, in that the latter is about the presence and absence of legal, that is formal, recognition, and so elevates the significance of legal form.

This chapter focuses on the political character of sovereignty. It is about the contrast between the legal approach to sovereignty which necessarily sees the solution to a problem in terms of making rules (and, in our *Rechtstaat* tradition, making rules within a moral framework), and the political approach to sovereignty which is about negotiating a space for politics. It is about confirming the priority of the political meaning over the legal meaning of sovereignty, and recognising how the political meaning of sovereignty has been shrouded by the key role attributed to the legal in the modern state *Rechtstaat* tradition by identifying conception with concept.

The post-state political conception of sovereignty outlined in Chapter 1 takes as crucial that the political character of sovereignty takes precedence over the legal character, such that legal sovereignty is the juridical sedimentation of political and politically arrived-at rules. However, it is worth noting the cultural specificity of this proposal. In political societies which incorporate religious principles into the political realm, such as in some Muslim countries that give priority to Sharia law, the balance between legal and political sovereignty is different. In such societies there is still an important role for political sovereignty, in sanctioning the priority of Sharia law, and in the constituent power of the people as such. But in this case legal sovereignty is substantially enhanced, not just because more weight is given to the idea of law but because political authority is taken to have a legal rather than secular and popular source. Currently there is also a case for arguing that in the USA Christian fundamentalist tenets have seriously encroached upon the long-standing idea of a secular state, and that the battleground to introduce explicitly Christian values is fought precisely through domestic and constitutional law in that country, for instance over abortion, nominees to the Supreme Court, the teaching of 'intelligent design' in schools, as well as in the 'crusade' of the war on terror in US foreign policy.

Loughlin's portrayal of sovereignty as 'a quintessentially political concept', and as 'a representation of the autonomy of the political, and as providing the foundational concept of the discipline of public law' (Loughlin 2003, 56) strengthens the argument made here, in focusing on the political role of sovereignty, and its priority over the legal aspect. He argues that 'sovereignty has been devised for the purpose of giving expression to the distinctively political bond between a group of people and its mode of governance', and that sovereign will is expressed principally through law (Loughlin 2003, 56–7). He also notes that '[p]roperly understood, political power does not reside in any specific locus, whether that be the king, the people or an institution such as parliament'. Rather, political power 'is generated from the particular quality of the relationship that evolves between the sovereign and subject, government and citizens. Political power generated through the apparatus of rule must be conceived as being relational' (Loughlin 2003, 65). Loughlin clarifies the meaning of 'relational' here through a quote from Croce, that in 'the relationship between ruler and ruled', sovereignty 'belongs to neither but to the relationship itself' (Loughlin 2003, 69). Loughlin's points are useful, not just in underlining the relational quality of politics but also in presenting the authority relationship discussed in the Introduction in a way that does not simply assume a benign and benevolent goodwill. Rather than ushering in a saccharine harmony, the authority relationship is precisely one in which contestation and dissent can and need to be voiced.

Loughlin also endorses the priority of political over legal sovereignty in an interesting argument in which he contends that sovereignty is not without its own inherent constraints, derived from the very nature of political sovereignty in the sense of the relation between rulers and ruled. As he notes, such 'limitations are derived from the basic tenets of sovereignty'. Without 'the limits implied by those tenets, sovereignty could not be identified as a representation of the autonomy of the political and thereby distinguished from the power that economic wealth, feudal dominion or despotism confers', he maintains. Loughlin holds that while law 'plays a critical role in explicating in the form of rules, regulations, rights and responsibilities the character of sovereignty authority', the 'determination of the limits to sovereignty authority, even when articulated by courts, must be political'. The limits of sovereignty are a matter of a political system 'authoritatively expressing its will', a will which is ultimately above the law (Loughlin 2003, 79). He also notes that the 'underlying relationship between rulers and ruled is one that lawyers – working on the assumption of the ultimate authority of the normative framework – have a tendency to suppress' (Loughlin 2003, 70). The political conception of sovereignty 'generally remains below the level of juristic consciousness', but is 'nevertheless one that is basic to an understanding of sovereignty, even in the juristic sense', because it is the one that makes the crucial link between rulers and ruled (Loughlin 2003, 71).

The modern distinction between legal and political sovereignty is, on close analysis, a very narrow one. This critique is not the same as that applied to the idea of the pre-eminence of legal sovereignty derived from positivist theories of law. That view presents law mistakenly as nothing more than positive law, 'law as a system of enacted rules' as 'an autonomous practice' (Loughlin 2003, 77), and focused only on competence. But like that critique, this one highlights the importance of the underlying political work that is going on. In the context of the state form of polity it distinguishes between the final authority of the sovereign people or sovereign assembly on the one hand and the final authority of the law that expresses political sovereignty. The sovereignty of the law and rule of law is regarded as foundational for political sovereignty to operate. As well as taking place in the context of the state political form this distinction is also indebted to the *Rechtstaat* conception of the relation between law and politics, of law expressing moral norms in the context of the state, and politics being about the struggle and debate to identify such moral norms and will them into law. What legal and political sovereignty also share, in this distinction, is a focus on ruler sovereignty, on the notion of being the highest authority to act and having freedom from all subordinate and lesser authorities to do so. This chapter puts forward another aspect of political sovereignty from ruler sovereignty, which is a condition for stable and viable political community and a crucial part of political identity. The idea of 'political sovereignty' is not about the question of ultimate authority but the equally important but largely unacknowledged way that the shaping of the development of norms and values which condition political action takes place.

Foucault denounces the juridical character of sovereignty, and indeed many of the conceptions of sovereignty discussed in the canon are heavily marked by a pre-eminence given to the idea of law and of the *Rechtstaat*. However, when Brown *et al* attend to the difference inherited from the Romans between *ius* (customary law) and *lex* (enacted law) that was still enormously influential into the early modern period, it prompts the sense that a way forward for reconceptualising sovereignty may be found in revitalising the notion of *ius*. In a relational and interactive conception of sovereignty there is an affinity between the groundedness of relationality and the idea of customary law. Revitalising customary law also moves away from the idea of the necessity of enacted law being the key mark of sovereignty. Brown *et al* describe how under Roman law, every '*lex*, being enacted at a particular time, is law only after it has been enacted. And, because it has been enacted, it can be amended or repealed'. While civil law, 'which governs relations between Roman citizens, is *lex*', the law governing 'relations between citizens and foreigners – that is, aliens living under Roman authority – was not the product of legislation'. Law concern-

ing citizens and foreigners was 'originally case law emerging from the decisions of administrators and judges handling disputes between the two
classes of persons. It is, therefore, a body of common or customary law'.
Brown *et al* describe how the 'Romans called this customary law governing
relations between members of different *gentes* or peoples *ius gentium*'. Then,
in 'late medieval and early modern Europe, *ius gentium* meant the customary law common to all or most civil societies. It is positive law in the
sense of being a social practice, not in being *lex* described by a sovereign'
(Brown *et al* 2002, 319).

The deeply political nature of the concept of sovereignty throws new
light on the distinction between *de facto* and *de jure* sovereignty. This point
builds on the one made in Chapter 2 about the *de facto/de jure* distinction.
The distinction trades on the inherent tension between and complementarity of political and legal sovereignty in the orthodox conception. Weak
states are held to have *de jure* sovereignty, the legal framework and international recognition, without the popular legitimacy or capacity to use
it in practice, either because another state holds *de facto* sovereignty or
because the basis for creating the state was weak, for instance in some
decolonisation projects, so the story goes. Other states are held to have
de facto status (on the ground workability) without the *de jure* (legal and
formal) standing to complement it, for instance if a state seizes part of
another states or seizes power without legal sanction, or states shunned by
the 'international community' like North Korea. In both these cases *de jure*
refers to external recognition or lack of it (which is a political matter), and
de facto refers to internal capacity or lack of it (which is also political).
De jure can also refer to the internal relationship between rulers and ruled
(for instance when a vote is close, and contested between polarised parties
or interests). These problems are not mirror images of each other, but point
to different forms of lack. The *de facto/de jure* distinction is not just a legal
matter, and does not simply line up with politics and law respectively. The
distinction is a deeply political one, and it is not a dichotomy because
states (according to the state sovereignty conception) need both to be
fully sovereign, and because neither one is favoured over the other – either
one without the other is equally unacceptable in sovereignty terms. The
de facto/de jure distinction is portrayed as exemplifying the role and importance of legitimacy in the concept of sovereignty, but it is also used to
either sum up or mask the political nature of judgements about who has
and who does not have sovereignty and power.

The political property of the concept of sovereignty identified here provides a deeper understanding of the distinction about sovereignty highlighted for instance by Franklin in relation to Locke, between constituent
power and ordinary power (see Prokhovnik 2008 forthcoming). The meaningfulness of the link between constituent and ordinary power, between
the power of the people as the ultimate lawmaking authority and the

legislative, executive and judicial branches of government, depends precisely upon the successful conditional settlement holding the specific content given to politics and the border between what is political and what is unpolitical. This is a key function we ask sovereignty to perform. One practical consequence that follows from the way the ordinary and constituent power distinction is made in modern polities is the decision in democracies about whether that distinction and connection is expressed in direct or representative form. Neil Walker also notes illuminatingly that, in Foucault's terms, 'sovereignty expresses both the power that enacts law and the law that restrains power – (political) ruler sovereignty and (legal) rule sovereignty – *pouvoir constituant* and *pouvoir constitué*'. Walker makes the case that for 'many, including Foucault, this double claim is testimony to the conceptual incoherence of sovereignty' but, Walker argues, 'it can also be viewed more constructively, as the conceptual key to sovereignty as a dynamic process of mutual constitution and mutual containment of law and politics'. If the term sovereignty is taken as 'expressive reminder' of the interdependence and mutual underpinning of law and politics, then the paradox dissolves (Walker 2003b, 19–20).

The condition of sovereignty identified here is also related to but different from the notion of *Kompetenz-Kompetenz* in the German law tradition, referring to the second-order competence to specify the first-order boundaries of the law. While both ideas are about borders and edges, and while the two are not unconnected, they are also distinct. *Kompetenz-Kompetenz* is more narrowly legal in focus, the second-order competence providing an answer to the limits, if any, of the law. The mystery of sovereignty, in contrast, is specifically about the content of the political and the political-unpolitical border.

The meaning of political sovereignty developed here also throws light on the question of the division of labour between sovereignty and a constitution. Although sovereignty and constitutionalism are closely aligned concepts, it is sovereignty which we invest with the function of deciding what is political and the boundary with the unpolitical. Rob Walker rightly insists that sovereignty is 'a highly complex and variable practice' rather than being just 'an inert constitutional principle' (Walker 1999, xiii). We use a principle of sovereignty, expressed in a constitution, to effect a distribution of powers, a coordination of institutions, an assigning of entitlements, and an allocation of values. Sovereignty and constitutionalism are contiguous, in some sense overlapping political concepts. A constitution does not have to have, in itself, a guiding principle – sovereignty provides this. Bellamy and Castiglione note Jon Elster's definition of the functions of constitutions, and this reinforces the sense of the closeness or overlap between the two. From 'a purely technical point of view written constitutions have three main functions: (1) to define and protect rights; (2) to establish a map of political powers; and (3) to fix the procedures for constitutional revision' (Bellamy and Castiglione 1997, 597). Moreover, while some theorists of cosmopolitanism put forward the idea of replacing sovereignty with constitutionalism, the problem with this proposal, as Schmitt understood, is that jurisdictional bodies are precisely not in a position to offer a decision in problematic cases that the law cannot adjudicate on. Where the problem is political the legal is impotent.

Political sovereignty in this sense is a condition of the concept, not a new conception

In drawing out this mystery at the heart of the sovereignty concept, this chapter is not simply adding yet another conception of sovereignty. This mystery of sovereignty is a general observation about the concept and not a full-fledged conception that lacks a historical grounding. What is being reinforced here is the tight link between the very concept of sovereignty and the condition of the political realm in a political society.

At the same time it is possible to spell out a general property of sovereignty without falling into the aridity of abstract conceptual analysis. There is a place for conceptual analysis but it must be complemented by historical analysis as well, in order to gain the full richness of the concept. The continuing salience of sovereignty as a political concept depends not only on demonstrating that it has multiple conceptions and untangling legal and international relations definitions from political theory ones. It depends also on disclosing the political work that we define sovereignty as doing for us. This formulation of the 'mystery' of sovereignty has the benefit of encompassing the variety of historical conceptions, and takes into account and thus is common ground between the understandings of sovereignty utilised in the different discourses discussed earlier. This meaning of political sovereignty also benefits from not being culturally-specific. It applies more widely than political communities with flourishing political domains and strong democratic traditions of citizen participation in the western sense. Even in totalitarian states there is an element of political sovereignty in this sense, because even in such regimes there is a clear sense of court politics even if not open politics, and there are older values and norms which inform the meaning of the political.

The argument here is very much about reconnecting sovereignty to politics, but not in the critical IR theory or critical security studies ways, which usefully exhibit how naturalised practices are political. The proposal developed here suggests that sovereignty as a concept is political in that its very work as a concept is intimately about the condition of politics, the content of politics, the context of politics, and the limits of politics. This chapter argues for the politicalness of political concepts – which is in itself perhaps unexceptional. But the argument is that the effect of that 'politicalness of political concepts' on the meaning of sovereignty is profound.

A question that is often asked of sovereignty is whether it represents a set of rules that either can or cannot be bent, do or do not have flexibility. This chapter sets out to demonstrate that it is specific conceptions of sovereignty that establish sets of rules, most familiarly the state conception of sovereignty, but that we can also discern analytically the way we use sovereignty to distinguish for us the meaning, scope and limits of politics.

The proposal put forward in this chapter does not universalise sovereignty. Its scope is more limited, arguing that, as far as we know and in history, the concept of sovereignty has a function in fixing the meaning and scope of the political. The meaning of the political – for instance what counts as political, which things are construed as temporarily or permanently on the political agenda, the scope of politics, etc. – represents a mass of shifting sands. In specifying a property of the concept rather than a new conception, the aim in this book is to attempt among other things to describe and analyse a bird's-eye perspective, but not a God's-eye view.

It follows from the way that political sovereignty in this sense is a property of the concept rather than a new conception, that the 'mystery of sovereignty' is a mystery for two further reasons, and both are related to the depoliticisation of the meaning of sovereignty in political theory. This meaning of political sovereignty is a mystery in the sense that the political functions we ask sovereignty to perform for us have been not only overlooked but mystified and shrouded by the universalised state sovereignty form and the universalising mainstream political theory discourse. This meaning of political sovereignty does not 'ontologise' a particular conception as foundational of political analysis, as happened with the state form. It is also a mystery because this form of political sovereignty raises the question of the politics of politics, the second-order question of competing views about the nature and limits of political activity, and the answers to second-order questions about politics are most often taken as given.

The political property of sovereignty is an organising principle, establishing order. As Reus-Smit sums up sovereignty is 'an intersubjective organising principle' (Reus-Smit 2001a, 527) involving mutual recognition. By an ongoing process of sovereigntising, the character of law, politics, governing, morality, international relations, and economics are established and conversely, in turn sanction the character of sovereignty in the polity. We use sovereignty as an organising principle for the public realm (notwithstanding that, according to the dominant liberal ideology, economic relations take place in the private sphere). In the West this sovereigntising process has also operated to identify, but in a negative sense, religion. Bodin and Schmitt emphasised the relation with law; Spinoza the relation with politics; Hobbes and Foucault the relation with governing; Rousseau and Hegel the relation with morality; Kant the relation with international relations; and Locke the relation with economics (see Prokhovnik 2008 forthcoming). But as well as being an organising principle, this meaning of political sovereignty is also a normative principle establishing, reinforcing or reforming dominant values, and also a functional principle.

Neil Walker is correct to identify the concept of sovereignty with a 'general ordering claim' (Walker 2003b, 7) rather than with the substantive practices of power and practical competencies and capacities that they enable in domestic and international politics. The kind of political sovereignty identified here is part of that 'general ordering claim' and is not equivalent with political practices. Because we use the term sovereignty to sum up this 'general ordering claim', it follows that we also use it to 'explain and justify the world', as 'a plausible mechanism to help make sense of the social world', as 'part of the metalanguage of explanation and political imagination' (Walker 2003b, 10).

The theories of sovereignty of Hobbes and Spinoza, representing crucially contrasting articulations within the range of the principal theories, can both be accommodated within this notion of political sovereignty as a property of the concept. For Hobbes and many other theorists, sovereignty establishes a fixed order, by instituting an inflexible hierarchy within the integrity of the whole, and within which the holder(s) of sovereignty form an indivisible unity, whose rule is subject to no other. For Hobbes, sovereignty thereby narrowly constrains the realm of politics. For Spinoza and others, sovereignty defines order by the orderly balance between different holders of a shared sovereignty in a dynamic tension, which generates a positively-embraced political realm.

Conditional, contingent, unstable and indeterminate

Part of the political import of sovereignty that this chapter highlights is that politics has no natural content, and so the necessary role of what we call politics in a world of irreducible plurality, uncertainty and contingency, of dealing with questions of living together, collective concerns, what we share in common, and how to deal with difference and those who dissent.

The content of politics (the things it deals with), the ways of conducting politics, the limits of politics, and the boundary between the political and the unpolitical are all contingent in the sense that they are all open to different determinations. There is no overall universal logic that says they must be this way rather than that. The claims of democratic politics, for instance, are made precisely because they are claims and not given by nature, reality, power, or a foundational rational logic. It is not simply 'natural' that, as democratic politics holds, the content of politics should focus on redistribution and equality, that its procedures should be open to all and participatory, that its limits should be the limits of perceived publicly-relevant equality, and that the boundary between political and unpolitical should be capable of being renegotiated by the people. All these categories are contestable and interactive, and shaped by specific cultural, political and historical traditions and dispositions of power, and so arranged differently in different polities. We need to attend, for example, to the way the political mindset expressed in the political language and shared assumptions of the seventeenth-century Northern Netherlanders differs from mindset, language and assumptions of the twenty-first-century Briton. Political sovereignty in the way it is described here alerts us to the specificity of the conditional definition of 'the political' in any particular polity, the importance of that specificity, and that it is not based on the actions of particular agents.

Political sovereignty in this sense is not a declaration, a performative use of language, a speech act, but a consensus but not a unity, a conditional settlement, upon which political practices and linguistic communication run smoothly. Typically it emerges through the organic process of the formation of political identity, not fully subject to purely rational debate, containing tensions and incoherencies, with different parts (and combinations of parts) of it articulated and rearticulated and reproduced over time. This meaning of political sovereignty is not simply equivalent to political culture, political custom, traditional practice, and the habitual language and mindset of a political community, because it is also subject to 'rationalist' and other ideas and principles and explicitly-defended egalitarian and conservative moral values and social norms.

Another aspect of the 'mystery' of political sovereignty arises from it *not* being judicified in a treaty, protocol, pact, or treaty. It is a practice, an implicit acknowledgment, rather than an explicit legal rule. It remains political in the sense of slightly unstable and ambiguous if looked at closely rather than legal (codified), a fluid rather than a solid. This political sovereignty is necessarily implicit because this is the only way sovereignty can define the boundary between the political and the unpolitical. Political sovereignty in this sense is necessarily a given, even though its provisions can be contested.

An important part of the 'mystery' of sovereignty refers to something that applies much more widely. The conditional settlement of the content and boundaries of the political is a necessary feature of life, along with the way we have habitual forms of action such as, on getting up in the morning we brush our teeth and have breakfast without stopping to think about whether these are things we really want to do. Life would be insufferable if we had to rethink afresh each action, idea and belief each time we encountered it. We individually, intersubjectively, and collectively develop habits and practices, preconceptions through which to filter all the information with which we are bombarded, patterns of social relations, social norms and values, and refer to customs, traditions and conventions to orient us. Such modes of being able to operate in the world are necessary and not in themselves oppressive, but are also the source of relations of dominance and subordination. They are also one rather than the source of the untrumpeted way habits move from being conditional settlements to being 'natural', neutral and entrenched, 'internalized and institutionalized' and so 'resistant to change' (Marcussen *et al* 2001, 102), such that the conditionality is erased and lost from view.

The proposal outlined here also recognises the contingency of the distinction, made differently in different polities across time and place, between what is seen as politically salient and what is regarded as unpolitical, politically neutral and given. For instance, the status of gender differences have changed in many contemporary cultures from being taken as given and biological to being seen as politically salient and the effects of difference contested. There is an ongoing process and dynamic of meaning, through interaction with political events and contestations, legal transformations (like the European Convention on Human Rights), and economic changes.

The emphasis Lindahl places on sovereignty as expressing the unity of a political community, and of the modern state conception of sovereignty (distinguished from a conception for instance based on religious authority) as 'the contingent unity of a political community' (Lindahl 2003, 88), is useful. His point is that, because the unity of the people cannot literally be demonstrated (neither the 'all' the people nor their unity), and is necessarily an idea and a symbol of participation in the political arena, the work of sovereignty is precisely to express and symbolise that idea. His emphasis on politics is valuable in highlighting that sovereignty as a political concept focuses on the political life of a polity (having a stake in even if not participating in policy-making, mediating between interests and power relations, pursuing a common good, redistribution and redressing inequalities, allowing contestation and dissent) as the key bond shared by members of the polity, and that this unity refers as much to a multi-level polity as it does to a state-centric one. Lindhal's statement about the link between government and sovereignty is also a way in which the mystery of sovereignty is exemplified. He maintains that 'there is no government without a sovereign in the sense of a final arbiter in the event of an irresolvable conflict about the content of unity' (Lindahl 2003, 105).

The way the mystery of sovereignty establishes the parameters for the meaning of political activity, what can count as political and what cannot (what constitute legitimate questions and answers), and the limits of what is political, the border with what is not political, is provisionally uncontested. Connolly enriches this account by pointing to the inherent instability of the content of the political, in pointing to the traditions, values and practices that help shape it in concrete instances. He gives the example of the police in American cities who 'both express and help to shape the ethos of sovereignty. They can find evidence or plant it...intimidate a section of the populace or act even-handedly, depending upon the unstable confluence of legal rulings given to them, the larger ethos in which they participate, and the professional police ethos carved out of dangers, ethnic loyalties and hostilities in the city' (Connolly 2004, 31).

Richmond discusses the way in which Kelsen's theory of sovereignty supports a deeply political reading of sovereignty. She notes that 'Kelsen argues that the concept of sovereignty is rooted in the presumption that the state in question is supreme', but that this presumption 'is underpinned not by logical arguments but by the "political design" to preserve the "notion that the state represents, in absolute terms, the highest legal community"' (Richmond 1997, 416). At bottom the source of the authority of claims to sovereignty cannot be legal in origin but are political. This is one of the meanings of sovereignty as a mystery, in that the concept necessarily contains an indeterminacy about its content because of its politically-defined (and so, differently in different places and times) character.

Another part of why sovereignty is a mystery is because the meaning, scope and limits of politics are under constant review, being negotiated and renegotiated over time. In 2006, for instance, part of what made hotly-debated issues in British politics and elsewhere about Terror bills, ID cards, and incitement to race hatred so vehemently discussed is precisely what it meant for the meaning, scope and limits of politics in a particular polity. Because politics has no natural, bedrock, foundational content that can be relied upon, the meaning, scope and limits of politics are unstable, constructed and volatile, and this is part of why sovereignty remains a mystery.

The historical specificity of this idea

This section of the chapter spells out how the historical specificity of the proposal for political sovereignty developed here follows from it being a property of the concept. The section also details how the realist conception denies that specificity.

The historicity of sovereignty leads to the recognition of the necessary multiplicity of its conceptions. There will always be a place for the concept of sovereignty, to define politics, distribute political powers, and set the limits of the political, and to perform these functions slightly differently with respect to the domestic and international realms, however defined and whatever the perceived relationship between them. What the concept of sovereignty does specifically in the international or external realm, for instance, is to define the 'logic of organisation' (Spruyt 1994, 16). Whatever conception it is expressed in, and however the concept is reconfigured and reformulated, while there is politics there has to be sovereignty. Moreover, the resilience of sovereignty does not depend upon its tethering to the state form.

The proposal offered here concerns the identification of a property of the concept of sovereignty itself and so suggests that this property is common to all conceptions of sovereignty, independent of historical context. At the same time it is clear that identifying this property occurs in a historical and political context. The idea of the mystery of sovereignty seeks to redress the depoliticisation and myopia of sovereignty in its modern state form.

What is being outlined here is a property of sovereignty suppressed or denied in the *Rechtstaat* conception of sovereignty. While the rule of law is important, it is now recognised as governed by political decisions rather than by a putatively universal moral principle. In Huysmans's distinction, it is a question of 'the legitimacy of political decisions declaring law and commanding obedience', rather than a question of 'the legality of deciding and implementing law' (Huysmans 2003, 213).

One reason for seeking to identify this political mystery of sovereignty is to distinguish the problems associated with its modern state form from other possible conceptions of sovereignty. So, while Rob Walker is right that 'the claims of modern sovereignty are insufficient to answer all questions about the character and location of political authority in contemporary circumstances' (Walker 1999, xii), having in mind recent trends in economic life, technology, and transnational politics, nevertheless a reconceptualised sovereignty – one that recognises explicitly the political functions sovereignty performs for us – is possible.

The idea of sovereignty as the absence of any higher authority in both domestic and international affairs, is not only merely legal (nobody has the right (though they may well have the ability) to issue orders to them). This conception also, and this is the crux of the matter, confers upon states a privileged position in international affairs. The state and the Westphalian settlement were created co-constitutively over time, through phases, into a realist paradigm. What is left out of the account is the political function sovereignty plays, logically prior to and presupposed by the legal and realist definition. Furthermore, the modern state definition of sovereignty conflates the distinction between legal and political sovereignty.

The modern realist vision of the state and of its account of state sovereignty radically depoliticised and reified the notion of the state political form, making it look natural, transhistorical and inevitable. It is important that this 'mystery' part of the political meaning of sovereignty is specifically targeted at the previous dominant, state, form, to reinforce the way in which we use sovereignty to conditionally set the content and limits of the political.

According to the realist view, sovereignty is something that states have. Then sovereignty is defined only in terms of things states (as a particular form of political organisational unit) have and have in relation to other states. As a result of this fusion of horizons in the meanings of 'state' and 'sovereignty' and the limit placed on the meaning of sovereignty, the functions of sovereignty in relation to political units more broadly are ignored. The modern realist function of sovereignty to primarily act, at least for rich Western states, as gate-keeper between inside and outside, is not altogether eliminated in the relational conception developed in Chapters 1 and 2. But that gate-keeping function is altered by the context in which it is seen. For a start, the post-state is more flexible and is conceived as having a permeable skin rather than fortress wall at its boundary. And, secondly, by emphasising the political functions of sovereignty we can see the gate-keeper function in a new perspective, one which supplies an (accountable) reason for setting the content and limits of the political where they are. It involves a recognition that gate-keeping is a political business. For instance, as questions of migration and refugee status have come back onto the political agenda in recent years, so there needs to be debate about whether the boundary between the political and unpolitical needs to be redrawn. The aim of this reconception of sovereignty is not to abolish the modern state as such but to refashion it in the light of a renewed understanding of the political functions of sovereignty. Sovereignty is no longer regarded as a transhistorical constant but as the function by which we set out the scope of politics.

The mystery of sovereignty identified here is different from but related to the idea of an untenable paradox of sovereignty that Connolly points to, the idea that it is self-contradictory that 'a democratic state seeking to honour the rule of law is also one with a sovereign power uncertainly situated within and above the law' (Connolly 2004, 24). Historically we can see that the development of the modern notion of the rule of law in a *Rechtstaat* necessarily holds within it – as protection as well as risk – that an aspect of sovereignty must be that it can reflect upon and change the law. Schmitt's notion of the exception, as well as the long-standing tension in the sovereignty canon between state and popular sovereignty, both arise directly out of this reliance on law in the moral and rational *Rechtstaat*. The untenability of sovereignty refers to a particular conception of it, whereas the mystery of sovereignty refers to a condition inherent in the concept itself. But the reason the current work identifies a mystery rather than a paradox about sovereignty also lies in its focus on politics rather than in a confusion of politics with democratic procedures. The use of sovereignty to distribute the parameters of political action points to the agency and choice (even if embedded into a habitual and normalised practice) in having sovereignty to perform this function, rather than to any specific set of political procedures and institutions.

Edkins and Pin-Fat (1999, 2) recognise an important feature of sovereignty when they argue that 'the relationship between sovereignty and subjectivity is an intensely political one'. However, their conclusion, that it is possible to 'talk of politics without the fixity such an authorizing concept imposes', that is, 'that it is only without a "sovereign" that a rethinking of the political is possible' (Edkins and Pin-Fat 1999, 3), is in terms of the current book's thinking to throw the baby out with the bathwater, the concept along with the modern state conception of it. We do indeed use the idea of sovereignty to provide some specific cultural parameters to the meaning and scope and limits of the messy business of politics in flux, but this does not necessitate the view of imposition, oppression, masking and stifling the real play of social antagonism.

These two views rest on different understandings of politics and the political. According to the view Edkins and Pin-Fat represent, politics as a sub-system of social relations in interaction with other sub-systems like the economy and culture, is distinguished from the political as the 'moment of openness and undecidability' when the 'very structuring principle of society' is called into question and somehow access is gained to an under-lying reality disguised and muffled by normal politics. The view of this book is that there is no such dichotomy between politics and the political, between tainted social construction and 'true' underlying social reality, that convulsions in the political can be regressive as well as emancipatory, that the desire to establish a politics that is free of sovereign power (Edkins and Pin-Fat 2004, 3) rests on a confusion between concept (sovereignty) and conception (modern state sovereignty) as well as on a craving induced by Foucault's reduction of politics to social power relations, and that pro-gressive politics can be found in both ongoing gains in the normal course of politics as well as in extraordinary events.

Nevertheless the line of thinking that Edkins and Pin-Fat pursue is valu-able in their insistence that retheorising the political does involve reflecting upon the crucial importance of the link between sovereignty and subject-ivity. Likewise, retheorising sovereignty involves reflecting again on politics and the role we have it perform for us. Connolly detects an ambiguity between 'effective and expressive sovereignty', an 'equivocation in the idea of sovereignty between acting with final authority and acting with irre-sistible power', final authority and irresistible effect (Connolly 2004, 30–1). This is useful in reminding us of the different aspects of sovereignty that affect how a political community conducts its politics.

Part of the reason for pursuing this perspective is the attempt to put liberal state sovereignty into a broader context and to render that concep-tion political. One obstacle to recognising the political character of sov-ereignty in the sense developed here includes that while the relation with law is important liberal sovereignty equates the *Rechtstaat* with law. Another obstacle is the liberal problem of distinguishing legal and political sovereignty, and yet another is the state form. With state sovereignty, the sovereignty question is only granted to states, not to other political societies such as tribes, ethnic groups, communes, and isolated islands and regions.

The political property of sovereignty outlined here focuses on the functions that the idea of sovereignty performs for us in relation to both domestic and international politics. But this property is also a value, a normative theory (though not a moral theory in the ordinary sense of the word), in that it implies that making overt and explicit the political functions of sovereignty is a good thing, is good for politics, strengthening its transparency and accountability. The implication is that it is valuable and worthwhile to acknowledge the construction of political realms, their scope and content and limits. This implication of the meaning of political sovereignty advanced here also affects the character of the post-state proposal. Bartelson notes the historicity of the state conception of sovereignty when he argues convincingly that the state as a political form is 'ultimately nothing but a claim to authority that authorises itself by containing its negation in the form of hypothetical rival claims to the same authority' (Bartelson 2001, 187). The idea of the post-state contains the sense that political forms, *and* economic, non-governmental, and legal forms, are not properly subject to reification, naturalisation and depoliticisation, but should be acknowledged as contingent and historical.

What is also key to this property of the sovereignty concept, then, is the idea that not only, as Bartelson rightly observes, have 'most human societies...confronted problems of power and authority, and where they should be located' (Bartelson 1995, 3). They have also confronted the underlying problem of the scope of the content, character, scope and limits of what counts as political. To settle what is legitimately contestable, open to interpretation, debate, dispute, or struggle, to establish or reform procedures for these things and their limits, and to specify what is taken as unpolitical and given, is to exercise political sovereignty in this sense. To ordain or ratify relations with other political communities, and who (person, elite, assembly) or what (gods, symbolic ritual or thing) is to decide such questions, is to exercise political sovereignty. Human societies have in different ways used political sovereignty in this sense to designate how fundamental rules are implemented, to give meaning to questions of authority and power and how claims about them can be made.

Other benefits of this meaning of political sovereignty

Finally, four other benefits of this meaning of political sovereignty are worth noting. This notion does not reify sovereignty, does not proceed by vicious imposition, applies also to other institutions beyond the state, and supplies an alternative to the social contract idea.

This reconceptualisation puts politics at centre stage in the discussion of sovereignty, toppling the profound and overwhelming centrality given to law in the modern period, both by the fundamental moral and ordering function given to law in the political theory discourse on sovereignty and by the very absence of law in the modern realist vision of international politics (and its positing of this arena as in opposition to the sphere of the legal and the ordered inside the state). This conception redresses the deep reification and naturalisation of the state sovereignty form, the way in which, as Bartelson observes, 'the concept of the state was removed from the domain of the politically contestable, as was the question of authority in general' (Bartelson 2001, 183). Because political sovereignty as described here is not a thing in itself but a meta-architecture, prevents it from being be reified.

The way in which sovereignty is a mystery is different from the kind of mystification and reification of the state and of ruler sovereignty based on authority that has been a strong feature of the mainstream political theory tradition. The mystery of sovereignty refers, rather, to our everyday need to treat some things as given and normal while still knowing at some level that they can be challenged and remade.

In addition, sovereignty is not reified in this characterisation because it is we who ask sovereignty to carry this complex meaning. Sovereignty functions for us to outline the border between the political and the unpolitical, and the ways in which politics can be expressed. Keeping a taken-for-granted in mind as ultimately still political avoids the reification of sovereignty. But we also need to recognise that in practice over time conceptions of sovereignty as unpolitical become congealed and normalised. This becomes apparent when claims that sovereignty is not a neutral but a political concept are resisted. Three examples are the idea of fixed sovereignty in discourses about or presupposing of the erosion of the sovereignty of the nation-state; the politics over sovereignty and the European Union; and the highlighting in Britain of challenges to some of the effects of sovereignty made by refugees and asylum seekers in recent years. These examples also all show that, while the character of sovereignty as both political and outside politics is primarily an insight into 'internal' sovereignty (sovereignty having been recognised as much more political in the critical IR discourse of 'external' sovereignty), specifying this character of sovereignty also acts to bring together the 'internal' and 'external' dimensions. These examples all also show how deeply sovereignty is a political concept.

This meaning of political sovereignty pinpoints how, as both a practice and a concept, sovereignty functions to specify a place 'beyond politics and beyond doubt'. But whether particular conceptions of sovereignty are then also used to create 'a voice of interpretation and judgment from which truth and power are thought to emanate as one' (Ashley and Walker 1990, 368), needs to be established on a case-by-case basis. Just as not all inequalities are politically relevant and not all distinctions are dichotomies that rank and polarise, so not all sovereignty claims impose viciously exclusionary hegemonic paradigms. The logic of the concept of sovereignty, like the logic of inequality and distinction, is not necessarily always political in the sense of always needing to be contested. Like inequality and distinction, sovereignty does function to privilege some practices, values, and interpretations over others, but this process is not always one of vicious imposition. Sovereignty can legitimately be about authority as well as about power, about exemplary practice as well as about exclusionary barriers. Norms and conventions play a positive as well as a negative role.

It follows from this meaning of political sovereignty that sovereignty provides a kind of coherence, but of a different kind from the structural coherence that the state form imposes. It is not associated with the state form and is compatible with a diversity of forms of political community. Dewey's insight is useful in this respect, that the condition of sovereignty is a function of all institutions. He says, '[e]very institution...has its sovereignty, or authority, and its laws and rights. It is only a false abstraction which makes us conceive of sovereignty, or authority, and law and rights as inhering only in some supreme organisation, as the national state' (cited in Loughlin 2003, 55). Runciman supports this view, that sovereignty is a function, and must be attached to some association (Runciman 2003, 29), which could be a state, a post-state or some other political form. Loughlin is correct to draw attention to sovereignty as 'a representation of the autonomy of the political' as well as noting its role in 'providing the foundational concept of the discipline of public law', and on this basis to argue that statements about the erosion, evasion or of moving beyond sovereignty are misconceived. His definition, that 'sovereignty has been devised for the purpose of giving expression to the distinctively political bond between a group of people and its mode of governance' (Loughlin 2003, 56), is also helpful in suggesting that sovereignty is not only about ruler sovereignty but also about political identity.

This notion of political sovereignty is also a useful alternative to the vexed social contract tradition that buttresses the idea of constitutionalism. Lindhal points to the circular logic involved in contract theories. He notes that 'the contractarian interpretation of popular sovereignty encounters an insurmountable obstacle in its effort to account for the unity of a polity'. Lindhal argues persuasively that 'social contract will not even function as the "virtual" foundation of a community because who ought to participate in its founding act can only be settled by already presupposing the polity's normative foundation' (Lindhal 2003, 94–5). The political property of the sovereignty concept that has been the subject of this chapter starts, by contrast, with the processes, conventions, vocabulary and values of politics, and the boundaries of the political that already exist in a political community and recognises their conditionality and the scope for their reform or renewal.

Part II
Practice

5
Less is More: Sovereignty in Europe

Pagden expresses a widely-held view, that in order for the European Union (EU) to move from a legal to a political identity, the 'peoples of Europe will have to abandon the ancient concept of sovereignty' (Pagden 2002, 28). This chapter argues on the contrary that a successfully reconceptualised sovereignty for Europe, in the EU, can be envisaged as being neither absolute nor obsolete, but needs to be pictured as less not more. This sounds counter-intuitive, but only because our tradition assumes a centralising and hierarchising logic, with a legal model of sovereignty represented in the highest, absolute and unassailable law-making authority and a political model of a sovereign as a king above and separate from the ruled.

The chapter argues against the two main integrative logics, against both those on the one hand who advocate a federalist logic and those on the other who are keen on allowing functionalist integration to lead to a supranational body. Both of these views ultimately follow the same logic tied to the assumption that sovereignty can only mean state sovereignty. However, there are many historical precedents for a very different way of conceptualising sovereignty in Europe, two of which are found in Spinoza and the seventeenth-century United Provinces search for political balance, and in the US pre-civil war empty-centred conception described by Deudney. Like Weiler (1999), the present chapter argues for drawing on the resources in earlier European traditions for thinking about the future of Europe. There are aspects of those examples that are durable beyond the nation-state form. In particular, the Spinoza example provides a model for a process that *constructs* the EU without going as far as *constituting* it in a constituent process, and for a construction that does perfectly well without a moralising constitution. This chapter presents an alternative to the view (outlined in different forms by Held, Linklater, Habermas, etc.) according to which any political field above the nation-state simply 'scales up' from the state form.

This chapter recommends the view that the political identity of the European Union can and should be conceptualised on the basis of the idea 'less is more'. That is, the political identity of the EU is best achieved not by giving primary attention to an elaborated edifice of EU institutions, to the legal order, to a constitution, nor by addressing the democratic deficit. In addition, it is neither necessary nor desirable to seek to construct a common 'European' culture, let alone a 'European nationalism' (Chebel D'Appollonia 2002). A viable EU political identity is best achieved by celebrating the diverse and multiple centres of political identity in the partners and keeping the organisation at EU level minimal. In addition, the argument of this chapter is that the discussion of the EU takes place in a context neither simply of state sovereignty nor post-sovereignty (the idea that state sovereignty is redundant or has been eroded) since, as Bellamy notes, these two views 'turn out to be two sides of the same coin' (Bellamy 2003, 169). The coherence of the minimalist EU level can be obtained by taking seriously political sovereignty as described in the previous chapter.

It is the concept of sovereignty that thus best provides the (conditional) settlement of the distinctive statement or embedded given of the content and limits of politics at the EU level. Rather than relying on the rhetorical device of a constitution (because if it does not already express embedded values the words are dead on the paper), and rather than leaving political identity to the lawyers (doomed to failure again because of a category mistake between politics and law) or EU functionalists (because, although attempting to build political identity organically from the complex of interactions, such a route will never adequately reach sovereignty), this chapter proposes that attention be focused directly on the question of *sovereignty* in Europe. The 'less is more' proposal also provides a way forward from the dichotomous thinking that has led to the stalemate position described by Shaw as the 'unresolved debate between conceptions of the EU and national legal orders as binary opposites in which one but not both can be sovereign' (Shaw 2001, 75).

The focus of this chapter is complex. It is concerned with putting forward a positive way of conceptualising sovereignty in the EU in the light of several things – the construction of European governance in the EU, the construction of an EU political identity, and the way these things are discussed, understood and constructed in various fields of European studies including integration studies and EU legal studies. In this way the context of the chapter is the dual one of the EU and the politics of discourses.

The chapter has several interlinked purposes. It is about an empirical case study, moving on in the book from theory to practice. Sovereignty is not only something discussed by academics, but is presently being constructed in the context of and concurrently with the forging of a multi-state political entity, and has real effects in the real world. While this chapter seeks to make a contribution to political theory and does not attempt to be a contribution to EU constitutional law, integration theory, or EU policy-making, the proposal made here can be regarded as opportune, occurring at a time that has seen the decisive non-ratification of the Constitutional Treaty in 2005 with 'no' votes in France and the Netherlands, the (at least temporary) halting of the process towards constitutionalisation, and a rethinking of the way forward for European political identity.

The chapter is also a test case for a particular reconceptualisation of sovereignty in two senses. It recommends utilising, more than is often done in an abstract discourse, the legacy of historical examples of sovereignty, and in particular draws upon the value of Spinoza's theory of sovereignty, which was trenchantly polycentric and avowedly anti state-centric. It also serves to implement some of the theoretical developments discussed and outlined in Chapters 1, 2, 3 and 4, specifically in relation to rethinking internal-external as relational rather than dichotomous in a post-state environment, seeking to move beyond the liberal stranglehold over the sovereignty debate that champions independence and autonomy and denies relational connection and interdependence, proposing the disaggregation or 'unbundling' of the elements of sovereignty such that they can be assigned in a different fashion, and reinstating the importance of the political and political imagination as a source of dynamism at the centre of the construction of sovereignty. Leaving sovereignty to the lawyers and constitutionalists is most likely to lead to a socially-conservative discourse in which politics is absent.

The argument of this chapter takes as its starting point the conviction that it is valuable to see the question of sovereignty in the EU as a political question rather than just a legal or institutional one, or one just about ruler sovereignty. Mainstream discussion of sovereignty in the EU has focused largely on the questions of who is going to rule and the idea of 'sovereignty over' (ruler sovereignty), where supreme authority will lie (legal sovereignty), the democratic deficit (popular sovereignty), and governmental institution-building. For instance Wallace typifies the view that equates sovereignty only with governmental competences when he argues that in the EU sovereignty 'is increasingly held in common: pooled among governments, negotiated by thousands of officials through hundreds of multilateral committees, compromised through acceptance of regulations and court judgment'. According to Wallace, in 'many of the central responsibilities of national governments, European states can do little without the acquiescence and approval of their neighbours'. It is, he argues, an 'inherently untidy and inefficient system, built on sustaining the illusion that governments can themselves provide their voters with benefits – security, prosperity, regulation of economic and social interchange – which can in practice be won only through common action with others' (Wallace 1999, 506).

Wallace's reference to an 'emerging post-sovereign European order' (Wallace 1999, 520) misses the point that in all political forms, however complex and however different from the conventional nation state, sovereignty has an important political role to play. To call the emerging European order 'post-sovereign' is simply to equate sovereignty with state sovereignty, to confuse conception with concept. While the case can certainly be made that the EU's 'disaggregated policy networks and disjointed and opaque policy-making processes' are problematic (Wallace 1999, 520), it is a problem about accountability and scrutiny rather than for sovereignty.

What has been overlooked and unacknowledged in this way of approaching sovereignty in the EU is the political work that sovereignty does. Attention to sovereignty as political provides a way of indeed 'unbundling' the dimensions of sovereignty in the complex context of the EU. This chapter argues for attending to the political functions sovereignty performs for the measure of integration we want, rather than expecting further institution-building, law, a constitution, and a non-existent demos to do this work for us. By calling upon sovereignty to do its job we can stem the centralising tide of institution-building and legal regulation. A focus on political sovereignty also provides a preferable alternative to the model put forward by Bellamy and Castiglione, based they say not on an idealised cosmopolitan utopia but on a 'de-nationalising of nationalism and a de-sovereigntising of sovereignty [of member states] stemming from the neo-republican mixed and balanced constitution'. Bellamy and Castiglione's approval of 'the plurality of demoi and legal systems that have both legitimated and fostered European integration' (Bellamy and Castiglione 2004, 190), is common ground with the present argument, but rather than seeking to bleach out sovereignty from the equation and rely on constitutionalism, this chapter argues for using the neglected resources of political sovereignty at the European level.

After exploring the importance of the measure of indeterminacy that characterises study of the EU, and indicating the significance of the architectural metaphor, the body of the chapter makes the case for sovereignty in the EU to be understood in terms of 'less is more'. This involves articulation of the notion of pooled or shared authority and the 'unbundling' of sovereign powers, and outlining the benefits of seeing the EU in terms of a complex confederalism. It also involves analysing the meaning of political sovereignty in relation to the EU, and clarifying the relevance of the term 'post-state'. Then, after setting out a critique of constitutionalism, and emphasising how sovereignty at the EU level differs from the international level, the value of Spinoza's conception of sovereignty for the EU is considered.

Having set out the argument, a set of contextual aspects that frame the debate will also be outlined. One important aspect of the context for understanding the meaning and potential of sovereignty in the debate over the future shape of contemporary Europe will have already been discussed, namely the openness of meaning construction in relation to the EU. There are also seven other aspects of the context that have a bearing on shaping the meaning of the proposal presented here. The first contextual factor is about the diversity of European traditions through which ideas and developments are sifted and understood, and the second is that to some extent the sense of the 'loss' of sovereignty by European nation-states in the twentieth century occurs independently of the growth of the European Union. The third concerns European reactions to the idea of the loss of national sovereignty. The fourth aspect of the context is about the influence of interpretations and misinterpretations of Hobbes and Spinoza. The fifth aspect refers to the dichotomous logic that has been a characteristic feature of thinking about the EU. The sixth aspect concerns the question of whether the EU has an independent legal personality, and the seventh examines the role of the nation-state in the debate.

Indeterminacy

One of the most striking features of the literature on European integration is the depth of the opportunity, the dynamic uncertainty and mutability, the openness and contingency, the contestability in meaning formation that confronts us in reconfiguring sovereignty for the EU.

The indeterminacy in the meaning of the political form of the European Union is important not only because it signals that there is still room to help shape its overall design and meaning, but also because there is scope to make the case that the meaning of the EU is indeterminate because it is lacking a sense of sovereignty. Political theory in the context of the EU is faced with an indeterminacy that does not generally affect 'normal' political theory in the given, 'obvious' context of the state. Associated with this case is the sense that indeterminacy has persisted because writers and actors have been looking for determinacy in the wrong place – in law and a constitution, and in a greater measure of 'democracy'. In addition, given the inherent tensions and ambiguities in the relations between EU partners (tensions which Spinoza, for example, in the United Provinces regarded as fruitful and constructive) there will perhaps always be an indeterminacy about the meaning of the EU, but it would be lessened by the acknowledgment of a conditional sovereignty settlement as outlined here.

In particular, the indeterminacy of the meaning of the EU refers to a cluster of features. The meaning of the EU is indeterminate because the EU is a new kind of polity whose features, construction, and 'naming' remain work in progress. It is not clear where the story is going. There are fewer constraints on interpretation than we find when dealing with other polities. It is indeterminate because of the more general way in which conceptualisation helps shape concrete practice (ideas precede reality), because we are dealing with practices rather than 'things', and because the struggle for conceptual dominance is still ongoing. On this point Neil Walker sums up the dialectical logic at work, the 'double-sided method of modelling the polity', between the importance of a 'discourse for capturing emergent trends' and the crucial need for 'a presumptively authoritative and open-ended means to frame new possibilities' (Walker 2005, 600). The indeterminacy is also a particularly acute case of the 'double hermeneutic' whereby all interpretation of the social world is affected by the interpretations and perceptions of the social actors who articulate and help to constitute it (Walker 2003b, 16–17). The meaning of the EU is also indeterminate because it is constructed both through intentional acts and unintentional actions that have unpredictable effects. The process of construction is not purely rational. It is also indeterminate because there is no overall consensus about its guiding purposes, institutional design, role of democratic participation, what to do about sovereignty, and the relation between law and politics. It is indeterminate because it is not clear when the EU would be deemed finished and what the finished product would look like. Perhaps it is finished now. It is indeterminate because political sovereignty has not yet been established. It seems indeterminate because less is more, such that some would always see it as incomplete without a hierarchical unity and constitution.

Weiler, Neil Walker, Diez, Chryssochoou, Drulák, and Richmond all point to valuable aspects of this indeterminacy of meaning. Weiler, for instance, pays tribute to the way the formation of the EU takes places as much in debates between contested discursive positions, in 'conceptualisation and imagination' as in institutions and rules (Weiler 1999, 223). Walker highlights the extent to which legal and political integration is theorised through three competing lenses, a state-centred one that regards the EU as a proto-state or, on the 'other side of the Westphalian coin', viewed through realist and intergovernmentalist assumptions as an 'elaborately tailored international model', or in terms of a '*sui generis* third way' of conceiving transnational law and politics. Walker's point draws attention to the downside of indeterminacy, namely the strength of the tendency of recourse to old patterns of explanation to read and interpret new developments, and so to 'a self-vindicating narrowing of the horizons' (Walker 2005, 588). At stake here is, in part, the innate conservatism of cleaving to familiar patterns of explanation, but also, as Walker also notes, the presence of a non-rational factor at work in theorising the EU, of 'responding to data overload by trimming its theoretical ambitions' (Walker 2005, 585).

Diez confirms the centrality of language in establishing the meaning and 'reality' of the EU. Competing classifications and acts of 'naming', of the EU as a '"postmodern" or "regulatory state", a "confederatio", "consortio" or "condominio", a system of "multi-level governance" or a "multiperspectival polity"', are not descriptions of reality but conceptualisations, exercises in 'linguistic construction', since that 'reality is not so readily observable'. Such categorisations are 'not mere descriptions of an unknown polity, but take part in the construction of the polity itself' as well as structuring our preconceptions, and so 'are not politically innocent'. Struggles for power are reflected in the process of 'naming' (Diez 2001b, 85–6). Any '"description" of European governance participates in the struggle to fix the latter's meaning, and thus is a political act' (Diez 2001b, 91). For instance, the designation 'multi-level governance' assumes the existence of local, regional, national and European governance levels and multi-level governance becomes a self-fulfilling prophesy. In contrast, operating as though the EU were a 'network polity' without 'levels' radically changes the nature of the thing described (Diez 2001b, 91–2).

Neil Walker also makes the valuable point that the indeterminacy characteristic of the EU is in part due to the way it is not only a 'work in progress' but is also developing as a unique form of polity. It is more circumscribed than a state and less circumscribed than a traditional international order. The EU is a 'normatively incomplete polity'. It is 'restricted to certain purposes, however broadly these be prescribed', and unlike a state it 'does not possess theoretically unlimited competence to deal with all and any of the affairs of its citizens'. At the same time, the EU is 'normatively open-ended', because 'unlike a classical international order, it is not presumptively confined to a determinate range of objectives' (Walker 2005, 590). This form of indeterminacy results from one of the many ways in which the EU cannot be satisfactorily understood in terms of either the state or international sides of the Westphalian model, nor in terms of the dichotomy it sets up to exhaust the range of possibilities. The EU is a unique 'work in progress' towards an end which is neither a state nor an international order.

Chryssochoou, likewise, emphasises the issue at stake when he observes that underlying the obstacles to 'conceptual consensus over the elusive ontology of the EU is that its conceptualisation rests on competing normative orders, accounting for different "structures of meaning"'. Theorising this 'most complex polity that human agency has ever devised' (quoted in Chryssochoou 2002, 341) is not just about analysing choices for governmental and legal institution-building and practices but about a struggle between competing visions of reality to instantiate, articulate and understand the choices. This chapter argues that it is precisely one of the functions that sovereignty performs for us, to register and hold the outcome of that struggle.

Drulák (2005) also confirms this point. His work is important in pointing up the contingent aspect of meaning-formation in general and in the EU in particular. Drulák's case study concerns the discursive conditions of political action in debates that took place prior to the Constitutional Convention and the European Constitutional Treaty, about the future of the EU. These debates included delegates from the accession countries as well as from the member states. Drulák identifies the significant use of a network of conceptual metaphors by the speakers at the debate, of motion ('moving forward', 'accelerate the train', 'continuous process'), equilibrium ('balance of power', 'cooperation between member states'), container ('forging Europe'), and joint-stock company ('Europe able to deliver', 'ownership of Europe by citizens'). He shows that such metaphors are not just embellishments for rhetorical purposes and are not simply instances of EU technocratic short-cuts like terms such as 'direct effect', 'acquis communautaire' and 'sub-sidiarity'. Drulák makes a strong case that such metaphors powerfully helped to create a common understanding among the transnational group of delegates and did important work in shaping political options and decisions.

Richmond's (1997) starting-point in tackling the question specifically of the character of European Community law is that, contrary to the received view, the meaning of the Community legal order is indeterminate and depends upon a process of theory-building to impose order on empirical evidence. The 'is' and the 'ought' are intertwined because concepts must be used to interpret experience, and she quotes Roger Cotterrell that '[c]oncepts need to be formed in advance – a priori – in order to organise empirical evidence'. Concepts not only 'determine what is empirically relevant but also reflect a view of why it is relevant' (quoted in Richmond 1997, 379). Richmond underlines that the criteria for deciding whether or not the EU represents an independent legal order, a new level of legal order in Europe, are not simply natural and given. They are themselves multiple, contradictory and ambiguous, and so in dispute and radically subject to interpretation. Understanding sovereignty in the context of the EU, as well as understanding other relevant legal concepts like 'legal order', 'consti-tution', 'supremacy' and 'competence', necessarily involves interpretation, choices of concepts and theory, and the construction of meaning. She shows that, in understanding the EU legal order and questions of sov-ereignty, what matters is not simply who has power and how they exer-cise it, but the ongoing struggle for conceptual definition and the way indeterminacy in the meaning of key concepts keeps open a range of interpretive options and choices (Richmond 1997, 420).

Conflicting understandings of the projected Constitutional Treaty in 2005 is a case in point here. Rosamond and Wincott take the view that the Constitutional Treaty did not amount to an attempt to inaugurate a new supranational constitution. It was, rather, a 'simplification and rational-isation' of the existing treaties, together with an attempt to 'reorder' the 'three pillar' framework into a single structure. They estimate that the 'core matter' of the Treaty document, notwithstanding public perception to the contrary, 'was already *in situ* well before the ratification debacle' (Rosamond and Wincott 2006, 1). Gamble, in contrast, detects a broader ambition for the Treaty. He argues that while the European Convention preceding the Constitutional Treaty did not make a Claim of Right ('We, the people of Europe...') it did 'propose a draft treaty establishing a constitution for the EU' (Gamble 2006, 36). However, Gamble agrees with Rosamond and Wincott that what has been lost in the rejection of the Constitutional Treaty in 2005 is not new substantive economic and social policies but 'new mechanisms for subjecting the institutions of the Commission to greater democracy and accountability, and to allow the EU to become subject to its citizens rather than to its political class' (Gamble 2006, 40).

While these scholars have radically different interpretations of the significance of the Constitution and the significance of its rejection, what remains crucial and ambiguous (and perhaps necessarily so, with conflicting evidence at stake) is whether the Constitution was framed around an 'internal claim to validity' (Richmond 1997, 386), where its validity in its own terms was sufficient, or whether it was made within the terms of mutual commitments between international actors, and whether there is an appetite to attempt to reformulate a constitution based on an 'internal claim to validity' in the future. The 'meaning' of the Constitution and the process that preceded it cannot simply be established by recourse to empirical evidence, to analysing the documents more closely. What also matters here is not whether the document represented a written constitution but whether it inaugurated or will inaugurate (for instance as Neil Walker spells out, on the basis of a new form of 'differentiated integration' (Walker 1998) between core and peripheral members) a new basis of validation, shifting from member states acting under international law to an EU legal system in its own right. According to the perspective Richmond convincingly propounds, it is no accident that, for instance, Rosamond and Wincott, and Gamble, present different views of the situation.

Another example of indeterminacy arises from the enlargement of the EU in 2004, from 15 to 25 states. This round of enlargement has had two opposite effects whose outcomes are indeterminate. It has strengthened the pressure for greater intergovernmental cooperation, to take account of the voices of all the member states. It has also led to increased calls for greater supranational reform, to ensure effective governance and decision-making through the EU's institutions, especially in the Commission and, expressed in the greater use of qualified majority voting, in the Council of Ministers.

'Integration' is used conceptually in two separate ways, and this makes the term interestingly ambiguous. It is taken to mean the progressive deepening of relations and a more and more articulated EU structure, and so there are pro-integrationists and anti-integrationists. It is also taken more broadly to be the name for thinking about and negotiating relations and structure itself, without any view whether a looser or tighter from of polity will result, without any normative commitment to deepening the convergence of authority, and without any teleological framework towards unity for the debate.

Thus another example of indeterminacy relates to the term, 'integration', and its ambiguity in the context of EU studies. It is often assumed that 'integration' means actively working towards closer kinds of relation rather than being satisfied with more distant kinds of relation. Integration has also, as Christiansen *et al* (2001, 13) highlight, been 'understood as "integration through law"...by the substantial community of EU law scholars for decades'. However, these dominant meanings of integration take place within a broader field of meanings. It can mean progress towards a teleological end and have a normative connotation, as a deliberate process of polity formation, or it can be a merely descriptive term that focuses on cooperation without implying an outcome at any particular level of harmonisation. 'Integration' can pre-suppose full or close forms of incorporation such as merger, fusion, blending, unification, assimilation and inter-penetration, or common obedience to a higher power. Alternatively, it can mean (light touch or partial) integration in the form of cooperation on specific policy-sectoral areas only or, on the analogy with multiculturalism, a celebration of differences within a 'thinner' commitment to overall overarching principles or institutions or procedures. While the meaning of integration remains in the balance there is a tendency to presume that it means more rather than less interactivity and intertwining as well as a common subscription to an EU identity. In putting forward the idea of 'less is more' this chapter seeks to challenge and put a brake on that presumption.

A final important example of indeterminacy that is relevant to EU studies is found in the ambiguous meaning of 'federalism'. This term refers, for instance, to the move towards a federation of states rather than a looser structure such as a confederation, the crucial difference being that the former is characterised by the primacy of central government over state or provincial governments while in the latter the primacy of the parts over the central government is what matters. Centre and periphery are reversed. But in the second meaning, 'federalism' is a generic name for all kinds of decentralised polities, including the loosest of confederations.

It is important to bear in mind the high degree and multiple kinds of indeterminacy that occur in discussing the meaning of the EU as a political entity. This recognition attunes us not only to the opportunity available in reconceptualising the EU and its political sovereignty, but also alerts us to be suspicious of arguments which present the present form of the EU as fixed and 'natural'.

The architectural metaphor

The phrase 'less is more' has been used to describe the radical late nineteenth- and early twentieth-century movement of minimalism in residential, corporate and public architecture, as well as in fine art, design, and sculpture.

Minimalists had a clear and distinctive approach to the organisation and arrangement of form, and regarded architecture and design as integrated. In some respects the minimalist movement is aligned with Cubism and Abstractionism, and it was enlivened by the potential offered by using industrial materials such as galvanised steel and by the effect of light on the surfaces and shapes formed by its clean lines. In architecture the movement is associated in particular with two innovative German architects – Mies van der Rohe (Ludwig Mies), and Adolf Loos for whom ornament is crime.

Van der Rohe, a contemporary of Le Corbusier, was influenced by Frank Lloyd Wright and the Bauhaus school. His guiding threads were the interconnected ideas of 'almost nothing', that God was in the detail, the aim of gaining a precise mastery of form, and the prescription to forget the architecture and concentrate on the form of the composition. The objective of proponents of the minimalist school was the repudiation of the idea of art as a vehicle for the self-expression of the artist. Their aim was a conceptual simplicity, expressed in the stripping away of everything that was not essential to the form. A minimalist composition emerges from the interaction of light, space and form. The objective of such artists was to disclose the immanence of meaning, to peel away the 'noise' that deflects from the way meaning can be discerned in the very shapes and the play of light on them. The aesthetic effect of their work was to create, depending on your point of view, either an intense and potent immanence or a neutral emptiness, an aloofness, and an almost mechanistic sense of design.

Minimalist practitioners were committed to clarity, literalness, simplicity, conceptual rigour, and equilibrium. They valued highly the way that, by abjuring embellishment of all kinds the power of the simple essentials was potently disclosed. Less adornment led to the perception of the implicit power of the form more fully. According to this view, decorative clutter and fussy patterns are superficial and prevent the underlying elegance of carefully-designed architectural simplicity to shine through. The minimalist approach rests on the belief that all good architecture is elegant and contains a simplicity which is worth highlighting. That is, architecture is not just something to achieve the utilitarian building which can then be beautified with decorative detail, by shrouding the utilitarian structure which has no intrinsic worth. In other words, the role of architecture in built environments is being elevated to the highest aesthetic priority, above decoration and art and craft. Without decorative clutter we can better see clean and clear lines and textures and colours, which are the three most important elements of the overall effect of the *space*. This approach promises that it can reveal deeper levels of meaning, now allowed to come to the top of perception and consciousness.

The 'less is more' metaphor works in several ways in relation to sovereignty in Europe. It highlights the role of ideas and theory in creating the immanence of meaning. It is a powerful metaphor for the dispensability of the move towards constitutionalisation. Thirdly, while in the minimalist architectural school 'less is more' means highlighting form and doing away with other elements, in this chapter it refers to having less institutional structure (the analogue with form) and relying instead on the power and dynamic of debate, discussion, talk and inter-subjectively derived meanings at different lower levels, and working positively with the different cultural inheritances of the post-states involved. The case is made here that political sovereignty provides the stable framework for such dynamic and highly-charged political processes. The metaphor also means that standing back from the 'noise' of entrenched interests that carry political weight gives us the opportunity to appreciate what is important, allows the voices of the unheard to come through. It also means that hierarchy gives way to a flatter pattern of interrelationships, and that the value of each thing can be more fully appreciated, rather than some things being supreme and taking priority. Furthermore, architectural metaphors are particularly appropriate to a structure like the EU, and this one suggests that a better structure will be created from *less* push to a centralising integration.

Less is more

The argument takes as its starting-point the view that clinging to a reading of the European Union through the lense of the dominant state conception of sovereignty, and so being transfixed by the options of whether power in Europe lies (or should lie) with the member states or is (or should be) supra-national, is a red herring. In positive terms the idea of 'less is more' comprehends a cluster of features. It means pooled, shared or jointly-used authority expressed in the 'unbundling' of sovereign powers and coopera-tion between partners, and a complex form of confederal government. It is in the context of these features that political sovereignty (as described in the previous chapter) at the EU level makes sense and offers a real contri-bution to the debate. The sense in which 'post-state/s' are involved is clarified. Other features are the critique of constitutionalism and of an over-inflated legal role, the difference between sovereignty at the EU level and the sovereignty-less international sphere, and what can be learned from Spinoza's understanding of sovereignty in relation to the United Provinces.

Pooled authority

The idea of pooled authority in the context of the EU can refer to two simultaneous processes, together with reassurance about the legal under-pinning of the first of the processes, and the notion of the 'faces' which member states present to different audiences. After examining the idea of pooled or shared authority and the 'unbundling' of sovereign powers (building on the argument in Chapter 2) and their legal support, we will turn to the notion of the multiple 'faces' of member states. The overall argument of this section of the chapter is that (notwithstanding the fears of some member states) pooling policy-sectoral governance areas does not necessarily trespass upon the 'ultimate authority' of member states' ruler sovereignty; that the unbundling of political sovereignty can be accomplished so that member states not only have their own political identities but also contribute to the identity of the EU; and that the move from two to three faces does not warrant conclusions about the loss of sovereignty.

In order to establish the legitimacy of the notion of 'pooled authority' we will first make a case for its validity in terms of the strong presumption that sovereignty is absolute and cannot be divided in any way, and in the light of the modesty of the proposal. Then we will examine how a plausible notion of 'pooled authority' operates in the context of the EU.

It does not follow from the idea of sovereignty as absolute that it cannot be pooled or shared. Pooling sovereignty does not require that it be divided, for final authority over the pooled sectoral areas remains with member states. Pooling authority does not entail pooling ruler sovereignty. Here, eurosceptics and little-England nationalists are joined with legal positivists who misconceive legal sovereignty as having priority over political sovereignty and who inflate the significance of the body of law developed by the European Court of Justice (ECJ). Once the pre-eminence of political sovereignty is brought back properly into focus, and the relationship between member states governments and their peoples reaffirmed, then it is clear that the governance and regulation of designated policy sectors can be shared and pooled without endangering (political) sovereignty.

A more radical idea of unbundling sovereignty, on the grounds that historically it has had the effect of setting up an 'ideological barrier' permitting 'dominant particular interests to masquerade as the general will', lacks plausibility. According to this idea, described by Neil Walker, sovereignty should be unbundled to the point where the boundaries of the sovereign polity as 'the boundaries of political initiative and legal norm-generation' are swept away in favour of the 'bottom-up democratic experimentalism' of a 'directly-deliberative polyarchy', a process of 'continuous reflection, adaptation and renegotiation' (Walker 2005, 594). This more radical idea, as well as leading to great political instability, does not recognise the role played in all polities of a conditionally-settled understanding of the content and parameters of politically salient issues, of the necessity for a commonly-agreed political language and values or (more modestly) a commonly-used set of working assumptions, at least until they are challenged and renegotiated. This view does not endorse the capture of power by dominant interests but acknowledges that it is a feature of liberal democracies that power differentials are a dimension of social life in a framework in which they can be specifically challenged and remedied. The *conditionally*-settled understanding referred to in the notion of political sovereignty commends the contingent and provisional character of any such settlement.

In Britain in particular the national tradition of centralised, unified and hierarchical sovereignty has led to a lack of imagination in reconceptualising sovereignty. However, many contemporary examples exist of alternatives to indivisibility, perhaps the most prominent being the political system in the United States where the powers of the president, Congress, and judiciary are balanced and checked against one another within the framework of the constitution.

Franklin, for instance, makes a strong case that Bodin and the subsequent tradition on sovereignty that followed his logic, was simply wrong in the assertion that sovereignty must be indivisible. He notes that there are three other alternatives – federal decentralisation, shared sovereignty and distributed sovereignty. These are all more radical than the case developed here. They deal with different forms of distribution of the legislative and executive powers, while the pooled authority envisaged here concerns only the joint use of policy-sectoral areas. Shared sovereignty in Franklin's terms results in what he calls a 'compound polyarchy', where each politically-relevant group retain their own identity within the whole. One example might be, as he cites, where 'the king, the senate, and the people, or any two of these...participate with different weights in any given governmental function' (Franklin 1992, xviii), and another is the roles in the American system of both the president and Congress in making legislation. Distributed sovereignty refers, he notes, to a system of 'constitutional co-ordination of co-equal parts', in which 'the rights of sovereignty [are distributed] to different partners separately'. Franklin goes on to detail how this 'entails express or implied coordinating rules by which the powers thus separated, and above all the legislative power, are adjusted to each other's function'. Moreover, he argues, it 'supposes, more specifically, that the legislature, although supreme in making rules, cannot apply them, and cannot control directly that authority which is constitutionally charged with their execution' (Franklin 1992, xix).

The notion of pooled authority has similarities with but also envisages a less radical distribution of sovereignty than the notion of republican constitution that Bellamy seeks to recommend for conceptualising the EU. In distinctively republican regimes, he argues, the separation of powers (which distributes sovereignty functions) and the balance of power (in a multiplicity of decision-making sites) are the two 'central mechanisms' which 'facilitate the distribution and sharing of power'. The 'first, distributive, mechanism reduces the discretionary aspect of the law, preventing it degenerating into a mere command. The second, sharing, mechanism encourages the law to track the interests of those to whom it applies and gives them a sense of ownership over it' (Bellamy 2003, 181).

In the context of the EU, then, pooled authority, then, refers here on the one hand to the disaggregation at member state level of some policy-sectoral governance functions, and so their reaggregation in different form at EU level. This can occur without the alienation of the 'ultimate authority' claim of ruler sovereignty by member states, and critically, pooling does not involve the blurring of the ruler sovereignty of member states. The legal underpinning of this situation also does not involve a breach of member state sovereignty. At the same time it refers to the notional disaggregation of sovereignty at the EU level, with the ultimate authority of ruler sovereignty held at member state level, legal sovereignty shared between the EU and member states, and forms of political sovereignty expressed at both EU and member state levels. Neil Walker makes the important distinction that while, in the state-centred conception of sovereignty a 'non-exclusive order is typically a dependent one', in the EU context this is not the case because here there is 'overlap without subsumption' (Walker 2002, 345–6). This understanding chimes with the view quoted by Chryssochoou (2002, 347) that highlights the importance of having 'a right to participate in the management of common arrangements with other states' over 'the traditional right to exclusive management'. Lindahl also makes a useful case for the coherence of sovereignty in the context of multi-level and multi-centred EU governance, in terms of a 'compound of decentralisation, horizontality, participation, deliberation and pluralism' (Lindahl 2003, 91).

In this two-fold process, sovereignty *over* (a population, a territory, functional policy sectors) is complemented by sovereignty *of* (the integrity of the whole, constituting the whole as a polity, the political identity). From the perspective of the EU, both the EU level and member states exercise aspects of sovereignty 'over' and 'of', and this represents a form of 'sharing' or 'pooling' of authority. This is entirely compatible with what, at member state level, Neil Walker calls (as noted in the Introduction) the 'irreducible core, the non-negotiable given of any sovereign order'. He draws attention to the two facets of this 'core'. A 'sovereign order must assume its own continuing or self-amending sovereignty within its sphere of authority (rules of recognition and change)'. This corresponds to what has here been called ruler sovereignty. At the same time, a sovereign order must also 'retain interpretive autonomy (rules of adjudication), deciding the boundaries of that sphere of authority' (Walker 2003b, 28). This relates to what has been here termed political sovereignty.

Werner and De Wilde phrase the unbundling thesis well, making a similar distinction to that between ultimate authority and sectoral governance. They distinguish between sovereign status and sovereign rights, noting that a 'successful claim to sovereignty establishes a relation between a status' such as supreme authority or independence, and 'a bundle of rights, powers and responsibilities related to that status', such as the rights to make treaties and to immunity. The 'claimed status' is indivisible and 'cannot be partly handed over or pooled', while the 'rights and powers linked to that status' can be transferred or shared with 'other states or international organisations' (Werner and De Wilde 2001, 303).

The unbundling of sovereignty powers could, in theory, have several different outcomes. The unbundling that is envisaged here means that sovereignty is not transferred and not transferred all of a piece. Some competencies are pooled, shared, or used jointly while others are retained by member partners and, crucially, the authority to pool competencies in specific areas is preserved by member states. In this way the autonomy that is part of the claim to sovereignty remains intact and the exclusivity (another part of the traditional territorial-state claim to sovereignty) is retained in some areas but not in others. In the context of the EU it is some of the competencies traditionally associated with internal sovereignty that are at stake here (though not taxation policy), while those associated with external sovereignty, such as foreign policy, the authority to make war and peace, and the authority to enter into international alliances and agreements, remain in the hands of member states. Those competencies that are pooled, shared, or used jointly are employed not simply with other member states but in a network that also includes national and transnational interest groups and regional representatives.

The idea of sovereign authority exercised by different bodies is not a new one. As Loughlin argues the constitutional separation of legislative, executive and judicial powers (as well as in all kinds of federal systems of government where powers are devolved and not just decentralised) does not 'amount to a division of sovereignty: sovereignty divided is sovereignty destroyed'. But separations of power can be understood rather as 'an explication, rather than a division, of sovereignty' (Loughlin 2003, 70). The policy-sectoral pooling of sovereignty in the case of the EU operates on the same principle, the only difference being that it is pooled across member states (not just any old states) rather than internally in one state. Indeed, policy-sectoral governance pooling on the model of self-regulating multi-level governance networks can be seen as a form of devolution rather than as an alienation of sovereignty.

The principles of pooling and 'delinking' are not new and are not necessarily threatening. Keating, for instance, makes a strong case for 'delinking' the accountability and deliberative activities at the EU level. He argues that, while the European Parliament 'is probably as good as most national parliaments' in 'scrutinising executive institutions and holding them to account', it does not 'sustain a pan-European deliberative community or help form a pan-European democratic will'. His assessment is that it 'probably never will, and possibly never should'. However it is possible to 'delink these activities. Accountability and scrutiny may take a variety of forms – audit, legal control, parliamentary investigation, adversary politics – and work at various levels'. On the other hand, he notes, '[d]eliberative democracy and will formation can similarly occur at various levels. In some cases, the state remains the main focus', and he cites Denmark, Portugal and Ireland as prime examples, while in Belgium deliberation is conducted primarily on the lines of the two linguistic communities, and in multinational Spain and the UK the different nations have deliberative assemblies (Keating 2003, 206).

Pooled authority brings with it a change in approach from competition to cooperation. Sørensen points to other ways in which sovereignty in the EU context (what he calls the postmodern game) differs from that in the orthodox Westphalian framework. For instance, he says, while 'in the Westphalian game, the rule of reciprocity is basically that of equal or fair competition, in the post-modern game it is cooperation rather than competition' and he gives the example of aid to poorer regions within the EU (Sørensen 1999, 603). The proposal put forward here builds upon existing features of the EU's manner of conducting politics, such as subsidiarity, state veto, and qualified majority voting. Moreover, the chances of effectiveness for its other features are increased by the existing indeterminacy and uncertainty in EU politics, described so well by Richmond.

Pooled authority operates not only in policy sectoral governance areas but also in terms of the legal framework that underpins it. Neil Walker's work here is important, in making a convincing case that with the European Union we already have a robust example of 'a multi-dimensional configuration of authority' (Walker 2003b, 9). The idea that the unbundling of different aspects of sovereignty is appropriate to the EU situation is supported by a parallel recognition in EU legal theory. Walker argues that the development of forms of 'structural variability' (in Maastricht's Three Pillar architecture), 'jurisdictional variability' (non-unanimous member state involvement in the single currency), and 'differentiated integration' (between member states) in the EU 'clearly casts doubt on the plausibility of a traditional Kelsenian or Hartian notion of a legal order'. The traditional notion conceived of a legal order as 'a hierarchical structure of norms organized around a point of legally self-validating sovereignty assumed or claimed to be grounded in social or political authority' (Walker 2005, 591–2).

Shaw draws out well the consequence of the outcome of the interconnected process of the pooling and unbundling of sovereignty. If 'legal orders can be overlapping and do not stand in a hierarchy or an arrangement which is either strict or fixed', she argues, then 'it is possible to see the EU as an entity of "interlocking normative spheres"; what is significant is that no particular sphere is seen as privileged or predominant' (Shaw 2001, 75). The key role of political sovereignty in facilitating this conjunction is outlined later.

Fears about the loss of sovereignty in the EU are sometimes based on confusion about the relationship between legal and political sovereignty.

Commentators such as Held *et al* (1999) maintain that the development of greater institutional integration in the international arena (of which the EU is an example), leading to the granting by states of jurisdictional competence to supranational bodies, amounts to the transfer of sovereignty. Against this, however, as Loughlin argues persuasively, such accounts focus on legal sovereignty and neglect the ongoing importance of the dynamic of (conventional) political sovereignty as the relation between rulers and ruled that underpins legal authority. Bearing in mind the pre-eminence of political sovereignty, such grants are not transfers and 'can just as easily be explained as an extension or augmentation of sovereignty'. So long as the 'question of "ultimate" authority is not significantly affected by these novel institutional arrangements, they do not entrench on sovereignty'. The crucial point is that, given the priority of political sovereignty over legal sovereignty, 'shared competence or transferred jurisdiction does not entail shared or transferred sovereignty' (Loughlin 2003, 81). What is pooled is not everything, but some of the 'internal' aspects of ruler sovereignty while a new political sovereignty for the EU is constructed.

The final element of the proposal for pooled authority concerns the integrity of the 'faces' that member states present. The strength of this point means that the debate about the feasibility of shared sovereignty does not really hinge after all on the quality of the 'pooled authority' argument.

Along with the pooling of some sovereign powers, the member states retain their traditional state sovereignty in a very real sense. As members of the EU they pool areas of authority, but as polities facing other audiences, whether their domestic electorates, membership of other international bodies, or in relations with other states in international politics, these states remain and are indeed enhanced as traditional sovereign states. Werner and De Wilde make a strong case that the pooling of sovereignty by EU member states is not the crucial consideration in deciding whether they have lost sovereignty or not. They see as critical that EU member states 'are still regarded as sovereign states by other actors in international society and they are still able to claim certain rights and powers in virtue of their being sovereign'. They argue that because the 'reality of sovereignty consists in its use and acceptance, it is pointless to wonder whether the member states' are 'still really sovereign' (Werner and De Wilde 2001, 306–7). The pooling of sovereign powers in the context of the EU does not affect the sovereignty of states in other internal and external contexts. This holds, notwithstanding that in the EU 'the degree to which powers have been handed over is unprecedented', and that some aspects of powers traditionally regarded as 'essential for the sovereignty of the state', such as immigration, internal security and the determination of states of emergency, have been shared. This is the case also despite the 'claim of the European Court of Justice that Community law constitutes an "independent legal order"' (Werner and De Wilde 2001, 303–4).

Crucial to this argument is the recognition that the identity of the member states as *member* states is often overlooked in the rush to either confirm or deny that they remain member *states*. Their status as *member* states is something they share, whatever the differences in background, wealth, international status, cultural norms, political languages, and social values. The EU states remain member *states* but they are also *member* states. This is crucially significant and the status of the states as member states is often neglected. The idea of the 'member state' is an important concept. Members are states in respect of their own peoples, states in international politics, and states within intergovernmental bodies such as the G8. But they are, in addition, members of the EU and members in relation to each other. Instead of the dual faces of the conventional state, looking outward to the international realm and inward to the domestic sphere, EU member states now have three faces, the third one looking towards the European construct. The three faces are no more in tension than the two faces of the conventional state are. Furthermore, value added does not mean value taken away in zero-sum fashion. The net result is that in place of the conventional notionally minimal and normatively neutral 'coexistence' between Westphalian states, a more complex pattern of relationship, and one which acknowledges relationship over the non-relationship of coexistence, is developed.

Diez follows up the point about the importance of member states' relations with their own internal audiences. He notes that the EU is a 'multi-perspectival polity' on two grounds, first through its 'lack of a single centre of decision-making', and second 'because it allows for conceptualizations from various angles'. Diez argues that 'the future development of the EU will not depend solely on member states' interests, but also on the translatability of the discourses on European governance that the relevant political actors are embedded in' (Diez 2001b, 97). But where Werner and De Wilde did not regard the diversity and incommensurability of those internal discourses as a problem, Diez implies that some level of symmetry is required for a smoothly-running EU.

Philpott's observation that neither the EU nor the member states 'enjoys absolute sovereignty' (Philpott 1999, 586), raises an interesting point in relation to pooled authority. In practice the network of connections between countries, alliances, dependencies, and geopolitical situations, means that countries, including the most powerful, have always been involved in meshes of relation that seemingly go against the formal possession of their sovereignty. However, this has not been seen, in itself, as a factor that derogates from the principle of sovereign status, and *that* fact has been an important aspect of the meaning of sovereignty as a political concept. The flaw with the 'argument from reality' – that member states have no reason to fear pooled authority because forms of pooling, sharing and interconnection have always routinely been the case – is that political concepts such as sovereignty and pooled authority require for their force, if a mismatch between theory and practice is to be avoided, that the potency of the ideas is recognised in political practice.

The idea of the importance of the multiple faces presented by member states opens up the question of what, if anything, should be done about it. The conduct of states subscribing to the Westphalian model, on the issue of the two faces of states and the possible disjunction between statements made for domestic consumption or for an international audience, has been to tacitly acknowledge the two faces but not see any salient consequences flowing to this. Sometimes more explicit acknowledgment is granted as in, for example, the media reports in 2006 that 'Bush's aggressive speech was aimed at an American audience and isn't taken to have consequences for his allies in Iraq'. Now there is something to be said for a more overt recognition by EU member states of their interdependence – an extension of the interdependence between states that is hidden in international politics behind the fiction of states' absolute sovereign self-governing independence. The resolute refusal to acknowledge interdependence can issue in relevant claims of hypocritical conduct. There is also something to be said for maintaining and indeed extending the fiction to cover the three faces of EU member states. The fiction of sovereign independence means that infringements of independence can be identified for what they are, just as the fiction of individualism acts as an (imperfect) bulwark against unjustified interference. Although such fictions do not in themselves make the world a fairer place it is possible, using them, to identify more readily forms of intervention that should be held to account.

Complex confederalism

Goldsmith identifies as a key feature of sovereignty that it 'excludes appeals outside the system, requiring that all questions be (legally) finally decidable within the system (that is, by its agencies or agencies designated by it)'. It follows, he says, that 'a state with a constitution that provided for an ultimately authoritative procedure (such as enactment by the crown in parliament or by a legislature followed by approval by some proportion of the electorate in a referendum or by some other process) would still possess sovereignty'. So too, he argues, would 'a state which restricted final decisions to the "concurrent" agreement of two distinct authorities (eg enactment by both federal and regional authorities)'. So, again, would 'a state which distributed final decisions on different subjects to different authorities as the British North American Act gave the Canadian federal government power over criminal justice but reserved commerce to the provinces'. He adds that 'such systems may not always exclude the possibility that the empowered authorities will disagree and they may or may not attempt to provide a procedure for reconciling or resolving such disagreements' (Goldsmith 1993, 784–5).

Confederal governance is a key feature of the 'less is more' proposal, in that the minimalism of the architectural style is mirrored in the confederalist, as Lister puts it, 'minimalist mandate that leaves most governmental powers to be exercised independently by its member states' (Lister 1996, 34). But in the context of the EU what is required is a complex confederalism.

We noted earlier that the term 'federalism' can apply to federal as opposed to confederal polities, but that it is also used as a generic term to distinguish any form of decentralised polity from a centralised one. This point has more than academic importance. The question of whether or not the EU has been moving towards a federal state has been understood in very different terms, for instance in Germany and Britain. As Koslowski (2001, 40) summarises, while 'the Germans tend to view federalism in terms of power-sharing and limited central government, the British tend to associate federalism with the loss of sovereignty and an overbearing Leviathan'. Indeed, in the German case the constitution distributes ultimate powers to both federal and state levels. This radical difference in understanding the term federalism in Germany and Britain, as signalling decentralisation and centralisation respectively, affects the discussion of it here. It is the more exacting first meaning (that is, confederal rather than federal) that is relevant here, endorsing the idea of a union of self-governing states. This section of the chapter will describe the complex confederal proposal and discuss its fit with the EU situation. The proposal is 'complex' because of the novel legal situation in the EU, the identity of its components as *member* states, and because of the role of policy-sectoral and regional networks. The active role of sub-national group in the EU, sometimes bypassing states, and the emphasis on sectoral governance through networks that include interest groups and NGOs as well as government representatives, complicates the picture.

A key part of the advocacy of confederalism is a positive defence of pluralism. Neil Walker sums up Weiler's valuable 'normative pluralism', his sense that one 'cannot conceive of an acceptable ethic of political responsibility for the new Europe other than in terms of mutual recognition and respect between national and supranational sites of authority', regardless of where one comes down on the question of where ultimate authority might lie (Walker 2001, 570). The robust assertion of normative pluralism as a positive feature of the EU, in contrast to the defensive insistence on state independence, together with the complexity of the confederalism advocated here, distances the present proposal simply from traditional intergovernmentalism.

The idea of the EU as a confederation has not been given sufficient weight in the discourse on EU studies. The key point is that, as Lister confirms, in confederal unions, 'the central authorities are kept subordinate to those of its member states' (Lister 1996, 2). The value of the idea of a confederation, is that it offers a range of middle ways between the international status of the single sovereign states and federation. In formal terms, a confederation is an international body in which the component states retain full international personality. Thus confederal status offers member states some pooling of authority in certain limited and specified fields without losing international personality as sovereign states. The proposal for 'less is more' expresses that status. A federation, in contrast, is a national political body constituted by its states and with a much larger role dedicated to its centralised institutions. The federal level of the polity mediates between its components and the international sphere. A confederation is, by contrast, a set of states whose members, rather than the central institutions, retain control over foreign affairs. Executive power, and in particular military power, is exercised at decentralised locations. The primary legal order for citizens is that which exists at component state rather than confederal level. It does not have its own police or armed forces, whatever coordinating bodies it might have.

In a confederation the balance is weighted in favour of states operating on the basis of mutual commitments, made under their adherence to the norm of international law that treaties embody legally binding norms, rather than on the basis of direct obligation to a positive federal law. However, the EU doctrines of direct effect and supremacy of Community law would seem to significantly modify that position. The outcome is, Richmond argues, that the question remains an open one whether the initial international legal character of multipartite agreements has decisively changed, by a process of creeping constitutionalisation, into a position where Community law now represents an effective and autonomous legal order that 'is validated by a basic norm presupposed in relation to it' (Richmond 1997, 398). While Richmond was writing ten years ago, the failure of the Constitutional Treaty means that her assessment remains valid and that the situation has not decisively changed, based on her highlighting of the indeterminacy and uncertainty that are still important features of the EU.

The proposal advocated here is that the EU is becoming and should be encouraged to endorse what is a new political form which, on a spectrum from federation to confederation, is closer to the confederal end. This is a complex confederalism because in standard confederations legal authority is not as complexly distributed as in the case of the EU. It remains a complex confederalism rather than an instance of federalism because, as discussed later, there is a strong case that the degree of legal integration does not infringe the maintenance of ruler sovereignty at member state level.

The idea of complex confederalism has three elements. This picture of the EU retains aspects of a confederation, such as the independent legal personality of the member states and that the primary focus of political life remains at member state level, both summed up in the notion of the absence of state-centrality. The polity would be a confederal 'union of states'. Lister, coming at the matter from the international end (rather than the usual comparison between federal and confederal states), usefully highlights the similarities between a confederation and the United Nations and other intergovernmental organisations. He describes a confederation as 'an IGO with teeth', empowered 'to carry out, with the joint participation of its member states, a limited range of sovereign functions on their behalf', jointly rather than separately, and to take actions which its member states are obliged to accept rather than simply issuing recommendations (Lister 1996, 11). At the same time this new political form would recognise that its institutions are knitted together more closely than in a conventional confederation, especially in that it has developed at least to some extent an independent legal identity in its own right. However, and this is the third element, in addition to the importance of member states, the significance of regions and regional networks and of policy sectoral networks across states for collective policy coordination, both need to be fully acknowledged at the political level.

The form of complex confederalism supported here, then is, in Neil Walker's words, 'more than a mere association of states but less than a state' (Walker 2001, 567), and is based on a strong critique of the state-centred perspective. It envisages a multi-level, multi-dimensional order; a non-hierarchical and complex overlapping set of authorities; no pivotal, central point or fulcrum; and the possibility of mixed agreements between member states. This positive confederal proposal is also complex in that, as Lister notes in relation to the EU, some 'of its features appear to be federal, others confederal, and still others [for instance on foreign policy] seem to be on the level of IGO-type voluntary cooperation' (Lister 1996, 81).

There are similarities between complex confederalism and consociationalism, but the latter is a non-state centric approach closer on the spectrum to federalism than is confederalism. Neil Walker defines consociationalism as the model whereby member states are the relatively autonomous 'pillars' of the divided polity (Walker 2001, 573). However Koslowski, taking up a position closer to the federal end of the spectrum, outlines a form of European consociationalism that could frame 'the "end state" of European integration as a polity between confederation and a federal state'. Consociationalism there is identified by its four features, of 'executive power-showing, or grand coalition, a high degree of autonomy for parts of the society, proportionality and minority veto'. Koslowski does identify a very useful feature that is also shared with complex confederalism when he describes a consociationalist political association as a stable polity which at the same time is 'characterized by continual internal contestation' (Koslowski 2001, 47). This feature, as we will see later, is a distinctive mark of the polity advocated by Spinoza.

Coming now to the fit of complex confederalism with the EU, Diez (2001a, 20) underlines how the openness of meaning of the EU works in favour of a confederal construction of it. He identifies a variety of constructions of European governance, broadening out the range from the conventional dichotomy of intergovernmental and supranational alternatives, and includes the intergovernmental cooperation of nation states, a free trade area, a federal state, two Eurosceptic constructions that affirm economic cooperation with the idea of the quasi-natural market but which proscribe political cooperation – liberal economic community and social democratic economic community – and network.

Lister specifies the 'confederal balance' of the EU as one that 'satisfies the need for a minimal level of political, economic, and technical integration while simultaneously conceding as much autonomy as possible to the member states in the spheres where they are heterogeneous'. He notes that the 'main guarantee that the confederal compact will be respected and upheld by all concerned' lies in the 'fact that the heads of government of the member states run the union' (Lister 1996, 57). The point is an important one because it runs up against the issue of the 'democratic deficit'. It is precisely because the member state governments (through the Council of Europe and Council of Ministers) fulfil this key function described by Lister that the 'democratic deficit' has been identified. The argument developed here takes the view that, in the contest over control of the EU, the decisive role of the member state governments is to be strongly favoured over direct democratic participation and accountability that overrides state boundaries, since the former is one of the most important guarantees of confederal status (another being the principle of subsidiarity). It ensures that the confederation does not slip towards federation, whereas the latter (direct democratic participation) turns the confederation categorically into a state-type polity.

The fit of complex confederalism to the EU is supported at the academic level as well as in the working of EU institutions. Diez confirms that the trend in European studies in recent years has been 'in opposition to "centralisation" and a further unitary development of the EU'. This trend is supported by the way that the emerging Euro-speak has 'focused on subsidiarity and flexibility' (Diez 2001b, 95), whether in the form of a core Europe, 'concentric circles', or greater elasticity.

Political sovereignty

As well as outlining a conception of sovereignty for the EU, this chapter is concerned to comment on the characterisation of a tension between those on the political left being associated with a concern that the EU has a democratic deficit, and those on the right being aligned to a primary commitment to the member nation states. In this way, ideologically, supranationalism is identified with the left and intergovernmentalism is identified with the right. It is those on the left who are wedded to an imagination of the EU as only and necessarily the state writ large, to another domestic analogy, such that democratic participation can only be meaningful if it is expressed at the level of the EU itself, and that oversight and political accountability cannot be left to the member states to carry out. Progressive politics demands direct rather than mediated representation, so the argument goes. It is those on the right who are wedded to an imagination of the EU limited to the primacy of the modern (now old) state, such that decision-making should remain vested to as large a degree as possible in member states. First, it is an irony that left and right are thought to be lined up this way, and second, both these views are blinkered and tied to a conservative and outdated view of the state and of sovereignty. The theory recommended here represents a third path, based on the post-state.

Weiler (1999) rightly contends that the new Europe does not need a sovereign in the sense of a central location of ultimate authority, and that the new Europe is and should be a complex overlapping pluralistic political form. But it would be mistaken to conclude from this argument that the EU can therefore do without a conception of sovereignty altogether, and to look for political identity instead in a 'revitalised democracy'.

The proposal for political sovereignty builds on the idea of the recognition of the political property of the concept of sovereignty discussed in the previous chapter, and involves two things. In the face of the dominance of lawyers in the thinking guiding the development of the EU over the past three decades and their misapprehension that legal thinking is autonomous, the argument here want to reaffirm with Loughlin the priority of orthodox political, ruler sovereignty (political *capacity,* expressed in the relation between rulers and ruled) over legal sovereignty (jurisdictional *competence*). The effect of this reaffirmation is that sovereignty, in Loughlin's words, 'is not directly affected by increasingly elaborate institutional arrangements of governance' which refine and develop jurisdictional competence, since 'sovereignty, at its most basic, is an expression of the political relationship between the people and' their member states (Loughlin 2003, 82–3). Secondly the proposal argues that at the EU level, political sovereignty in the form of the setting out of the content and limits of the political, is a necessary condition for the minimal political identity that is all that is required for a viable EU and far preferable to the construction of a constitutional document.

In the previous chapter a case was made for a meaning of political sovereignty that is valuable in alerting us to the specificity of 'the political' in any particular polity. In the context of the EU this means that current responses are not adequate. Political sovereignty can no longer (as it has been) simply be ignored, overridden by discourses of jurisdictional competence and legal institution-building, subsumed under constitutionalism, or absorbed into calls for a European demos. There are already distinctive ways in which politics is conducted in the EU (for instance, through mutual accommodation and bargaining, but also through creative tension), and new ways in which the limits of politics are imagined. Moreover, there are opportunities in the EU to rethink the way in which the boundary between the political and unpolitical is charted. The substantive content of politics in the EU is still under dispute. Again, while political sovereignty typically develops organically in a state polity, and in parallel with but not determined by the question of ruler sovereignty, the character of political sovereignty in the context of the EU is distinctively different. In the case of the EU, political sovereignty is not mirrored by ruler sovereignty since ruler sovereignty remains at member state level (together with the member states' own political sovereignty). The ideas of pooled authority and complex confederalism are closely connected with envisaging political sovereignty in the EU in this sense.

Neil Walker's work is valuable in seeking to revitalise the concept of sovereignty in theorising the EU and for conceptualising EU as polycentric. He argues convincingly that the term 'sovereignty' is helpful for comprehending not only the 'one-dimensional pattern of state-centred authority' but is also 'capable of illuminating more or less complex configurations of authority' (Walker 1998, 356). However, the pre-eminence he accords to legal over political sovereignty is misplaced because it does not fully take into account the way legal sovereignty gains its legitimacy from political decisions. It is worth analysing his reasoning in some detail. He contends that legal and political sovereignty are not different sides of the same coin and should not be collapsed into a single definition. He goes on to claim the priority of the legal over the political conception for thinking about the EU, on the grounds that the latter is only 'a measure of the capacity to command of a government elite, or in its popular variant, of the capacity of the wider community to ensure that its interests are secured', and so is 'at best...a marker of a certain empirical state of affairs'. Moreover, Walker maintains, in trying to conceptualise the EU in terms of multiple centres of authority, on the basis of a 'heterarchical rather than hierarchical political space' the idea of political sovereignty – as an ultimate source of authority – is of no help. The political conception, he contends, only 'seeks to describe rather than to explain power relations', 'lacks theoretical purchase', and is 'both theoretically empty and empirically redundant'. Legal sovereignty, on the other hand, he holds 'is a more helpful device in explaining a complex configuration of political authority' because law is institutionally autonomous (and so provides 'an internally coherent system of rules' that permits it to be discussed independently of 'other levers and incidents of political power'), and because law is a form of normative power that allows it to make significant claims to decision-making authority (Walker 1998, 357).

When Walker states that the articulation of a claim to ultimate legal authority 'takes the form of fundamental practices, propositions or assumptions' (Walker 1998, 360), we can note that such practices, propositions and assumptions are deeply political, both because they are indeterminate and contestable and because they are formed by a political rather than a legal process. All such forms of embedding values are political and in this way (although Walker wanted to deny this) the political is prior to the legal. But most importantly, it is the work of sovereignty to carry for us the unique set of values and the legacy of meanings associated with them.

The proposal made here, for 'less is more', argues for a minimal content for political sovereignty at the EU level mirroring the priority of politics in the member states seen as *member* states. The proposal also demonstrates that political sovereignty in this sense, while in part deliberative and explicitly constructed, is also crucially in part tacit, organically developed, and not agency-based. While political sovereignty in the sense developed here typically emerges as part of an organic development of political identity (and this is where the mystery arose), there is no reason why it could not be initially constructed through a process of debate and discussion. Sovereignty expresses the sense in which a polity has an identity, a unity in the sense of integrity (and so which may be non-hierarchical), a coherence (which may be multi-centred), an integration (which may be decentralised), and political sovereignty as described above provides that sense and exhausts the need at the EU level. Once political sovereignty in this sense is acknowledged, there is no need for other political attempts – either in the form of constitutionalism or a European demos – and the attempt by lawyers to make legal sovereignty pre-eminent is shown to be misguided.

Proponents who see the building of greater democracy as the means of constructing a European identity argue that what is crucially lacking in the EU is the legitimacy provided by the 'constituent power of the people (or nation)'. This view is correct insofar as it identifies that there is currently no European demos, but wrong in that the constituent power of the people of the different member states can still be understood as providing the necessary legitimacy for political sovereignty. One reason for rejecting the advocacy of a 'European demos' is precisely that it interrupts and weakens the link between popular sovereignty and state sovereignty. In giving recognition to the political sovereignty of the EU we are not setting up a founding myth such as nation-state polities have. Instead of the myth of 'the people', the constituent power of the EU, that is, the founding agent of the political compact, remains with the member states. In the democracies that constitute the EU (remembering that the existence of thriving democratic procedures and institutions is one of the conditions of membership) state sovereignty is understood as necessarily founded upon and expressing the popular sovereignty of the people. The idea of a 'European demos' impairs the popular sovereignty of the member states both directly and indirectly. It weakens the force of popular sovereignty in the link between popular and state sovereignty in the member states, and it enfeebles the role of the member states in the EU. Maintaining the value of popular sovereignty is particularly important in mass industrial societies. As the scale of political life is broadened and the number of people involved increases, so the significance of political elites in political decision-making becomes greater. Moreover, as Neil Walker notes, critics of the EU tend to highlight its alleged shortcomings – a democratic deficit and problems around accountability, legitimacy, security, and equality – in terms of 'a statist template and against the benchmark of a (real or imagined) statist standard' (Walker 2002, 323). The same state-centred mindset is clear in discussions about sovereignty in Europe, for instance in Pagden's assumption, quoted at the beginning of this chapter, that in turning to the EU the concept of sovereignty would have to be abandoned. The proposal made here for reconceptualising political sovereignty moves beyond visualising the EU in state terms.

An important aspect of the kind of political sovereignty developed here is that it is not a speech act, a performative use of language, a declaration like a constitution. This was described in the last chapter as part of the 'mystery' of sovereignty. Those in favour of a European constitution think, over-optimistically, that the act of naming will itself give the EU legitimacy, and later in the chapter this disputed. Political sovereignty is not an act of naming but a conditional, for-the-time-being consensus and pre-conception upon which one operates and upon which practices run smoothly. It is more than an instrumental *modus vivendi* or pragmatic accommodation, settling crucially as it does the scope and limits of politics at the EU level.

Werner and De Wilde (2001, 299, 303) articulate the view that international cooperation has 'undermined the idea of sovereignty of the member states', that (and here assuming the primacy of internal over external sovereignty) the internal ability to rule in a set of integrated states such as the EU is compromised by 'overlapping authorities and competing competences'. The proposal put forward here supports the argument that, far from the EU having 'moved European politics beyond sovereignty', unbundling, sharing and pooling, and the construction of a political sovereignty at EU level, amount to a reconceptualised but no less valuable and powerful form of sovereignty both for its members and for the EU as an agent in international politics.

Neil Walker argues for a conception of the EU as 'a plurality of sovereign unities' in which 'the coherence of the whole is always precarious and derivative', reliant on 'various bridging mechanisms' between the 'diverse sites of sovereign authority'. According to this 'multiplicity' conception, there can be, as he says, 'no final "authority of authorities" – no *über*sovereign' (Walker 2005, 592). The proposal put forward in this chapter both agrees and disagrees with Walker's insightful view and the difference from Walker rests on a clear distinction between ruler sovereignty and what I am calling political sovereignty. In terms of ruler sovereignty Walker is right to emphasise that the idea of an übersovereign does not fit with the way the EU is or should be developing. At the same time, however, the ruler sovereignty of the partners is now the ultimate authority to 'unbundle' or 'rebundle', to distribute or withdraw from shared consideration the composite and disaggregated aspects of authority. But in terms of political sovereignty, the (conditional) consensus about the content of what counts as political, the parameters and limits of the political, the boundary between what is open to contestation and what is taken as given or as merely legal or social or cultural or economic, then there is a need for such a consensus as part of the EU identity. The EU with (an even tacit) political sovereignty providing coherence for the framework of multiple ruler sovereignties is a central part of what is meant here by 'less is more'. According to this scheme, legal sovereignty remains firmly in the service of ruler and political sovereignty. The alternative of 'a poly-centred structure of political authority' together with an 'encompassing EU-wide or EU-and-state wide legal authority', a conception that 'implies a downgrading of the importance of sovereignty' (Walker 2005, 592–3) would not, on this reckoning, convincingly sustain the political identities of the members within the minimal coherence provided by the whole.

This new political form is a sovereign body precisely because it is at this level of Europe and this level only that the parameters are established of the content of politics and where and how politics operates, what was called in the previous chapter the neglected dimension of the 'mystery' of sovereignty. The normative purpose and identity of the EU are summed up in its political sovereignty in this sense. But what it establishes is that politics mostly takes place at state, regional and local levels, and in distinctive forms in different places (for instance the street protests that are a feature of French political life but do not have the same role or meaning in British practice). Weiler's notion (1999) of the recognition of multiple *demoi* – part of what is at stake here – is a good one. Not only does the idea of multiple *demoi* indicate the plurality of places, the variety of member states where the primary sense of belonging, political identity, and participatory citizenship are forged and acted out, where the primary legal system operates, where tax-raising powers are held, and where foreign policy decisions are made. This notion also captures a new sense of including an assessment of the similarities with and differences from the *demoi* of other member states as part of one's own experience of democracy and citizenship at the level of the nation-state, and the sense that one has plural membership, a perception of multiple and intersecting centres of belonging instead of just one. In this way the sovereignty of the new political form does not involve the forging of either a strong European political identity nor of a strong European demos, and so the proposal presented here deliberately stops short of the more elaborated ideals advocated by MacCormick (1999) and Siedentop (2000).

The 'less is more' tag stresses that one can construct a political sovereignty and then look to the immanence of meaning it provides, as a preferable alternative to attempting to vest meaning explicitly in a constitution that then becomes an object captured and interpreted according to legal criteria. This is a model of a political entity of 'interlocking normative spheres' (Bankowski and Christodoulidis 1998, 342), which is deliberately without a single, central reference point, and which maintains the pluralism and heterogeneity that is a feature of Europe's cultural history. Thus, for instance, 'I become a European and more specifically a Scottish European for being European is part of my Scottish identity. The French, the English and others will do likewise' (Bankowski and Christodoulidis 1998, 353). It also follows that the term 'integration', in the discourse on 'European integration', is now recognised as having assumed a road to completeness and a fixed horizon, but in truth presupposes no necessary teleology of progress and consummation. One of the problems with a constitution is that it would seek to itself provide that reference point.

In the context of contemporary Europe important contributions to a reconceptualised sovereignty along relational and interactive lines include the elegant insights of Weiler, Deudney, and Preuss, drawn from past and present examples. The kind of political form they envisage is thrown into relief by the clumsy liberal internationalism of Habermas's recommendation of a 'future Federal Republic of European States...connected with the overlapping consensus of a common, supranationally shared political culture of the European community' (Habermas 1995, 264). Weiler for instance argues, in a way that directly takes issue with the idea of a 'common, supranationally shared political culture of the European community', that 'there is no European Demos – not a people not a nation'. Weiler makes the case that '[n]either the subjective elements (the sense of shared collective identity and loyalty) nor the objective conditions which could produce them...exist'. By objective conditions he has in mind 'the kind of homogeneity of the organic national cultural conditions on which peoplehood in the European tradition depend such as shared culture, a shared sense of history, a shared means of communication' (Weiler 1996, 523). Weiler convincingly outlines a 'multiple demos concept' in which citizenship in and so sovereignty of the different European nation-states is not replaced by a pan-European definition.

Preuss argues robustly that the European Union 'is *not* a state, not even a federal state,...is *not* a traditional alliance of states,...is *not* a confederacy' (Preuss, 1996, 549). Rather it is a political form that is dynamic, heterogeneous and non-hierarchical, and polycentric (Preuss 1996, 550). Preuss's argument opens up a space between the state and the liberal internationalism of the state-writ-large onto the region or the world. This is a space in which the examples of the Philadelphian system and the seventeenth-century United Provinces deserve further consideration. 'In contrast to most federal states', Preuss argues in positive and plausible fashion, European 'Union citizenship is not likely to supersede national citizenship or to make it a status of minor importance'. Rather, 'both statuses will co-exist, representing two different principles of political organisation' (Preuss 1996, 551).

'Post-state', 'post-states', and the three faces of member states

Studying the EU and proposing a reconceptualisation of sovereignty in relation to it raises urgently the question of the character of the EU polity and of its component polities. The idea of post-states and other actors in a recast international realm was introduced in Chapter 1 and this chapter adapts the term to meet the peculiar situation with respect to the EU. If the EU is to be envisaged not on the model of the state but in terms of pooled authority, complex confederalism, and with ruler sovereignty held by component polities but political sovereignty informing both levels, is the EU a post-state? Moreover, are the changes to member states sufficient to conclude that the component polities are now post-states? The designation of 'post-state' and 'post-states' is not used lightly or merely as an aspiration but in order to account for important changes in theoretical focus. This section of the chapter will argue that it is valuable to think of the EU and of its component polities as post-states, though in different ways. The EU can helpfully be regarded as a post-state because of its uniquely polycentric and 'less is more' character, while its component polities are best visualised as post-states – in their third face – because member states are now not the only significant political actors on the EU stage. Ultimate authority is held by member states (some of that authority as states and some as post-states) but some governance powers and functions (but not authority) are devolved to both regions and to the EU.

Wallace describes the range of attributions to the status of the EU as a political body, contrasted with the unitary character of the modern state. The EU has been seen as a '"quasi-state", or as an "international state"; or as a post-modern pattern of government in a post-modern European order'. It has also been regarded as a *Verstaatenbund*, a potential federation, as used by the German Constitutional Court (Wallace 1999, 518–19). The term 'post-state' for the EU provides a better fit than does any of these titles.

What does it mean to call the EU a 'post-state'? Firstly it points to the way in which the EU conception of sovereignty developed here is 'not state-centric'. 'Not state-centric' highlights the way it is not based on the model of the state (or any member state) writ large. It also emphasises that this conception does not require a constitution or a demos, and is not based on hierarchy. But it presupposes that something resembling states are still its building blocks, that the sovereignty of states is not eroded but is indeed enhanced by its sharing, and that the EU operates within a conventional idea of international politics (as it does for instance on the question of border controls). This post-state view is not to be confused with Bellamy and Castiglione's (1998) category of 'postnationalists', which refers to those who advocate a European federalism not on the basis of the state write large but as an alternative to the nation-state political form.

Shaw also uses the term 'postnationalist'. He makes the case that the contemporary world is one in which 'states are highly interdependent and are not the only *loci* and foci of political activity and processes' (Shaw 2001, 74). International economic management is expanding and intensifying, evidenced for instance by the restructuring of the IMF as 'world economic watchdog' (*Guardian* 24 April 2006). One of the debates stimulated by such trends is about 'postnationalism', which refers to both the 'denial of nationalism' and its exclusionary practices, as well as the attempt to 'recover and rethink some of the core values of nationalism' (Shaw 2001, 74) in a world in which local and regional forms of sub-national politics gain importance.

In terms of the EU's face towards the international sphere, Spruyt's argument (1994, 193), that the development of the EU does not necessarily pose a challenge to the state system but rather can be seen as further empowering it, is more convincing that Shaw's. The case made in this chapter is not that we now inhabit a 'post-Westphalian' order but that the EU's new form of polity is (for better or ill) simply mapped onto the dominant interpretation of the international order as just one more tolerated anomaly. This is especially so in that member states of the EU continue unimpaired as sovereign nation-states in international politics. The situation is most adequately described in terms of 'something added' rather than 'transformation'. The EU polity transcends the statist template but does not necessarily thereby break the grip of the realist reading of international politics in terms of sovereign states with two faces. Whether the model established by the EU has the effect of leading to a rethinking of the role of the state and its position as the dominant form of polity remains to be seen. But it is likely that in the short term the impact of the model of the EU is likely to be only on geo-politically significant regional areas that wish to establish closer coordination, rather than on the pre-eminence of the nation-state.

It is still a powerful 'background assumption' to debates about European integration that it is nation-states, 'cultural-linguistically defined polities' that are in some sense 'about to merge into a larger polity' (Friese and Wagner 2002, 345). The proposal set out here argues strongly against that view being either necessary or desirable. However, in arguing for the modification of component polities as post-states only in their third face, it is important to emphasise that this proposal does not normatively endorse the image of the nation or nationalist state beloved of conservatives. Diez's observation on how the notion of subsidiarity in EU legal discourse serves to 'reify' the nation state through 'its sole stress on member states' competences' (Diez 2001b, 95), indicates that conservatism is reinforced by some EU practices. The proposal here would be that member states recognise the multicultural, multiethnic and multi-religious composition of their populations, and that immigration stimulated by these member states being part of the EU places a duty on them to find non-exclusionary ways of conducting relations with especially long-term guest workers.

Aspects of the work of writers like Deudney, Weiler and Preuss all point to the possibility of a reconceptualised sovereignty in which the changed role and character of the state is recognised. The positive role of the state is now as a focus of multiple identities rather than the sole definer of a single identity. Werner and De Wilde argue convincingly that the process of EU integration has had the effect of helping to reconceptualise sovereignty away from its taking of territoriality as an essential component. They note that the participation of a tiny and relatively insignificant state like Luxembourg in the process of EU integration 'has not dashed their sovereignty, but rather defined the focus of the sovereignty debate'. The EU process has 'institutionalized the power struggle in international relations' so that questions of 'law and institutional positions' have become more important than territorial questions in interstate relations (Werner and De Wilde 2001, 305).

It is important to recognise the role played by policy-sectoral networks and of EU institutions like the Commission and ECJ as agents, and thus to acknowledge that states are not the only players in EU politics. The idea of 'network governance' goes a step beyond this by conceptualising the EU in terms of both territorial categories and functional categories that crosscut the territorial pattern. It is nevertheless clear as Offe and others argue that nation-states remain the key centres of democratic participation and 'relations of association' based on trust and solidarity. In a sense the new political form of the EU hangs onto some of the intergovernmentalist logic, leaving executive authority intact but without the hegemony of the state form, but also takes something from the functionalist logic, in emphasising the transnational basis of sectoral governance and regulation, but without the sense of this involving a creep towards a super-state. In addition, in this account of the EU as a 'post-state', sectoral networks do not have the same political status as states and regions. Their purpose is economic rather than political governance, and they do not lead to economically-determined political outcomes. However, sectoral networks (like regions and regional networks) gain a measure of coherence from operating and being governed under the umbrella of the new political form.

However, while the notion of the EU as a 'post-state' acknowledges the level of intergovernmental bargaining, the role of governance actors at different levels and sectoral interest groups, and a more active level of interaction between state actors and between state and other actors, writers like Diez and Neil Walker remind us of the continuing potency of entrenched methods of operating and thinking. Thus, while it is important to take account of the significance of policy-sectoral networks alongside the value of member states in the governance of the EU, Diez underlines the powerful nature of the legacy of functionalist language in conceptualising the EU. While many scholars in integrationist studies have moved on to endorse the idea of multi-level governance, the language of the functionalist explanation continues to carry a strong negative connotation in the public's conception of the EU as 'a monster bureaucracy concerned with technical matters that increasingly' spill over into 'the everyday life of its citizens without their formal consent', which shapes public opinion and influences the actions taken by member states in the light of it. Diez also confirms the political role played by the dominant discourse that serves to conceptualise the EU, in that other groups play a largely unacknowledged part in EU governance because the dominant languages do not include them. For instance, 'non-governmental organizations are heavily involved in the making of EC policies' (Diez 2001b, 93).

Neil Walker notes the impact of New Public Management methodologies on redefining institutional design in the emerging EU, and the 'trend away from the conception of centrally institutionalized administrative steering tied to a holistic conception of the public interest' (Walker 2005, 585). The traditional 'command-and-control' Community method was of proposals coming from the Commission and being followed up in legislation through the parliament and Council. Now 'New Modes of Governance' are being discussed in the EU, and particularly the 'Open Method of Co-ordination' to replace or supplement the traditional method of governance, whose decision-making structure is based on 'standard setting, voluntary national compliance and mutual learning' (Walker 2005, 584). However, Walker argues, several features of the distinctive EU set-up work against too radical a reconceptualisation. These include the 'restrictions imposed by limited EU competence', and the 'dispersed transnational framework for establishing standards and engineering compliance'. As a result, reaching towards 'norms of good governance' in the EU is more likely to take place through 'older forms of transnational governance' rather than through models developed at national level (Walker 2005, 585). While Walker's research demonstrates the lag between new ideas and their implementation, this line of argument also indicates the extremely significant point, that in the area of conceptualising EU administration the state template (on whichever side of the Westphalian coin) does not form the default explanatory position.

Critique of constitutionalism and law

The argument of this section of the chapter is that political sovereignty performs more adequately than does the proposal of a constitution, the function of providing the EU with the minimal political identity it needs, and that the project by European lawyers to 'constitutionalise' the EU is misconceived. The critique of moving toward an EU constitution rests on five interrelated arguments: the co-constitution of modern constitutionalism and the hierarchical modern state; the rationalist basis of modern constitutionalism; the legitimacy of member states in a polycentric EU; the stronger case provided by the idea of 'political sovereignty'; and the conservatism of legal discourse. The close connection between the critiques of constitutionalism and of law here are demonstrated by Shaw. She quotes approvingly Shapiro's critical review of a legal work on the then European Community. The nub of Shapiro's criticism is that the book, 'presents the Community as a juristic idea; the written constitution as a sacred text; the professional commentary as a legal truth; ...and the constitutional court as the disembodied voice of right reason and constitutional teleology' (quoted in Shaw 2001, 67).

The first argument, then, is that the instrument of a constitution is closely associated with the hierarchical political structure of a modern state. While this book argues for a reconceived relational sovereignty beyond its traditional association with the state, it is less easy to seriously rethink constitutionalism for a polity that is not a state because of the importance of legal and political hierarchy to the meaning of constitutionalism. Modern constitutionalism is also strongly allied to the idea of state-building and polity-formation, whereas in an important sense and especially in the 'less is more' sense, the EU is not a substantive exercise in polity-building, let alone state-construction.

This criticism, then, concerns the state-centredness of constitutionalism and its consequent lack of utility for conceptualising a polity that is not a conventional state. The discourse on the 'constitutionalisation' of the EU as a post-state polity may look innocent enough. But it is to be strongly resisted, not only because it models the EU on the state form (and so thinks the EU must have a constitution as one of the essential accoutrements of polity-hood), but also because it further promotes the misconception that the process of integration must be led by legal thinking and that political identity will follow in the wake of legal clarity. If one takes the 'post-state' status seriously and innovatively, then neither of these things is necessary.

Ferrajoli sums up the approach to constitutionalism that is being rejected here. He argues that the 'sole democratic foundation of the unity and cohesion of a political system is its constitution, and the type of allegiance it alone can generate – the so-called "constitutional patriotism"'. He draws the conclusion from this that 'the future of Europe as a political entity depends to a great extent on developing a constituent process open to public debate, aimed at framing a European constitution' (quoted in Shaw 2001, 77). In response, Shaw points to the value of Tully's criticism, that in 'societies composed of diverse groups, dominant groups engaging with the traditions of modern constitutionalism seek to "assimilate, integrate or transcend" differences, rather than to "recognise and affirm" cultural diversity' (Shaw 2001, 78).

Shaw underlines that the categories of modern constitutional and democratic thought and the assumptions made there about political community are tied to the context of relatively homogenous nation states and do not fit well with the situation of a diversity of member states as found in the EU case. Shaw argues persuasively that, as a result, constitutionalism 'cannot on its own provide the answers' to the precise nature and detailed character of this 'emergent postnational non-state polity' that is being developed within the wide domain of 'more than an international organization but less than a state' (Shaw 2001, 73).

The second argument in the critique of constitutionalism concerns its rationalist and so universalist basis. The target of criticism here is modern constitutionalism with its combination in one rationalist and socially engineered document of institutional design with normative principles.

Constitutionalism is guided, or misguided, by a rationalistic impulse on two counts. Such thinking considers that the task is achieved once a rationally spelled out design and set of normative principles is laid out. However, Weiler has comprehensively shown that the result of rationalist thinking in conceptualising the EU is simply empty aspirations and clichés. Secondly, the constitutionalist position misleadingly thinks that a rational articulation has the power to override all the presuppositions and entrenched ways of doing and understanding things whereas, as Diez notes, 'we all [necessarily and unavoidably] enter into a conversation with a set of preconceptions from which we set out to reconstruct other articulations' (Diez 2001b, 94).

Neil Walker addresses the criticism of constitutionalism that centres on the way its ability to mould political community is overestimated – such 'top-down command logic' being 'the crowning conceit of a legocentric model of social engineering' (Walker 2002, 327) – especially because it 'neglects the cultivation of a broader discourse of political community', and because constitutional discourse does not get to the heart of 'political imagination' (Walker 2002, 325). In the terms developed in this chapter, it is not warranted that constitutionalism is regarded as being logically prior to sovereignty, for as Walker insists political sovereignty plays a 'meta-constitutional' role as an 'ultimate source and formative influence' for a modern constitution that may or may not develop. What are also suspect here are constitutionalism's capacity to act as a 'placatory discourse', a technocratic secular religion that enervates 'real political engagement' (Walker 2002, 325), and the 'republican conceit' of Habermas and others that 'law can somehow "contain" politics' and 'deliver an expansively participatory version of popular sovereignty' (Walker 2002, 326). Those who follow a Habermasian line and emphasise the 'community-mobilizing potential' (Walker 2005, 600) of a constitution place too great a faith in the writing of a document and confuse the way in which a constitution can sum up retrospectively a consolidated political consensus with an artificial attempt to create such a consensus. They also confuse a constitution with political sovereignty.

Koslowski (2001, 48) highlights other problems with the rationalist belief that informs constitutionalist thinking. Instead of establishing a constitution on purely rational and intended principles, such thinking in fact runs 'the risk of its construction on the rubble of taken-for-granted social institutions' which may be deeply conservative in orientation. Moreover, such rationalism leaves open the way for the development of 'unintended federal political relationships' developed through the struggle between bureaucratic elites, policy-sectoral networks and member states.

A very powerful form of rationalism at work in EU studies is the legocentrism of legal rationalism. Neil Walker points to 'the unusual centrality of law in the task of supranational polity-building' in the EU (Walker 2005, 586). This partly explains the inflated role accorded to law in the future development of the EU and helps to account for the seeming naturalness of the move in the direction of constitutionalism. This situation has come about, in part, because of the way the EU appears incoherent, in terms of the familiar models, both an incomplete polity and more open-ended than the realist international order. This sense of the '"unsaturated" political and legal capacity' of the EU has meant that the 'exploitation of this latest potential is peculiarly amenable to conscious [legocentric] design'. The centrality of law has also come about to compensate, from the legal point of view, for 'the weakness of its cultural supports and political steering mechanisms'. However, from a political theorist's point of view the supposed 'fragmentation, fragility and volatility of the political dimension in the making of the European polity' (Walker 2005, 590), is not a weakness but a necessary extended process of debate and negotiation in order to arrive at a settlement of political sovereignty, which is crucial to the formation of the EU's identity.

Ward makes another valuable point about legal rationalism. On the overestimation of the role of law and constitutionalism in European integration, Ward articulates the allure to many commentators of constitutionalism, in that it seems to offer 'the retrospective legitimation of juristic power by establishing a putatively authoritative constitutional "discourse"'. He notes that it is 'something of an article of faith – at least among European lawyers – that the European Community was secured by law, by the role of the European Court of Justice developing all kinds of doctrines, of supremacy, of direct effect, and so on. The lawyers, it is implied, have made the Community what it is today' (Ward 2001, 25). Ward argues that the '"new" Europe has been too easily distracted by the temptations of constitutionalism', and has mistakenly sought to cobble together a public philosophy from the collection of treaties and their scattered proclamations about democracy and fundamental freedoms and economic aspirations. The idea of a public philosophy stands for him for a 'state of mind, something refined by the political imagination', and he contends that the future of Europe does not depend upon 'the integrity of its political, economic, or even constitutional order', and that the EU's legitimacy cannot be 'secured by the right phraseology in the right treaty articles' (Ward 2001, 25). Ward is right to argue that legitimacy must precede a constitution, but also that agreement on what he calls a public philosophy and what I am calling the content, parameters and limits of politics, is prior and, in my view, when established, makes the constitution redundant.

Schmitt is useful here not just in theorising the legitimacy and importance of political conflict, but in helping to show the limits of legal constitutionalism as an instrument or method for the EU project. His point about the limits of legalism and constitutionalism is closely linked indeed to the importance of politics and conflict for Schmitt. What is needed is less integration not more. Schmitt's views on the limits of liberal legal theory's reliance on constitutionalism, which underpins his concepts of exception and decisionism, and his recognition of the political nature of political conflict, have great potential for the future of sovereignty (see Prokhovnik 2008 forthcoming).

The third argument in the critique of constitutionalism is that, if the best way forward for the EU is as a poly-centric polity and the absence of centrality on the part of the EU institutions, then the main reason for a constitution, to give legitimacy to the work of the EU institutions, is removed because legitimacy remains primarily with national governments.

Neil Walker rehearses an important range of criticisms of constitutionalism that address this point, coming to the conclusion that constitutionalism represents a 'debased conceptual currency' (Walker 2002, 319). On this basis he puts forward his own idea of a 'constitutionalism pluralism' for the EU arranged non-hierarchically across a number of sites of constitutional discourse and authority. The advocacy of constitutional pluralism is designed by Walker to recognise that the different sites (conceived of horizontally across the EU and member states) are 'distinct constitutional sites', and that this implies a crucial 'incommensurability of the knowledge and authority (or sovereignty) claims emanating from these sites' (Walker 2002, 338).

Walker has here pinpointed as aspect of pluralism that is rarely recognised. Moreover, Walker emphasises that insofar as the constitutional pluralism concerns the relation between the EU and member states, it is a 'plurality of unities' (Walker 2002, 357) that is involved.

The fourth argument in the critique of constitutionalism is that 'political sovereignty' in the sense proposed in Chapter 4 provides a stronger form of minimal coherence for the EU political entity than does the combination of the very possibly empty rhetoric of a constitution and its role as a single authoritative document. The rhetoric is likely to be hollow in the absence of a constituent people, and in the light of conflicting imperatives which work against the meaningful articulation of sufficiently broad, general, and detailed common values. The ongoing process of treaty reform has its own logic and does not need to be interpreted as a constitutional refinement procedure. It follows from Bankowski and Christodoulidis's (1998, 349) description of law and politics as different and separate 'systems of meaning', that trying to hypothesise and set up the political meaning of Europe in legal terms involves a category mistake.

In rejecting constitutionalism this argument is not denying the importance in democratic government and politics of constitutional safeguards and restrictions expressed in the rule of law, legitimate majority rule, a separation of powers, and governmental accountability and scrutiny, and of a clear sense of institutional design and allocation of competences. The aim here, however, is to underline that a high-profile written constitutional document taken to be the ultimate political and legal reference point, the expression of a social contract, the touchstone of EU political identity, and the embodiment of the moral aspirations and purposes of 'the people', is neither desirable nor necessary to achieve those safeguards and restrictions. The kind of constitutional document being rejected here is one associated with summing up in an exclusive and exhaustive fashion the relation between rulers and ruled on a nation-state state. The argument here is that there is a growing consensus among scholars that such a degree of constitutional bindingness and normativity has not been reached in the EU, and that it need not be aspired to, especially if the role of political sovereignty is recognised.

The biggest problem with the recourse to either constitutionalism or addressing the democratic deficit is that these responses to the need to reinvigorate the EU and give it an overall credibility do so by suppressing the more fundamental option provided by reconceptualising sovereignty. It is only when an adequate conception of sovereignty is in place that one can clarify the need or not to constitutionalise and the need or not to do something about democratic representation.

Political sovereignty, in setting agreed norms and parameters for the content and limits and the political, acts precisely as a source of legitimacy, establishes and embeds an ontology for the EU and a means of orienting the direction its politics should take, without recourse to a constitution. The problems with giving primacy to the instrument of a constitution are its capture by legal over political thinking, that it will not 'take' unless the work of political sovereignty is already done, and the impulse in a constitution to move towards a superstate. The constitutional path utilises an unquenchable 'more is more' logic that has a tendency towards ever greater consistency, homogeneity and synthesis, and so sets up an immense problem for the recognition of and respect for difference. As Weiler argues, the absence of a formal constitution can be valued as uniquely European, its 'most original political asset and its deepest set of values' (referred to in Lacroix 2002, 955). With political sovereignty as the source of legitimacy a constitution is redundant, and a strong message is given that the EU remains a composite entity, subject to its partners and not the 'unilateral act of one people'. While there are affinities with the approach described by Chryssochoou, what is envisaged here is more radical than that depicted by Chryssochoou as the 'paradigm shift from "policy to polity"', and as a 'critical "normative turn" in EU studies' (Chryssochoou 2002, 343–4).

The critique of the contractarian basis of constitutionalism identified in the previous chapter has particular resonance in relation to the EU. The urge for a constitution to fulfil a 'constituent process' and which assumes that a constitution holds the consent of the ruled may be appropriate in a homogeneous nation state but such tightly binding mechanisms are both wholly inappropriate in a more politically and culturally open and diverse polity like the EU and wholly unnecessary when the mechanism of political sovereignty is available.

It is an illusion that modern constitutionalism, because it is expressed in a tangible document whereas sovereignty is expressed through a claim about ultimate authority, is any more 'real' than sovereignty in establishing and sustaining the political identity of the polity as a polity. Both equally rest on claims to legitimacy to establish their political credentials. In addition, Philpott's idea (1999, 574) concerning the 'claims about obligation' that 'polities agree upon', in some ways resembles the proposal put forward here about political sovereignty in the EU. But Philpott's designation of this in terms of constitutionalism is, I think, misplaced, in the same way as Bellamy and Castiglione overrate constitutionalism. It is an important aspect of this EU conception of sovereignty as 'less is more' that it is *not* codified, set out in a charter, treaty, protocol or pact, that it remains political in character and is not captured by legal interpretation and meaning. As described in the previous chapter, this is an aspect of what is meant by the 'mystery' of sovereignty.

The fifth argument in the critique of constitutionalism and law concerns the conservatism of legal discourse. The innate conservatism of legal discourse refers to the way that only two traditional options are available for dealing with questions of sovereignty – international and constitutional law. As a result the parameters in which the EU can be conceptualised are narrow and deterministic – either in terms of relations between states under international law or in terms of constitutionalising a polity. The split between international and constitutional law is taken as a given, following a realist internal/external division, and in the mainstream legal discourse it is unproblematised. In addition, constitutional law assumes a 'rule-hierarchy' according to which constitutional law is primary and sets the context for any other level of law.

The damaging consequences of fostering legal thinking as the primary vehicle of integration are that in its innate conservatism it promotes hierarchical thinking with the ranking of legal rules and prescriptions, it ends up with a hollow centre because political identity has not been attended to, and it promotes a narrow vision of integration as moving towards unity on the state model. This is expressed in what Neil Walker calls 'the neat unitarian geometry of international law' (Walker 2001, 564).

Walker also articulates well the criticism of constitutionalism that centres on the normative bias in constitutionalism in favour of uniformity and against recognising the claims of 'difference', the 'presumption of homogeneity' (Walker 2002, 330), and thus the way it is 'systematically skewed against the recognition and support of diverse identities' (Walker 2002, 329). He also outlines succinctly the criticism of the ease with which particular interest groups can provide a dominant interpretation of the constitution that suits their interests, as evidenced in the 'unending battle for the body and soul of the American constitution' (Walker 2002, 328). While Walker is keen to salvage or reconceptualise constitutionalism in a form that fits the challenge of the EU, the dominant discourse for relating constitutionalism to the EU remains subject to the criticisms he discusses.

Bankowski and Christodoulidis (1998, 341) identify another of the problems with this legalistic approach when they observe that 'law's integrity as a guiding ideal cannot cope with the uneasy co-existence or inter-locking of normative orders'. Legal thinking is inherently unsympathetic to the idea of sovereignty shared between interconnected member states, unhappy with 'contestability over jurisdiction and competence', finding it difficult to conceptualise legal coherence on these terms at all.

The legal logic practice of testing the validity of a legal norm by seeing if it can be traced back through a hierarchy of norms to a basic norm, also demonstrates the conservative disposition of legal thinking. This practice seeks to identify the source of legitimacy in a basic norm and automatically eschews innovation and originality that cannot be so justified. This practice illustrates an important difference between legal and political thinking and underlines why the investigation of sovereignty carried out here as an inquiry that highlights its political aspects must not be reduced to a legal basis. The matter is complicated in that it may be that the search to track back to a basic norm is a rhetorical rather than substantive feature of legal thinking and discourse, in that any potential legal proposal could in theory be given such a pedigree through a complex hierarchy of norms. On the other hand, the upshot of this conservative disposition of legal discourse may be that the search for origins is more likely to lead back to a position that leans towards a confederal rather than to a federal designation for the EU.

Ward considers the conservatism of legal thinking in another sense. He argues that the attachment shown toward treaties and constitutionalism, in building the EU, results from a 'longing' for the 'allurements of a revitalised *respublica Christiana* that', after Nietzsche's pronouncement of the death of God, 'it does not quite believe in' (Ward 2001, 25). Equally seriously, he points out that a constitution can also be a 'placatory discourse', an 'apologetic approximation' that is 'designed to enervate real political engagement' (Ward 2001, 28), a piece of decorative embellishment that prevents the recognition and development of immanent meaning.

Different from international realm

The features of the 'less is more' proposal examined so far have been pooled authority and unbundled sovereignty, complex confederalism, 'political sovereignty', 'post-states', and the critique of constitutionalism. Those features have concentrated on analysing the differences between the EU and conventional states. But another distinctive aspect of conceptualising sovereignty at the level of the EU as political sovereignty in a 'less is more' form which is worth spelling out is that neither can the EU be envisaged as international politics writ small. A key feature of the dominant interpretation of the international realm is that there is no overall sovereignty in terms of an agreed condition of the parameters, content and limits of politics at this level. In this sense there is, strictly speaking, no such thing as 'global politics'.

Werner and De Wilde argue strongly that the EU as a novel and unique polity does not exhaust the sovereignty-value of its member states, and that because the EU is developing within the realm of international politics and has not changed that context, that the traditional state sovereignty of member states continues un-eroded and un-pooled in the face of other (internal and external) audiences. Looked at from the perspective of international politics, what has happened between the member states of the EU is that '[i]nternational anarchy has been abolished and replaced by a complicated structure of overlapping authorities and competing competencies'. The result 'is not a federation, since there is no single authority' – sometimes France and Germany shape outcomes, sometimes EU institutions like the ECJ and the Commission, and sometimes a 'mixture rules'. Werner and De Wilde draw attention to the potent analogy that holds between the EU and other multi-purpose IGOs. In particular they argue that the EU represents a strong version of the example of the UN, where ad hoc 'alliances in international politics, law and economics have been replaced by firmly institutionalized members only clubs'. Their crucial point is that while international society has been strengthened 'to a point unique in history', it remains 'sovereignty-based'. After all, they note, in a 'post-sovereign world', IGOs including the EU, would not 'exist as institutional facts' (Werner and De Wilde 2001, 306).

These observations also demonstrate that in recent debates about sovereignty in Europe, it is the internal dimension of sovereignty rather than the external dimension which preoccupies the defenders of national sovereignty. When Michael Portillo in 1994 assured the British people that British sovereignty was safe with John Major as Prime Minister, it is not with Britain's ability (or, rather, inability) to pursue autonomously chosen policies on the world stage, accountable only to the British electorate, with which he was concerned. The debate turned upon the erosion of internal sovereignty of Britain to Europe, and it is in this context that Spinoza's perspective has more to offer than Hobbes's, as we shall see.

But what is the significance of the fact that it is *international* rather than domestic constitutional law, by international treaties, that lawyers in the EU have used to construct the EU? This point works in favour of a confederal future. As Hartley observes, the EU legal system is not self-sustaining but is dependent on other legal systems, namely those of international law and the legal systems of member states. In consequence, the treaties do not establish an independent Grundnorm (Hartley 2001, 226). The highest courts in Germany and Denmark have affirmed that EU law only applies there if the German Parliament and Danish Constitution respectively say it does, and that both countries retain the status of sovereign, independent, states (Hartley 2001, 232). Moreover, the European Court of Justice has claimed to have established a 'new legal order', separate from 'ordinary' international law, and the Constitutional Courts of Germany and Italy have accepted this. This means that the member states, acting unanimously, have the power to dissolve the Union, simply through a new treaty ending the earlier ones. This is the case notwithstanding that member states have agreed to 'direct effect' and 'supremacy' of European law, since these agreements were made and could be retracted by member states. This logic means that partial repeal of the earlier treaties, and repeal of particular provisions, is also possible (Hartley 2001, 234), and there is no provision in EU treaties specifying that Community law prevails over member-state law (Hartley 2001, 242). Despite 'overzealous judges and lawyers' in the early days of the Community, who 'believed they were laying the foundations of a new superstate', it remains clear that EU treaties are still treaties under international law (Hartley 2001, 245).

Huysmans makes a valuable point when he contrasts the problem of unity in the domestic sphere, in 'maintaining the rule of law, retaining a monopoly of the legitimate use of violence, and binding people into an imaginary community', with the problem of unity in the international system, revolving around 'the question of guaranteeing the existence of a plurality – the international society of sovereign states' (Huysmans 2003, 212). There are resemblances between this characterisation of the problem of unity in the international and the way forward for reconceptualising sovereignty in Europe proposed here. One of the differences between the international realm and Europe, of course, is that at the international level there is no normative impulse behind the guaranteeing of plurality – rather, plurality is a functional requirement that instrumentally benefits the protection of the interests of states.

Spinoza

Gray raises an objection from the liberal perspective to 'all republican views' on the grounds that republican politics are based on ethnic homogeneity, ethnic nationalism, small ethnic nation-states, and that such states promote partition and division (Gray 2000, 127). Putting the fairness or unfairness of Gray's challenge to one side, the model drawn here from Spinoza's republicanism is not based on any of the qualities Gray identifies.

There is a widespread assumption that the appropriate context in which to analyse European integration is, in Friese and Wagner's words, 'the historically rare event of the deliberate founding of a polity' (Friese and Wagner 2002, 353). What Spinoza provides us with is a strong counterbalance to the assumption that that polity should resemble a state. Spinoza expressed the commonsense of his time, but which has subsequently been radically misunderstood. He strongly supported the view that in the case of the United Provinces comprehensive polity-formation on the model of the state was neither necessary nor desirable. This view is developed in Prokhovnik (2008 forthcoming). Spinoza and the United Provinces stand as a potent example that shows the lie to the assumption that a move toward a state-like polity in Europe is somehow necessary and is indeed the only possible logic. A crucial part of the idea of 'less is more' is that such a model of polity-formation is not the only possible logic available.

There are several examples of theorists drawing upon the resources of European political philosophy to conceptualise the new Europe. For instance Habermas uses historical examples in his desire to instil republican principles into the European polity, and other moves to promote democratic, social democratic welfare principles are well known. The example offered by Spinoza is distinctive because it brings to bear a valuable way of thinking about politics that has been radically neglected.

There are several historical precedents (Spinoza's United Provinces, Onuf's parallel between the US federation of 1787 and Kant's theory, Tully's Iroquois federation, and Deudney's characterisation of the 'Philadelphia system') for a conception of sovereignty which deliberately suppresses state-centrality, and instead fosters the positive aspects of conflict between member states recognised as different and diverse. In this multidimensional confederalism (instead of member states all and only relating to the central body, the centre acts with respect to internal sovereignty only to promote difference), sovereignty is neither absolute nor obsolete. And sovereignty, *vis-à-vis* external actors on the international political stage, is not alienated but partially pooled, creating broader opportunities for independent action and control for 'Europe'.

Onuf (1998) draws a parallel between the US federation in 1787 of the 13 Euro-American states and the 'continental' idea of federation put forward by Kant. Tully also uses Kant and notes that the European Union 'is arguably the very organisation that was supposed to unfold in accord with the Kantian idea' (Tully 2002, 351). However, he notes imperialist resonances which are attached to the Kantian cosmopolitan idea, and thus the shortcomings of the line of argument that 'suggest[s] that the Union of Europe in our time ought to be viewed in the light of Kant's idea of federalism'. He also identifies that 'the Kantian idea of free states and federation is not culturally neutral but is the bearer of processes of a homogenizing or assimilating European cultural identity' (Tully 2002, 339). Tully uses the Kantian idea 'as a critical ideal rather than as a regulative ideal' or normative standard (Tully 2002, 334) in order to argue for 'cultural pluralism' both within and across states. By applying Kant's 'critical "attitude" to one of his own ideas' (Tully 2002, 335), Tully takes up the notion of cultural pluralism as a means to overcome the presumption that all other societies 'are described and ranked from the standpoint of the European level' (Tully 2002, 341). Tully also discusses another model for the EU and contends that the 'Iroquois federation and its constitution, The Great Law of Peace, is a better heuristic for global federalism than the Kantian idea precisely because it respects and recognises cultural diversity' (Tully 2002, 353).

Deudney's examination of the 'Philadelphian system', based on the American model used between the 1780s and the 1860s, contains a strong case for its contemporary relevance in a reconceptualised sovereignty. He elicits the value of the Philadelphian system as a viable alternative to both the now-problematic realist Westphalian sovereign state order and the liberal internationalist image of the federal state. As Deudney notes, the latter vision 'reinforces the more essential realist claim about the universal applicability of the state form' (Deudney 1996, 230). In contrast with the internally-hierarchical sovereignty of the Westphalian order, a Philadelphian sovereignty contains as positive elements both 'a toleration of diversity and central-state incapacity' (Deudney 1996, 229). The toleration of diversity recalls Rob Walker's critique of the patterns of inclusion and exclusion that characterise state sovereignty, and the idea of central-state incapacity as a valued feature is closely related to the notion of a diffusion of governance functions.

Deudney identifies the reason for the disfavour into which this system has fallen in an erroneous reading of the intention of the original model.

According to the misreading of this piece of history, he says, 'the thirteen states joined to create a federal state, when in fact they only federated to erect an organised states' union' (Deudney 1996, 230). Crucial to Deudney's theory is the idea that the 'key to understanding the Philadelphian system is republicanism' (Deudney 1996, 192). The features of republicanism he highlights are popular sovereignty, civic virtue as self-restraint (of individual self-interest), absence of state-centrality, legal proceduralism and constitutionalism. There is a close resemblance between Deudney's description very similar to that of the Philadelphian system – '[m]ore than a confederation of states in anarchy, and less than a state with extensive devolution' (Deudney 1996, 204) – and the situation obtaining in the United Provinces in the seventeenth century. It is crucially distinctive of sovereignty in both the Philadelphian example and in the Dutch Republic that, as a positive virtue, the centre did not rule over the parts.

The value of the Spinozan notion of sovereignty (1951) is that it provides a model in which powers are shared between sovereign bodies, in institutions which reaffirm their separateness (see Prokhovnik 2004, 2008 forthcoming). Thus instead of forging a hierarchy with sovereignty as the pinnacle, the Spinozan idea rests upon a minimally-confederal constitution whose parts are in dynamic tension. In federal systems such as in the United States or in Australia, legislative, judicial and executive powers are distributed between federal and different state governments, areas of competence being shared or shared out between them. In the case of the United Provinces in the seventeenth century, however, the relationship between the 'confederal' and provincial levels was very different. Independent 'confederal' powers, independent of the powers of the provinces, were extremely closely restricted, indicative among other things, of the deliberate rejection by the Northern Netherlanders of the idea of a centralised state. Rather than attempting to harmonise differences, the Spinozan notion reflects the practice of upholding the constructiveness of difference in the same positive spirit as envisaged in contemporary political theory by Iris Marion Young (1990) and William Connolly (1991). At the same time, in Spinoza because the different constituent parts have many common interests, and none is hegemonic over the others, the resulting 'confederal' organisation has an identity, an aspect of which is its independence of legal, economic and military power external to itself or its member states, which makes it more than simply an intergovernmental structure. Furthermore, it was the United Provinces rather than the separate provinces which made treaties with other European states, indicating a limited independent legal identity for the confederation.

The Spinozan contribution to the re-imagining of the European political space is indeed a theory that contains elements of a polity, association, and confederation. The Spinozan theory presents a model for a vibrant Europe that is based on the entrenched rights of its component political units and which does not depend upon the legitimacy of a European demos. Indeed this model argues strongly against the construction of stronger institutions for democracy, citizenship and representation, as well as challenging the trend towards 'hypercentralisation' of modern mass industrial societies. It also holds that scrutiny of European political elites can operate just as effectively through checks and balances built into the confederal system, rather than through the direct democratic accountability of periodic elections.

Spinoza's view of sovereignty is outlined in his two political works published in the 1670s. While many Spinoza commentators concur, largely uncritically, that his political thought largely follows that of Hobbes, the differences from Hobbes, comprehensible in the context of the political culture in the United Provinces in which Spinoza was writing, are startling. The most important thing that Spinoza's theory of sovereignty offers to this discussion is the 'immanence of meaning' disclosed in the political shape of the balance of polycentricity as the source of political legitimacy. Without the 'noise' of embellishments like a laboured, explicit constitution, but instead listening to the work that sovereignty does in (conditionally) settling the content, parameters, and limits of the political, politics as a contest of interests or of norms and values can operate more freely. Politics occurs at multiple levels but is not dominated, in this view, either by a search for ultimate democratic legitimacy in some manufactured 'transnational public sphere', or by a desire to pin down the conception to some specified territorialised entity. This approach avoids the pitfalls of the legalistic and litigious culture such as has developed in the US as a way of interacting with and interpreting constitutional provisions. It also eschews the trap of the associated temptation to slide towards the formation of a superstate.

Spinoza's vision of shared sovereignty on the basis of a dynamic tension between the partners, celebrated a political practice which was regarded as having not only been successful in defeating the Spanish, but also in having been the basis of the subsequent economic power of the United Provinces as a world force in the seventeenth century. It also crucially concerned a political dominion which was resolutely not a modern nation state. There was no common source of national unity but rather a self-conscious multiplicity of independent and indeed competing local loyalties and codes of law, and no systematic centralisation of administrative powers. Moreover, its territorial boundaries were fluid. For instance the province of Drente joined the Union of Utrecht in 1579 but left again the following year. Another example is that the eastern provinces of Gelderland and Overijssel were often overrun by Spanish and later French troops, without the integrity of the United Provinces being affected. Again, no attempt was made by the United Provinces which constituted the Northern Netherlands to recover the southern provinces in the name of the integrity of the Netherlands as a whole. Spinoza's strategies for and commitment to a dynamic balance that holds the multiple political centres in tension and cooperation, resonate strongly with the desire of many European elites and citizens of members states alike to marry difference and equality in Europe.

Spinoza's view of sovereignty has much to offer in the contemporary debate about the future political organisation of Europe, specifically to those on the one hand who simply want to defend the old state sovereignty, and to those on the other hand who want to dismiss the issue of sovereignty altogether. Spinoza's notion of shared or pooled sovereignty endorses separateness. It affirms the value, in discussion about the future direction of Europe, of a renewed heterogeneity in political forms. The value of this proposal is especially useful in the light of the self-fulfilling prophesy (however misguided) that significant global interconnectedness is occurring. It is also valuable in the face of complex events in and renewed interrelationship between Eastern and Western Europe with the timetable of further accession states to the EU, and in view of the construction of the idea of the EU as a western bulwark against the global reach of the power of the United States.

The proposal for sovereignty in the context of the EU put forward here, using some elements of Spinoza's theory, is certainly pluralistic and polycentric. But that description needs to be qualified in that, upon that plurality and polycentricity, is a pattern of (minimal) centralised and (maximal) decentralised features such that at the decentralised level there is a radical equality between the political members. This point thus differs from the idea of an undifferentiated pluralism.

The suggestion put forward here is that by drawing upon Spinoza's rather than Hobbes's idea of sovereignty, the stark alternatives posed by on the one hand the broadly federalist thrust which recognises that an automatic spillover of sovereignty envisaged by functionalists will not occur, and on the other hand by the (state-centric) defenders of national sovereignty, can both be avoided. This is meant as a contribution to the debate about the reconceptualisation of European political identity rather than as a contribution to the discussion of specific European institutions and practical arrangements. Both of these diametrically opposed positions utilise a part of Hobbes's notion of sovereignty. For both the federalist camp and the defenders of national sovereignty, the defining characteristic of sovereignty is its absoluteness. That is, it represents an abstract unity which cannot be shared, divided or limited, but is identified in a particular person or assembly. Not only the defenders of national sovereignty, but also the federalists, seem to argue that 'ultimate' or 'final' legislative, judicial and executive powers should be vested somewhere specific – in either national or European institutions respectively.

For Hobbes sovereignty cannot lie in a constitution but must lie in the figure and office of the sovereign. However, Hobbes endorses the notion of the rule of law and while the sovereign cannot be subject to any particular laws, he is subject to the principle of the rule of law, for instance when Hobbes makes the case for the importance of the publicity of laws, and laws not being applied retrospectively. Another qualification to the stricture that sovereignty lies only with the sovereign is, as Tully notes, that even Hobbes concedes the authority of custom, but for him 'custom has its authority only in virtue of its recognition by the sovereign, not vice versa' (Tully 1995, 67).

Spinoza's notion of sovereignty could not be 'applied' to contemporary Europe in some easy fashion as a simple solution. Important differences exist between the contexts of the United Provinces in the seventeenth century and contemporary Europe, significant amongst which must be the current lack of an unselfconscious tradition as the basis of political life in modern Europe, and the contemporary presence of rationalist, liberal and democratic presuppositions about the future form that Europe could take. Nevertheless Spinoza and the history of the United Provinces do represent another legitimate strand of European intellectual and political history with much to offer.

Philpott takes the view that in High Medieval Europe, under the *Respublica Christiana*, there was 'no supreme authority within a territory, manifestly no sovereignty' (Philpott 1999, 579). However, we can see from the example of Spinoza and the United Provinces that sovereignty was effectively unbundled but that there existed, at the level of the United Provinces, a clear sense of political sovereignty as a 'less is more' tacit but strong agreement about the parameters, content and limits of politics. The view Philpott endorses is unreasonably narrow not only in equating sovereignty with the state sovereignty of the later period and reading back onto the earlier period a 'lack' or 'absence', but also in not recognising the clear reality of political sovereignty in the case of the United Provinces' complex arrangements.

In practical terms for Europe, the Spinozan 'less is more' theory could be expressed in terms of decentralised confederalism, a political form that emphasises that the power of central government has been severely curtailed, and which rejects the hierarchical unitary state form. This model stresses an antipathy towards centralisation of political control and power and so sets up supreme powers at different levels. From this point of view, sovereignty is neither unitary nor delegated and, at the EU level some is pooled. This proposal also prioritises those matters which are within the competence of member states and regions within them, and so beyond the scope of the EU, rather than beginning from the position of matters outside the smaller units. This model also contains three independent levels – states, semi-autonomous regions, and EU – but crucially tax-raising powers are held at state level. This form of decentralised confederalism is best placed to recognise, acknowledge, and celebrate

territorial and non-territorial cultural, ethnic, linguistic and regional differences, unifies the constituent parts without destroying the identity of
each, is responsive to regional and local needs and demands, increases
the weight given to each citizen participating in the smaller units, and is
a successful way to define and guarantee complex and multiple centre-
periphery relations.

Neil Walker makes an important point when he identifies the ways in
which the EU already accommodates (but does not fully acknowledge)
'differentiated integration', such as the various opt-outs and proposals for
a 'multi-speed Europe', and analyses the implications of differentiated
integration becoming a more widespread feature of the EU architecture in
terms of three levels of legal order (states, EU, and arrangements between
groups of states for particular policy-sectors). Walker's argument recalls the
complex arrangements that co-existed under the United Provinces whereby
the character of participation by provinces differed according to a number
of factors. Different groupings of provinces had common cause through
geographical proximity, predominantly rural or urban economies, levels of
wealth and poverty, different cultural, linguistic and religious tradition, a
history of isolation or of being overrun by invading armies, and the self-
suppression of Holland from political dominance. Like Spinoza, Weiler
holds the view that, as Walker puts it, 'it is in the competition and interaction of different sovereignties that pluralist ideas, institutions and
attitudes emerge and achieve momentum' (Walker 2001, 570). However,
neither in the case of the United Provinces, nor in the EU to date, does the
evidence support Walker's claim that these examples amount to 'a third
level of claims to sovereignty' (Walker 1998, 362).

Context

There are a range of important contextual factors that form a tacit framework in which this conceptualisation of the identity of the EU takes place.
The most significant of these factors, the indeterminacy of the meaning
of the EU, the formation of intersubjective and constructed meanings, and
the opportunities and constraints indeterminacy poses, was discussed
above. In a sense the contextual factors described here represent the
obverse of the indeterminacy, the sometimes invisible 'givens' that help
shape the way that the developing EU is theorised. For instance, the debate
about normative political theory in relation to the EU is framed by dominant assumptions (Friese and Wagner 2002, 361) about the value of individualist liberal and rationalist principles, the latter concerned to make the
EU an 'effective' polity. Early discussion of the EU also took place within
the organising principles of realist international relations but Friese and
Wagner (2002, 342) confirm that there has been a shift towards analysing
the EU as a 'polity in its own right', using the tools of policy analysis, insti-

tutional analysis and political theory. There is now a field of study which analyses European integration in the light of the history of theories of European integration, marking a course from earlier optiministically-framed federalist and functionalist 'spillover' imperatives and realist IR assumptions, to greater recognition of the EU as a novel and unique form of complex and compound polity, using its own history in order to try and understand what it is and where it is going. Neil Walker also testifies to the 'context- and practice-dependence of EU theorizing' more broadly (Walker 2005, 584) and it is in this light that a set of other contextual issues is discussed here.

Different European traditions

Pagden indicates the length and nature of the historical context that helps shape the EU. Europeans have, on the one hand, he notes, 'more than a shared past; they have a shared history of antagonisms to overcome', which go back to 'remote struggles for control of Europe or for empire overseas' as well as the more commonly recognised impact of the two twentieth-century world wars (Pagden 2002, 20). On the other hand, the Peace of Westphalia, the Treaty of Utrecht, the post-Napoleonic European settlement, the Zollverein, and Voltaire's vision of Europe all attest to the history of joint endeavour in 'Europe' that influences our understanding of what has been and can be.

Reimagining sovereignty in Europe already takes place against the backdrop of understandings of Europe formed from several sources, from international law, from integration theories, from competing theories of international relations (including neo-liberal institutionalism but especially realism), from the perspectives of different member states. This chapter adds the view of theories of sovereignty and in particular that of Spinoza. In addition, there is also a special resonance attached to the reconceptualisation of sovereignty in the context of the EU. In the mainstream triumphalist story of modernity and the West the growth of the sovereign state and the development of states in European states coincides. In particular the idea of civilised states in the eighteenth and nineteenth centuries, which still has strong echoes today, was identified with European states. Reimagining sovereignty in the new political form (still under discussion) of the EU carries the resonance of the sense of Europe once again embarked on a project that serves as a benignly virtuous model for other parts of the world. This chapter holds that it is important to be aware, in reconceptualising sovereignty in the context of the EU, of these reverberations with the past and does not foster a sense of enlightened superiority, of Europe in a normative sense 'in the lead' and 'most advanced', as Hettne puts it (Hettne 2002, 325).

The UK is the only country in Europe in which national political representatives correspond to territorial constituencies. In other countries representatives for parliamentary assemblies are chosen from party lists according to each party's share of the vote. This very much affects the way representative government is conceived. The stronger representative procedure, together with the cardinal notion of the sovereignty of Parliament and the lack of a written constitution, contribute to the British sense that closer involvement in the EU automatically means a loss of sovereignty, control, and representation.

Marcussen *et al* also analyse the differences between member states' conceptions of Europe, in the light of their different contexts and histories. They note the 'dramatic shift' that took place in the 1980s and 1990s when French political elites 'increasingly incorporated "Europe"' into the 'nation state identity of the Fifth Republic'. They refer to the way '(West) German political elites have shared a consensual and thoroughly Europeanized version of German nation state identity since the end of the 1950s as a way of overcoming the country's own past'. And they confirm that the 'nation state identity which continues to dominate the British political discourse on Europe', which has 'remained virtually the same since the 1950s', still constitutes Europe as the 'albeit friendly, "other"' (Marcussen *et al* 2001, 101). Diez also notes that in the 1960s, the EEC was commonly referred to in Britain as the 'Common Market' while in Germany it was known as the '*Gemeinschaft*' or 'Community' (Diez 2001b, 89).

The backdrop of understandings of Europe is also expressed in that each member state of the EU brings to the discussion of sovereignty in the European Union the legacy of its own historical and contemporary debates specifically about its own national sovereignty. As a result the development of the EU and the meaning of reconceptualising sovereignty within it are mediated at times dramatically differently through the different political, cultural and institutional histories of member states and indeed regions. Ziller (2003) and Aziz (2003) bring out this point clearly in relation to France and Germany respectively. In France the terms of the debate had been dominated by the competing domestic claims of national and popular sovereignty, but now the key issue is the question of the possibility of shared sovereignty in the face of the continuing authority of Bodin and others who prohibit such a thing. In Germany the debate about Germany in Europe occurs against the background of the broader question of Germany's reclaiming of sovereignty since re-unification in 1990. Diez (2001a, 28) argues convincingly that in the UK under New Labour the dominant conceptualisation of European governance is one of the EU as an economic community, although a shift has occurred from advocating a liberal to advocating a social democratic version of it, with an intergovernmentalist viewpoint still prevailing in most non-economic policy areas.

Marcussen *et al* (2001, 105) also discuss the broader ideological trends which influence the variety of ways in which member states regard the

EU. For instance the liberal nationalist view of a Europe of nation states is prevalent in Britain, while Europe as a modern liberal democratic polity with a social market economy is the view articulated in Germany and France. The idea of a wider Europe as a community of values was strongly present in the early Cold War years and re-emergent in France and Germany. Europe as a democratic socialist 'third force' between capitalism and communism has carried force, as has the idea of a Christian Europe that recognises its social obligations, expressed by Christian Democratic parties. Marcussen *et al* note that the first and second of these ideological predispositions have been strongest in 1990s debates.

'Globalisation'

Even though some of the claims for the power and importance of globalisation have been overstated, and have masked just another phase in the systematic expansion of capitalism, the way in which governments have adapted their conduct through a belief in globalisation has rendered it to some extent a self-fulfilling prophesy. The *idea* of the development of increasingly interconnected global systems of production, trade and finance, supported by technological networks in communications, information and transport, as well as international, transnational and multinational economic, military and legal organisations, has had the effect of undermining and constraining the autonomy of the governments of nation states to make and carry out their policies, despite the legal sovereignty of strong states remaining intact. The upshot of this line of argument is that Europe can be seen as deliberately constructed as an instance of regionalism in the face of (presumed and then perceived) global pressures. Wallace voices the sceptical view convincingly that, in response to the notion that globalisation appears to amount to little more than a form of economic determinism, the development of Europe since the 1950s does not furnish evidence for such a viewpoint. In considering the slogan, 'politicians are determining the rhetoric, but industrialists are determining the reality', Wallace urges that 'the experience of the past 30 years suggests that the relationship between political and economic development is by no means as straightforward as' some 'were arguing in the optimistic years after the signing of the Rome Treaty'. Politics, he stresses, 'follows its *own* logic, not simply those of economics and technology' (Wallace 1999, 7).

Rosamond discusses the differences in studying and understanding the EU that arise from whether the 'parent' discipline of EU studies is conceptualised as being international relations/globalisation or comparative politics. When IR is considered the parent discipline then the key question is the degree of greater or less integration, whereas when comparative politics is prioritised the key question is the politics of distribution in the context of the policy environment (Rosamond 2001, 159). Rosamond advocates that the 'now pervasive metaphor' of multi-level governance should be understood not just in terms of an EU system with distinct policy-making levels, but as a 'highly fluid system of governance, characterized by the complex interpenetration of the national, subnational and supra-national', in a manner that overcomes the 'counterproductive "inside-outside" dichotomy' (Rosamond 2001, 159–60).

Moreover, the habituation of governments to the idea of globalisation, even if ungrounded, and the links between such habituation and European restructuring, is one element making redundant the absolutist notion of sovereignty held by federalists and defenders of national sovereignty alike. It is in this light that negative comments on sovereignty in modern political developments in Europe can be read. For example, Beitz concludes that sovereignty is 'an anachronism' and 'less and less illuminating' (Beitz 1994, 128). Puhovski takes the view that the legitimation value of sovereignty is useful only within the international community, that is, as external sovereignty (Puhovski 1994, 202). Pogge argues that the concentration of sovereignty and governmental authority is 'no longer defensible' (Pogge 1994, 99).

National sovereignty

The next contextual element for rethinking sovereignty is that the early development of the EEC itself, in the particular economic links and policies agreed by member states, the federalist logic, and the functionalist impulse, have all, since its conception, raised the alarm for the defence of national sovereignty. De Gaulle in the early years and now Britain are seen as the champions of this perspective. The functionalist impulse has been aligned with a vision of Europe on supranational and now transnational terms, while the federalist logic has been associated with an intergovernmentalist view that mistakenly regards isolation as a key element of sovereignty. Rosamond emphasises the centrality of the theory and practice of state sovereignty in governing 'both the analysis of European integration and the approach of political actors to the EU itself'. The state-centric sovereignty discourse, he notes, 'has been integral to the evolution of the EU and its institutions as well as to the analysis of the EU' (Rosamond 1995, 394).

Hobbes

The options for conceptualising and reconceptualising sovereignty in Europe can draw upon continuities and patterns of historical resources of ideas which form another element of context. One example is the research on the connection between legal and political theory in the Weimar Republic and recent theorising of the EU as a supranational polity (Walker 2005, 595). But in particular those options can be fruitfully and drama-tically posed in terms of the theories of Hobbes (or rather, one narrow reading of his theory) and Spinoza. Hobbes's definition of sovereignty in *Leviathan* has been taken as pivotal for 350 years, in two respects. It has been taken as fundamental in the received understanding of both the theory and practice of the development of the nation state. And it has been decisive in the authority accorded to the realist theory of international relations. Thus Hobbes's view of sovereignty has been taken as critical to the internal and external self-definition of the state in modern Western political thought. Furthermore, both these factors have played a crucial, but increasingly strained, part in helping to support the dominant definition of the parameters of the discussion about contemporary Europe.

As the generation of the EU has developed, as an identity cutting across the political relationships within and between member states, as well as being an identity fostered by state actors pursuing national interests, a crisis in the meaning of sovereignty followed. The narrow notion of sovereignty taken from Hobbes no longer provides the theoretical legitimacy of and authority for the emerging political configuration. However, the narrow interpretation of Hobbes's definition is still visible in the formation of the views expressed, that the conventions require that 'central to contemporary political thought and reality, is the idea of the autonomous territorial state as the pre-eminent mode of political organisation' (Pogge 1994, 99); that sovereignty equals state power, the 'permanent formalisation of the superiority of the state' (Puhovski 1994, 202); and that sovereignty is the 'essential element of statehood', with internal and external dimensions (Beitz 1994, 127).

The dominance which Hobbes's theory (or, rather, a limited reading of it) has maintained for three and a half centuries, fused as it has been seen to be with the notion of the nation-state, has overshadowed another view which is relevant to contemporary discussion about the role of sovereignty in Europe. The argument developed in this chapter is that a theory of sovereignty can be detached from the necessity of regarding sovereignty as absolute in Hobbes's sense. It is true that in *Leviathan* sovereignty is presented by Hobbes as indivisible, complete, supreme, unified, independent and unqualified. It is the outcome of a rational and conceptual theory, deliberately universalist and eschewing the impact of history or custom, and so involves no intentional preconditions. Hobbes's sovereignty sets up a radically egalitarian commonwealth, of citizens equal in their political obligations (Hobbes 1946, Chapters 16–21, 29). The concept of sovereignty in *Leviathan* is built upon a relationship of authority and obligation *between* citizens in the presence of an impartial positive law, and not (as is mistakenly supposed) upon an identification primarily of a holder of coercive power. The concept of sovereignty is tellingly captured in the artificial, multi-figured image of the sovereign Leviathan.

However, and this is where the conventional reading has been limited, sovereignty is neither unconditional nor unrestricted for Hobbes. It is conditional externally upon the sovereign's ability to represent a self-determining commonwealth and so prevent foreign conquest or civil war.

It is also informally restricted internally in two ways – by the implicit advocacy of governing according to positive law (since members are bound to observe the civil laws of their particular commonwealth), and (though somewhat ambiguously) by the duty imposed by the laws of nature in settled conditions, for the sovereign to transpose natural law into positive law.

Hobbes presents his readers with the stark choice of accepting either his version of absolute authority, which fuses state with popular sovereignty, or the instability and insecurity afforded by any form of mixed or divided sovereignty. In contrast Spinoza offers a vision of shared sovereignty, closely modelled on the United Provinces, which reaffirms the separateness of the provinces, and of the cities within them, and holds them in dynamic tension, principally in the institution of the Estates General assembly (Spinoza 1951, 370–2). In terms of contemporary debates about the future political form of Europe, Spinoza's perspective provides useful support for modern theorists who recommend, for instance, the vertical dispersal of sovereignty (Pogge 1994).

The canon of political theories of sovereignty demonstrates that distinctively different conceptions of sovereignty have been put forward over time, and the historicity of those conceptions challenges the universalised character attributed to Hobbes's conception of absolute sovereignty. The existence of multiple robust political conceptions (see Prokhovnik 2008 forthcoming) also shows that sovereignty cannot be reduced to economic or functionalist categories. Furthermore, the Spinozan example shows that conceptions of sovereignty need not be limited to being identified with nation state sovereignty, in the way that broadly speaking both federalists and defenders of traditional sovereignty assume.

By untangling the fusion that has taken place in the conventional discussion of sovereignty, whereby it has been identified solely with the development of the nation state and with an absolutist definition, this chapter supports the view that a positive way forward for Europe is nevertheless possible. While it has been argued that Spinoza's view of sovereignty cannot be 'applied' in any simple way to contemporary Europe, its existence, and the successful political practice of the United Provinces it describes, provide further support for the argument that the future of Europe does not necessarily herald the end of sovereignty.

Beyond dichotomies – federalism/functionalism, intergovernmental/ supranational, deepening/widening

The fifth dimension of the context for reconceptualising sovereignty in the EU explicitly addresses the dualistic logic that has characterised much of the discussion in the past and highlights proposals which attempt to supplant that logic. For instance, Weiler poses supranationalism as the alternative to federalism, and as a way of retaining the pluralism of intergovernmentalism. But this logic neglects to recognise the ways in which supranationalism is a form of federalism, a way of merging member states into a single, unified larger whole. The dualistic logic is evident in particular in the politics of how much power is retained by member states and how much is transferred to the EU. The debate on this key issue has often been conducted in terms of a choice between two polar opposites. This chapter takes the view that the most satisfactory approach to that issue is to conduct the debate instead in terms of a non-dichotomous balance and convergence of powers.

This fifth aspect of the context refers most prominently to the way the federalist and functionalist views that have dominated the discussion of European integration. Both follow, either according to a design or by a functional process, a centralising logic which seeks to map hierarchy and a legal/legislative focal point for sovereign authority onto 'Europe' in the image of the nation state writ large. As Weiler notes, the subsequent debate between Euroskeptics and Europhiles often amounts to 'not a debate of opposites but of equals – equals in their inability to understand political and social organisation in non-statal, national terms' (quoted in Lacroix 2002, 954). This logic, on the federalist side, leads to the barricading of an ossified state sovereignty system. On the functionalist side, which simply extrapolates from the old nation-state sovereignty and transposes 'the pluralist polity from the national to the regional level' (Rosamond 1995, 395) and exploits economic and political spillover, the logic leads indeed to the destruction of member state sovereignties through homogenisation and enforced consensus, without providing, in a manner recognisable to individuals, the elements of autonomy, independence and accountability, or the sense of sovereign identity, at Union level. The federalist and functionalist positions were also supported by competing bipolar views of the character and fate of the nation state. The idea of nation-states as 'obstinate entities' that are 'more or less immune to non-state factors' was pitted against the view of the 'withering away of the state' (Rosamond 1995, 395).

Alongside the federalist/functionalist debate views on the role of the state in Europe fell into opposed intergovernmentalist and supranationalist camps. Intergovernmentalism (often associated with a realist IR perspective) presupposed that, in the EU, states simply pursued their own interests (formed solely by domestic political processes) in the context of the international treaties and an EU institutional framework formulated by states, and that the EU consists simply of inter-state transactions. The state focus makes recognition of a greater role by the Commission and other EU institutions, and of interest groups, both impossible and threatening. The two debates are closely interlinked, the federalist and intergovernmentalist positions being allied to the realist commitment to the unaltered state form while the functionalist and supranationalist views were premised on the idea and strategy of teleological change.

'Less is More: Sovereignty in Europe' develops ideas in the current litera-ture that what is needed is not a 'European sovereignty', the outcome of an attempt to manufacture an explicit and unified European identity and European citizenship, but a conception of sovereignty that fits the poly-centric character of Europe. The EU is more than a contemporary system of interstate cooperation. Neil Walker's conception of 'necessarily inter-connected sites of a plural political configuration' (Walker 2001, 575) offers a welcome answer to the previous traditions of dichotomous thinking in the literature.

Under the umbrella of the dichotomy between intergovernmentalists and supranationalists (in my terms) Walker (1998) summarises a number of ways of negotiating between the two poles of uniformity and Europe a la carte, including a multi-speed Europe, a Europe of concentric circles, a Europe of flexible integration with a common commitment to core free-doms and flexible commitment to policy-sectoral integration, a distinction between case-by-case flexibility, predetermined flexibility and enhanced cooperation, a distinction between constructive abstention and positive entitlement, the distinction between opting in and opting out, and the dis-tinction between deep and shallow integration. Most of these alternatives work within the logic of two dimensions of legal authority, at member state and EU levels, but at the more flexible end before a la carte there is the possibility of a third, intermediate, level of claims to sovereignty among the various new open partnerships.

Another positive move has been the development of the view over the last decade that the key questions in European integration has moved from deepening towards ever closer union to broadening European political identity. The move towards a Constitutional Treaty has been halted by 'a wave of (national) plebiscitary scepticism' (Rosamond and Wincott 2006, 2), at least in its present form, and an ambitious enlargement programme for the inclusion of accession states is underway. The focus of debate has to some extent moved on from the old functionalist/federalist alternatives, with greater emphasis on subsidiarity and the consolidation of European policymaking as applying to named policy sectoral areas (such as agri-culture, fishing, monetary policy) on the one hand, and on qualified major-ity voting and the principles of supremacy and direct effect expressed in the judgments of the European Court of Justice on the other. There has recently been a strong appetite for multi-level governance and the sharing or pooling of sovereignty in specific policy areas (Hallstrom 2003), and this picks up aspects of both sides of the debate.

There has also been a cooling of zeal for deepening integration with the end of the Cold War and the enlargement of the EU to include a range of former Soviet states (Su 2004). Debate between supranationalists and inter-governmentalists is now not between the opposite ends of the spectrum, 'whether there should be a federal centre at all' and 'whether nation states should continue to exist', but the much narrower and fine-grained one about 'what the division of powers should be' between the two positions (Gamble 2006, 41). Consensus building, and agency network governance resulting in a shift from 'intergovernmentalism' to 'transgovernmentalism', are now distinctive features of European politics as is, as Gamble sums it up, 'practical multi-lateral cooperation to solve particular problems' (Gamble 2006, 37). The embrace of a network model of governance with a range of interest groups involved in developing, say, fisheries policy, is also a distinctive feature. However, the idea of lack of state-centrality put forward in this chapter, it will become clear, is very different from the 'Governance School' identified by Diez, which holds the view that the EU 'represents a political system in which binding decisions are made without a single decision-making centre' but where 'policies are made in a complex web of interaction by territorially as well as functionally differentiated actors' (Diez 2001a, 10). Moreover, current debate also continues between supporters of the European 'social model' of capitalism for Europe and supporters of an Anglo-American neo-liberal model, as it does over the idea of a two-speed Europe, and over the idea of the EU redefined as primarily 'the enabler of European civil society and European networks' (Gamble 2006, 38).

Another move beyond dichotomous thinking is exhibited by Weiler. As part of thinking of the EU in explicitly relational terms he identifies three political arenas, modes of governance, and opportunities for democratic control, in the EU, none of which is privileged over the others (1999, 271). The first mode of governance he identifies is intergovernmental and so international, and consists of diplomatic practice, summits and treaty-making between member states. The particular problems for democracy at this level concern elites and the jealous guarding by member states of their role as primary sites for democratic representation. The second mode occurs at the EU or 'supranational' institutional level and involves the politics of EU legislation. Its particular problems revolve around elites and bureaucracy. The third is 'Comitology' administrative practices at the 'infranational' level, concerned with processes regulating policy sectoral networks, and the political latitude they contain. The primary problem for democracy at this level is about transparency.

Independent legal personality?

The sixth element in the context for reconceptionalising sovereignty revolves around the debate among lawyers over whether the EU represents a new legal order independent of both member states and of international law. The resolution of this legal debate has been regarded not only by lawyers but by others as well as foundational for the meaning of the EU. In a sense this is another example of dichotomous logic in conceptualising the EU, and it is clear that the EU can develop in a way that, in crucial respects, international and domestic constitutional law overlap. It is also clear that the foundational status accorded to the resolution of this question is illusory. As we saw in the sections on indeterminacy and the critique of law and constitutionalism, the uniqueness of the EU means that no wholly definitive answer is possible. And, secondly, the question is wrong to assume that it can be answered by reference to some external touchstone because, in a very real sense, the way the EU is conceived helps shape its construction, and at present it is conceived in at least three different ways. So while it is interesting and important to explore this question, the outcome of the discussion cannot be decisive.

Neil Walker sums up well Weiler's notable contribution in stressing the importance of breaking out of 'a mind-set which views the question of ultimate authority as crucial, as one in which the winner takes all (Liberties with the power of auto-interpretation included!)'. Rather than perpetuating a 'preoccupation with the one true foundation of the European legal order, his approach instead emphasises the range of key legal authority sites, both state and supra-state, within the European legal space'. At the same time Weiler does not hold that 'the different authority claims of the states and the EU are simply incommensurable', and affirms that it continues to be the case that 'the sovereignty-in-the-last-instance of the Member States may in some sense remain an objective, inter-systemic truth' (Walker 2001, 569).

Walker argues persuasively that none of the familiar forms of explanation do justice to the 'degree of interpenetration of national and European legal orders'. One commonplace off-the-peg account assumes a set of separate legal orders and conceives of their relationship either in terms of 'episodic "conflicts" of private international law' or in terms of monist or dualist ways of linking national law and public international law. But this account is, as Walker says, 'inadequate to grasp the dense complexity of the relevant ties'. The other mainstream line of reasoning is to conceive that, beyond a 'certain threshold of density in their relations', legal orders either become fused or one absorbs or colonises the other. But explanations in terms of these methods of moving towards a 'single monopolistic sovereign authority' (Walker 2005, 589) do not coherently capture what is happening in the EU either.

In her useful article on the politics of the law in the EU, Richmond teases out the complexity of the issues involved. She valuably does not attempt to assimilate or shy away from the fact of the conflicting evidence supplied by different actors (European Court of Justice, other EU actors, the German Federal Constitutional Court), authorities (Kelsen, Hart) and academic commentators. Her evidence and arguments allow one to reflect that, on balance, the Community remains closer to a confederation than to anything else. Even though the EU has moved towards federation in that it now has some powers of direct effect and of enforcement and powers to execute sanctions, and has enlarged its own competence in foreign affairs, it has no police or armed forces of its own, which some observers regard as definitive. The position still holds that the Community may be a new legal order but it remains a legal order within international law rather than within domestic law. Were the EU to institute a constitution, and crucially one that was based on an *internal* claim to validity, and one which took away the power of member states under international law to amend or revoke their treaty obligations, then the balance might tip towards a federation. Overall, the limited extent of the formal degree of centralisation registers that the EU is still closer to a confederation. However, the direction in which the EU is heading as an 'independent legal order' (that is, independent of its member states) means that the conventional spectrum of legal communities may need to be revised to account for the EU as a new category 'not constituted by international law but...not a federation' (Richmond 1997, 385–6).

The question of whether the EU is an independent legal order also turns upon whether its principles, values and ethical core, and the juridical norms that, as Richmond says, supply the 'obligatory, normative character of law' (Richmond 1997, 387) which underpin them, depend upon a 'basic norm' that gains its validity from the EU, from the member states separately, or from international law. This 'basic norm' could be an ethical, religious or other meta-legal norm, or the norm that is regarded as structuring power relationships, which establishes the fundamental cognitive presupposition to obey the law and regulates the construction of general legal norms. Richmond observes that, in the case of the EU, the basic norm in this sense is 'particularly diffuse' in origin, 'spread between the various Community Treaties, Conventions and even decisions of the Council' (Richmond 1997, 392). The character of the EU's legal order will also vary according to whether precedence (and so the basic norm) is attributed to the legal order of the member states, international law, or Community law, and whether the other two sources of law are seen as in a chain or following equally but separately from the one given priority. Different commentators, political actors, and EU decisions seem to assume different relationships here (Richmond 1997, 414). The orthodox concept of sovereignty cannot be invoked here to decide the issue since its definition is not a neutral but a political and contested matter that involves choice. Indeed, Richmond significantly concludes, sovereignty 'can play no part in a neutral conceptual modelling of the relationship between the Community, its member States and international law' (Richmond 1997, 415). The development of the EU exposes the political nature of the distribution of legal competences to state, EU, and international levels, whereas before the advent of the Community the validity of the state as the source of legal authority seemed simply natural (Richmond 1997, 416). One of the ways in which this chapter is important for the discussion of the reconceptualisation of sovereignty is precisely that the emergence of the EU as a political and legal community uncovers the contingent basis of the modern and realist equation of sovereignty with state sovereignty.

Richmond also brings out that the identity of the Community legal order is also described differently by different actors and authorities, and by the same actors at different times (Richmond 1997, 385). Again the issue of the relative strengths of and hierarchy between international law, Community basic norm, member states' legal systems, and custom, is deeply contested with evidence available for different viewpoints, and radically affects the interpretation of the character of the Community legal order now. Furthermore, the identity of the Community legal order depends not only on how much authority and competence has been delegated by member states but also on the extent to which the Community legal order has become a system with its own systemic validity (Richmond 1997, 396). Richmond also uses the example of the intentionally legally-indeterminate meaning of 'subsidiarity' by member states in the Maastricht Treaty to show how they successfully sought to avoid the question of ceding sovereignty and to preserve state powers (Richmond 1997, 417). This example illustrates how the meanings of the EU legal order and of sovereignty remain ultimately political rather than legal questions. In addition, definition of the EU legal order will vary according to whether one holds a dualist or monist view of the relation between international and national legal systems, as independent and separate or as one system such that the 'norms of international law are immediately valid within the national order' (Richmond 1997, 408). The consequences for sovereignty are enormously important since for a monist the sovereignty of the nation state is conferred by international law whereas for the dualist it is self-validating.

This debate provides further support for the argument against the realist interpretation of international relations. For the realist view is, as the discussion of internal/external in Chapter 1 showed, also a view of domestic politics, and of the relation between them. The significance of the realist dualist mode lies in that, according to the realist logic, domestic law and politics are pre-eminent over international law, but one of the key reasons for stating this is in order to specify the international realm as a separate realm from the domestic. Actions taken in the international realm are ultimately sanctioned by the domestic justification for sovereignty. This is a nice argument which allows the realist view to avoid external sanctions. In the discussion of sovereignty in international relations theory (let alone in political theory) the distinction between dualist and monist views is not taken into account but it has big effects. What matters here is not that the conferral of the authority of sovereignty is made by one or other legal sources but that there are two very different origins with very different effects.

Nation-state

The seventh and final aspect of the European context for reconceptualising sovereignty is that the perception of the problem of the defence of national sovereignty is further compounded not only by being bound up with a narrow version of Hobbes's definition, but also by being bound up historically with significance accorded to the nation state, such that sovereignty is simply defined as the powers held by the particular governmental unit called the nation state. This is made explicit by Camilleri and Falk, when they argue that the history of sovereignty 'parallels the evolution of the modern state. More particularly, it reflects the evolving relationship between state and civil society, between political authority and community' (Camilleri and Falk 1992, 11). This definition is circular and so does not throw enough light on what sovereignty is or can be.

It is commonly assumed that the historical roots of the EU are the different European nation-states but claims for the importance of the prior coherence of the European space under Christendom and humanism, and the impact of the cultural movement of the Renaissance and the intellectual movement of the various European Enlightenments, for the contemporary European identity are also made. Such claims tend to undermine, however, recognition of the extent to which the EU is multicultural and multi-religious.

Hegel argues very strongly for the retention of individual states as the focus of sovereignty. However, he has in mind the retention in the early nineteenth century of the patchwork of German states against the aim of Prussia to forego its autonomy and incorporate to form a union with the other German states (Knox 1967, 208n). Hegel maintains that awareness of the individuality of one's political identity is manifested 'in the state as a relation to other states, each of which is autonomous *vis-à-vis* the others'. He adds, with Prussia in mind, that '[t]hose who talk of the "wishes" of a collection of people constituting a more or less autonomous state with its own centre, of its "wishes" to renounce this centre and its autonomy in order to unite with others to form a new whole, have very little knowledge of the nature of a collection or of the feeling of selfhood which a nation possesses in its independence' (Hegel 1967, 208).

However, in an important sense, sovereignty is not a fact or a universal, but an essentially contested concept and a claim about the way political power is or should be exercised. Moreover, the orthodox history of the nation state and the status accorded to Hobbes's definition, are themselves linked. The way in which the meaning of sovereignty has been tied conceptually to the historical existence of the nation state has been a serious obstacle to reconceptualising sovereignty in Europe. The mainstream international relations and political theory discourses have compounded the problem. The realist model of an abstract and ahistorical sovereignty dominates. In political theory some elements of Hobbes's theory (his conceptualisation of the abstract individual, the state of nature, mechanism/materialism) have been plucked out to form a paradigm, again one that is abstract and ahistorical. All of this has stood in the way of envisaging a wider perspective in which the discussion of sovereignty in contemporary debate can take place.

Bibliography

Hannah Arendt (1977) *Between Past and Future: Eight Exercises in Political Thought*, London, Penguin.

David Armitage (1998) 'Literature and Empire', in Nicholas Canny (ed.) *The Origins of Empire. Volume 1 British Overseas Enterprise to the Close of the Seventeenth Century*, Oxford, Oxford University Press.

Richard Ashley (1987) 'The Geopolitics of Geopolitical Space: Toward a Critical Social Theory of International Politics', *Alternatives*, Vol. 12.

Richard Ashley and R.B.J. Walker (1990) 'Reading Dissidence/Writing the Discipline: Crisis and the Question of Sovereignty in International Studies', *International Studies Quarterly*, Vol. 34.

Georgina Ashworth (1995) (ed.) *A Diplomacy of the Oppressed. New Directions in International Feminism*, London, Zed.

Iain Atack (2005) *The Ethics of Peace and War. From State Security to World Community*, Edinburgh, Edinburgh University Press.

Miriam Aziz (2003) 'Sovereignty *Über Alles*: (Re)Configuring the German Legal Order', in Neil Walker (ed.) *Sovereignty in Transition*, Oxford, Hart.

V Bader (1995) 'Citizenship and Exclusion', *Political Theory*, Vol. 23.

Terence Ball (1988) *Transforming Political Discourse*, Oxford, Blackwell.

Terence Ball (1995) *Reappraising Political Theory. Revisionist Studies in the History of Political Thought*, Oxford, Clarendon Press.

Terence Ball (1997) 'Political Theory and Conceptual Change', in Andrew Vincent (ed.) *Political Theory. Tradition and Diversity*, Cambridge, Cambridge University Press.

Zenon Bankowski and Emilios Christodoulidis (1998) 'The European Union as an Essentially Contested Project', *European Law Journal*, Vol. 4.

Jens Bartelson (1995) *The Genealogy of Sovereignty*, Cambridge, Cambridge University Press.

Jens Bartelson (2001) *The Critique of the State*, Cambridge, Cambridge University Press.

Charles Beitz (1994) 'Cosmopolitan Liberty and the States System', in Chris Brown (ed.) *Political Restructuring in Europe. Ethical Perspectives*, London, Routledge.

Richard Bellamy (2003) 'Sovereignty, Post-Sovereignty and Pre-Sovereignty: Three Models of the State, Democracy and Rights within the EU', in Neil Walker (ed.) *Sovereignty in Transition*, Oxford, Hart.

Richard Bellamy and Dario Castiglione (1997) 'Review Article: Constitutionalism and Democracy – Political Theory and the American Constitution', *British Journal of Political Science*, Vol. 27.

Richard Bellamy and Dario Castiglione (1998) 'Between Cosmopolis and Community: Three Models of Rights and Democracy with the European Union', in D. Archibugi, D. Held and M. Kôlher (eds) *Transnational Democracy*, Cambridge, Polity.

Richard Bellamy and Dario Castiglione (2004) 'Lacroix's European Constitutional Patriotism: A Response', *Political Studies*, Vol. 52.

Seyla Benhabib, in S. Benhabib and D. Cornell (eds) (1987) *Feminism as Critique*, Cambridge, Polity.

Stanley Benn (1955) 'The Uses of "Sovereignty"', *Political Studies*, 3.

R.N. Berki (1971) 'Perspectives in the Marxian Critique of Hegel's Political Philosophy', in Z.A. Pelczynski (ed.) *Hegel's Political Philosophy. Problems and Perspectives*, Cambridge, Cambridge University Press.

Isaiah Berlin (1991) 'Two Concepts of Liberty', in D. Miller (ed.) *Liberty*, Oxford, Oxford University Press.

Thomas Biersteker and Cynthia Weber (1996) 'The Social Construction of State Sovereignty', in T. Biersteker and C. Weber (eds) *State Sovereignty as Social Construct*, Cambridge, Cambridge University Press.

Thomas Biersteker and Cynthia Weber (eds) (1996) *State Sovereignty as Social Construct*, Cambridge, Cambridge University Press.

Max Black (1995) *Models and Metaphors. Studies in Language and Philosophy*, Ithaca, Cornell University Press.

Jean Bodin (1992) *On Sovereignty. Four Chapters from 'The Six Books of the Commonwealth'* (ed.) Julian Franklin, Cambridge, Cambridge University Press.

James Bohman and Matthias Lutz-Bachmann (1997) 'Introduction', in J. Bohman and M. Lutz-Bachmann (eds) *Perpetual Peace. Essays on Kant's Cosmopolitan Ideal*, Cambridge MA, MIT Press.

Laura Brace (1997) 'Imagining the Boundaries of the Sovereign Self', in Laura Brace and John Hoffman (eds) *Reclaiming Sovereignty*, London, Pinter Press.

Chris Brown (1992) *International Relations Theory. New Normative Approaches*, New York, Harvester Wheatsheaf.

Chris Brown (2002) *Sovereignty, Rights and Justice. International Political Theory Today*, Cambridge, Polity.

Chris Brown (2005) *Understanding International Relations*, Basingstoke, Palgrave Macmillan.

Chris Brown, Terry Nardin and Nicholas Rengger (2002) 'Introduction', in C. Brown, T. Nardin and N. Rengger (eds) *International Relations in Political Thought. Texts from the Ancient Greeks to the First World War*, Cambridge, Cambridge University Press.

Wendy Brown (1987) 'Where is the Sex in Political Theory?', in *Women and Politics*, Vol. 7.

Wendy Brown (2000) 'Suffering Rights as Paradoxes', *Constellations*, Vol. 7.

Govert Buijs (2003) '"*Que les Latins appellant* maiestatem": An Exploration into the Theological Background of the Concept of Sovereignty', in Neil Walker (ed.) *Sovereignty in Transition*, Oxford, Hart.

Hedley Bull (1966) 'Society and Anarchy in International Relations', in H. Butterfield and M. Wight (eds) *Diplomatic Investigations. Essays in the Theory of International Relations*, London, Allen & Unwin.

Herbert Butterfield (1966) 'Society and Anarchy in International Relations', in H. Butterfield and M. Wight (eds) *Diplomatic Investigations. Essays in the Theory of International Politics*, London, Allen & Unwin.

Joseph Camilleri and J. Falk (1992) *The End of Sovereignty? The Politics of a Shrinking and Fragmenting World*, Aldershot, Edward Elgar.

Marta Cartabia (2003) 'The Legacy of Sovereignty in Italian Constitutional Debate', in Neil Walker (ed.) *Sovereignty in Transition*, Oxford, Hart.

Terrell Carver (1996) '"Public Man" and the Critique of Masculinities', *Political Theory*, Vol. 24.

David Chandler (2003) 'New Rights for Old? Cosmopolitan Citizenship and the Critique of State Sovereignty', *Political Studies*, Vol. 51.

David Chandler (2004) 'Building Global Civil Society "From Below"?', *Millennium*, Vol. 33.

Ariane Chebel D'Appollonia (2002) 'European Nationalism and European Union', in Anthony Pagden (ed.) *The Idea of Europe. From Antiquity to the European Union*, Cambridge, Cambridge University Press.

Paul Chilton (2004) *Analysing Political Discourse. Theory and Practice*, London, Routledge.

Thomas Christiansen, Knud Erik Jorgensen and Antje Wiener (2001) 'Introduction', in Thomas Christiansen, Knud Erik Jorgensen and Antje Wiener (eds) *The Social Construction of Europe*, London, Sage.

Dimitris Chryssochoou (2002) 'Europe's Republican Moment', *European Integration*, Vol. 24.

Janet Coleman (2005) 'Pre-Modern Property and Self-Ownership Before and After Locke', *European Journal of Political Theory*, Vol. 4.

Conal Condren (1994) 'The Paradoxes of Recontextualization in Early Modern Intellectual History', *The Historical Journal*, Vol. 37.

Conal Condren (1997) 'Political Theory and the Problem of Anachronism', in Andrew Vincent (ed.) *Political Theory. Tradition and Diversity*, Cambridge, Cambridge University Press.

William Connolly (1984) (ed.) *Legitimacy and the State*, Oxford, Blackwell.

William Connolly (1991) *Identity/Difference*, Ithaca, Cornell University Press.

William Connolly (1993) *The Terms of Political Discourse*, 2nd edn., Oxford, Blackwell.

William Connolly (1995) *The Ethos of Pluralization*, Minneapolis, University of Minnesota Press.

William Connolly (2004) 'The Complexity of Sovereignty', in J. Edkins, V. Pin-Fat and M. Shapiro (eds) *Sovereign Lives. Power in Global Politics*, New York, Routledge.

Diana Coole (2005) 'Rethinking Agency: A Phenomenological Approach to Embodiment and Agentic Capacity', *Political Studies*, 53.

David Cooper (1971) 'Hegel's Theory of Punishment', in Z.A. Pelczynski (ed.) *Hegel's Political Philosophy. Problems and Perspectives*, Cambridge, Cambridge University Press.

Charles Covell (2004) *Hobbes, Realism and the Tradition of International Law*, Basingstoke, Palgrave Macmillan.

Daniel Deudney (1996) 'Binding Sovereigns: Authorities, Structures, and Geopolitics in Philadelphian systems', in T. Biersteker and C. Weber (eds) *State Sovereignty as Social Construct*, Cambridge, Cambridge University Press.

Thomas Diez (2001a) 'Europe as a Discursive Battleground. Discourse Analysis and European Integration Studies', *Conflict and Cooperation*, Vol. 36.

Thomas Diez (2001b) 'Speaking "Europe": The Politics of Integration Discourse', in Thomas Christiansen, Knud Erik Jorgensen and Antje Wiener (eds) *The Social Construction of Europe*, London, Sage.

Michael Dillon (2004) 'Correlating Sovereign and Biopower', in J. Edkins, V. Pin-Fat and M. Shapiro (eds) *Sovereign Lives. Power in Global Politics*, New York, Routledge.

Petr Drulák (2005) 'Identifying and Assessing Metaphors: The Discourse on European Future', unpublished paper delivered to Workshop 14, 'Metaphor in Political Science', ECPR Joint Sessions, Granada, 14–19 April 2005.

Ivo Duchacek, Daniel Latouche, and Garth Stevenson (eds) (1988) *Perforated Sovereignties and International Relations. Trans-Sovereign Contacts of Subnational Governments*, New York, Greenwood Press.

Alfred Dufour (1991) 'Pufendorf', in J.H. Burns (ed.) *Cambridge History of Political Thought 1450–1700*, Cambridge, Cambridge University Press.

John Dunn (1994) 'Introduction', *Political Studies Special Issue*, 'Contemporary Crisis of the Nation State?', 42.

Alison Edgley (1995) 'Chomsky and the State', *Politics*, Vol. 15.

Jenny Edkins and Veronique Pin-Fat (1999) 'The Subject of the Political', in J. Edkins, N. Persram and V. Pin-Fat (eds) *Sovereignty and Subjectivity*, Boulder, Colorado, Lynne Rienner.

Jenny Edkins and Veronique Pin-Fat (2004) 'Introduction. Life, Power, Resistance', in J. Edkins, V. Pin-Fat and M. Shapiro (eds) *Sovereign Lives. Power in Global Politics*, New York, Routledge.

Jean Elshtain (1987) *Women and War*, New York, Basic Books.

Bardo Fassbender (2003) 'Sovereignty and Constitutionalism in International Law', in Neil Walker (ed.) *Sovereignty in Transition*, Oxford, Hart.

Markus Fischer (1992) 'Feudal Europe, 800–1300: Communal Discourse and Conflictual Practices', *International Organisation*, Vol. 46.

Michel Foucault (1977) *Discipline and Punish: The Birth of the Prison*, London, Allen Lane.

Michel Foucault (1980) *Power/Knowledge: Selected Interviews and Other Writings 1972–77*, Colin Gordon (ed.), Harlow, Essex, Pearson Educational.

Michel Foucault (1986) 'Disciplinary Power and Subjection', in Steven Lukes (ed.) *Power*, Oxford, Oxford University Press.

Michel Foucault (1994) 'Two Lectures', in Michael Kelly (ed.) *Critique and Power. Recasting the Foucault/Habermas Debate*, Cambridge MA, MIT Press.

Michel Foucault (2003) '*Society Must Be Defended*' *Lectures at the College de France, 1975–76*, Mauro Bertani and Alessandro Fontana (eds), London, Allen Lane.

M. Fowler and J. Bunck (1996) 'What Constitutes the Sovereign State?', *Review of International Studies*, Vol. 22.

Antonio Franceschet (2002) *Kant and Liberal Internationalism. Sovereignty, Justice, and Global Reform*, Basingstoke, Palgrave Macmillan.

Julian Franklin (1992) 'Introduction', in Jean Bodin (ed.), *On Sovereignty. Four Chapters from 'The Six Books of the Commonwealth'*, Julian Franklin, Cambridge, Cambridge University Press.

Elizabeth Frazer (1997) 'Method Matters: Feminism, Interpretation and Politics', in Andrew Vincent (ed.) *Political Theory. Tradition and Diversity*, Cambridge, Cambridge University Press.

Elizabeth Frazer and Nicola Lacey (1993) *The Politics of Community*, London, Harvester Wheatsheaf.

Heidrun Friese and Peter Wagner (2002) 'The Nascent Political Philosophy of the European Polity', *Journal of Political Philosophy*, Vol. 10.

Hans-Georg Gadamer (1975) *Truth and Method*, London, Sheed and Ward.

Hans-Georg Gadamer (1987) 'The Problem of Historical Consciousness', in Paul Rabinow and William Sullivan (eds) *Interpretive Social Science. A Second Look*, Berkeley, University of California Press.

Andrew Gamble (2006) 'The European Disunion', *British Journal of Politics and International Relations*, Vol. 8.

Moira Gatens (1996) *Imaginary Bodies. Ethics, Power and Corporeality*, London, Routledge.

Clifford Geertz (1973a) 'Thick Description: Toward an Interpretive Theory of Culture', in Clifford Geertz, *The Interpretation of Cultures*, New York, Basic Books.

Clifford Geertz (1973b) 'The Impact of the Concept of Culture on the Concept of Man', in Clifford Geertz, *The Interpretation of Cultures*, New York, Basic Books.

Clifford Geertz (1973c) 'The Politics of Meaning', in Clifford Geertz, *The Interpretation of Cultures*, New York, Basic Books.

Anthony Giddens (1990) *The Consequences of Modernity*, Cambridge, Polity.

C. Gilligan (1993) *In A Different Voice*, Cambridge MA, Harvard University Press.

M.M. Goldsmith (1993) 'Hobbes's "Mortal God": Is There a Fallacy in Hobbes's Theory of Sovereignty?', in P. King (ed.) *Thomas Hobbes. Critical Assessments, Volume 3 Politics and Law*, London, Routledge.

John Gray (2000) *Two Faces of Liberalism*, New York, New Press.

Elizabeth Grosz (1990) 'Philosophy', in S. Gunew (ed.) *Feminist Knowledges. Critique and Construct*, London, Routledge.

Elizabeth Grosz (1994) *Volatile Bodies. Towards a Corporeal Feminism*, Indiana University Press.

Jurgen Habermas (1991) *Moral Consciousness and Communicative Action*, Cambridge MA, MIT University Press.

Jurgen Habermas (1995) 'Citizenship and National Identity: Some Reflections on the Future of Europe', in R. Beiner (ed.) *Theorising Citizenship*, New York, State University of New York Press.

Janet Halley (2006) *Split Decisions*, Princeton, Princeton University Press.

Lars Hallstrom (2003) 'Support for European Federalism? An Elite View', *European Integration*, Vol. 25.

Iain Hampsher-Monk (1992) *A History of Modern Political Thought*, Oxford.

Donna Haraway (2000) *How Like a Leaf*, London, Routledge.

Alan Harding (1994) 'The Origins of Concept of the State', *History of Political Thought*, 40.

Michael Hardt and Antonio Negri (2000) *Empire*, Cambridge MA, Harvard University Press.

Michael Hardt and Antonio Negri (2004) *Multitude. War and Democracy in the Age of Empire*, London, Penguin.

Trevor Hartley (2001) 'The Constitutional Foundations of The European Union', *Law Quarterly Review*, Vol. 117.

Helen Haste (1993) *The Sexual Metaphor*, London, Harvester Wheatsheaf.

G.W.F. Hegel (1964) *Hegel's Political Writings*, Z.A. Pelczynski (ed.), trans. T.M. Knox, Oxford, Clarendon Press.

G.W.F. Hegel (1967) *Philosophy of Right*, trans. T.M. Knox, Oxford, Oxford University Press.

David Held (2004) *Global Covenant – The Social Democratic Alternative to the Washington Consensus*, Cambridge, Polity.

David Held, Anthony McGrew, David Goldblatt and Jonathan Perraton (1999) *Global Transformations: Politics, Economics and Culture*, Cambridge, Polity Press.

Bjorn Hettne (2002) 'The Europeanisation of Europe: Endogenous and Exogenous Dimensions', *European Integration*, Vol. 24.

F.H. Hinsley (1969) 'The Concept of Sovereignty and the Relations Between States', in W.J. Stankiewicz (ed.) *In Defense of Sovereignty*, Oxford, Oxford University Press.

F.H. Hinsley (1986) *Sovereignty*, Cambridge.

Paul Hirst and Grahame Thompson (1996) *Globalisation in Question*, Cambridge, Polity.

Thomas Hobbes (1946) *Leviathan*, M. Oakeshott (ed.), Oxford, Blackwell.

Thomas Hobbes (1991) *Hobbes. 'Leviathan'*, R. Tuck (ed.), Cambridge, Cambridge University Press.

John Hoffman (1996) 'What on Earth have Sovereignty and the State to do with the Question of Gender?', in I. Hampsher-Monk and J. Stanyer (eds) *Contemporary Political Studies 1996*, Belfast, Political Studies Association.

John Hoffman (1997) 'Can We Define Sovereignty?', *Politics*, Vol. 17.

John Hoffman (1998) *Sovereignty*, Buckingham, Open University Press.

J. Hood-Williams (1996) 'Goodbye to Sex and Gender', *Sociological Review*, Vol. 44.

Kimberly Hutchings (1996) 'The Death of the Sovereign Individual: Reflections on Feminist Analyses of Political and Moral Agency', in M. Griffiths and M. Whitford (eds) *Women's Philosophy Review*, Special Issue, Nottingham, University of Nottingham.

Kimberly Hutchings (1999) *International Political Theory. Rethinking Ethics in a Global Era*, London, Sage.

Jef Huysmans (1999) 'Know Your Schmitt: A Godfather of Truth and the Spectre of Nazism', *Review of International Studies*, 25.

Jef Huysmans (2003) 'Discussing Sovereignty and Transnational Politics', in Neil Walker (ed.) *Sovereignty in Transition*, Oxford, Hart.

Jef Huysmans (2005) 'Introduction', in J. Huysmans, A. Dobson, R. Prokhovnik (eds) *The Politics of Protection*, London, Routledge.

N. Inayatullah and D. Blaney (1995) 'Realising Sovereignty', *Review of International Studies*, Vol. 21.

Robert Jackson (1990) *Quasi-States: Sovereignty, International Relations and the Third World*, Cambridge, Cambridge University Press.

Robert Jackson (1999) 'Introduction: Sovereignty at the Millennium', *Political Studies*, Vol. 47.

Alan James (1986) *Sovereign Statehood*, London, Allen & Unwin.

Alan James (1999) 'The Practice of Sovereign Statehood in Contemporary International Society', *Political Studies*, Vol. 47.

Kathleen Jones (1990) 'Citizenship in a Woman-Friendly Polity', *Signs*, Vol. 15.

Bertrand De Jouvenal (1957) *Sovereignty. An Inquiry into the Political Good*, Cambridge, Cambridge University Press.

Immanuel Kant (1952) *The Critique of Judgement*, trans. J.C. Meredith, Oxford, Clarendon Press.

Immanuel Kant (1997) *Political Writings*, H.S. Reiss (ed.), trans. H.B. Nisbet Cambridge, Cambridge University Press.

Immanuel Kant (1999) 'Appendix' to the *Metaphysics of Morals*, in Mary Gregor (ed.) and trans. *Immanuel Kant. Practical Philosophy*, Cambridge, Cambridge University Press.

G. Kaplan and L. Rogers (1990) 'The Definition of Male and Female: Biological Reductionism and the Sanctions of Normality', in S. Gunew (ed.) *Feminist Knowledge, Critique and Construct*, London, Routledge.

Paul Keal (2003) *European Conquest and the Rights of Indigenous Peoples. The Moral Backwardness of International Society*, Cambridge, Cambridge University Press.

Michael Keating (2003) 'Sovereignty and Plurinational Democracy: Problems in Political Science', in Neil Walker (ed.) *Sovereignty in Transition*, Oxford, Hart.

T.M. Knox (1967) 'Translator's Forward' and translator's notes, in G.W.F. Hegel *Philosophy of Right*, trans. T.M. Knox, Oxford, Oxford University Press.

Martti Koskenniemi (2001) *The Gentle Civilizer of Nations: The Rise and Fall of International Law 1870–1960*, Cambridge, Cambridge University Press.

Rey Koslowski (2001) 'Understanding the European Union as a Federal Polity', in Thomas Christiansen, Knud Erik Jorgensen and Antje Wiener (eds) *The Social Construction of Europe*, London, Sage.

Stephen Krasner (1995/6) 'Compromising Westphalia', *International Security*, Vol. 20.

Stephen Krasner (2001) 'Problematic Sovereignty', in S. Krasner (ed.) *Problematic Sovereignty. Contested Rules and Political Possibilities*, Columbia University Press, New York.

F. Kratochwil (1995) 'Sovereignty as *Dominium*: Is There a Right of Humanitarian Intervention', in G. Lyons and M. Mastanduno (eds) *Beyond Westphalia? State Sovereignty and International Intervention*, Baltimore, Johns Hopkins University Press.

Jill Krause (1994) 'Inclusion/Exclusion: Political Theory, International Theory', in P. Dunleavy and J. Stanyer (eds) *Contemporary Political Studies 1994*, Belfast, Political Studies Association.

Justine Lacroix (2002) 'For a European Constitutional Patriotism', *Political Studies*, Vol. 50.

George Lakoff and Mark Johnson (1980) *Metaphors We Live By*, Chicago, University of Chicago Press.

Thomas Laqueur (1990) *Making Sex. Body and Gender from the Greeks to Freud*, Harvard, Harvard University Press.

Hans Lindahl (2003) 'Sovereignty and Representation in the European Union', in Neil Walker (ed.) *Sovereignty in Transition*, Oxford, Hart.

Andrew Linklater (1992) 'The Question of the Next Stage in International Relations Theory: A Critical Theoretical Point of View', *Millennium*, 21.

Andrew Linklater (1998) *The Transformation of Political Community. Ethical Foundations of the Post-Westphalian Era*, Cambridge, Polity.

Randy Lippert (2005) *Sanctuary, Sovereignty, Sacrifice: Canadian Sanctuary Incidents, Power, and Law*, UBC Press, Vancouver.

Frederick Lister (1996) *The European Union, the United Nations, and the Revival of Confederal Governance*, Greenwood Press, Westport Conn.

Ruth Lister (1995) 'Dilemmas of Engendering Citizenship', *Economy and Society*, Vol. 24.

Ruth Lister (1997) *Citizenship. Feminist Perspectives*, Basingstoke, Macmillan.

Genevieve Lloyd (1989) 'Woman as Other: Sex, Gender and Subjectivity', *Australian Feminist Studies*, Vol. 10.

Genevieve Lloyd (1993) *The Man of Reason. 'Male' and 'Female' in Western Philosophy*, 2nd edn., University of Minnesota Press.

John Locke (1965) *Two Treatises of Government*, Peter Laslett (ed.), New York, Mentor.

John Locke (1988) *Two Treatises of Government*, Cambridge, Cambridge University Press.

Martin Loughlin (2003) 'Ten Tenets of Sovereignty', in Neil Walker (ed.) *Sovereignty in Transition*, Oxford, Hart.

G. Lyons and M. Mastanduno (1995) 'Introduction: International Intervention, State Sovereignty, and the Future of International Society', in G. Lyons and M. Mastanduno (eds) *Beyond Westphalia? State Sovereignty and International Intervention*, Baltimore, Johns Hopkins University Press.

G. MacCallum (1991) 'Negative and Positive Freedom', in D. Miller, *Liberty*, Oxford, Oxford University Press.

Neil MacCormick (1999) *Questioning Sovereignty: Law, State and Nation in the European Commonwealth*, Oxford, Oxford University Press.

Anthony McGrew (1992) 'Conceptualising Global Politics', in A. McGrew *et al* (eds) *Global Politics*, Cambridge, Polity.

A. MacIntyre (1981) *After Virtue*, London, Duckworth.

Iain MacKenzie (2005) 'General Introduction', in Iain MacKenzie (ed.) *Political Concepts. A Reader and Guide*, Edinburgh, Edinburgh University Press.

Noel Malcolm (1991) *Sense on Sovereignty*, London, Centre for Policy Studies.

Noel Malcolm (2002) *Aspects of Hobbes*, Oxford, Clarendon Press.

Martin Marcussen, Thomas Risse, Daniela Engelmann-Martin, Hans Joachim Knopf and Klaus Roscher (2001) 'Constructing Europe? The Evolution of Nation-State Identities', in Thomas Christiansen, Knud Erik Jorgensen and Antje Wiener (eds) *The Social Construction of Europe*, London, Sage.

T.H. Marshall (1950) *Citizenship and Social Class*, Cambridge, Cambridge University Press.

Karl Marx (1975) 'Economic and Philosophical Manuscripts', in L. Colletti (ed.), *Karl Marx Early Writings*, Harmondsworth, Penguin.

John Stuart Mill (1974) *On Liberty*, Harmondsworth, Penguin.

David Miller (1989) 'In What Sense Must Socialism Be Communitarian?', in E.F. Paul, F.D. Miller, J. Paul and D. Greenberg (eds) *Socialism*, Oxford, Blackwell.

H. Brinton Milward (1996) 'Symposium on the Hollow State: Capacity, Control, and Performance in Interorganisational Settings', *Journal of Public Administration Research and Theory*, Vol. 6.

M. Molloy (1995) 'Imagining (the) Difference: Gender, Ethnicity and Metaphors of Nation', *Feminist Review*, Vol. 51.

Hans Morganthau (1964) 'The intellectual and political functions of a theory of international relations', in H.V. Harrison (ed.) *The Role of Theory in International Relations*, Princeton, Van Nostrand.

Chantal Mouffe (1992) 'Preface: Democratic Politics Today', in C. Mouffe (ed.) *Dimensions of Radical Democracy*, Verso, London.

Jan Müller (1999) 'Carl Schmitt's Method: Between Ideology, Demonology and Myth', *Journal of Political ideologies*, Vol. 4.

T. Nardin and D. Mapel (1992) *Traditions of International Ethics*, Cambridge, Cambridge University Press.

L. Neack and R. Knudson (1996) 'Re-Imagining the Sovereign State: Beginning an Interdisciplinary Dialogue', *Alternatives*, Vol. 21.

Mark Neocleous (2003) *Imagining the State*, Maidenhead, Open University Press.

Robert Nozick (1974) *Anarchy, State and Utopia*, Oxford, Blackwell.

Martha Nussbaum (1995) 'Human Capabilities, Female Human Beings', in M. Nussbaum and J. Glover (eds) *Women, Culture and Development. A Study of Human Capabilities*, Oxford, Clarendon Press.

Julia O'Connell Davidson (1997) 'Does She Do Queening?: Prostitution, Sovereignty and Community', in L. Brace and J. Hoffman (eds) *Reclaiming Sovereignty*, London, Pinter.

Onora O'Neill (1992) 'Vindicating Reason', in Paul Guyer (ed.) *The Cambridge Companion to Kant*, Cambridge, Cambridge University Press.

Nicholas Onuf (1995) 'Intervention for the Common Good', in G. Lyons and M. Mastanduno (eds) *Beyond Westphalia? State Sovereignty and International Intervention*, Baltimore, Johns Hopkins University Press.

Nicholas Onuf (1998) *The Republican Legacy in International Thought*, Cambridge, Cambridge University Press.

Anthony Pagden (1998) 'The Struggle for Legitimacy and the Image of Empire in the Atlantic to c. 1700', in Nicholas Canny (ed.) *The Origins of Empire. Volume 1 British Overseas Enterprise to the Close of the Seventeenth Century*, Oxford, Oxford University Press.

Anthony Pagden (2002) 'Introduction', in Anthony Pagden (ed.) *The Idea of Europe. From Antiquity to the European Union*, Cambridge, Cambridge University Press.

Carole Pateman (1988) *The Sexual Contract*, Stanford, Stanford University Press.

Daniel Philpott (1995) 'Sovereignty. An Introduction and Brief History', *Journal of International Affairs*, Vol. 48.

Daniel Philpott (1999) 'Westphalia, Authority, and International Society', *Political Studies*, Vol. 47.

Daniel Philpott (2001) *Revolutions in Sovereignty. How Ideas Shaped Modern International Relations*, Princeton, Princeton University Press.

Christopher Pierson (1996) *The Modern State*, London, Routledge.

Val Plumwood (1993) 'The Politics of Reason: Towards a Feminist Logic', *Australasian Journal of Philosophy*, Vol. 71.

Thomas Pogge (1994) 'Cosmopolitanism and Sovereignty', in Chris Brown (ed.) *Political Restructuring in Europe. Ethical Perspectives*, London, Routledge.

Ulrich Preuss (1996) 'Two Challenges to European Citizenship', *Political Studies*, Vol. 44.

Ulrich K. Preuss, Michelle Everson, Mathias Koenig-Archibugi and Edwige Lefebvre (2003) 'Traditions of Citizenship in the European Union', *Citizenship Studies*, Vol. 7.

Raia Prokhovnik (1991) *Rhetoric and Philosophy in Hobbes's 'Leviathan'*, New York, Garland Press.

Raia Prokhovnik (1996) 'Internal/External: the State of Sovereignty', *Contemporary Politics*, Vol. 2.

Raia Prokhovnik (1998) 'Public and Private Citizenship: From Gender Invisibility to Feminist Inclusiveness', *Feminist Review*, Vol. 60.

Raia Prokhovnik (1999) 'The State of Liberal Sovereignty', *British Journal of Politics and International Relations*, Vol. 1.

Raia Prokhovnik (2002) *Rational Woman. A Feminist Critique of Dichotomy*, 2nd edn, Manchester, Manchester University Press.

Raia Prokhovnik (2004) *Spinoza and Republicanism*, Basingstoke, Palgrave Macmillan.

Raia Prokhovnik (2005) 'Hobbes's Artifice as Social Construction', *Hobbes Studies*, Vol. 18.

Raia Prokhovnik (2008 forthcoming) *Sovereignty: History and Theory*.

Zarko Puhovski (1994) 'The Moral Basis of Political Restructuring', in Chris Brown (ed.) *Political Restructuring in Europe. Ethical Perspectives*, London, Routledge.

Paul Rabinow and William Sullivan (eds) (1987) *Interpretive Social Science. A Second Look*, Berkeley, University of California Press.

D.D. Raphael (1990) *Problems of Political Philosophy*, London, Palgrave.

John Rawls (1972) *Theory of Justice*, Oxford, Oxford University Press.

John Rawls (1993a) *Political Liberalism*, New York, Columbia University Press.

John Rawls (1993b) 'The Law of Peoples', in S. Shute and S. Hurley (eds) *On Human Rights*, New York, Basic Books.

Christian Reus-Smit (2001a) 'Human Rights and the Social Construction of Sovereignty', *Review of International Studies*, Vol. 27.

Christian Reus-Smit (2001b) 'The Strange Death of Liberal International Theory', *European Journal of International Law*, Vol. 12.

I.A. Richards (1967) *The Philosophy of Rhetoric*, Oxford, Oxford University Press.

Catherine Richmond (1997) 'Preserving the Identity Crisis: Autonomy, System and Sovereignty in European Law', *Law and Philosophy*, Vol. 16.

Melvin Richter (2005) 'A Family of Political Concepts. Tyranny, Despotism, Bonapartism, Caesarism, Dictatorship, 1750–1917', *European Journal of Political Theory*, Vol. 4.

Paul Ricoeur (1973) 'The Model of the Text: Meaningful Action Considered as a Text', *New Literary History*, Vol. 5.

R. Robertson (1990) 'Mapping the Global Condition', in M. Featherstone (ed.) *Global Culture*, London, Sage.

Bert Van Roermund (2003) 'Sovereignty: Unpopular and Popular', in Neil Walker (ed.) *Sovereignty in Transition*, Oxford, Hart.

Ben Rosamond (1995) 'Mapping the European Condition. The Theory of Integration and the Integration of Theory', *European Journal of International Relations*, Vol. 1.

Ben Rosamond (2001) 'Discourses of Globalization and European Identities', in Thomas Christiansen, Knud Erik Jorgensen and Antje Wiener (eds) *The Social Construction of Europe*, London, Sage.

Ben Rosamond and Daniel Wincott (2006) 'Constitutionalism, European Integration and British Political Economy', *British Journal of Politics and International Relations*, Vol. 8.

Justin Rosenberg (2000) *The Follies of Globalisation Theory*, London, Verso.

Jean-Jacques Rousseau (1968) *The Social Contract*, trans. Cranston Maurice, London, Penguin.

David Runciman (2003) 'The Concept of the State: the Sovereignty of a Fiction', in Q. Skinner and B. Strath (eds) *States and Citizens*, Cambridge, Cambridge University Press.

Michael Sandel (1982) *Liberalism and the Limits and Justice*, Cambridge, Cambridge University Press.

M. Sawer (1996) 'Gender, Metaphor and the State', *Feminist Review*, Vol. 52.

J. Scanlan and O. Kent (1988) 'The Force of Moral Arguments for a Just Immigration Policy in a Hobbesian Universe. The Contemporary American Example', in M. Gibney (ed.) *Open Borders? Closed Societies?*, New York, Greenwood Press.

Carl Schmitt (1976) *The Concept of the Political*, New Jersey, Rutgers University Press.

Carl Schmitt (1985) *Political Theology. Four Chapters on the Concept of Sovereignty*, Cambridge MA, MIT Press.

Carl Schmitt (1986) *Political Romanticism*, Cambridge MA, MIT Press.

Carl Schmitt (1988) *The Crisis of Parliamentary Democracy*, Cambridge MA, MIT Press.

Carl Schmitt (1996) *The Leviathan in the State Theory of Thomas Hobbes. Meaning and Failure of a Political Symbol*, trans. George Schwab and Erna Hilfstein, Westport, Conn., Greenwood Press.

Lynn Segal (1994) *Straight Sex*, London, Virago.

Jo Shaw (2001) 'Postnational Constitutionalism in the European Union', in Thomas Christiansen, Knud Erik Jorgensen and Antje Wiener (eds) *The Social Construction of Europe*, London, Sage.

Martin Shaw (1991) 'State theory and the post-Cold War world', in M. Banks and M. Shaw (eds) *State and Society in International Relations*, London, Harvester Wheatsheaf.

Martin Shaw (1994) *Global Society and International Relations*, Cambridge, Polity.

Larry Siedentop (2000) *Democracy in Europe*, Harmondsworth, Penguin.

Robert Simon (2002) 'Introduction: Social and Political Philosophy – Sorting Out the Issues', in Robert Simon (ed.) *The Blackwell Guide to Social and Political Philosophy*, Oxford, Blackwell.

Gerry Simpson (2004) *Great Powers and Outlaw States. Unequal Sovereign in the International Legal Order*, Cambridge, Cambridge University Press.

Quentin Skinner (1975) 'Hermeneutics and the Role of History', *New Literary History*, Vol. 7.

Quentin Skinner (1978) *The Foundations of Modern Political Thought. Volume Two: The Age of Reformation*, Cambridge, Cambridge University Press.

Quentin Skinner (1988) 'A Reply to My Critics', in James Tully (ed.) *Meaning and Context: Quentin Skinner and His Critics*, Cambridge, Polity.

Quentin Skinner (1989) 'Language and Political Change', in T. Ball, J. Farr and R. Hanson (eds) *Political Innovation and Conceptual Change*, Cambridge, Cambridge University Press.

Quentin Skinner (1992) 'On Justice, the Common Good and the Priority of Liberty', in C. Mouffe (ed.) *Dimensions of Radical Democracy*, London, Verso.

Carole Smith (2000) 'The Sovereign State v Foucault: Law and Disciplinary Power', *Sociological Review*, Vol. 48 (2).

Georg Sørensen (1999) 'Sovereignty: Change and Continuity in a Fundamental Institution', *Political Studies*, Vol. 47.

B. Spinoza (1951) *B. de Spinoza. A Theologico-Political Treatise. A Political Treatise*, R.H.M. Elwes (ed.), New York.

B. Spinoza (1955) *Benedict de Spinoza. On the Improvement of the Understanding, The Ethics, Correspondence*, R.H.M. Elwes (ed.), New York.

Baruch Spinoza: Theological-Political Treatise (1998) trans. S. Shirley, Indianapolis, Hackett Publishing Company.

Hendrik Spruyt (1994) *The Sovereign State and Its Competitors. An Analysis of Systems Change*, Princeton, Princeton University Press.

W.J. Stankiewicz (1969) 'In Defense of Sovereignty: A Critique and an Interpretation', in W.J. Stankiewicz (ed.) *In Defense of Sovereignty*, New York, Oxford University Press.

Stanley Stewart (1997) *Old Serpent Nile. A Journey to the Source*, London, Flamingo.

Tracy Strong (2005) 'Forward', *Carl Schmitt 'Political Theology*, trans. G. Schwab, Chicago, University of Chicago Press.

Hungdah Su (2004) 'Can Constitution-Building Advance European Integration? A Three-Pillared Institutionalist Analysis', *European Integration*, Vol. 26.

Adam Swift (2001) *Political Philosophy*, Cambridge, Polity.

Christine Sylvester (1994) *Feminist Theory and International Relations in a Postmodern Era*, Cambridge, Cambridge University Press.

'Symposium on Care and Justice' (1995) *Hypatia*, Vol. 10.

M. Tapper (1986) 'Can a Feminist be a Liberal?', *Australasian Journal of Philosophy*, Vol. 64.

Charles Taylor (1987) 'Interpretation and the Sciences of Man', in Paul Rabinow and William Sullivan (eds) *Interpretive Social Science. A Second Look*, Berkeley, University of California Press.

Charles Taylor (1990) *Sources of the Self*, Cambridge, Cambridge University Press.

Charles Taylor (1992) *Multiculturalism and 'The Politics of Recognition'*, Princeton, Princeton University Press.

Lucy Taylor (1997) 'The Citizen, Her Sovereignty and Democratization: Lessons from Chile', in Laura Brace and John Hoffman (eds) *Reclaiming Sovereignty*, London, Pinter Press.

Paul Taylor (1999) 'The United Nations in the 1990s: Proactive Cosmopolitanism and the Issue of Sovereignty', *Political Studies*, Vol. 47.

Benno Teschke (2003) *The Myth of 1648. Class, Geopolitics, and the Making of Modern International Relations*, London, Verso.

Joan Tronto (1993) *Moral Boundaries*, New York, Routledge.

James Tully (1995) *Strange Multiplicity. Constitutionalism in an Age of Diversity*, Cambridge, Cambridge University Press.

James Tully (1999) 'To Think and Act Differently: Foucault's Four Reciprocal Objections to Habermas' Theory', in S. Ashenden and D. Owen (eds) *Foucault contra Habermas. Recasting the Dialogue between Genealogy and Critical Theory*, London, Sage.

James Tully (2002) 'The Kantian Idea of Europe: Critical and Cosmopolitan Perspectives', in A. Pagden (ed.) *The Idea of Europe. From Antiquity to the European Union*, Cambridge, Cambridge University Press.

Andrew Vincent (1987) *Theories of the State*, Oxford, Blackwell.

Sylvia Walby (1994) 'Is Citizenship Gendered?', *Sociology*, Vol. 28.

Neil Walker (1998) 'Sovereignty and Differentiated Integration in the European Union', *European Law Journal*, Vol. 4.

Neil Walker (2001) 'All Dressed Up', *Oxford Journal of Legal Studies*, Vol. 21.

Neil Walker (2002) 'The Idea of Constitutional Pluralism', *Modern Law Review*, Vol. 65.

Neil Walker (2003a) 'Preface', in Neil Walker (ed.) *Sovereignty in Transition*, Oxford, Hart.

Neil Walker (2003b) 'Late Sovereignty in the European Union', in Neil Walker (ed.) *Sovereignty in Transition*, Oxford, Hart.

Neil Walker (2005) 'Legal Theory and the European Union: A 25th Anniversary Essay', *Oxford Journal of Legal Studies*, Vol. 25.

R.B.J. Walker (1993) *Inside/Outside. International Relations as Political Theory*, Cambridge, Cambridge University Press.

R.B.J. Walker (1995) 'From International Relations to World Politics', in J. Camilleri, A. Jarvis and A. Paolini (eds) *The State in Transition: Reimagining Political Space*, Boulder, Colorado, Lynne Rienner.

R.B.J. Walker (1999) 'Foreward', in Jenny Edkins, Nalini Persram and Veronique Pin-Fat (eds) *Sovereignty and Subjectivity*, Boulder, Colorado, Lynne Rienner.

R.B.J. Walker (2004) 'Conclusion. Sovereignties, Exceptions, Worlds', in J. Edkins, V. Pin-Fat and M. Shapiro (eds) *Sovereign Lives. Power in Global Politics*, New York, Routledge.

R.B.J. Walker (2006) 'On the Protection of Nature and the Nature of Protection', in J. Huysmans, A. Dobson and R. Prokhovnik (eds) *The Politics of Protection*, London, Routledge.

R. Walker and S. Mendlovitz (1990) *Contending Sovereignties: Rethinking Political Community*, Boulder, Lynne Rienner.

William Wallace (1999) 'The Sharing of Sovereignty: the European Paradox', *Political Studies*, Vol. 47.

Michael Walzer (1967) 'On the Role of Symbolism in Political Thought', *Political Science Quarterly*, Vol. 82.

I. Wallerstein (1983) *Historical Capitalism*, London, Verso.

Ian Ward (2001) 'Beyond Constitutionalism: The Search for a European Political Imagination', *European Law Journal*, Vol. 7.

Cynthia Weber (1994) 'Good Girls, Little Girls and Bad Girls: Male Paranoia in Robert Keohane's Critique of Feminist International Relations', *Millennium*, 23.

Cynthia Weber (1995) *Simulating Sovereignty. Intervention, the State and Symbolic Exchange*, Cambridge, Cambridge University Press.

Max Weber (1949) '"Objectivity" in Social Science and Social Policy', in M. Weber *The Methodology of the Social Sciences*, New York, Free Press.

Joseph Weiler (1996) 'European Neo-constitutionalism: in Search of Foundations for the European Constitutional Order', *Political Studies*, Vol. 44, Special Issue.

Joseph Weiler (1999) *The Constitution of Europe: 'Do the New Clothes Have an Emperor?' And Other Essays on European Integration*, Cambridge, Cambridge University Press.

Alexander Wendt (1992) 'Anarchy is What States Make of It: The Social Construction of Power Politics', *International Organisation*, Vol. 46.

Alexander Wendt (1999) *Social Theory of International Politics*, Cambridge, Cambridge University Press.

Wouter G. Werner and Jaap H. De Wilde (2001) 'The Endurance of Sovereignty', *European Journal of International Relations*, Vol. 7.

Martin Wight (1966) 'Why is There No International Theory?', in H. Butterfield and M. Wight (eds) *Diplomatic Investigations. Essays in the Theory of International Politics*, London, Allen & Unwin.

Michael Williams (2004) 'Why Ideas Matter in International Relations: Hans Morganthau, Classical Realism, and the Moral Construction of Power Politics', *International Organisation*, Vol. 58.

Jonathan Wolff (1996) *An Introduction to Political Philosophy*, Oxford, Oxford University Press.

Iris Marion Young (1990) *Justice and the Politics of Difference*, Princeton, Princeton University Press.

Jacques Ziller (2003) 'Sovereignty in France: Getting Rid of the Mal de Bodin', in Neil Walker (ed.) *Sovereignty in Transition*, Oxford, Hart.

Slavoj Zizek (1999) *The Zizek Reader* (eds) Elizabeth Wright and Edmond Wright, Oxford, Blackwell.

Index

9 781403 913234